# THE *Language* OF BUSINESS ENGLISH

## *Grammar & Functions*

**Business Management English Series:**

Brieger, N. and J. Comfort
*Production and Operations**

Brieger, N. and J. Comfort
*Personnel**

Brieger, N. and J. Comfort
*Language Reference for Business English*

Comfort, J. and N. Brieger
*Marketing**

Comfort, J. and N. Brieger
*Finance**

***Other ESP titles of interest include:***

Adamson, D.
*Starting English for Business**

Brieger, N and J. Comfort
*Early Business Contacts**

Brieger, N. and J. Comfort
*Developing Business Contacts**

Brieger, N. and J. Comfort
*Advanced Business Contacts**

Brieger, N. and J. Comfort
*Technical Contacts**

Brieger, N. and J. Comfort
*Social Contacts**

Brieger, N. and J. Comfort
*Business Issues*

Brieger, N. and A. Cornish
*Secretarial Contacts**

Davies, S. *et al.*
*Bilingual Handbooks of Business Correspondence and Communication*

Goddard, C.
*Business Idioms International**

Minkoff, P
*Executive Skills**

Sneyd, M.
*International Banking and Finance**
*Accounting**
*Insurance**

St John, M-J.
*Marketing*
*Advertising and the Promotion Industry*

*Includes audio cassette(s)

# THE *Language* OF BUSINESS ENGLISH

## *Grammar & Functions*

Nick Brieger and Simon Sweeney

Prentice Hall

New York London Toronto Sydney Tokyo Singapore

PRENTICE HALL INTERNATIONAL ENGLISH LANGUAGE TEACHING

## *Acknowledgements*

The authors would like to thank colleagues at York Associates for their advice on pedagogic matters and Steve Hick for his technical assistance.

First published 1994 by
Prentice Hall International
Campus 400, Maylands Avenue
Hemel Hempstead
Hertfordshire HP2 7EZ
A division of
Simon & Schuster International Group

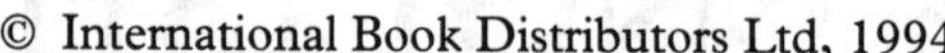



Designed by Ken Vail Graphic Design, Cambridge
Printed and bound in Great Britain by
BPC Paulton Books Ltd, Paulton, Bristol

**Library of Congress Cataloguing-in-Publication Data**
Brieger, Nick.
The language of business English: reference and practice / Nick Brieger and Simon Sweeney.
p. cm.
ISBN 0-13-042516-8
1. English language–Business English–Problems, exercises, etc.
2. English language–Grammar–Problems, exercises, etc.
I. Sweeney, Simon. II. Title.
PE1115.B684 1993
428.2'02465–dc20 93-30937
CIP

**British Library Cataloging in Publication Data**
A catalogue record for this book is available from the British Library.

ISBN 0-13-042516-8

5 4 3 98 97 96

# CONTENTS

# CONTENTS

## *Adjectives and adverbs*



## *Determiners*



## *Prepositions*



## *Information-handling*



## *Expressing attitudes*



## *Describing logical and personal relations*



## *Suasion*

# INTRODUCTION

## Targets and objectives

*The Language of Business English* is aimed at students who need to develop and practise their Business English language skills. More specifically, the material is relevant for learners, at intermediate level or above, who need to extend their knowledge of grammar and functions so that they become more accurate and their use of language is more appropriate in a range of key business contexts.

*The Language of Business English* can be used together with any Business English course book to provide more detailed explanations and supplementary exercises in the grammar and functions of Business English. It is suitable for both classroom and self-study use.

## Organisation of material

There are 90 units and 11 appendices:
Units 1–72 Grammar
Units 73–90 Functions
Appendices 1–11 provide additional notes on business vocabulary, grammar and functions.

Each unit consists of:

1. Language presentation through:
   - sample sentences to show the language forms in use;
   - an explanation of the language forms;
   - a description of the uses of these forms.
2. Practice through:
   - controlled exercises to develop an awareness of the language forms;
   - guided exercises to practise expressing the range of meanings conveyed by these forms;
   - a transfer activity which provides a framework for further free practice of the language presented in the unit.
3. Answers to the controlled and guided exercises.

## Selection of material

The book may be used either in class or for self-study. For classroom use, teachers should choose units to supplement the language areas covered by the Business English course book being followed, either to consolidate the presentation of language forms or to provide additional exercises. For self-study use, students should choose units according to their own interests or to problems they or their teachers have identified. For both teachers and students, the contents at the front of the book and the detailed index at the end will help to locate appropriate units.

## Using a unit

Having chosen a unit, you should work through the presentation by:
- reading through the sample sentences and noting the use of the language forms (Section A);
- studying the language forms presented (Section B);
- studying the uses of these forms (Section C).

Next, you should move on to the practice exercises. There are three types of exercises: controlled, guided and transfer.

Before you start an exercise:
- make sure you clearly understand the task;
- look at any examples that have been given;
- refer back to the language forms and uses, if necessary.

After you have finished a controlled or guided exercise, check your answer with the key at the back of the book.

Controlled exercises have only one possible solution; guided exercises (M) have a suggested answer. If your answers to a controlled exercise are wrong, look again at the Form and Uses sections (B and C). If your answers to a guided exercise are different from those suggested, check if your answers are possible alternatives. If you are not sure, then ask your teacher.

We have used the following conventions which are convenient and simple as short forms:

V1 = the infinitive without **to**
V2 = the past simple form
V3 = the past participle
AmE = American English
BrE = British English

◄—|—► (present) a time line on which the past lies to the left and the future to the right.

Finally, a few words about the transfer activities. The reason for including these in a practice book is that they act as a bridge to **your** world by providing an opportunity to transfer to your own personal situation the language presented and practised in the previous exercises.

# GRAMMATICAL TERMS AND CONVENTIONS

**Active**
A verb or verb phrase which is not in the passive voice, e.g. *The government increased taxes* or *Taxes increased* (see also Passive and Voice).

**Agent**
The doer of an action in a passive sentence introduced by *by*, e.g. *The mistake was discovered by the accountant.*

**Article**
The words *the* or *a/an* which stand before a noun or the zero article, e.g. *the manager, a department, subsidiaries.*

**Aspect**
The feature of a verb which shows its time characteristics, i.e. when an activity or state is seen to take place. We have two aspects in English: continuous (see Continuous) and perfect (see Perfect).

**Auxiliary verb**
The verbs *be, have* and *do* when used in the following constructions:
- continuous verbs (be), e.g. *Sales are increasing at the moment.*
- passive verbs (be), e.g. *The factory was sold last year.*
- the perfect (have and had), e.g. *We have already placed an order.*
- negative and interrogative verbs in the present and past simple tenses (do), e.g. *We don't agree with your proposal. What do you think?*

**Bare infinitive** (see Infinitive)

**Clause**
A group of words containing a subject and verb and acting as a full sentence or part of a sentence. The verb may be a finite verb, e.g. *The company has been operating for 10 years* (finite clause) or a non-finite verb, e.g. *Having founded the company, ...* (non-finite clause).

**Conjunction**
A word which links words, phrases or clauses, e.g. *and, but, because.*

**Connector**
A word which links clauses which are separated by a full stop or a semi-colon, e.g. *however, therefore, similarly.*

**Continuous (aspect)**
A verb construction comprising *be* + V1 *...ing* (see also Simple).

**Copula (copular verb)**
The name given to a group of linking verbs like *be*, which take a subject complement. The subject complement tells us what the subject is, e.g. *He is the Managing Director*, or what the subject becomes, e.g. *He became the Managing Director.* Copular verbs also take an adjective complement rather than an adverb complement, e.g. *The new premises seem very comfortable.*

**Demonstrative**
The words *this, that, these* and *those*, when they are used in a noun phrase, e.g. *This presentation consists of 4 parts.*

**Derivation**
A word whose form originates in another word, e.g. *management* is derived from the verb *manage.*

**Determiner**
A class of words which includes articles, possessive pronouns, demonstratives and quantifiers.

**Direct object** (see Object)

**Direct speech** (see also Indirect speech)
A way of showing the actual words spoken, e.g. *'I declare the meeting closed.'* Quotation marks are commonly used to show direct speech.

**Finite verb**
A verb or verb phrase in one of the tenses.

**Full verb** (see Finite verb)

**Genitive**
A noun, written with an apostrophe, and indicating possession or a similar relationship, e.g. *the chairman's decision, last year's results, the countries' economies.*

**Indirect speech**
A way of showing what someone else has said by using our own words, e.g. *The chairman announced that the next meeting would be the following week* (see also Direct speech).

**Infinitive** (or bare infinitive) (V1)
The non-finite base form of a verb, e.g. *be, make, develop.*

**Infinitive + to**
The non-finite base form of a verb with the particle *to*, e.g. *to be, to make, to develop.*

**Interrogative**
A group of words which asks a question.

**Intransitive verb**
A verb which cannot take a direct object, e.g. *Production increased by 5 per cent last year.* Some verbs can be both intransitive and transitive (see Transitive verb).

**Main verb**
A verb which is neither a modal verb nor an auxiliary verb. *Be, have* and *do* can be either main verbs or auxiliary verbs, depending on their use.

**Modal verb**
The following verbs and their negative forms are modals:
*will* *can* *shall* *may* *must*
*would* *could* *should* *might*
Modal verbs take a bare infinitive. The following verbs also take a bare infinitive:
*needn't* *daren't*

# GRAMMATICAL TERMS AND CONVENTIONS

**Object**
An obligatory noun or noun phrase after a transitive verb, e.g. *We increased production by 5 per cent last year.*

**Participle**
A non-finite verb formed with V1 + *ing* (present participle) or V3 (past participle).

**Particle**
A grammatical word which does not belong to the main classes, e.g. *to* (in the infinitive) or *not*.

**Passive**
A passive construction contains a verb or verb phrase comprising *be* + V3, where the doer of the action is expressed as the agent rather than the subject, e.g. *The last government increased taxes* (active) versus *Taxes were increased by the last government* (passive) (see also Voice).

**Perfect (aspect)**
A verb construction comprising *has/have* + V3 which places the activity or event in a different time zone from the time of speaking or writing.
The present perfect combines the present tense and the perfect aspect. It indicates that the action is seen as completed by reference to now, the time of speaking or writing, e.g. *We have already seen the report.*
The past perfect combines the past tense and the perfect aspect. It indicates that the action is seen as completed by reference to an earlier point of time, e.g. *We had already seen the report* (see also Continuous and Simple).

**Phrasal verb**
A verb phrase comprising a verb + adverb.

**Phrase**
A group of words, but less than a clause, i.e. not containing a subject and verb.

**Pronoun**
A word which takes the position of a noun or noun phrase, e.g. *he, my, this, who.*

**Quantifier**
A word which describes quantity and amount, e.g. *all, many, some, few* and *no.*

**Question tag**
A short question, added to a statement, which turns the statement into a question, e.g. *We sent the goods last week, didn't we?*

**Relative clause**
A clause beginning with a relative pronoun (*who, whom, whose, which, that* or zero) or a relative adverb (*when, where, why*).

**Reported speech** (see Indirect speech)

**Simple**
A verb construction in either the present simple or past simple tense (see also Continuous and Perfect).

**Subjunctive**
A finite verb form used to describe non-factual or hypothetical meaning. It may be realised either by the bare infinitive or *were*, e.g. *The shareholders demanded that the chairman resign. If I were him, I would resign immediately.*

**Tense**
The grammatical form of verbs which differentiates, e.g. the present from the past.

**Time line**
A line which shows the three real-world times of past, present and future, in order to show tense in terms of their relative position on the line.

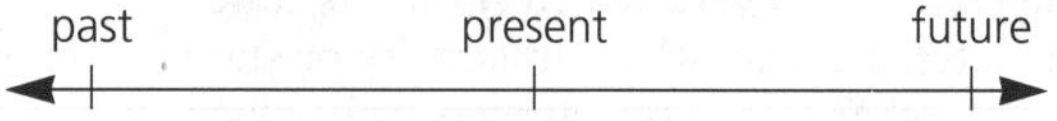


**Time marker**
A phrase to describe the timing of an event, e.g. *last year, at the moment, next week.*

**Transitive**
A main verb which takes a direct object is described as transitive, e.g. *We increased production by 5 per cent last year.* Some verbs can be both transitive and intransitive (see Intransitive verb).

**V1**
The infinitive form of a verb, e.g. *help.*

**V2**
The past tense form of a verb, e.g. *helped.*

**V3**
The past participle form of a verb, e.g. *helped.*

**Verb ...ed**
The verb form comprising V1 + *ed*, e.g. *helped.*

**Verb ...ing**
The verb form comprising V1 + *ing*, e.g. *helping.*

**Voice**
The grammatical category of either active or passive verb form.

**Wh-question**
A question beginning with a *wh*-word, i.e. *who, what, which, when, where, why,* also *how* and *how* phrases.

**Yes/no question**
A question form to which the answer must be *yes* or *no*, i.e. not a *wh*-question.

# PART 1

# GRAMMAR

# UNIT 1

## THE PRESENT CONTINUOUS

*See also* **Unit 2 – The present simple**
**Unit 8 – The future with will**
**Unit 9 – The future with going to**

### A *Sample sentences*

- The company is expanding at the moment.
- At present we are recruiting a new Production Director.
- What is happening in the Marketing Department? We are just finishing the market research.
- We are launching the new model next month.

### B *Form*

The present continuous comprises two parts:
the present tense of **to be** + V1 ... *ing*

| 1 Positive form | 2 Negative form | 3 Interrogative form |
|---|---|---|
| I **am/'m checking** the figures. | I **am not/'m not expecting** a reply today. | **Am** I **doing** it correctly? |
| We/you/they **are checking** ... | We/you/they **are not/aren't expecting** ... | **Are** we/you/they **doing** ...? |
| He/she/it **is/'s checking** ... | He/she/it **is not/isn't expecting** ... | **Is** he/she/it **doing** ...? |

### C *Uses*

We use the present continuous to talk about:
– activities at or around the time of speaking
– temporary activities in the present
– fixed arrangements in the future

1 To indicate an activity at the moment of speaking:
A: What are you doing?
B: I'm writing a job application.

2 To indicate an activity around the time of speaking:
We are setting up a number of independent profit centres.

3 To indicate the temporary nature of an activity:
I'm helping the sales team at the moment (but normally I work on other activities).

4 To indicate a fixed arrangement in the future:
We are presenting the new company structure at next month's meeting.

***Notes***

1 With C1, 2 and 3, we can use the following time expressions (present time markers):
*at the/this moment* *currently*
*at present* *now*

2 With C4, we normally use a word or expressions to show that we mean future time. This avoids confusion with the present time:
Which project are you working on *next week*? (future)
*cf.* Which project are you working on? (present)

# THE PRESENT CONTINUOUS

## Exercise 1

*Make six sentences based on the following options.*

| Time expression | Subject | Present continuous | Object |
|---|---|---|---|
| Now<br>At the moment<br>At present<br>Currently | I<br>we<br>our department<br>they | is planning<br>are working<br>am designing<br>are installing | with our R & D department<br>a new project<br>new solutions<br>a new network |

## Exercise 2

*Read the following text. It contains five examples of the present continuous tense. Classify them according to different uses shown in the box below.*

The department is presently undergoing (1) major reorganisation. We are reducing (2) the number of office staff and relocating (3) some personnel in other departments. This month we are also advertising (4) for two new senior management posts. Our present director is leaving (5) at the end of the year.

| *activity at or around the time of speaking* | *temporary activity in the present* | *fixed arrangement in the future* |
|---|---|---|

## Exercise 3

*Read the following dialogue.*

Michael: What are you doing now, John?
John: I'm finishing preparations for our meeting tomorrow morning.
Michael: Is Patrizia coming?
John: Yes, she's arriving this evening.
Michael: Oh good. What are you doing this evening?
John: Nothing.
Michael: Well, I'm meeting Felix, to discuss the trip to Japan next week. Could you join us?
John: Er, no, I don't think so …

*Complete the following sentences:*

**1** *Now John is* ______________________________.

**2** *Tomorrow morning, Michael, John and Patrizia* ______________________________.

**3** *Tonight Michael* ______________________________.

**4** *Tonight John isn't* ______________________________.

**5** *Next week they* ______________________________.

## Transfer

*What are you doing now?*
*What are you doing tomorrow?*
*Think of a friend or colleague. What is he/she doing now?*
*Where are you going on Tuesday next week?*
*Are you working on any special project at the moment?*

# UNIT 2

## THE PRESENT SIMPLE

*See also* **Unit 1 – The present continuous (see C4)**
**Unit 8 – The future with will**
**Unit 9 – The future with going to**
**Unit 54 – Expressions of frequency**

## A *Sample sentences*

- The annual report contains a lot of background information about the company.
- We usually raise our prices at the beginning of the year. How often do you raise yours?
- These figures don't add up.
- The meeting starts at 9.00 on the dot.

## B *Form*

The present simple comprises:
one part in the positive, i.e. V1(s)
two parts in the negative and interrogative, i.e. **do/does** + V1

| 1 Positive form | 2 Negative form | 3 Interrogative form |
|---|---|---|
| I **work** in different departments. | I **don't produce** a monthly report. | **Do** I **need** more information? |
| We/you/they **work** ... | We/you/they **don't produce** ... | **Do** we/you/they **need** ...? |
| He/she/it **works** ... | He/she/it **doesn't produce** ... | **Does** he/she/it **need** ...? |

## C *Uses*

We use the present simple to talk about:
- characteristic or typical activities
- situations which are permanent
- fixed schedules in the future

1 To indicate a general or permanent activity:
The company manufactures a wide range of plastics.

2 To describe a truth or current belief:
Company cultures evolve and develop.

3 To describe how often an activity is done:
How often do you visit your American plant? – I always go there twice a year.

4 To indicate a fixed schedule in the future:
When does the new plant open? – It opens officially on 1st July.

5 With non-continuous verbs:
Our current prospectus contains information about prices and delivery.
(*not*: is containing)

The following verbs are usually only used in the simple form:
*hope know understand like love mean forget contain imagine*
*remember prefer suppose want belong concern consist of cost*
*equal have involve depend on owe possess own remain require*

***Notes***

1 Remember the **s** in the third person singular, i.e.:
positive – works    negative – doesn't work    interrogative – does ... work?

2 With C1 and 2, no adverb of time is needed.

3 With C3, we use time expressions to indicate how often something happens:
*always usually often sometimes rarely/seldom hardly ever never*

4 Note the position of indefinite frequency markers:
Absenteeism *usually* increases before Christmas. (before the verb)
*Usually* absenteeism increases before Christmas. (at the beginning of the sentence)
Absenteeism is *usually* up before Christmas. (after the verb **to be**)

## Exercise 1

*Complete the following text with the correct form of a verb from the list in the box.*

| employ | use | supply | work | develop |
|---|---|---|---|---|

Softcraft produces computer software for business applications. The company ____________ programmes for general business applications. In addition, Softcraft ____________ customised software for individual requirements. Softcraft ____________ 85 people. About 40 of these ____________ in programme development. The company also ____________ external consultants.

## Exercise 2

*Write sentences to complete a dialogue based on the flow chart below.*

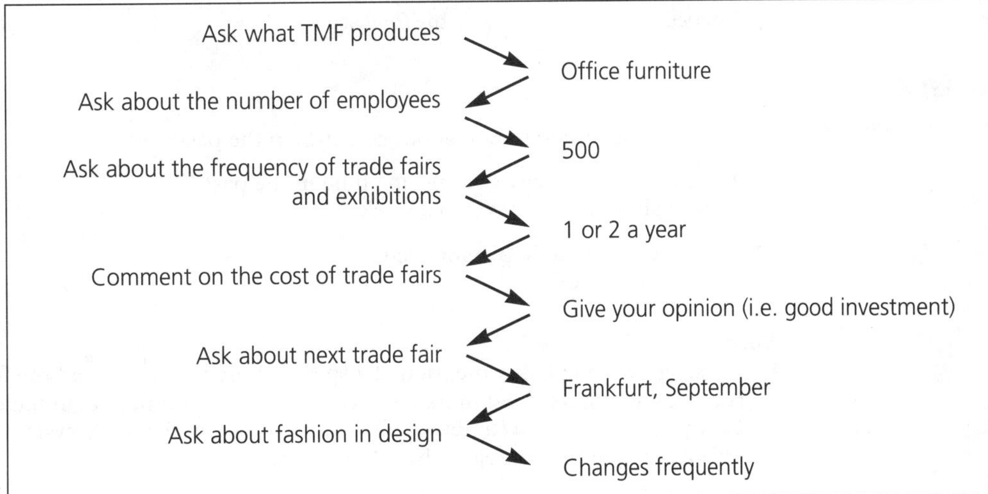

Ask what TMF produces
Office furniture
Ask about the number of employees
500
Ask about the frequency of trade fairs and exhibitions
1 or 2 a year
Comment on the cost of trade fairs
Give your opinion (i.e. good investment)
Ask about next trade fair
Frankfurt, September
Ask about fashion in design
Changes frequently


## Exercise 3

*Use a frequency adverb from the list below to make sentences using the given prompts.*

| | | |
|---|---|---|
| *always* | *frequently* | *usually* |
| *often* | *sometimes* | *occasionally* |
| *rarely* | *hardly ever* | *never* |

1 We/provide/good service
2 I/have/face-to-face meetings/new customers
3 Our company/employ/external consultants
4 I/be/busy in summer
5 He/have/meetings/in the morning
6 I/see/the Senior Vice-President
7 We/write/reports

## Transfer

*Read the following text.*

```
Our company produces electronic components for washing machines.
We are based in Singapore and we have subsidiaries in Korea,
Malaysia and Japan. We sell our products throughout Europe and
our biggest customers are in Europe. At present we are setting
up a new distribution centre in France. Our department is
working on the design plans and at the moment I am studying
different plant layouts.
```

*Use the model above to write a similar description of your own company and your present activities, or a company you know well.*

# UNIT 3

## THE PAST SIMPLE

*See also* Unit 5 – The present perfect simple

### A *Sample sentences*

- Last year the labour laws changed.
- During the year we installed a new management accounting system.
- When did you finish stocktaking? – We put the final details into the system three days ago.
- At that time we didn't need to ask the bank for an overdraft.

### B *Form*

The past simple comprises:
one part in the positive, i.e. V2
two parts in the negative and interrogative, i.e. **did** + V1

| 1 Positive form | 2 Negative form | 3 Interrogative form |
|---|---|---|
| Last year I/you/he/she/it/we/they **worked** in personnel. | At that time I/you/he/she/it/we/they **didn't know** the forecast. | **Did** I/you/he/she/it/we/they **fill** in the form correctly? |

### C *Uses*

We use the past simple to talk about activities in the past.

1 To indicate an activity at a specific time in the past:
I heard about the takeover last week.

2 To ask when an activity happened:
When did you retire?

***Notes***

1 Once we have explicitly mentioned a specific time in the past, all the following activities are understood to happen within that time frame, i.e. in the past:
Last year we *introduced* a new quality control system. After the system *came* into force, we *reduced* the number of rejects by 10 per cent.

2 Typical past time markers include:

| | |
|---|---|
| *yesterday* | *on* + day/date, e.g. on Monday, on 21 January |
| *ago* | *in* + month/year, e.g. in July, in 1983 |
| *last* | *at that time* |

3 **Already** and **recently**
In American English **already** is used with the past simple:
We already appointed a new president.
In British English the present perfect is used (see Unit 5).

**Recently** is used with both the past simple and the present perfect:
I talked to our bank manager recently. (at a specific time in the recent past)
I haven't needed to talk to our bank manager recently. (in a period of time from the recent past till today)

## Exercise 1

*Complete the following paragraph with a correct form of the verb in brackets.*

*On Monday Diano S.p.A. ____________ (report) increased profits for the year. Exports ____________ (climb) by 20 per cent last year but domestic sales ____________ (fall) by 5 per cent. Two months ago the company ____________ (set up) new sales offices in France and Singapore. On the Milan Stock Exchange yesterday the company's share price ____________ (rise) by 300 lire to L. 2,155.*

## Exercise 2

*A journalist interviews a company director about a joint venture with Fallon Inc., an American company. Complete the sentences with an appropriate form of the verb given in brackets.*

J : *When ____________ (begin) negotiations?*

D: *We ____________ (start) three months ago.*

J : *And you reached agreement this morning?*

D: *That's right.*

J : *Was the original idea yours or Fallon's?*

D: *At first we ____________ (approach) Fallon and we ____________ (put forward) some outline proposals.*

J : *____________ (have) any major problems?*

D: *No, as you know, we ____________ (meet) many times and we ____________ (reach) agreement yesterday.*

## Exercise 3

*Look at the following chart which shows the history of a joint venture between two companies. Write a short paragraph which explains the main events.*

| | |
|---|---|
| Jan 1992 ↓ | TELCO reports profits of $28m (increase of 25 per cent) |
| June 1992 ↓ | TeleResearch (TR) produces prototype of Linco Mobile Phone |
| Oct 1992 ↓ | TR offers Telco a licence agreement |
| Nov 1992 | Telco offers to buy Linco Mobile Phone for $2.5m ↓ |
| | TR rejects offer ↓ |
| Jan 1993 | Telco suggests joint venture ↓ |
| | negotiations begin ↓ |
| June 1993 | Telco and TR form a joint venture company, Linco. |

## Transfer

*Write six sentences describing either:*

- the history of a project you know well
- your educational and/or professional background.

# UNIT 4

## THE PAST CONTINUOUS

*See also* Unit 3 – The past simple

## A *Sample sentences*

- We were trying to find alternative work, when they went on strike.
- While we were seeking a solution, they were doing everything to oppose us.
- A: Which team were you working with last year?
  B: With Paul's team. We were trying to cut fuel costs.

## B *Form*

The past continuous comprises two parts:
the past tense of **to be** + V1 …*ing*

| 1 Positive form | 2 Negative form | 3 Interrogative form |
|---|---|---|
| I **was checking** the stock. | I **was not/wasn't expecting** a delivery. | What **was** I **doing** at this time last year? |
| We/you/they **were checking** … | We/you/they **were not/weren't expecting** … | What **were** we/you/they **doing** …? |
| He/she/it **was checking** … | He/she/it **was not/wasn't expecting** … | What **was** he/she/it **doing** …? |

## C *Uses*

We use the past continuous to provide a past time frame for another activity.

**Timeframing:**
The Health and Safety Committee were discussing hazards when the fire started.

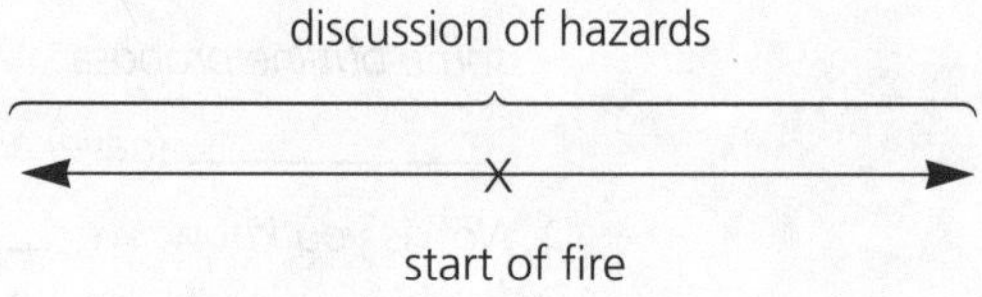

The fire started at a past point of time (X) within a period.

discussion of hazards

X

start of fire

What were you doing at this time last year?

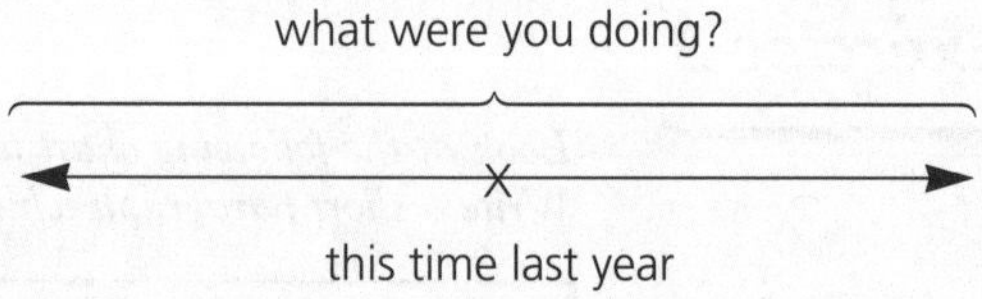

This time last year = a past point of time within a time frame; 'what were you doing' indicates a past period of time and provides a time frame for 'at this time last year'.

what were you doing?

X

this time last year

While the fire brigade were fighting the fire, we were trying to save some of our works of art.

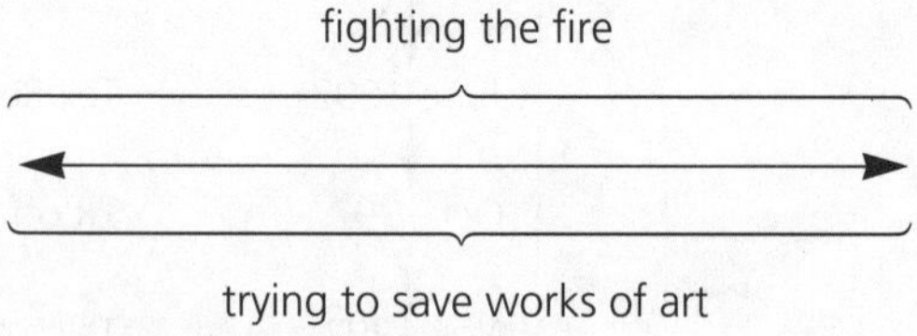

Here 'trying to save works of art' is not at a point of time (X), but lasts for a period of time (indicated by the lower brace).

fighting the fire

trying to save works of art

In fact the two actions happened at the same time and for the same period. Therefore, both verbs are in the past continuous.

***Notes***

1 The past continuous does not indicate an activity that lasted for a long time:
I was working with John for 10 years.(✗) I worked with John for 10 years.(✓)
I was working with John when the fire broke out.(✓)

2 Expressions with the preposition **during** can be changed to clauses with **while** + past continuous:
During the product launch, two members of the team resigned.
While we were launching the product, two members of the team resigned.

## THE PAST CONTINUOUS

### Exercise 1

*How many sentence combinations can you make based on the following alternatives?*

| | | | | | | |
|---|---|---|---|---|---|---|
| The manager<br>Mrs Ford<br>The production team<br>I | was<br>were | designing<br>writing<br>researching | new ideas<br>a new plant<br>a report | when | they<br>he<br>the Director<br>I<br>she | resigned<br>abandoned the project<br>found a solution |

### Exercise 2

*Complete the following sentences by choosing a suitable form of the verb in brackets. Use either the past simple or the past continuous.*

1 *We ___________ (review) safety procedures when the accident ___________ (happen).*
2 *While we ___________ (clean) the tanks the chemicals ___________ (pollute) the river.*
3 *The plant ___________ (operate) at full capacity before the explosion ___________ (happen).*
4 *We ___________ (turn off) the supply because the pipe ___________ (leak).*
5 *As the equipment ___________ (get old) we ___________ (decide) to replace it.*
6 *When the fire ___________ (start) she ___________ (wear) protective clothing.*
7 *While the company ___________ (investigate) the accident the government ___________ (introduce) new regulations.*
8 *The risk of explosion ___________ (be) highest precisely when workers ___________ (repair) the pipe.*

### Exercise 3

*Below is an extract from a report on an accident at a construction site. Complete the text by choosing an appropriate form of each verb in brackets. Use either the past simple or the past continuous.*

> On Monday at 16.30 a construction worker was hurt at the Iribas plant. The foreman said that four men ___________ (work) on a roof when a crane ___________ (hit) the wall of the building. One of the men ___________ (slip) and ___________ (fall) to the ground. The crane driver ___________ (try) to lift a metal pipe when he ___________ (lose) control. A preliminary report identifies three factors which contributed to the accident: the injured worker ___________ (not/wear) a safety harness. The crane ___________ (work) in a prohibited area. It ___________ (rain), so work should have been stopped.

### Transfer

*Think of your own career or work. Make sentences in which a past action occurs within a given time period.*

*Example:*
*We were doing a lot of work with Japanese suppliers when Imtel bought the company.*

# UNIT 5

## THE PRESENT PERFECT SIMPLE

***See also*** **Unit 3 – The past simple**
**Unit 6 – The present perfect continuous**

### A *Sample sentences*

- ◆ Business confidence has dropped as a result of the recession.
- ◆ Have you seen the new legislation on environmental protection?
- ◆ The markets haven't increased at all this year.
- ◆ We have led the field in this market niche since the early 1990s.

### B *Form*

The present perfect simple comprises two parts:
**has/have** + V3

| 1 Positive form | 2 Negative form | 3 Interrogative form |
|---|---|---|
| I/you/we/they **have/'ve finished** the project. | I/you/we/they **have not/ haven't** + V3 | **Have** I/you/we/they + V3? |
| He/she/it **has/'s finished** the project. | He/she/it **has not/hasn't** + V3 | **Has** he/she/it + V3? |

### C *Uses*

In meaning, the present perfect belongs to the present tenses. This is because in the various uses the meaning is always linked to the present, rather than the past.

1 To indicate an activity at some non-specific time in the past with an impact or result in the present or future:
The government has reduced interest rates. (present result = rates are now lower)
*cf.* The government reduced interest rates last week. (specific time in the past)
We have recruited six new workers. (present result = six new employees)
*cf.* We recruited six new workers at the beginning of May. (specific time in the past)

2 To indicate an activity within a period of time which is not yet finished, i.e. unfinished time:
Quality has improved this year. (The year is not yet finished.)
*cf.* Quality improved last year. (Last year is finished.)

3 To indicate an activity which started in the past and continues to the present:
So far/Up to now we have purchased three companies. (in the period between then and now)
She has worked as Purchasing Manager since 1989. (She started in 1989 and she is still Purchasing Manager today.)
The company has operated from this site for five years. (It started operations here five years ago and is still operating here today.)

***Notes***

1 As the activity in C1 happened at a non-specific time in the past, no time marker is used.

2 In C2, typical time markers are:
*this morning/week/month/year* *today* *now*

**Just** and **just now** are considered as present time markers, and are used with the present perfect:
We have just signed the acceptance certificate.

**Recently** can also be used with the present perfect (see also Unit 3, Note 3):
We have recently changed over to Microsoft Windows.

**Already** and **yet** both provide a frame of unfinished time; the time frame starts at an unspecified point in the past and continues to the present. **Already** is typically used in positive sentences; **yet** in negative and interrogative sentences:
Have you made an appointment yet? (between then and now)
We have already recruited someone for the post. (between then and now)

3 In C3, typical time markers are:
*since* (to indicate the starting point), *for* (to indicate the period)
She has worked here since 1991. (starting point)
She has worked here for seven years. (period)

# THE PRESENT PERFECT SIMPLE

## Exercise 1

*Make six sentences based on the following options.*

| | | | | |
|---|---|---|---|---|
| Mennis plc<br>I<br>We<br>Paolo<br>Mr Joyce<br>She | has<br>has not<br>have<br>have not | called<br>contacted<br>sent<br>ordered<br>arrived<br>spoken | you<br>us<br>the goods<br>anything<br>to Frank | yet<br>recently<br>today |

## Exercise 2

*Complete the following extract by choosing the correct form of the verb in brackets. Use either the past simple or the present perfect simple.*

*Last year our company ___________ (report) a small increase in profits. This year we ___________ (see) continued improvement and our turnover ___________ (rise) by 15 per cent. This is very good news in a difficult world market. In fact internationally, the market ___________ (fall). Naturally, our costs ___________ (go up) and so the rise in profits is not so great. It is true that our domestic performance ___________ (be helped) by the collapse of our competitor, Capra & Pecora, which ___________ (go out of business) in January.*

## Exercise 3

*JBM is a Financial Services Company. The Managing Director is Martina Pavlovski. Here is an extract from a speech she made to shareholders at the AGM.*

*Read the extract from her speech and place the different actions in bold in the appropriate column in the box below, according to the meaning in the context. The first one has been done for you.*

'For our sector, **recent times have been difficult**. However, it is clear that we are not alone. **The world economy has suffered a downturn** and all sectors of industry have experienced difficulties. But this year **we have already seen signs of improvement**; I am sure you know that especially **in Asia there has been increased growth** and this will benefit us greatly. Also, turning to insurance, **we have been involved in the insurance market** for only a relatively short time, but it is good to see that **this sector has grown rapidly** since 1991.'

| Activity at some non-specific time in the past with an impact or result in the present or future. | Activity within a period of time which is not yet finished. | Activity which started in the past and continues to the present. |
|---|---|---|
| | | recent times have been difficult |

## Transfer

*Make sentences about the recent economic performance of either your own company, an industry you know about, or the economy of your country. You can use both the present perfect and the past simple.*

# UNIT 6

## THE PRESENT PERFECT CONTINUOUS

*See also* Unit 3 – The past simple
Unit 5 – The present perfect simple

### A *Sample sentences*

A: How long have you been leasing this coffee machine?
B: Well, I suppose we've been leasing it for about 3 years. We've been using it quite a lot.
A: And has the coffee tasted okay?
B: Well, it's been tasting a bit weak recently.
A: That's because the coffee powder hasn't been dropping through properly.

### B *Form*

The present perfect continuous comprises two parts:
the present perfect of **to be** + V1 ...*ing*

| 1 Positive form | 2 Negative form | 3 Interrogative form |
|---|---|---|
| I/you/we/they **have/'ve been using** the agency.<br>He/she/it **has/'s been using** the agency. | I/you/we/they **have not been /haven't been** + V1 ...ing<br>He/she/it **has not been/ hasn't been** + V1 ...ing | **Have** I/you/we/they **been** + V1 ...ing?<br>**Has** he/she/it **been** + V1 ...ing? |

### C *Uses*

The present perfect continuous belongs to the present tenses because, in its uses, the meaning is always linked to the present, rather than the past. We use the present perfect continuous:

1 To indicate an activity at some non-specific time in the past with an impact or result in the present or future:
We have been reviewing our software development programme.
Here, the verb phrase 'have been reviewing' indicates an action over a period of time.
*cf.* We've just finished reviewing our software development programme.
Here, the verb phrase 'have finished reviewing' indicates an action at a point of time. 'To finish' cannot happen over a period of time; it indicates an instantaneous action. We use the present perfect continuous for verb phrases which can happen over a period of time.

2 To indicate an activity which started in the past and continues to the present:
We have been developing quality toys here since 1953.
Again the verb phrase 'have been developing' indicates an action over a period of time; in this case the period of time is specified.

Compare the following sentences:
Since the beginning of the year we have tested three new applications.
We have been testing three new applications since the beginning of the year.
In the first sentence we are interested in the fact that the tests are now finished and that we can now come to some conclusions, or move on to a new stage in the development cycle; in the second sentence we are interested in the action itself – the testing – and its duration.

# THE PRESENT PERFECT CONTINUOUS

## Exercise 1

*Make three sentences from each of the following prompts in the present perfect continuous. Make first a positive statement, then a negative statement and finally a question.*

You/work/Paulus & Company/for many years
They/sell/shares/since January

## Exercise 2

*Read the following sentences. Decide which show examples of actions which continued over a period of time and which show actions which occurred at specific points in time. Write 'period' or 'point'.*

1 *George has been working too hard recently.* ________
2 *He has made a lot of mistakes.* ________
3 *He has been travelling all over the country.* ________
4 *He's even had a couple of minor road accidents.* ________
5 *He's asked for some time off work.* ________
6 *We've been thinking of ways to help him.* ________

## Exercise 3

*Use the following prompts to produce a short internal memo about recruitment problems in a clothing distribution company.*

**MEMO**

To: B.J. McCusker
(Sales)

From: H.V.

Subject: Recruitment of Sales Director
(Northern Region)

We/to advertise/for six months/national newspapers. We/to interview/five candidates but/to be not able to fill/position.

This month/to place/an advertisement/Sales & Marketing Journal.

I/to talk to/'Head Hunting' agency. This seems to be an increasingly probable solution. Any comments?

## Transfer

*Describe a decision connected with your own work. Use examples of both the present perfect simple and the continuous form.*

*Example:*
ABC has decided to change the management structure. They have been thinking about this for a long time.

# UNIT 7

## THE PAST PERFECT

***See also*** **Unit 3 – The past simple**
**Units 10 and 11 – The conditionals (1) and (2)**
**Unit 46 – Clauses of time**

## A *Sample sentences*

- When we installed the new software, it had already become obsolete.
- Once we had identified our weaknesses, we devised an action plan to counter them.
- The Financial Controller reported that the company had had a satisfactory year.

## B *Form*

The past perfect is:

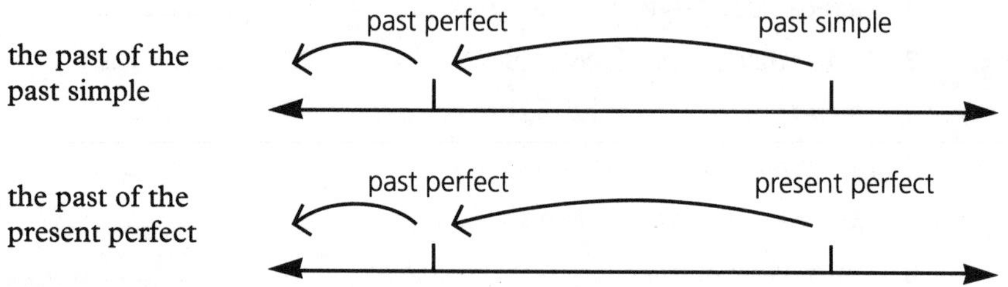


The past perfect comprises two parts:
**had** + V3

| 1 Positive form | 2 Negative form | 3 Interrogative form |
|---|---|---|
| I/you/he/she/it/we/they **had/'d finished** the project. | I/you/he/she/it/we/they **had not/hadn't** + V3 | **Had** I/you/he/she/it/we/they + V3? |

## C *Uses*

We use the past perfect to talk about activities which happened at a time before the past.

1 To indicate an activity at a time before the past:
As soon as we had announced the new chairman, our share prices went up.

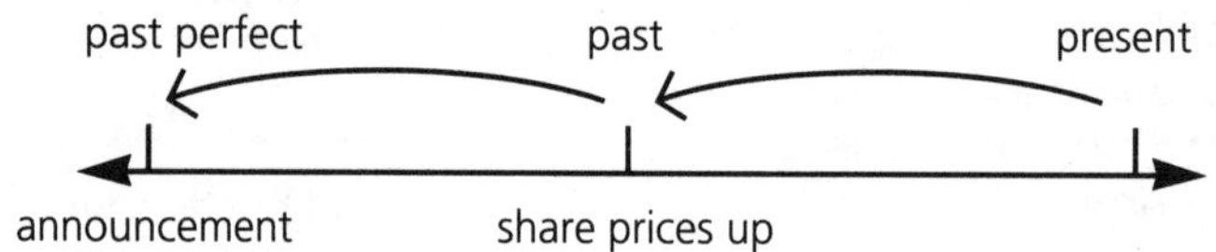


Before we appointed the new chairman, our share prices had been very low.

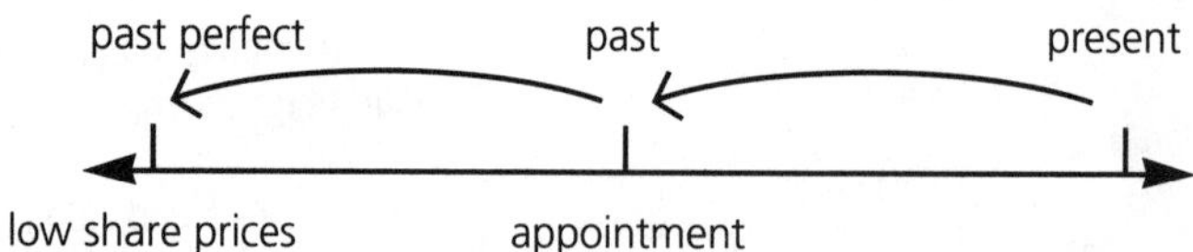


2 To report a present perfect tense after a past tense verb of speaking:
The Financial Controller said, 'We have had a good year.'
The Financial Controller said that they had had a good year.

The present perfect in the direct speech in the first sentence is changed to the past perfect in the indirect speech in the second sentence.

***Notes***

1 We often use a past simple form where the sequence of events is clear:
After the new logo was designed, our image definitely improved.
(The use of **after** makes it clear that the first event was the design of the new logo.)

2 We use the past perfect with the following time conjunctions:
*after before once until when as soon as*

# 7 TASKS

## THE PAST PERFECT

### Exercise 1

*Use the prompts below to write sentences which include a past perfect tense contrasted with a simple past tense. Use positive, negative and interrogative forms. Here is an example:*

speak to/agency//when they/change/the agreement

*We had spoken to the agency when they changed the agreement.*
*We hadn't spoken to the agency when they changed the agreement.*
*Had we spoken to the agency when they changed the agreement?*

1 plane/leave//when they/reach/airport
2 she/already/sign/contract//when you/call
3 You/send/report//before we/notice/mistake

### Exercise 2

*Look at the time lines below to make sentences which contrast two different actions. Use **already** in each sentence. The first has been done for you.*

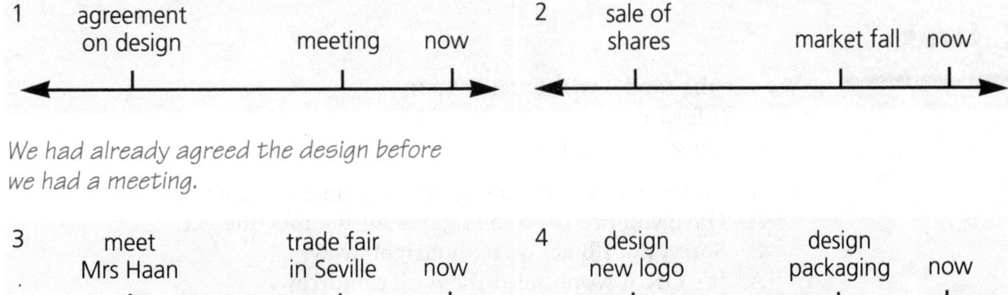


*We had already agreed the design before we had a meeting.*

### Exercise 3

*Your company has contracted an advertising agency to market your goods. You receive the following letter from them, describing preliminary results of a market research survey.*

*Imagine you telephone a colleague to tell him about these results. What would you say? Write five sentences using past perfect tenses.*

*Example:*
*More women than men had bought clothes in the previous week.*

**DTR Market Surveys**
King Richard Street
Coventry CV2 7RT
Telephone (0203) 542281
Fax (0203) 542020

Jean Tournier
KeeK Klothing
ST Paul's Avenue
Dublin 6
Irish Republic

Our Ref: K/JT7
Your Ref:

Dear Jean,

Re: KeeK Klothing Survey: Preliminary Results

We have now finished the first stage of analysing the results of our survey. I am preparing a full report to send to you.

We asked whether the respondents had bought clothes in the previous week, and divided the respondents by sex and into three age categories. The results are as follows:

| sex | 18-25 | 26-35 | 36-45 |
|---|---|---|---|
| male | 62% | 49% | 31% |
| female | 71% | 57% | 42% |

We were surprised by the large number in all categories but the margin of error was calculated at only ±5 per cent and the sample size was 850.

I'll phone you later to discuss this.

Best regards,

*Simon Deekes*
Simon Deekes
DTR Market Surveys Ltd

### Transfer

*Write four examples of sentences describing events affecting your work, in which a past tense is contrasted with a past perfect tense.*

*Example:*
*I had already worked in marketing before I joined my present company.*

# UNIT 8

## THE FUTURE with **WILL**

*See also* Unit 1 – The present continuous (section C4)
Unit 2 – The present simple (section C4)
Unit 9 – The future with **going to**
Unit 17 – **Will** and **would**

### A *Sample sentences*

- OK, I'll take the minutes of the meeting.
- I think I'll read the proposal of the external consultant first.
- They certainly won't reply until after the weekend.
- At the first stage, the machine will be completely overhauled.

### B *Form*

The future with **will** comprises two parts:
the modal **will** + V1

| 1 Positive form | 2 Negative form | 3 Interrogative form |
|---|---|---|
| I/you/he/she/it/we/they **will/'ll deliver** the goods tomorrow. | I/you/he/she/it/we/they **will not/won't be** at the meeting. | **Will** I/you/he/she/it/we/they **arrive** in time? |

### C *Uses*

We use the modal **will** to talk about:
– the future
– willingness (see Unit 17)

1 To indicate an activity decided at the time of speaking:
A: Have you prepared the figures for the meeting yet?
B: Sorry, no. I'll get on with it right away.
A: It's OK. I won't need them till tomorrow.
B: Right. I'll bring them to your office as soon as I've finished.

2 To indicate a neutral activity in the future or a part of a process:
The conference will begin next Monday at 9 o'clock.
First the minister will present a keynote speech about opportunities in Rotaronga.

3 After verbs of mental activity, e.g. *think*, *hope*, *expect*:
I expect that this decision will cause a lot of controversy.

4 After adverbs of certainty, probability and possibility:
The unions will probably call a meeting of their members as soon as they hear.

5 In the main clause of conditional sentences type I (see Unit 10):
Even if we back down, we won't be able to stop them. (*not*: even if we will back down…)

***Notes***

1 The contraction **'ll** can be used after all subjects (noun and pronoun) – but only in speech:
The new policy'll be in force next month.

2 Future time markers are:
*next …*
*on* + day/date, e.g. on Monday, on 21 January
*in* + month/year, e.g. in July, in 1999

3 In C3, the negative of 'I think he will' is usually 'I don't think he will':
We think they will say yes.
We don't think they will say yes. (*rather than*: We think they won't say yes.)

Notice also:
I think so. (positive) I don't think so. (negative)

Notice, however, the following equivalents:
We hope/expect (that) they will say yes. We hope/expect (that) they won't say no.

4 In C4, notice the word order (**will** and adverb) in the positive and negative sentences:
They will definitely accept the new pay award.
They definitely won't accept the new pay award.

# THE FUTURE with WILL

## Exercise 1

*Look again at the five uses of **will** explained on the opposite page. Then read the sentences below and categorise them according to type of use.*

1 I think I'll go to Athens soon.
2 Are you thirsty? I'll get you something to drink.
3 We'll watch a video, then we'll see the production plant.
4 Hold on – I'll just phone Marta to ask her.
5 When you come, I'll introduce you to Maria Penrose, our Finance Manager.
6 There'll probably be a fall in profits in the spring.
7 Perhaps I'll get to Sydney next year.
8 I expect you'll stay in a hotel, won't you?
9 John has arrived. I'll go to meet him.
10 The report will be ready on Monday.

## Exercise 2

*Write appropriate sentences to complete the following exchanges. Include a form of the word **will**. The first has been done for you.*

1 *Martin: Sara has arrived.*
*Kevin: (come)*
*I'll come at once.*

2 *Sara: What'll your talk be about?*
*Hanna: (cost savings)*
______________________________

3 *Emma: What do you think about the possibility of doing more business in Europe?*
*Fred: (easy)*
______________________________

4 *Isobel: The photocopier has broken down.*
*Piers: (repair man)*
______________________________

5 *Charlotte: Katrin is away today. She's at home.*
*Maeve: (telephone)*
______________________________

6 *Lee: If we go to Paris, who will we meet?*
*Dietmar: (not Bergit)*
______________________________

## Exercise 3

*Write sentences which use **will** and match the different uses indicated. The first has been done for you.*

1 A neutral activity in the future.
*The meeting will start at 9.00.*
2 After a verb of mental activity.
3 A neutral activity as part of a process, e.g. a presentation.
4 A neutral activity in the future.
5 Activity decided at the time of speaking.
6 In the main clause of conditional I sentences. (see Unit 10)

## Transfer

*Answer the following questions about your work.*

1 What special projects do you think you will be working on next year?
2 What are you doing later today?
3 Who'll you see tomorrow?
4 What do you expect you will be doing this time next year?
5 If business drops by 50 per cent will you lose your job?

# UNIT 9

## THE FUTURE with GOING TO

*See also* Unit 1 – The present continuous
Unit 2 – The present simple
Unit 8 – The future with **will**

### A *Sample sentences*

- The figures look pretty impressive! How are we going to maintain them?
- We are going to end the conference on Friday at 6 o'clock.
- The materials have just arrived. That means production isn't going to be delayed.
- When are you going to have that report ready?

### B *Form*

The future with **going to** comprises three parts:
**to be** + **going to** + V1

| 1 Positive form | | 2 Negative form | | 3 Interrogative form | |
|---|---|---|---|---|---|
| **I am**<br>He/she/it **is**<br>We/you/they **are** | **going to analyse** the results. | **I am not/I'm not**<br>He/she/it **is not/isn't**<br>He**'s**/she**'s**/it**'s not**<br>We/you/they **are not/ aren't**<br>We**'re**/you**'re**/they**'re not** | **going to analyse** the results. | **Am** I<br>**Is** he/she/it<br>**Are** you/we/they | **going to analyse** the results? |

### C *Uses*

We use **going to** to talk about activities in the future.

1 To indicate an action that has already been decided:
They are going to subcontract part of the assembly out next year.

2 To indicate an intention:
We are going to look for cheaper producers in the Far East.

3 To indicate a future activity based on the present situation:
Interest rates have just fallen. So we are certainly going to be able to make the investment.

***Notes***
Future time markers are:
*next* ...
*on* + day/date, e.g. on Monday, on 21 January
*in* + month/year, e.g. in July, in 1999

## THE FUTURE with GOING TO

### Exercise 1

*Look at three uses of the future with **going to** described on the previous page. Categorise the following examples in the box below.*

1 The international market is increasingly competitive. We are going to have to improve our sales performance.
2 Laconte & Cie are going to open a plant in Rouen.
3 There's no way this situation can continue. I'm going to insist on a different strategy.
4 There's going to be a new range of products very soon.
5 What are we going to do about the supply problem?
6 Fred's going to Singapore tomorrow.

| Sentence | Action already decided | Intention | Activity based on present situation |
|---|---|---|---|
| 1 | | | |
| 2 | | | |
| 3 | | | |
| 4 | | | |
| 5 | | | |
| 6 | | | |

### Exercise 2

*Look at the graph below. It shows sales and expected sales for three products, A, B and C. Complete the following paragraph.*

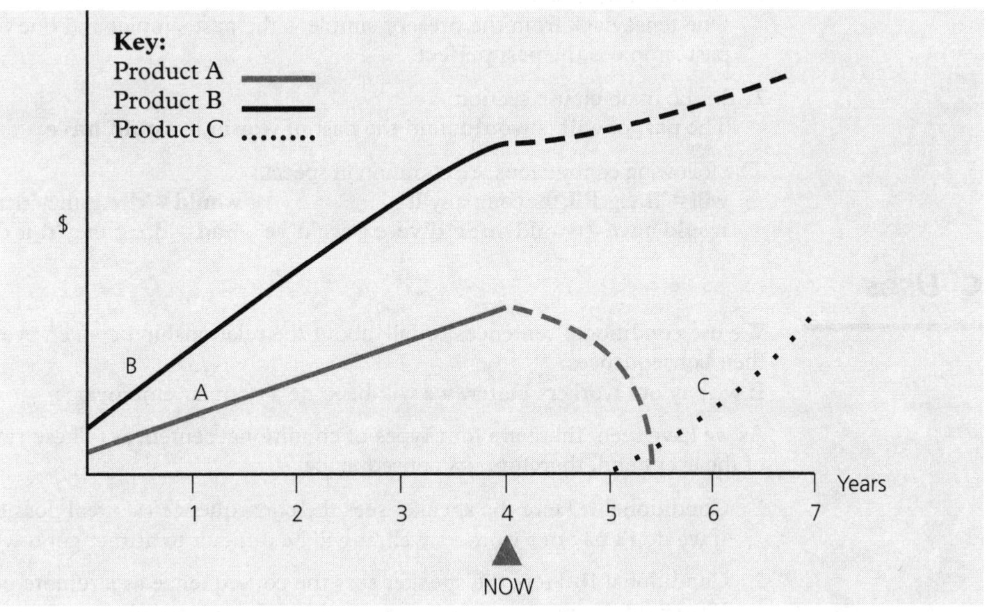


*'Product A is an old product, nearing the end of its life. As the graph shows, sales for Product A ____________ (fall) whereas sales for product B, which is very profitable, ____________ (rise). Because of this, we ____________ (cut) production of A and at the same time concentrate efforts on B. In addition, we ____________ (launch) a new product, C.'*

### Transfer

*Write sentences on any of the following:*

- your intentions
- an action already decided
- some future activity based on the present situation.

# UNIT 10

## THE CONDITIONALS (1)

*See also* Unit 11 – The conditionals (2)
Unit 17 – **Will and would**
Unit 19 – **Can and could**
Unit 21 – **Shall and should**

### A *Sample sentences*

- If we pay the tax on time, we won't be liable for any further payment.
- You would have to pay interest if you didn't settle the bill within 60 days.
- If they hadn't been able to reschedule the debt, they would certainly have gone bankrupt.
- If companies grow too quickly, they risk overheating.

### B *Form*

A conditional sentence comprises two clauses:
the **if** clause + the main clause

There are four principal types of conditional sentences: conditional I, conditional II, conditional III and universal conditions.

| Conditional | If clause | Main clause |
|---|---|---|
| I | present simple | future with **will** |
| II | past simple | conditional with **would** |
| III | past perfect | past conditional with **would have** |
| universal | present simple | present simple |

Notice the relationship between the tenses in the table above:

1 In the **if** clause section:
One tense back from the present simple is the past simple; and one tense back from the past simple is the past perfect.

2 In the main clause section:
The past of **will** is **would**; and the past of **would** is **would have**.

The following contractions are common in speech:
**will** = **'ll**, e.g. **I'll**, the company**'ll** — **would** = **'d**, e.g. they**'d**, it**'d**, the organisation**'d**
**would have** = **would've** or **'d've**, e.g. we**'d've** — **had** = **'d**, e.g. they**'d**, it**'d**, the organisation**'d**

### C *Uses*

We use conditional sentences to talk about the relationship between events and their consequences:
If we pay our workers better, we will become a popular employer.

As we have seen, there are four types of conditional sentences. These reflect the probability of the event and, therefore, its consequence.

1 Conditional I. Here the speaker sees the consequence as a real possibility:
If we don't pay our workers well, it will be difficult to attract good workers.

2 Conditional II. Here the speaker sees the consequence as a remote possibility:
If we paid our workers better, we would become a popular employer.

3 Conditional III. Here the speaker recognises that the consequence is an impossibility, i.e. cannot be fulfilled:
If we had paid our workers better, they wouldn't have left the company.

4 Universal conditions. Here the speaker indicates that the consequence always follows the event:
If a company pays well, it attracts good workers. (Good pay always attracts good workers.)

*Notes*

1 **Will** is a modal verb; in conditional I, other modal verbs can be used in the main clause, e.g. **may**, **can**, and **must**; similarly in conditionals II and III, the modal in the main clause can be **would** or **might** or **could** or **should**:
If payment comes/came late, we may/might make other arrangements.

2 There are certain polite formulae where we can use **would** or **could** after **if**:
We would be very grateful/much obliged if you would/could send us the information.

## Exercise 1

*Complete the missing part of each of the following conditional sentences.*

1 *If you ____________ (come) we'll discuss it in detail.*
2 *If we ____________ (reach) agreement we'd sign the contract the same day.*
3 *Unless there is a major problem, we ____________ (need) only one day.*
4 *If we have good advertising, the product ____________ (be) a success.*
5 *If there ____________ (be) an easy solution, we would have avoided the problems.*
6 *If we had taken your advice, we ____________ (spend) more money.*

## Exercise 2

*Look at the following scenarios showing events and their consequences. Write three conditional sentences for each situation, one for each of the three categories below. The first one has been done for you.*

– real possibilities
– remote possibilities
– impossibilities

| Events | | Consequences |
|---|---|---|
| 1 Increase in sales | → | Increase production |
| 2 Poor sales | → | Change distribution network |
| 3 High demand overseas | → | Increase Export Sales team |
| 4 World recession | → | Drop in world market |

1 *If there is an increase in sales we will increase production.*
*If there were an increase in sales we would increase production.*
*If there had been an increase in sales we would have increased production.*

## Exercise 3

*Imagine you work for Big Insurance Company, a subsidiary of International Credit Bank. You write to the bank's customers to tell them about the risks involved in not having insurance with Big Insurance Company.*

*In your letter you describe the consequences of various disasters. Write a sentence for each of the following events and possible consequences. The first has been done for you.*

1 accident → stop work
*If you had a serious accident you would have to stop work.*

2 stop work → no protection for family
3 period in hospital → no cover for hospital fees
4 house fire → insufficient cover to replace lost items
5 road accident → no cover for legal expenses
6 death → no life assurance
7 no life assurance → family with no money

## Transfer

1 *Write a note to a colleague or a friend suggesting an economy measure to reduce costs (conditional II).*
2 *Write another note to a colleague or friend describing a decision you took which had serious consequences.*
*Suggest what you should have done and what the alternative result would have been (conditional III).*
3 *Think of your own company or country and write sentences containing different conditionals.*

Example (company):

| | | |
|---|---|---|
| Conditional I | *investment now* → | *benefits in the future* |
| Conditional II | *new products* → | *new markets/increased market share* |
| Conditional III | *past investment* → | *bigger turnover* |

# UNIT 11

## THE CONDITIONALS (2)

*See also* Unit 10 – **The conditionals (1)**
Unit 17 – **Will and would**
Unit 19 – **Can and could**
Unit 21 – **Shall and should**

### A *Sample sentences*

- This drain on cash will only be a short-term problem, provided we take action soon.
- In the event that you can't sign the contract, please contact our legal department.
- Should this bill not be paid within 60 days, we reserve the right to reclaim the goods.

### B *Form*

The following words and expressions can also introduce conditional clauses or phrases:

*provided/providing (that)*   *on condition that*   *so long as*
These expressions mean 'if and only if'.

*in case*   *in the case of*   *in the event that*   *in the event of*
These expressions indicate that a future event may or may not happen.

*unless*
This word means 'if not'.

We can also use inverted constructions as alternatives to conditionals I, II and III.

Conditional I – inverted construction with **should**:
Should the supplier fail to deliver on time, a penalty clause will be applied.

Conditional II – inverted construction with the subjunctive **were** … **to**:
Were the supplier to deliver late, a penalty clause would be applied.

Conditional III – inverted construction with the past perfect:
Had the customer refused to accept the goods, we would have terminated the contract.

### C *Uses*

1 *provided/providing (that)*   *on condition that*   *so long as*
These expressions are used in conditional I and II constructions:
We will replace the equipment, on condition that the purchaser follows the service schedule.
The buyer would be entitled to a refund so long as he returned the goods within 7 days.

2 *in case*   *in the case of*   *in the event that*   *in the event of*
These expressions refer to future events and are used in conditional I constructions:
Customers are reminded to keep proof of purchase in case they wish to make a complaint.
Both **in** (**the**) **case of** and **in the event of** are used with a noun phrase:
In the event of loss, you must get a certificate from the police.

3 The inverted constructions are widely used in formal written documents, e.g. legal contracts or agreements.

## Exercise 1

*Look at the following extract from a tour operator's terms and conditions and underline the conditional markers.*

**Deposit and payment**
No holiday booking will be accepted unless accompanied by the necessary deposit. A confirmation will then be issued once the deposit has been received. The balance may be paid at any time provided it is not later than eight weeks before departure.

**Changes to bookings**
As you will appreciate, your holiday arrangements are planned many months in advance and on rare occasions it may be necessary to make changes. In the unfortunate event that we have to make major changes, you will be entitled to compensation as shown in Appendix 1. However, you will only be entitled to compensation on condition that you contact our office not later than seven days after notification of the proposed changes. Provided that we can substitute a holiday of similar quality, there will be no entitlement to compensation.

**Misbehaviour**
We reserve the absolute right to terminate without notice the holiday arrangements of any person in the case of misbehaviour likely to annoy other passengers.

**Should you have a problem**
Should you have a problem, remember that our representatives are on hand to help.

## Exercise 2

*Match a clause on the left with a clause on the right to make six sentences.*

1 In case of fire,
2 We will replace faulty goods,
3 We will continue trading
4 We will not renew our contract
5 We would certainly have reconsidered our prices
6 Please contact us

**a** so long as we have goods to sell.
**b** had you asked us.
**c** in case you have any questions.
**d** hotel guests should leave the building immediately.
**e** unless you are able to offer better conditions.
**f** provided that the customer returns them in an unused condition together with proof of purchase.

## Exercise 3

*Change the **if** constructions in the following legal contract clauses into inverted constructions.*

1 If the policyholder wishes to extend this policy, he must notify the company before the policy expiry date.
2 If the policyholder does not contact the company before the expiry date, the company shall be entitled to terminate the agreement.
3 If the policyholder subsequently decided to renew the policy, the company would be entitled to charge an introductory fee.
4 However, if the company decided not to renew the policy, for whatever reason, they must inform the policyholder within seven days.
5 If the company did not inform the policyholder within the specified time, they may not refuse to renew the policy.
6 The company may terminate the contract if the policyholder:
   **a** does not disclose all the relevant information;
   **b** did not complete all the sections;
   **c** had failed to pay the full premium by the agreed time.

## Transfer

*As we have seen in this unit, some conditional constructions are more commonly found in formal documents such as legal contracts.*

*Write six clauses from your contract of employment or invent six clauses for the contract you would like to have.*

# UNIT 12

## TENSE REVIEW

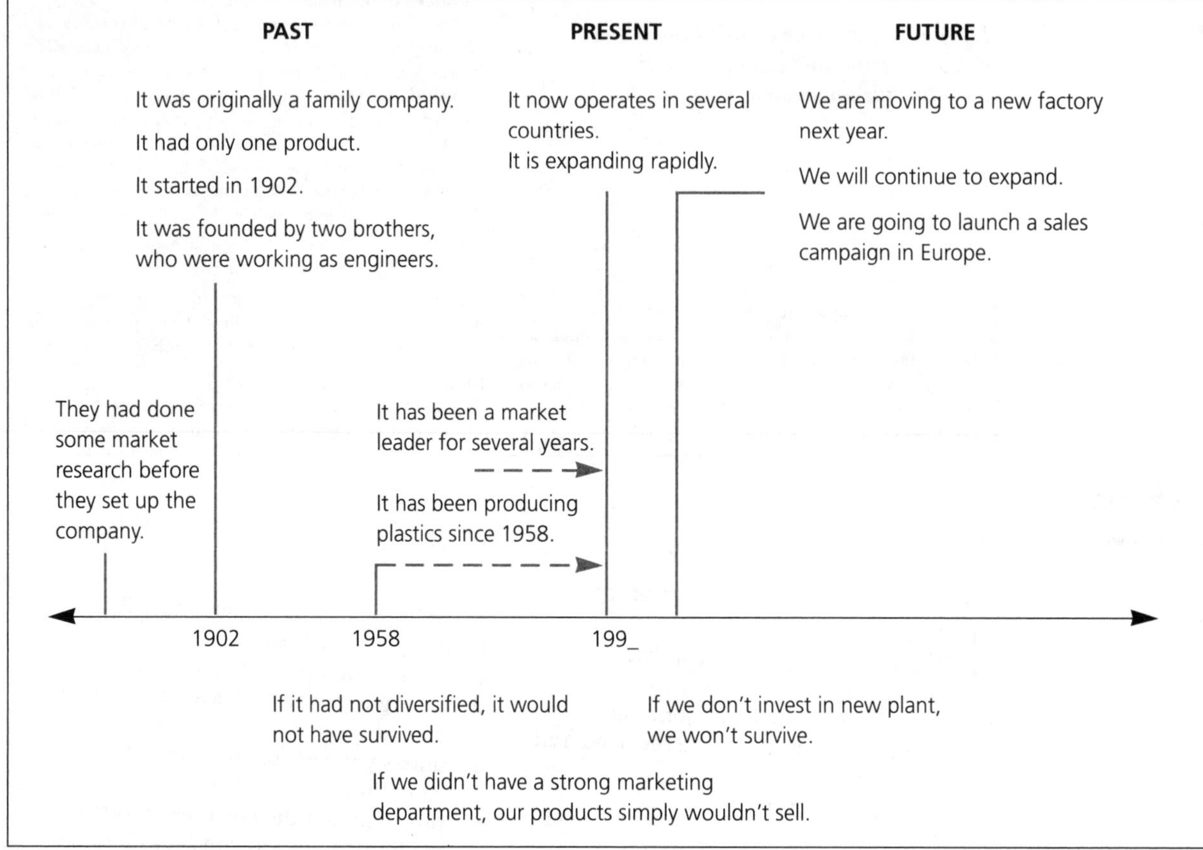

PAST
PRESENT
FUTURE
It was originally a family company.
It had only one product.
It started in 1902.
It was founded by two brothers, who were working as engineers.
It now operates in several countries.
It is expanding rapidly.
We are moving to a new factory next year.
We will continue to expand.
We are going to launch a sales campaign in Europe.
They had done some market research before they set up the company.
It has been a market leader for several years.
It has been producing plastics since 1958.
1902
1958
199_
If it had not diversified, it would not have survived.
If we don't invest in new plant, we won't survive.
If we didn't have a strong marketing department, our products simply wouldn't sell.

## Exercise 1

*Look at the following summary of the history of Mantegna S.p.A., an Italian engineering company. Write a short paragraph about the company, using as many different tenses as you can.*

| | |
|---|---|
| 1952 | Mantegna S.p.A. founded by Leonardo Mantegna. |
| 1952–55 | Small factory in Verona. Main product: steel pipes. |
| 1956 | New production plant in Milan. Began valve manufacturing. |
| 1975 | Head Office moved to Milan. |
| 1980 | Rejected attempted takeover by Echo Inc., Chicago. |
| 1981–90 | Sales offices established in 48 different countries. |
| 1990–now | Turnover $450m. Range of over 400 products.<br>Planning expansion into automotive sector.<br>Next year: new plant in United Kingdom.<br>In three years: new plant in Boston, Massachusetts. |

## Transfer

*Look at the diagram on the previous page. Think of the history of a company you know well and write a paragraph about it.*

# UNIT 13

## VERB …ING

*See also* Unit 14 – Infinitive
Unit 15 – Verb …**ing** or infinitive + **to**

### A *Sample sentences*

- The MD is responsible for running the company on a day-to-day basis.
- We look forward to competing in the Far East market.
- We will start designing our promotional literature next month.
- Advertising in the trade journals has created a lot of interest in our products.
- I am sure that this campaign is worth investing in.

### B *Form*

The verb …*ing* form comprises:
V1 + *ing*

It can be seen in:
– the present continuous verb, e.g. I **am going** (see Unit 1)
– adjective forms, e.g. an **interesting** product
– the present participle, e.g. I heard the MD **presenting** the results
– noun forms, e.g. We are interested in **increasing** our market share

The following section, 'Uses', deals with the noun form.

### C *Uses*

In noun forms, the verb …*ing* functions as a noun and can be called a *verbal noun* – a noun made from a verb. It is also called a *gerund*. We use it:
– as the subject or object of a verb
– after a preposition

1 As the subject of a verb:
Leading a team is a key management function.

2 As the object of certain verbs:
Certain verbs are followed by a verb …*ing* (and not an infinitive).
You should consider upgrading the system to make the software run faster.
That would involve redesigning many of the programmes.
These verbs include:
*acknowledge dislike miss risk avoid enjoy*
*postpone stop consider finish practise suggest*
*delay involve regret deny don't/doesn't mind*

3 After a preposition:
Prepositions are always followed by nouns, so can be followed by the verbal noun:
After reading through the accounts, we noticed a number of curious entries in your books.
We are interested in hearing about the new RD230.

4 After certain phrases:
*(not) worth have trouble/difficulty spend/waste time*
We've spent a lot of time getting the quality right.

***Note***
**To** can be either a preposition or a particle:
We are used to paying local prices. (preposition followed by verb …*ing*)
We used to pay the local supplier directly. (particle followed by infinitive)

## Exercise 1

*Read the following fax message and underline uses of the verb ...ing form. Then classify them according to use in the table below.*

| Subject of verb | Object of verb | After preposition | Continuous verb form |
|---|---|---|---|
| | | | |

GORLIZ & ZIMMERMAN

11436 S. Bundy Drive, Auckland 46032
Telephone (1) 503 786432, Fax (1) 503 786333

Fax to: Peter Anderson
Accounts Dept
From: Harriet Gorman

Dear Peter

Re: Harawi Project 1998

On checking the above file we find that you are correct in thinking the cost estimates for the coming year are excessive. We regret that in calculating labour costs some errors appeared in our analysis. We are presently repeating the study which involves reviewing all the figures.

Working in partnership with Harris & Co is proving very useful and we are sure that there will be many benefits. We look forward to having a joint meeting soon. We are also involved in calculating costs for the following year and will let you know as soon as they are finished.

We must meet soon, otherwise we risk not having everything ready for the MD in June, but it's not worth fixing a date today, as I don't yet know my movements for the rest of this month.
Best wishes,

*Harriet*
Harriet

## Exercise 2

*Complete the following sentences by adding subjects or objects with the verb ...ing form. Use the verbs given in the box.*

*lose hear launch meet clarify see*

1 *We are interested in __________ your plant.*

2 *__________ new products is essential for the survival of the company.*

3 *We look forward to __________ from you.*

4 *He suggested __________ us next month.*

5 *__________ our policy is an essential prerequisite to improving products.*

6 *By delaying we risk __________ the contract.*

## Exercise 3

*Hutchison & Hunt is a company which is losing money. The Chief Executive asked an external consultant to analyse its problems and make suggestions. Make sentences based on the notes below.*

| Problem | Solution |
|---|---|
| falling sales | change advertising, improve products |
| quality deficit | introduce new Quality Control system |
| old products | invest in more Research & Development |
| lack of money | have a rights issue |
| overstaffing | reduce workforce |

*Two have been done for you as examples.*

1 *The consultant said falling sales was a problem. She suggested changing the advertising strategy and improving the products.*

2 *She said there was a quality deficit. This could be improved by introducing a new quality control system.*

## Transfer

*Talk about your work or studies. Use the verb ...ing form.*

- current projects
- your responsibilities (use 'be responsible for')
- recent successes (use 'succeed in')
- likes, dislikes
- recent suggestions (use 'suggest')
- the future (use 'look forward to')

# UNIT 14

## INFINITIVE

*See also* Unit 13 – Verb ...ing
Unit 15 – Verb ...ing or infinitive + to

### A Sample sentences

- We plan to reduce our energy consumption in the New Year.
- We have decided not to renew the contract with that supplier.
- We appear to be making very good progress.
- The problem seems to have occurred during the night.
- It is essential to implement the solution as quickly as possible.
- To give every employee a share in this company would be financially impossible.

### B Form

There are three infinitive forms:

the *present simple infinitive* – V1
the *present continuous infinitive* – **to be** + V1 ...*ing*
the *present perfect infinitive* – **to have** + V3

We distinguish between the infinitive with **to** and the 'bare infinitive' (V1) without **to** (see Note 1).

### C Uses

We use the infinitive:
– as the subject or object of a verb
– after certain adjectives

1 As the subject of a verb:
To advertise in the national press is very expensive.

2 As the object of a verb:
We have agreed to postpone the decision until a later date.

3 After an adjective:
I am pleased to inform you that your application has been successful.
It would be easy for us to change to an alternative energy source.

4 The tenses:
We normally use the present simple infinitive to link two verbs:
We intend to send you the documents next week.
We use the present continuous infinitive to highlight that the action is happening at the time of speaking:
We seem to be going round in circles. (It seems that we are going round in circles.)
We use the present perfect infinitive to highlight that the action of the infinitive happened before the action of the first verb:
He is alleged to have committed the crime last Friday evening.
(It is alleged that he committed the crime last Friday evening.)
He was thought to have stolen the documents at that time.
(It was thought that he had stolen the documents at that time.)

***Notes***

1 The particle **to** is needed to link a full verb with an infinitive; the bare infinitive (V1) is used after modals:
*can/could may/might shall/should will/would must needn't*

Two exceptions are *help* and *dare,* when the bare infinitive may or may not be used:
We don't dare (to) put up our prices by more than the level of inflation.
After joining the department, she helped (to) introduce the new management practices.

2 In adjective + infinitive constructions, notice the use of the preposition **for**:
It would be good for you to spend some time abroad.

3 Notice the form of the negative infinitive:
We prefer not to divulge this information until the court case.
We have decided not to proceed with our project.

## Exercise 1

*The board of a car manufacturing company is discussing falling sales. Here is part of a talk by the Director of R & D. Identify all infinitives in the text then list them under the following headings:*

Present simple infinitive Present continuous infinitive Present perfect infinitive

'We need to increase research to develop a completely new model. To have begun the research earlier would have cost much less money. However, to delay now will cost even more. Some members of the board appear to be recommending simple modifications to the existing range. This is a very short-sighted strategy. To rely on old models during a fall in the market is quite wrong. We have to plan for the long-term development of our product range. As I said, it would have been better to have put more cash into the project two years ago. Now, to be talking about relying on continued production of a range that is declining is clearly not sensible.

'This, to me, is absolutely clear. If we want to be in control of the situation in the future, we have to understand it now.'

## Exercise 2

*Look at the internal memo opposite which concerns discussions before negotiations to fix an advertising contract.*

*Choose a verb from the box to complete the spaces in the text. The first has been done for you.*

*take on clarify reach resolve*
*be tell agree discuss want*

**MEMO**
**To:** TR
**From:** SA
**Date:** 14th May

Re. Advertising contract negotiation

It is going *to be* difficult __________ agreement with Emmy over the advertising material. Their principal negotiator, Stella Ragione, appears __________ a large downpayment on signature of contract – probably near 50 per cent. We plan __________ her that this is impossible. We are happy __________ the possibility of an advance but personally I believe it would be a mistake __________ to anything above 20 per cent. __________ our position immediately could save us time. I suggest we inform Miss Ragione of our views on the matter. We should also make it clear that Morreille Partnership (Marseille) are happy __________ the project and their reputation for high standards is as good as Emmy's. We need __________ this very soon, as time is short.

## Exercise 3

*Decide if the following sentences are grammatically correct or not. If they are wrong, correct them.*

1 We want to talk about the problem of transport.
2 We delayed to have a meeting.
3 We decided not to have a meeting.
4 We started to consider the alternatives.
5 We avoided to have an accident.

## Exercise 4

*Choose the correct infinitive form from the box to complete the phrases below.*

*increase begin decide commission put invest delay understand be*

1 __________ *the research earlier would have cost much more money.*
2 __________ *now will cost even more.*
3 *We have* __________ *on our priorities.*
4 *My impression is that* __________ *production is a high-risk strategy.*
5 __________ *more during a fall in the market is quite wrong.*
6 *It would have been better* __________ *more cash into the project two years ago.*
7 __________ *more market research would have helped.*

## Transfer

*Think of a problem you are/were personally involved with. Now answer these questions:*

- Is/was the problem getting worse?
- What do/did you plan to do to reach a solution?
- Think of another problem that you tried to solve, but failed. What should you have done?

# UNIT 15

## VERB ...ING or INFINITIVE + TO

*See also* Unit 13 – Verb ...ing
Unit 14 – Infinitive

### A *Sample sentences*

- We stopped producing the A32 last year.
- We stopped to produce the A33.
- Do you like using the new optical reader?
- We like to have a new product on the market each year.
- We would like to upgrade the RD200 next year.
- We are trying to start a quality circle in our German company.
- We have already tried introducing quality concepts into our foreign units.

### B *Form*

The verb phrase comprises two verbs. The second is:
a verb *...ing* or an infinitive

### C *Uses*

1 The meaning of the verb is different depending on the construction:
We stopped producing the A32 last year. (We stopped the production)
We stopped to produce the A33. (We stopped the production of something else in order to produce the A33)

2 The meaning of the verb changes slightly with the construction:
Do you like using the new optical reader? (Do you enjoy it?)
We like to have a new product on the market each year. (It is a good thing to do)

Other verbs are:
*remember forget try attempt regret*

We remembered to update the client database. (didn't forget)
I remember receiving the updated client database. (I received it and I remember it)
We are trying to start a quality circle in our German company. (attempting)
We have already tried introducing quality concepts into our foreign units. (experimented with)

3 There is no systematic difference in meaning between the two constructions:
We started to restructure the company some time ago.
We started restructuring the company some time ago.

Other verbs are:
*begin continue intend love prefer hate*

## VERB ...ING or INFINITIVE + TO

### Exercise 1

*Complete the following sentences.*

1 I'd like (attend) the conference.
2 I remember (meet) your colleague in Osaka.
3 I tried (phone) you last week but I think you were away.
4 We like (test) the goods before we despatch them.
5 We tried (ask) for payment on delivery but in practice we had to allow 30 days.
6 We would like (make) a formal agreement.

### Exercise 2

*Read the sentences given here and decide which of the given meanings is the correct one.*

1 We'd like to have a meeting.
   **a** We enjoy meetings.
   **b** We want a meeting.
   **c** It's good to have meetings.

2 We stopped to visit suppliers in Budapest.
   **a** We do not visit them any more.
   **b** We interrupted our journey so we could visit them.
   **c** We ended our journey by visiting them.

3 Have you tried sending goods by train?
   **a** Have you experimented with the idea of using the train?
   **b** Have you attempted to send goods by train?
   **c** Have you studied the possibility of sending goods by train?

4 We remembered to send publicity material with the goods.
   **a** We did send the material and I recall sending it.
   **b** We told you to send the material with the goods.
   **c** We did not forget to send the material with the goods.

### Exercise 3

*Rewrite the following sentences from a telephone call, replacing the phrases in brackets with a verb combination from the box below. Use either verb …ing or the infinitive* **+ *to*.**

*remember/send try/call stop/think like/contact*

1 I (attempted to call) you yesterday but without success.
2 I (recall that I sent) you a tender for the Apple Project but we have had no reply.
3 We (think it is a good idea to contact) potential customers to check their reactions to tenders.
4 I am sure that if you (delay your next move and think) about our offer you will agree that the price is fair.

### Transfer

*Make sentences about yourself using any of the following verbs.*

*prefer hate like try remember intend stop begin start love*

*Example:*
I like listening to music at home but I prefer going to concerts.

# UNIT 16

## VERB + OBJECT + INFINITIVE

*See also* Unit 13 – Verb ...ing
Unit 14 – Infinitive
Unit 15 – Verb ...ing or infinitive + to

### A *Sample sentences*

- We have asked the bank to notify us of all transactions.
- Last year HQ invited all the business units to send in their suggestions for training programmes.
- The new guidelines let us allocate our own budgets. In fact, they don't make us report outside our division.

### B *Form*

The construction comprises:
transitive verb + noun or pronoun object + infinitive.

### C *Uses*

1 Verbs which are always followed by an infinitive with **to**:
They want to work on the new plans immediately.
They want us to work on the new plans immediately.
(*not*: They want that we work on the new plans immediately.)

Other verbs are:
*ask* *expect* *would like* *would prefer*

2 Verbs which are followed by verb ...*ing* or an object + infinitive:
The council advised looking for an alternative site.
(*not*: The council advised to look for an alternative site.)
The council advised the company to look for an alternative site.

Other verbs are:
*allow* *permit* *recommend* *encourage*

3 Verbs which only take an object + infinitive:
The Director told them to improve productivity.
(*not*: The Director told to improve productivity.)

Other verbs are:
*enable* *persuade* *order* *warn* *invite*
Improved quality will enable us to sell our products throughout Europe.

4 Verbs which take an object + bare infinitive (without **to**):
The new personnel policy lets us take initiatives.

Such verbs are:
*make* *help* *let*
A consultant can help you (to) draw up a marketing plan.

***Notes***

1 Compare the following sentences:
He told them to reduce costs.
He said (to them) that they should reduce costs.
(*not*: He said them to reduce costs.)
**Tell** takes an object + infinitive; **say** takes an indirect object (optional) + a clause.

2 **Expect** can be followed by an infinitive or a clause:
We expect an announcement to be made next week.
We expect that an announcement will be made next week.

# VERB + OBJECT + INFINITIVE

## Exercise 1

*Read the short text. Underline examples of verb + object + infinitive constructions. The first has been done for you.*

**OFFICESPACE**

We will help you solve your space problems.
We invite you to share in a whole new concept in office design!
Our modern office systems allow you to create additional space at little extra expense. We can enable you to redesign working areas to maximum advantage! If you would like us to send you details of this amazing offer, fill in the reply coupon below.
Or if you would prefer to telephone us, simply ring 0800 and ask for Freefone Officespace.

## Exercise 2

*Make sentences based on the following words. Each sentence should contain a verb + object + infinitive construction.*

| | | | |
|---|---|---|---|
| *I* | *persuaded* | *purchasers* | *understand* |
| *Joanne* | *can help* | *new recruits* | *to resign* |
| *We* | *does not allow* | *the report* | *to come* |
| *She* | *want* | *me* | *to accept gifts* |
| *Henry* | *would prefer* | *you* | *to be destroyed* |

**1** *I* ____________________________________

**2** *Joanne* ________________________________

**3** *We* ___________________________________

**4** *She* __________________________________

**5** *Henry* ________________________________

## Exercise 3

*Decide if the sentences below are right or wrong. Mark them with a tick ☑ or a cross ☒. Then correct the mistakes where necessary.*

**1** *The report made us to review our forecasts.* ☐

**2** *The report failed to identify the cause of the accident.* ☐

**3** *This allows to make further investments.* ☐

**4** *We want that you respect the terms of the contract.* ☐

**5** *We asked them to advance the order by two months.* ☐

**6** *We would like that you come to the meeting.* ☐

**7** *The contract does not permit that we increase the price.* ☐

## Transfer

*Have you ever been persuaded to buy something you did not want?*
*Write a memo warning or advising someone not to be persuaded to do something.*

*Example:*

**MEMO**

**From:** PH
**To:** Fred

I advise you not to speak to Gubu Ltd. They will try to persuade you to order goods we do not want. I advise you to send them away.

**MEMO**

**From:**
**To:**

# UNIT 17

## WILL and WOULD

*See also* **Unit 8 – The future with will**
**Unit 10 – The conditionals (1)**
**Unit 11 – The conditionals (2)**
**Unit 90 – Requesting information and action**

### A *Sample sentences*

- I'll call you back later as soon as I've got the figures.
- We talked to them for hours, but they wouldn't renegotiate the terms.
- Would you reconsider your offer, please?
- Will you please let me see Anna's fax before the next meeting?

### B *Form*

**Will** and **would** are modals. **Would** is the past tense form of **will**. Both forms take a bare infinitive (V1).The contracted forms are **'ll** and **'d**.

The negative forms are **will not/would not**. The contracted forms are **won't/wouldn't**.

### C *Uses*

We use **will** and **would** to talk about willingness.

1 In requests for action or information:
Will you call me back later, please? (Are you willing to call me back later?)
Would you sit down, please?
The past tense form **would** is more remote (in time) and, therefore, less direct and more polite.

2 In replies to requests:
A: Will you call me back later, please?
B: Yes, of course I will. At what time? (Yes, of course I am willing to.)

3 In offers:
I'll fax the information to you immediately. (I offer to fax the information to you immediately.)

4 To express willingness and refusal:
A: How did the discussions go?
B: Quite well. They will accept our terms. (They are willing to accept our terms.)
A: And the payment period?
B: No, I'm afraid they wouldn't accept the 30-day clause. (They refused to accept the 30-day clause.)

***Notes***

1 In C1, **will** and **would** are only used in requests with the subject **you**.
2 In C2, we can use different subjects:
A: Will you confirm the arrangements, please?
B: Either I will or my secretary will.

## Exercise 1

*Here is a conversation in which two partners are discussing a contract for the transport of goods. Insert contractions where appropriate.*

A: This is the contract for the transport of the order to Singapore. Would you check it for me?
B: Of course. I will do it now.
A: You will see, they would not agree to pay the insurance.
B: Really? I think that other company, TransWorld, would pay it.
A: No, on the contrary, they would not. But if you like I will ask them.
B: No, do not. I am sure you are right.

## Exercise 2

*Look at the following dialogue. Complete the spaces with an appropriate word. Use contractions where appropriate.*

Helena: Oh, Martina. You know about the despatch of the KMB order tomorrow? ____________ you check that the transporters will arrive early?

Martina: Of course I ____________, I ____________ phone them now.

Helena: And do you know if they ____________ reach the ferry terminal in time for the 2 o'clock sailing?

Martina: I spoke to them yesterday. They said they ____________

Helena: And ____________ they agree to bring back the faulty goods?

Martina: No, they ____________ do that this time because the lorry is going on to Bari with other goods. They said they ____________ bring the faulty goods another time.

Helena: I see. That's a pity.

## Exercise 3

*Write appropriate sentences using the following prompts. Use* ***will*** *or* ***would*** *and contractions where appropriate.*

**1** Ask someone to help you book a flight to Manchester.

'Excuse me, ____________________________________________?'

**2** Someone asks you to phone a colleague, Ms Cain. What do you say?

'Of course ____________________________________________'

**3** You are telephoning a haulage company who are going to deliver some goods to you tomorrow. Offer to help them unload the goods.

'If you want, ____________________________________________'

**4** Answer the following. 'Will the ship arrive by the end of the month?'

'Yes ____________________________________________'

**5** Answer the following. 'Are they going to present all the documentation to the customs?'

'No ____________________________________________'

## Transfer

*Write the following sentences, including a form of* ***will*** *or* ***would*** *in each sentence.*

- a request for help
- a reply to a request
- an offer of help
- an expression of willingness to do something
- a refusal to do something

# UNIT 18

## MAY and MIGHT

*See also* Unit 19 – **Can and could**
Unit 20 – **Must, mustn't and needn't**
Unit 88 – Scale of likelihood

## A *Sample sentences*

- There may be a downturn in business later in the year.
- Because of the health risk, we might have to review safety procedures.
- May I just interrupt for a moment? Might I just point out a mistake in the figures?
- Confidential documents may not be photocopied without prior approval.
- The computer system has just crashed. I think we might have lost a lot of data.

## B *Form*

**May** and **might** are modals. In form, **might** is the past tense of **may**. Both verbs take a bare infinitive (V1). The negative forms are **may not** and **might not**. The contracted form of **might not** is **mightn't**.

## C *Uses*

We use **may** and **might** to talk about:
– possibility
– permission

1 Present possibility:
A: Can I speak to Peter Franks, please?
B: Yes, I think the meeting may/might be over now. (It is possible that the meeting is over now.)

Both **may** and **might** express present possibility. **May** expresses stronger possibility than **might**:
A: Can I speak to Peter Franks, please? He was in a meeting before.
B: Just one moment. I think the meeting may/might have finished now. (It is possible that the meeting has finished now.)

2 Future possibility:
Both **may** and **might** express future possibility. **May** expresses stronger possibility than **might**.
Next year we may/might relocate to outside London. (It is possible that we will relocate.)
By this time next year we may/might have relocated to outside London. (It is possible that by this time next year we will have relocated.)
If we relocate, we may/might still manage to reduce overheads. (It is still possible that we will manage to reduce overheads.)

3 In requests for permission:
May/might I just interrupt here? (Is it permitted for me to interrupt here?)
The past tense form **might** is more remote (in time) and, therefore, less direct and more polite.

4 In permission and prohibition:
A: May/might I make a comment at this point?
B: Yes, of course you may. (*not*: of course you might) (It is permitted for you to make a comment.)
Confidential documents may not be photocopied without prior approval. (*not*: documents might not) (Confidential documents are not permitted to be photocopied without prior approval.)

***Notes***

1 In C3, **may** and **might** are only used in requests with the subject **I**.

2 In C4, we can use different subjects:
A: May/might we point out a mistake in the figures?
B: Yes, of course you may or one of your colleagues may.

3 Normally we use **may** rather than **might** to indicate permission and prohibition. However, in indirect speech we can use **might** after a past tense verb of speaking:
The MD said that documents might be photocopied after approval had been given.
This sentence has two possible interpretations:
The MD said that it was permitted for documents to be photocopied.
The MD said that it was possible for documents to be photocopied.

# MAY and MIGHT

## Exercise 1

*Rewrite the underlined parts of the following sentences to form new sentences which include **may** or **might** and a negative form if necessary. Retain the original meaning.*

1 It is possible that stock levels will rise in the final quarter of the year.
2 I don't know if we have any SuperFix in stock.
3 We are considering changing to a just-in-time method of procurement.
4 It is possible that we will need to increase the quantity we hold in stock but there is a slight possibility that our present suppliers will not be able to meet our needs.
5 If the quality is not good enough it is possible that we will change our suppliers.
6 Is it okay if I check stock levels today instead of tomorrow?
7 If you check stock levels today instead of tomorrow there is a slight possibility that you will get inaccurate information for the month.
8 It is possible that we are already using that supplier.

## Exercise 2

*Below are six questions and answers. Complete the answers using **may** or **might**. Use a negative form if appropriate.*

1 *Q. Do you think this is a high risk product?*

*A. Yes, it ____________ damage our reputation.*

2 *Q. Why do you think we need to explain the project to the press?*

*A. If we don't, the public ____________ misunderstand our intentions.*

3 *Q. What are we going to do?*

*A. We'll have an 'open' day when everyone ____________ visit the factory.*

4 *Q. Why do you want to explain everything about the product?*

*A. If we don't, we ____________ get the support we want.*

5 *Q. Did you tell the press they were not invited?*

*A. No, I said they ____________ come.*

6 *Q. Do you think the newspapers will write about this problem?*

*A. I don't know. They ____________, or they ____________.*

## Transfer

1 *We use **may** or **might** to predict future events which we are not certain about. Make predictions about:*

- the future of the economy in your country
- unemployment
- manufacturing industries

2 *Now write about your plans for tomorrow. Describe something that you will possibly do and something else that there is a smaller possibility that you will do.*

# UNIT 19

## CAN and COULD

*See also* Unit 18 – **May** and **might**
Unit 20 – **Must, mustn't** and **needn't**
Unit 87 – Ability and inability

### A *Sample sentences*

- You can use your credit card to pay for phone calls.
- In the past almost anybody could sell insurance policies. Unless you are certified, you can't offer financial services.
- A: Can I help you?
  B: Yes, can you put me through to extension 234?
  A: I'm afraid I can't. The line is busy at the moment.
- If you don't accept the offer today, we can't guarantee that it will be available tomorrow.

### B *Form*

**Can** and **could** are modals. **Could** is the past tense form of **can**. Both verbs take a bare infinitive (V1).

The negative forms are **cannot** and **could not**; the contracted forms are **can't** and **couldn't**.

### C *Uses*

We use **can** and **could** to talk about:
- ability
- possibility
- permission

1 **Ability:**
We can start legal proceedings against ABC, if you wish.
(Present ability: we are able to start legal proceedings.)
Next year, after we move to new offices, we can install a complete network.
(Future ability: we will be able to install a complete network.)
When we were in the old building, we couldn't access all the files.
(Past ability: we were not able to access all the files.)

2 **Possibility:**
Both **can** and **could** express present and future possibility. **Can** expresses stronger possibility than **could**:
A large range of options can/could be identified for this company's future.
(Present possibility: it is possible to identify a large range of options.)
So, we have no idea what can/could happen to our positions next week.
(Future possibility)
The meeting has been going on for two hours, so they could have decided by now.
(*not*: they can have decided) (Present possibility in relation to earlier action: it is possible that they have decided.)
They didn't meet yesterday, so they can't/couldn't have made the decision then.
(Present impossibility in relation to earlier action: it is impossible that they made the decision yesterday.)

3 **Permission:**
Only employees with protective clothing can enter the building site.
(Present permission: only employees with protective clothing are permitted to enter.)
When I worked there, only the site manager could authorise outside visits.
(Past permission: only the site manager was permitted.)
It's a company rule – personnel can't take less than half an hour for lunch.
(Present prohibition: personnel are not permitted to take less than half an hour.)
When I worked there, personnel couldn't take less than half an hour for lunch.
(Past prohibition: personnel were not permitted to take less than half an hour.)

***Note***

1 As the **can** of possibility has the same meaning as the **may** of possibility, we can use **may** to avoid any possible ambiguity.
They can deliver on time (They are able to.)
They may deliver on time (It is possible that they will.)

## Exercise 1

*Rewrite the following sentences, changing the underlined words for new phrases including **can** or **could** and a negative form where appropriate.*

A: Is it possible for me to see you next week?
B: Of course it is possible. Are you able to come on Monday?
A: No, sorry, I'm unable to come then. If it is okay with you, it is possible for me to come on Tuesday.
B: Excellent. Is it possible for you to confirm by fax?
A: Certainly. It is possible for me to do that now. Oh, another question. Is it okay if I bring my colleague, Mr Lee Wang?
B: Of course it's okay. I look forward to meeting him.
A: Thanks very much. See you next week.

## Exercise 2

*Complete the unfinished sentences below based on the given prompts. Include **can** or **could** in your answer, and a negative form if appropriate. The first has been done for you.*

1 *Present possibility: Only lower-grade personnel/take part in the training course.*

*Only lower-grade personnel* can take part in the training course.

2 *Future possibility: they/find theory difficult.*

*They* ____________________

3 *Past permission: Manager told Piero/do the course.*

*The manager told Piero that* ____________________

4 *Future ability: After the course you/carry out major maintenance.*

*After the course you* ____________________

5 *Present impossibility in relation to earlier action: Course not available last year/so not possible that Gautier has this qualification.*

*This course was not available last year so Gautier* ____________________

6 *Past prohibition: The company cut back on training and told the department that spending on the course was not possible.*

*Due to company cuts, the department* ____________________

## Exercise 3

*Read the passage. Then put each example of **can** or **could** (numbered 1–7) into the correct column in the table below, depending on its use.*

During the first three years of the project the Board agreed we **could** (1) increase investment in the TT5 each year by 5%. Now we are told that we **can** (2) increase investment by only 3%. But we need to recruit more people. Without increased technical support we **cannot** (3) compete with our rivals who, with better resources, **could** (4) find solutions within one or two years. With more support we **could** (5) have produced a prototype last year. The board say we **can** (6) do this within six months – which is very optimistic. My view is that it **could** (7) take four years.

| Ability past present future | Possibility present future | Permission past present |
|---|---|---|
| | | |

## Transfer

1 *Write a short dialogue similar to the one in Exercise 1 in which you make an appointment with a colleague.*

2 *Think of the place where you work or study. Describe something that you do have permission to do and something that you do not have permission to do.*

# UNIT 20

## MUST, MUSTN'T and NEEDN'T

*See also* **Unit 18 – May and might**
**Unit 19 – Can and could**
**Unit 86 – Obligations and requirements**

### A *Sample sentences*

- The alarm system must be on at night; however, it needn't be on during the day.
- The money was sent a week ago; it must have arrived by now.
- We mustn't forget to include this news in the bulletin.

### B *Form*

**Must, mustn't** and **needn't** are modals. They take a bare infinitive (V1). We use the negatives **must not** and **need not** in writing and speech; we generally use the contracted forms **mustn't** and **needn't** only in speech. The positive of **needn't** is **need**. **Need** is a full verb and takes an infinitive + **to** (see Note 4).

### C *Uses*

We use **must, mustn't** and **needn't** to talk about:
– necessity to do something (obligation)
– necessity not to do something (prohibition)
– no necessity to do something
– logical deduction

1 Necessity to do something (obligation):
Investors must complete the application form below. (It is necessary that investors complete the form.)

2 Necessity not to do something (prohibition):
Unauthorised personnel must not pass this point. (It is necessary for them not to pass this point, i.e. they are prohibited.)

3 No necessity to do something:
I am not in a hurry; you needn't do it right now. (It is not necessary to do it right now.)

4 Logical deduction:
A: We ordered 5000 of these parts. There are only 2000 in this box. There must be another box somewhere! (It is a logical deduction, from the total number ordered that there is another box somewhere.)
B: That's true. But they needn't all have arrived in the same delivery. (It is not a logical deduction that they arrived in the same delivery.) In fact, now I remember! Cathy must have taken them.

***Notes***

1 The past of **must** (obligation) is **had to**; the past of **must** (logical deduction) is **must have** + V3:
They had to make the payment yesterday. (It was necessary to make the payment.)
They must have made the payment yesterday. (It is logically necessary that they made the payment yesterday because, for example, we received it today.)

2 The past of **mustn't** (prohibition) is **was/were not allowed/permitted to**:
I wasn't allowed to observe the meeting because they were discussing a sensitive issue.

3 **Mustn't** (prohibition), **can't** (no permission), and **may not** (no permission) have similar meanings:
In our new offices, employees mustn't/can't/may not smoke, except in certain areas.

4 The positive of the modal **needn't** is the full verb **need. Need** is followed by an infinitive + **to**:
We need to increase productivity next year.
In the negative, we have two possible constructions:
We don't need to increase productivity./We needn't increase productivity.
The past of **need** is **needed**; the past of **needn't** is **didn't need**. Both are followed by an infinitive + **to**:
They needed to remove the subassembly in order to do the maintenance.
They didn't need to remove the subassembly in order to do the maintenance.

# MUST, MUSTN'T and NEEDN'T

## Exercise 1

*Decide which of the following show examples of obligation (O+), no obligation (-O), prohibition (O-) or logical deduction (D).*

The colour of the plastic is not right. The liquid must have been too hot. This batch must be withdrawn but we needn't stop the production. Obviously we must check the temperature control. We mustn't leave it as it is or the same thing will happen tomorrow.

## Exercise 2

*Write sentences which describe the situations shown in the pictures.*

(obviously/not/pollute/rivers) (build/expensive purification plant) (make small changes to production methods)

## Exercise 3

*Change the following text into the past form.*

We must look at our production control procedures. We needn't examine every step in the process, but we must ask all employees how we can improve the system. Of course, the management fix the rules: but we have to implement them.

## Exercise 4

*Complete the following sentences with a modal form from the box below.*

*didn't need to must must have have to mustn't had to needn't*

1 *Miriam is late. She had another meeting this morning but it __________ finished by now.*
2 *The goods are faulty so we __________ pay for them.*
3 *The production costs are too high. We __________ reduce them.*
4 *The system is dangerous. We __________ continue using it.*
5 *The valve broke so we __________ replace it.*
6 *The supervisor says we __________ report any leakage. Last year we __________ report small leaks.*

## Transfer

*Write six sentences about your work environment. Your sentences should describe the following:*

- obligation
- prohibition
- no necessity to do something
- logical deduction

# UNIT 21

## SHALL and SHOULD

*See also*: **Unit 10 – The conditionals (1)**
**Unit 11 – The conditionals (2)**
**Unit 17 – Will and would**
**Unit 20 – Must, mustn't and needn't**
**Unit 89 – Advising and suggesting**

### A *Sample sentences*

- Shall I go through the minutes of the last meeting first?
- Should we leave that point until the end?
- The goods should arrive by the end of the week.
- You shouldn't sign the document until you have read it through.
- The supplier shall deliver the goods on or by the date specified in the agreement.
- Should you wish to discuss this further, please contact our London office.

### B *Form*

**Shall** and **should** are modals. Both verbs take a bare infinitive (V1).
The negative forms are **shall not** and **should not**; the contracted forms are **shan't** and **shouldn't**.

### C *Uses*

We use **shall** and **should** to:
– talk about the future
– make suggestions
– give advice
– express probability
– express obligation
– express a condition

1 The future. After **I** and **we**, we can use **shall** in place of **will**:
First I shall give a brief overview of last year's performance.

2 Making suggestions. We use **shall** and **should** followed by **I** or **we** in the question form:
Shall we get started?
Should I move on to the next point on the agenda now?
The past tense form **should** is more remote (in time) and, therefore, less direct and more polite.

3 Giving advice. We use **should** to give advice:
You should have this statement ready by the beginning of the month.
(It would be a good idea to have this statement ready by the beginning of the month.)
And you shouldn't include these figures here; it's bad accounting practice.
(It would be a good idea not to include these figures here.)

4 Expressing probability. We use **should** to express probability:
A: Can I speak to Judith Franks, please?
B: Yes, the meeting should be over now.
(Present probability: it is probable that the meeting is over now.)

The relocation should take place at the beginning of next year.
(Future probability: it is probable that the relocation will take place.)
They sent the payment yesterday; so it should have arrived by now.
(Present probability in relation to earlier action: it is probable that it has arrived by now.)

5 Expressing obligation (very formal).
We use **shall** to express obligation – particularly in official orders and legal documents:
The customer shall notify the supplier of any defects within five days.
(The customer must notify the supplier of any defects within five days.)
Workers shall not enter the building site unless wearing hard hats.
(Workers must not enter the building site.)

6 Expressing a condition. We can use an inverted construction with **should** in conditional I:
Should you wish to discuss this further, please contact our London office.
(If you wish to discuss this further, please contact our London office.)
The construction with **should** is rather formal. We use it in official letters and documents.

## Exercise 1

*Read the following dialogue and decide how the forms **shall** and **should** are used. Decide if they are used in suggestions (Sugg), talking about the future (Fut), advice (Ad), probability (Pr), obligation (Obl) or conditions (Cond).*

A: Shall we wait for Peter?
B: Yes, he should be along any moment.
A: Is he staying all morning?
B: He certainly should. We've important things to discuss.
A: While we're waiting, shall I show you the report?
B: No, I shall look at it in detail this afternoon. I think you shouldn't say anything about it until Peter's here. Should it be controversial, he'd want to be the first to know.

## Exercise 2

*Look at the pictures below. Match each one to a quote from the list.*

1 'Henry! You shouldn't drink before a meeting with the Vice-President!'
2 'Should the delivery be late, ABC will be entitled to compensation.'
3 'I think the Sales Team should resign!'
4 'The delivery should be before the end of August.'
5 'We shall have 50 per cent of market share in five years time.'
6 'Shall we finish now?'

## Exercise 3

*Rewrite the following sentences using **shall** or **should**. Use a negative form if appropriate.*

1 What about having some lunch now?
2 Is it a good idea for us to change the schedule?
3 I think it would be crazy for you to continue with this.
4 I think she will arrive at about 5 o'clock.
5 The report will probably be a good one.
6 If you want to see the machine in operation, please contact us.

## Exercise 4

*Here are the opening remarks of a Production Manager talking to some colleagues about two production lines in Italy. Change the underlined words for other phrases which include **shall** or **should**.*

'Friends, I'm going to talk about new production plans. First I'm going to talk about the 24-hour production line at the Friuli plant, then I want to say something about our new automated line at Rimini. So, Friuli. Production will probably start in June. I think it would be a good idea if we began with a low output – say about 50 per cent of capacity. In this way it is probable that any bugs will be eliminated early without creating chaos. Do you want me to describe the line in detail? If not, my advice is that you read the report that will almost certainly be ready at the end of next week. Now, if we start at 50 per cent capacity, the production output will be about the same as it is now for the initial period. This is not likely to be a big problem ...

## Transfer

*Write a short paragraph about your present situation. Include uses of **shall** or **should** in phrases which:*

- talk about the future
- make suggestions
- give advice
- express probability
- express obligation
- express a condition.

# UNIT 22

## ACTIVE

*See also* **Unit 23 – Passive**

## A *Sample sentences*

- The company decided to develop the RX200 two years ago.
- The company will launch the RX200 this year.
- Next year they will move into Eastern Europe.
- If the demand increases, they expect to have a 20 per cent market share in five years.
- They have been discussing the possibility of joint ventures.
- The Marketing Director has said that he would like to move quickly into the Far East.

## B *Form*

The active sentence contains:
– a subject
– an active verb form

The subject normally comes before the verb:
The organisation offers legal services.

The active verb is *transitive* or *intransitive*. A transitive verb is followed by a direct object, i.e. a noun phrase or a gerund. This object comes after a verb:
The organisation *offers* a wide range of legal services. (object: a wide range of legal services)
They *acknowledged* receiving the letter. (object: verb ...*ing*)

An intransitive verb is not followed by a direct object:
Next year they *will move* into Eastern Europe. (into Eastern Europe = prepositional phrase)
The demand for our products *is increasing*.

The active verb form can be:
– a full verb:
We *are developing* a new product.
– an infinitive:
We hope *to develop* a new product.
– verb ...*ing*:
They acknowledged *receiving* the letter.

The active verbs can be in different tenses and forms:
– full verbs (see Units 1, 2, 3, 5, 7)
– infinitives (see Unit 14)
– verb ...*ing* (see Unit 13).

## C *Uses*

We use the active form in both spoken and written language to describe events and activities. We use the passive form in spoken and written language to achieve a specific effect (see Unit 23). In general, the active creates a more personal effect:
First we discuss the client's problem. (Here 'we' can mean the speaker and the listeners or simply 'one' – an unidentified person.)
*cf.* First the client's problem is discussed. (passive and impersonal)

***Notes***

1 The normal word order in active sentences is:

| subject | verb | object | rest of the sentence |
|---|---|---|---|
| They | launched | the product | two years ago |

2 We use an active subject construction after **happen**, **arise**, and **occur**:
An explosion happened at the plant. (*not*: It happened an explosion at the plant.)
A problem arose during the installation. (*not*: It arose a problem during the installation.)

## Exercise 1

*Decide which of the following sentences contain a transitive verb (T) and which contain an intransitive one (I).*

1 The cost of living is rising faster than ten years ago. ☐
2 We need to reduce costs. ☐
3 Manufacturing companies are experiencing major problems. ☐
4 Service companies are doing better. ☐
5 Unemployment is increasing in the United States. ☐
6 Property values show a slight fall. ☐
7 In spite of the problems, economists are optimistic. ☐

## Exercise 2

*Here is an extract from a radio news report:*

The National Bank will probably decide today to raise the cost of borrowing. Interest rates will increase by 2.0 per cent. Many companies already have large debts and are paying heavy costs. Any new increase will definitely make problems worse. A representative of the Industrial Federation said 'Many businesses will close. Profits are non-existent for many companies. This new increase in the cost of borrowing is a disaster.'

*Use an appropriate form of one of the verbs in the box below to complete the sentences which follow.*

| *say* | *worsen* | *pay* | *be* | *raise* | *increase* |
|---|---|---|---|---|---|

1 *The bank* is going to raise *interest rates.*
2 *The cost of borrowing* ____________ *by 2 per cent.*
3 *Many companies* ____________ *heavy costs.*
4 *An interest rate rise* ____________ *industry's problems.*
5 *A representative* ____________ *the news* ____________ *a disaster.*

## Exercise 3

*The prompts below outline the steps that a company follows to process an order and despatch goods. Use the prompts to make six active sentences. Note: the prompts contain subject + verb + object.*

1 First/load/goods/lorry
2 After that/lorry/take goods/port
3 Then/driver/hand over/docket
4 Next/customs/sign/docket
5 Driver/keep/docket
6 Finally/we/file/docket

## Exercise 4

*Write a sentence for each of the prompts given below. Use an appropriate verb from the box and select an appropriate tense and either a negative or positive form. Each prompt contains a subject and an object and a time marker.*

| *repair* | *take* | *patrol* | *check* | *manufacture* | *cook* | *make* | *test* |
|---|---|---|---|---|---|---|---|

1 Vice-President/important decision/last week
2 Telephonist/too many private calls/recently
3 The nightwatchman/just/the factory
4 Plant/products/during the August holiday
5 Laboratory/new product/next week
6 Company doctor/employees/every month
7 Maintenance staff/production line/next Monday
8 Canteen staff/food/at the weekends

## Transfer

*Describe the typical actions and responsibilities you have in a normal day.*

# UNIT 23

## PASSIVE

*See also* Unit 22 – Active

## A *Sample sentences*

- The investment was made in the last quarter, but for some reason it hasn't been shown in the accounts.
- At the final stage, the finished products are stored in the warehouse ready for despatch.
- We would like the tax to be carried forward to next year.
- We are interested in being kept informed about new developments.

## B *Form*

| | Simple | Continuous |
|---|---|---|
| Present | they **are developed**<br>**to be** (present) + V3 | they **are being developed**<br>**to be** ( present) + **being** + V3 |
| Past | they **were developed**<br>**to be** (past) + V3 | they **were being developed**<br>**to be** (past) + **being** + V3 |
| Present perfect | they **have been developed**<br>**to be** (present perfect) + V3 | |
| Past perfect | they **had been developed**<br>**to be** (past perfect) + V3 | |
| Present infinitive | **to be developed**<br>**to be** + V3 | **to be being developed**<br>**to be** + **being** + V3 |
| Present perfect infinitive | **to have been developed**<br>**to be** (present perfect) + V3 | |

## C *Uses*

We use the passive:
- to avoid mentioning the doer
- to emphasise the doer with a 'by' phrase
- in process descriptions
- in impersonal language

1 Avoiding mentioning the doer:
The accounts have now been prepared.
We are not interested in who prepared the accounts; so an active sentence cannot be used.

2 Emphasising the doer:
The figures have been prepared by our new accountants.
In speech, we usually put the information to be emphasised at the end of a clause. We call this 'end-weight'. So here 'our new accountants' gets more focus than 'the figures'.

3 In process descriptions:
At the final stage, the finished products are packed into boxes.
We are not interested in the agent, but in the action.

4 In impersonal language:
Hard hats must be worn on the building site at all times.
The passive is widely used in formal written announcements, where an impersonal tone is intended.

## Exercise 1

*Create five passive sentences in different tenses, using the prompts in the table below.*

| | | |
|---|---|---|
| Staff | store | R & D staff |
| Finished products | manufacture | several locations |
| New products | open | warehouse |
| Goods | recruit | Corporation President |
| New plant | develop | Human Resources Dept |

## Exercise 2

*Describe what happens in the production process shown by the sequence of pictures below. Use the verbs below each picture.*

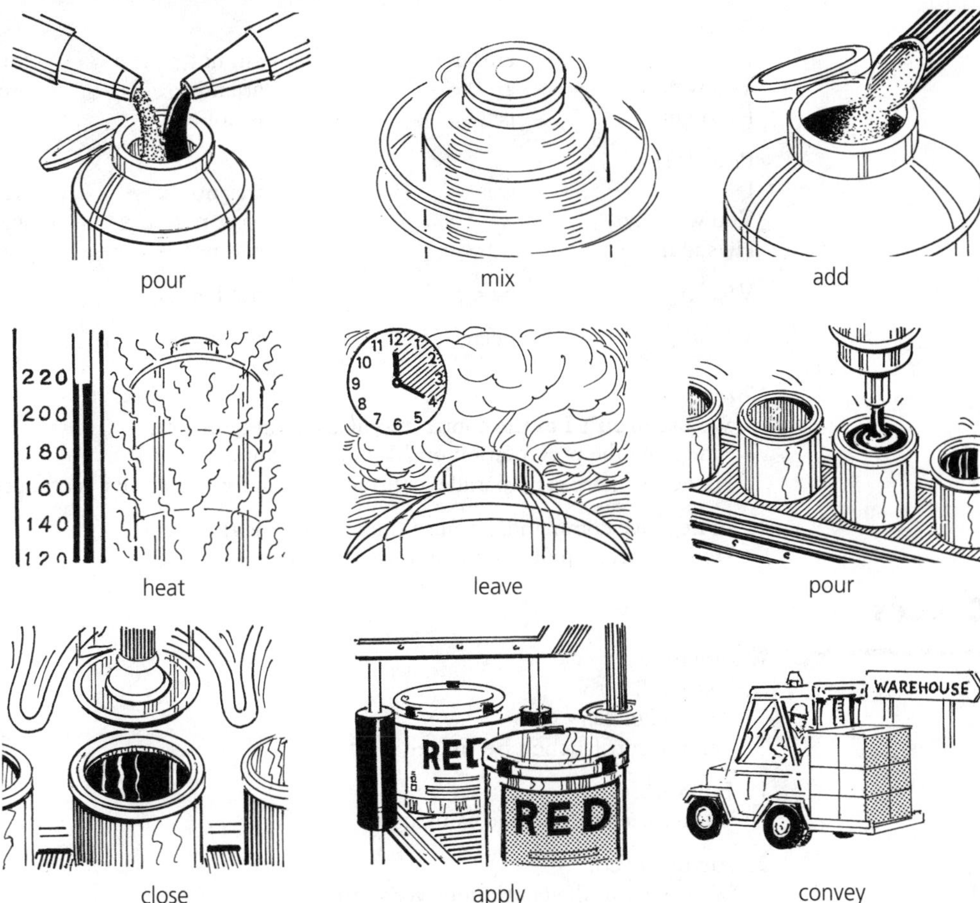


## Exercise 3

*Change the following from the active to the passive.*

1 We are going to make 50 per cent of our production at our Bahrain plant.
2 The company is expanding its range of services.
3 We are relocating our headquarters in Malaysia.
4 The Sales Manager increased the commission paid to agents.
5 Employees must wear protective clothing inside the production area.
6 We were considering the merger proposal for most of last year.

## Transfer

*Describe a process that you are familiar with. Has it changed in recent years? How was it different a few years ago?*

# UNIT 24

## BE (1)

*See also* Unit 1 – The present continuous
Unit 4 – The past continuous
Unit 6 – The present perfect continuous
Unit 23 – Passive
Unit 25 – **Be** (2)
Unit 51 – Adjectives versus adverbs

### A *Sample sentences*

- We are very interested in seeing your new product range.
- Have you ever been to Japan before?
- They are moving their offices to the new industrial estate.

### B *Form*

| **Positive** | | **Negative** | |
|---|---|---|---|
| | | **Uncontracted** | **Contracted** |
| Present | | | |
| I | am/'m | am not | (aren't)/'m not |
| You/we/they | are/'re | are not | aren't/'re not |
| He/she/it | is/'s | is not | isn't/'s not |
| Past (V2) | | | |
| I | was | was not | wasn't |
| You/we/they | were | were not | weren't |
| He/she/it | was | was not | wasn't |
| V1 …*ing* | being | not being | |
| V3 | been | not been | |

***Notes***

1 We use **aren't I** as the contracted negative in questions:
I'm giving the presentation on Monday morning, aren't I?
However, there is no parallel contracted form for declarative sentences.

2 In negative commands, we use the modal **don't**:
Don't expect a policy statement from the board.

### C *Uses*

We use **be**:
- as a full verb
- as an auxiliary verb
- in the construction **be to** (see Unit 25).

1 Full verb:
We are keen to start the campaign.

2 Auxiliary verb:
We use **be** in the continuous verb forms:
We are approaching a number of new suppliers.
and in the passive verb forms:
The prototype is being tested at the moment.

***Notes***

1 We use an adjective after **be**, not an adverb:
It is usual to subcontract parts of the project to outside companies.
*cf.* We usually subcontract parts of the project to outside companies.

2 We use **be** in the continuous form when we want to emphasise the verb's activity meaning:
Although the payment is overdue, we are being very patient. (We are behaving very patiently.)

## Exercise 1

*Complete the sentences below by filling in the correct forms of the verb **be**.*

We ____________ reviewing salaries at the moment. However they ____________ unlikely ____________ increased by more than the current rate of inflation, which ____________ 3 per cent. The future strength of the company depends on capital investment. When costs increase too much, capital investment ____________ reduced. This ____________ sure to affect the profitability and long-term strength of the company. We ____________ committed to the development of the company. This has always ____________ our objective and will continue ____________ so in the coming decade.

## Exercise 2

*This information appeared in a trade journal about the Greek company Papandreos Mechanica.*

There are four production plants. One is responsible for 50 per cent of the total production of the company. This one is in Athens. The smallest plant, in Thessalonika, is also the newest. It was opened in 1992. A new plant is to be opened near Athens next year.

*Imagine a newspaper journalist wants confirmation of this information and telephones the Public Relations department of Papandreos Mechanica. He asks a series of questions. Write down what he says. The first is done for you.*

1 There ___are___ four production plants, ___aren't there?___
2 One ____________ responsible for half the production ____________?
3 And that one ____________ in Athens, ____________?
4 The Thessalonika plant ____________ the smallest, ____________?
5 And ____________ the newest, ____________?
6 It ____________ opened in 1992, ____________?
7 And a new plant ____________ opened next year, ____________?

## Exercise 3

*Complete the letter by putting a suitable form of the verb **be** in the spaces.*

Dear Mr Antrobus

We ________ very pleased to hear that you ________ interested in our new TESPO-2 account. Unfortunately, the documentation ________ not ________ ready until next month. Therefore I ________ enclosing with this letter the preliminary details.

As you ________ no doubt aware, TESPO-1 ________ issued at the end of last summer and ________ a great success. We ________ confident that TESPO-2 ________ a great success, too.

We hope that this information ________ of use to you. However, if there ________ other aspects that you ________ interested in, we ________ delighted to talk to you by phone.

Yours sincerely

M Bailey

M Bailey
Investment Consultant

## Transfer

1 Is there a company in your town that employs more than 4000 people?

____________________________

2 Are there many small companies near where you live?

____________________________

3 Think of one of these companies. Is it a manufacturing company?

____________________________

4 This was a short Transfer exercise,

____________________________?

# UNIT 25

## BE (2)

*See also* Unit 24 – **Be (1)**

### A *Sample sentences*

- The MD is to visit the plant on Monday.
- There is no doubt that the situation is very dangerous.
- It is very difficult to stimulate consumer spending in the present economic climate.

### B *Form*

For the forms of the verb **be**, see Unit 24.

### C *Uses*

The verb phrase **be to** comprises the verb **be** + V1. For more information on V1 tenses and forms see Units 14 and 23.

1 We use the construction **be to**:
to indicate what must or must not happen:
All payments are to be made before the goods can be despatched.

to indicate what should happen:
The meeting is to start at 9 o'clock sharp.

to indicate what is going to happen:
The statement is to be made tomorrow about the company's trading position.

to indicate what cannot or could not happen:
The company is in the hands of the receiver. There's nothing to be done.

This construction is widely used in formal announcements such as directives, timetables and memos to indicate that an action is fixed either in time or by obligation.

2 **It is** versus **there is**
Compare the following sentences:
Our quality system needs reviewing. It is time to introduce new quality checks. (now)
Don't worry. There is time to introduce new quality checks. (enough time)
'It is time to do something' means 'we must do it now'; 'there is time to do something' means 'there is still enough time to do it'.

Now compare the following sentences:
A: Have you visited their head office?
B: Yes, it's in New York now, isn't it? (the head office)

A: Do you know their management structure?
B: Not really.
A: Well, there is an MD supported by a Finance Manager. (There exists an MD.)

A: We are moving to new offices, did you know?
B: Yes, I've heard. The problem is that it is not easy to find office space big enough for all our people. (To find office space is not easy.)

In the first exchange **it** refers to information that has already been identified, i.e. the head office. In the second exchange **there** introduces new information – the introductory **there**. The word **there** has no specific meaning; it indicates that the key information will follow, i.e. the management structure that B doesn't know.
*cf.* A: Do you know their management structure?
B: Yes, it's quite simple, isn't it? (B already knows 'it'.)

In the third exchange, the **it** is an 'empty **it**'. In order to give more emphasis to this information (that to find office space is not easy), we need to put it at the end of the sentence (see Unit 23, C2), resulting in the 'empty **it**' construction. Information at the end of a sentence carries more emphasis.

3 **There** can be followed by a singular or plural verb form, depending on the subject:
There was a company in Bradford that used to specialise in laminating.
There were three major manufacturers in the early 1980s.

## Exercise 1

*Are the following sentences right or wrong? If wrong, correct them.*

1 I am being a little over-optimistic, aren't I?
2 The situation is clearly more volatile than I expected.
3 Companies are meeting the challenge by be more cautious.
4 Our advice to new investors is: Don't be putting all your capital into one fund.
5 This service has been being offered to clients for twenty years now.

## Exercise 2

*Rewrite the underlined words in the sentences below using a construction with* **be**. *The first one has been done for you.*

1 The company's new headquarters are <u>under construction</u> just outside Brussels.
The company's new headquarters are being constructed just outside Brussels.
2 Originally the project <u>should</u> have been completed by the end of next year.
3 <u>Unfortunately</u>, the building company ran into some financial difficulties.
4 Finally, <u>they abandoned the project</u> after we demanded they keep to the deadline. (put into the passive)
5 <u>Because of the delay</u>, there is a lot of pressure on us to find a replacement.
6 At the moment <u>we are inviting interested companies</u> to submit tenders. (put into the passive)
7 Originally, all tenders <u>ought to</u> have been submitted by the end of last month.
8 <u>Honestly speaking</u>, we are unlikely to be in the new building on time.

## Exercise 3

*Use the words from the box to complete the text below. Write one word in each space.*

| there | are | were | it | is | will | they | be |
|---|---|---|---|---|---|---|---|

_______ _______ an airline in France called Air Europa. _______ _______ owned by a consortium of French, German, Danish and Dutch companies. _______ _______ too many airlines in Europe and _______ _______ likely that Air Europe _______ _______ bought out by one of the larger national carriers. _______ _______ a small company and _______ unlikely to remain independent. This _______ a common pattern in Europe where a few years ago _______ _______ many more airlines.

## Transfer

*Describe a company that you know well. You can start:*

There is a company I know well. It is called …

# UNIT 26

## VERBS of SPEAKING

*See also* **Unit 27 – Verbs of reporting**

### A *Sample sentences*

- He said that he would take up his appointment at the beginning of the year.
- I would like to tell you a little about our civil engineering project in Zambia.
- We are planning to discuss the new video conference system at our next meeting.
- A: Have you talked to Rosa about the timing of the Vienna project?
  B: Yes, I spoke to her about it yesterday. She said she'll try to delay the starting date.

### B *Form*

| V1 | V2 | V3 |
|---|---|---|
| say | said | said |
| tell | told | told |
| talk | talked | talked |
| speak | spoke | spoken |
| discuss | discussed | discussed |

### C *Uses*

**Say**
– to say (to someone) that …
He said (to us) that he would take up his appointment at the beginning of the year.
(*not*: He said us that he would take up his appointment.)

**Tell**
– to tell someone that …
– to tell someone to do something
– to tell someone something
He told us that the project was coming along well.
I told him to give us another report in six months.
I would like to tell you a little about our civil engineering project in Zambia.
(*not*: I would like to tell about/I would like to tell to you about …)

**Talk**
– to talk (to someone) about something (BrE)
– to talk (to/with someone) about something (AmE)
Have you talked to Rosa about the timing of the Vienna project?

**To talk** refers to a whole conversation. **Talk** is not a reporting verb. (*not*: He talked that he would like to see me.)

**Speak**
– to speak (to/with someone) about something
I spoke to her about the Vienna project yesterday.

**To speak** refers to a whole or part of a conversation.
Can I speak to Mr Jones, please? (*not*: Can I talk with Mr Jones, please?)
**Speak** is not a reporting verb. (*not*: She spoke that she would like more information about the project.)

**Discuss**
– to discuss something (with someone)
We are planning to discuss the new video conference system at our next meeting.
(*not*: We are planning to discuss about the new video conference system.)

# VERBS of SPEAKING

## Exercise 1

*Identify mistakes in the following text and correct them.*

The board met to discuss about the new financing arrangements. The Chairman told to the meeting that changes were necessary to reduce costs. He asked to the Finance Manager to describe the new plan. She first talked on the reasons for the changes. Then she told about the new plan.

## Exercise 2

*Complete the text by adding a correct form of one of the verbs in the box.*

| say | tell | talk | speak | discuss | ask |
|---|---|---|---|---|---|

*I first heard about the problem when Jane _______ me about it. We _______ it for an hour. I _______ her to _______ me the reasons but she couldn't _______ what the reasons were. We agreed to _______ about it again before the meeting next week.*

## Exercise 3

*Complete the conversation below.*

*Arione:* Pronto, Arione, SpA.

*Karamura:* Hello, this is Yu-Ling Wu, from Karamura. Can I _______ to Ms Rina Arione, please?

*Arione:* She's in a meeting just now. Can you _______ me what you want to _______ about?

*Karamura:* Certainly. I need to _______ our meeting next month. I would like to _______ Ms Arione for some suggestions for the agenda. When could I _______ to her?

*Arione:* I think she'll be free in about an hour. I'll _______ her to call you, shall I?

*Karamura:* Oh yes please. Did you _______ about an hour?

*Arione:* Yes, approximately. She'll call you then.

*Karamura:* Many thanks. Goodbye.

## Transfer

1 *Give an example of something you discussed recently.*

I recently ______________________________

2 *Say who you discussed this subject with.*

I ______________________________

3 *Say what you said.*

I ______________________________

4 *Say what you asked.*

I ______________________________

5 *What are you going to talk about next time you meet the person in Question 2 above?*

Next time we meet, we'll probably ______________________________

6 *Will you speak to this person tomorrow?*

I'll probably ______________________________

# UNIT 27

## VERBS of REPORTING

*See also* **Unit 16 – Verb + object + infinitive**
**Unit 26 – Verbs of speaking**
**Unit 39 – Reported speech (1)**
**Unit 40 – Reported speech (2)**

### A *Sample sentences*

- The banks announced that there would be a decrease in interest rates.
- He admitted giving information to one of our competitors.
- He asked us not to pass on this information to any third parties.

### B *Form*

Verbs of reporting can take different constructions. Below is the range of constructions and a range of verbs.

| | say | ask | admit | accept |
|---|---|---|---|---|
| infinitive with **to** (1) | | ✓ | | |
| **that** + clause (2) | ✓ | | ✓ | ✓ |
| verb …*ing* (3) | | | ✓ | |
| object (4) | | | ✓ | ✓ |
| object + infinitive with **to** (5) | | ✓ | | |

Here are some sample sentences which show the use of these verbs:
She said that the old version would be withdrawn shortly.
He asked to be informed of any developments.
They asked her to make them an offer.
He admitted all the charges against him.
He admitted giving the information to a competitor.
She admitted that they had lost a lot of money.

### C *Uses*

Below are some of the more common verbs of reporting, classified according to the constructions 1–5 in the table above.

1 These verbs take an infinitive with **to** (Type 1); if they take any other constructions as well, they are shown in brackets:

*agree* (2) *claim* (2, 4) *consent* *decline* (4) *demand* (2, 4) *promise* (2, 4) *propose* (2, 3, 4) *refuse* (2, 4) *swear* (2) *threaten* (2, 4)

2 These verbs take **that** + clause (Type 2); if they take any other constructions as well, they are shown in brackets:

*announce* (4) *assume* *believe* (4) *confirm* (4) *consider* (3, 4, 5) *declare* (5) *demonstrate* (4) *disclose* (4) *estimate* (4, 5) *explain* (4) *guess* (4, 5) *hold* *indicate* (4, 5) *inform* (4) *maintain* (4) *notify* (4) *presume* *prove* (4, 5) *report* (4, 5) *say* *show* (4, 5) *state* (4)

3 These verbs take a verb …*ing* (Type 3); if they take any other constructions as well, they are shown in brackets:

*admit* (2, 3, 4) *advise* (2, 4, 5) *authorise* (4, 5) *recommend* (2, 3, 4) *require* (2, 4, 5) *suggest* (2, 3, 4) *urge* (2, 4, 5)

4 These verbs only take an object (Type 4):

*describe* *outline* *present*

5 These verbs take an object + infinitive with **to** (Type 5); if they take any other constructions as well, they are shown in brackets:

*ask* (1, 4) *command* (4) *direct* (4) *instruct* (4) *invite* (4) *order* (2, 4) *persuade* (4) *tell* (4) *warn* (4)

## Exercise 1

*Complete the table below by adding ticks (✓) to indicate how each of the given verbs is used. Several of the verbs are used in more than one way.*

| | say | suggest | promise | require | explain | advise | warn | claim |
|---|---|---|---|---|---|---|---|---|
| infinitive + **to** (1) | | | | | | | | |
| **that** + clause (2) | | | | | | | | |
| verb …*ing* (3) | | | | | | | | |
| object (4) | | | | | | | | |
| object + infinitive with **to** (5) | | | | | | | | |

## Exercise 2

*Complete the text below with the correct form of an appropriate verb from the alternatives given. In some cases, more than one verb could be used.*

*urge recommend threaten accept agree admit promise indicate claim ask*

*The Health & Safety Committee has (1) __________ a full investigation into the accident on the drilling rig Puffin in the North Sea. The Minister for Energy has (2) __________ the Committee to produce an interim report. The company concerned, General Oil, has (3) __________ responsibility for the accident and has (4) __________ carrying out immediate safety checks on all similar installations. The government has (5) __________ to force the closure of the rig but the company (6) __________ this is not necessary. A member of the Committee, Grete Arnheim, has (7) __________ the company to (8) __________ to a full public enquiry. General Oil has (9) __________ that they do not think this is necessary but that they probably would (10) __________ the conclusions of an independent investigation.*

## Exercise 3

*Choose the correct ending for each of the phrases below. In some cases two alternatives are possible.*

1 The labour costs are too high so the Board recommend
  **a** to reduce the number of workers.
  **b** reducing the workforce.
  **c** the workforce to be reduced.

2 The R & D budget has been reduced and the Head of the Department has warned
  **a** to resign.
  **b** resigning.
  **c** that she will resign.

3 The problems require
  **a** looking for an immediate solution.
  **b** an immediate solution.
  **c** that we find an immediate solution.

4 We maintain
  **a** a high level of quality.
  **b** to keep a high level of quality.
  **c** having a high level of quality.

5 The results prove
  **a** doing investing was right.
  **b** that we were right to invest.
  **c** to invest was right.

## Transfer

*Think of your own work or studies. Write sentences about the last few days including any of the verbs in the box opposite.*

*suggest advise recommend invite instruct indicate prove report authorise ask threaten present propose show explain*

# UNIT 28

## VERBS of the SENSES

*See also* Unit 30 – Verbs + adjectives

### A *Sample sentences*

- We are going to look at the production costs in the meeting, but first we're going to watch a short video about production techniques.
- The new product range looks very good.
- Their terms sounded quite attractive to me.
- Mary, you don't look too well. What's the matter?

### B *Form*

There are five senses: sight, hearing, smell, taste and touch. Each sense has three activities associated with it:

*intentional* activity, e.g. to look at the figures
*unintentional* activity, e.g. to see an accident
describing the *current sensation*, e.g. to look attractive

| Sense | Intentional activity | Unintentional activity | Current sensation |
|---|---|---|---|
| sight | **look at** (a static object)<br>**watch** (a moving or changing object or activity) | **see** | **look** |
| hearing | **listen to** | **hear** | **sound** |
| smell | **smell** | **smell** | **smell** |
| taste | **taste** | **taste** | **taste** |
| feel | **touch/feel** | **touch/feel** | **feel** |

### C *Uses*

1 Intentional activity:
Let's look at the costs in more detail (The figures are a static object.)
If you look over to your right, you can watch all the operations on the screen. (The operations are an activity involving change.)
First I plan to listen to the comments of the shopfloor workers.
If you touch this new fabric, you can feel how soft it is.

***Note***
Sorry, I missed that. Can I see the previous transparency again? (experience visually, though without a lot of attention)

2 Unintentional activity:
Did you see the report about our company in the local newspaper?
I didn't hear what was said about the benefits of leasing.
Can you smell anything strange in here?

3 Current sensation:
These verbs of sensation are followed by adjectives.
You look great! Have you been on holiday?
They are in a very strong position now. Their results sounded excellent.
A: This is the new synthetic fabric.
B: Very attractive. Yes, and it feels very smooth, too.

***Notes***

1 We use **well** (adj.) to describe health and **good** to describe positive attributes:
He looks/feels very well. (healthy, not ill)
*cf.* The future looks very good. (positive, not bad)

2 We do not use the present continuous for unintentional activity and current sensation verbs:
Now do you see the screen on the right? (*not*: are you seeing?)
You needn't move the OHP. I can see quite well from here. (*not*: I am seeing.)

## Exercise 1

*Each of the sentences below contains a mistake. Underline the mistake and then write the correct form.*

1 After work I like looking at television.
2 I am smelling something strange. Is it a gas leak?
3 I want to look at the results but not in any detail.
4 I'm hearing you, please carry on.
5 This surface is feeling very good. What is it made of?
6 If you watch over here, I'll show you something interesting.
7 The wine is tasting good.

## Exercise 2

*Here is an agenda for a visit to a chemical manufacturer, Oxwell Laboratories.*

10.00 Welcome
10.15 Introduction: Presentation of Oxwell by Robin T. Robins, Vice-President
10.45 Video: *The Chemical Industry Market*
11.15 Discussion
11.45 Tour of Plant led by Joanna P. Tarrant, Vice-President, Production
13.00 Lunch

*At the beginning of the meeting, Sonny R. Spencer, Manager, Human Resources, introduces this programme. Fill in the spaces with appropriate verbs of the senses.*

*'Welcome to Oxwell. Now, I'd like to outline the programme for the morning. We're going to __________ a presentation by our Vice-President, Robin Robins. Then we'll __________ a video about the chemical industry market. Then we'll have an opportunity to talk about the video. After that at about 11.45 Joanna Tarrant will take us __________ the plant. You'll be able to __________ the production process in action. Then we'll have lunch and I promise you'll be able to __________ some local specialities.'*

## Exercise 3

*The following is part of a discussion between two managers of a soft drinks manufacturer. Fill in the spaces with the correct form of one of the verbs in the box.*

| watch | look | smell | taste | see | feel |
|---|---|---|---|---|---|

*Paul:* How do you __________ about the plans?

*Angela:* I'm optimistic. Do you want to __________ the latest forecasts?

*Paul:* I can't just now. I'll __________ at them tomorrow. I've got to go and __________ a demonstration of a new testing machine by Horrowitz & Co.

*Angela:* Before you go, the laboratory has produced a variation on the RT4 flavour for the new Zappo drink. Have you __________ it?

*Paul:* Yes, it was okay but it __________ like bad eggs!

## Transfer

*Where are you now? Answer the following questions.*

1 *What are you __________ at?*
2 *What can you __________ if you __________ out of the window?*
3 *Can you __________ anything? Flowers or perfume for example?*
4 *What did your last drink __________ like?*

# UNIT 29

## ARISE, RISE, RAISE, LIE and LAY

*See also* **Unit 75 – Describing trends**

### A *Sample sentences*

- If a problem arises during installation, call the helpline immediately.
- You can raise the alarm by breaking the glass on this device here.
- I'm afraid that the banks will have to raise interest rates again. That means they have risen three times this year.
- Installation is very simple. The cabinet just lies on the floor. After you've laid it there, leave it for about three hours to settle.

### B *Form*

| V1 | V2 | V3 |
|---|---|---|
| arise | arose | arisen |
| rise | rose | risen |
| raise | raised | raised |
| lie | lay | lain |
| lay | laid | laid |

### C *Uses*

Let's look at the uses of each of these verbs:

**Arise** is intransitive. It needs a subject.
A problem has arisen at the plant.
(*not*: It has arisen a problem.)

**Rise** is intransitive.
Interest rates rose by 2 per cent last year.
(*not*: The banks rose interest rates last year.)

**Raise** is transitive.
The bank has raised interest rates by 1 per cent.
(*not*: Interest rates have raised by 1 per cent.)

**Lie** is intransitive.
The cabinet just lies on the floor.
(*not*: First you lie the cabinet on the floor.)

**Lay** is transitive.
First lay the material on the floor.
(*not*: This material just lays on the floor.)

# ARISE, RISE, RAISE, LIE and LAY

## Exercise 1

*Mark the following as transitive (T) or intransitive (I).*

raise rise lay lie arise

## Exercise 2

*Select correct sentences from each group below. In some cases, two sentences are correct.*

1 **a** We arise different problems.
**b** Different problems arise.
**c** This arises another problem.

2 **a** The costs have risen every year.
**b** We have risen the costs every year.
**c** Every year has risen the costs.

3 **a** We can raise the prices.
**b** The prices can raise.
**c** The prices can be raised.

4 **a** If we lie the material directly on the floor it will be okay.
**b** If the material lies directly on the floor it will be okay.
**c** If the material is lied directly on the floor it will be okay.

5 **a** Lay the picture on the table and we'll see it clearly.
**b** If the picture is laid directly on the table we'll see it clearly.
**c** The picture lays on the table so we can see it clearly.

## Exercise 3

*Read the following dialogue. Then write a short memo to a colleague telling her what you have discussed.*

A: A problem has arisen over the travel arrangements to Switzerland.
B: Really? What's that?
A: The airline has raised its fares by 20 per cent so we're above the budget agreed.
B: Really? Well the problem lies in the budget being too small! We have rising costs and a budget that hasn't been raised in two years.
A: Could you get authorisation for the increased cost?
B: I'll send the Finance Department the details. I'll call you later.

**MEMO**

To: Finance Department
Re: Trip to Switzerland

## Transfer

*Write a short memo to a colleague about rising costs or a decision to raise prices, or a problem that has arisen in your work.*

# UNIT 30

## VERBS + ADJECTIVES

*See also* Unit 28 – Verbs of the senses

### A *Sample senses*

- The new working environment is very stressful.
- I have become very anxious about the future of the company.
- I am glad to report that the prices of raw materials have remained stable over the last year.
- I don't want to sound over-optimistic, but I am certain we have a winner with this new product.

### B *Form*

Verbs which take an adjective are called *linking* or *copular* verbs. We can divide them into:

– current verbs, which indicate what the subject is:
He is/appears/seems/sounds content in his new job.
– resulting verbs, which indicate what the subject becomes:
The directors became/got/grew anxious after the results were released.

| Current verbs | Resulting verbs |
|---|---|
| be | become |
| remain | fall |
| appear | turn |
| feel | get |
| look | go |
| prove | grow |
| seem | run |
| sound | |
| stay | |
| keep | |
| smell | |
| taste | |

### C *Uses*

1 Current verbs:
So far this year energy costs have remained/stayed constant.
Our new policy of energy conservation has proved very economical.
The contract we have negotiated sounds very secure.
Keep quiet about the overspend for the moment.
We feel very confident about our move into the US.

2 Resulting verbs:
The markets got very nervous after the unemployment figures were released.
I regret that the market has turned sour – just after our earlier success.
With the present volatility in the markets, share prices have run wild over the last few days.

## Exercise 1

*How many phrases can you make by combining the verbs in the lefthand column with the adjectives in the righthand column below?*

| | |
|---|---|
| feel | optimistic/pessimistic |
| sound | right/wrong |
| look | wild |
| turn | ill |
| prove | happy/unhappy |
| run | sweet/bitter |
| become | sceptical |
| seem | confident |
| appear | crazy |
| taste | absurd/sensible |
| fall | |
| go | |

## Exercise 2

*Complete the following sentences by choosing the most appropriate ending.*

1 Share prices are very volatile and the market
 **a** has grown pessimistic.
 **b** appears stable.
 **c** looks relaxed.

2 The company has invested a lot in new products and everyone
 **a** appears interesting.
 **b** appears confident.
 **c** is ill.

3 After looking at the splendid results the Board
 **a** is becoming anxious.
 **b** proved right.
 **c** feels excited about future prospects.

4 Paula has read the report on the product and says she
 **a** sounds interesting.
 **b** feels good.
 **c** remains pessimistic.

5 After a good start the project
 **a** went wrong.
 **b** fell ill.
 **c** sounded critical.

## Exercise 3

*Complete the letter by adding an appropriate form of the correct verb from the list below. Use each word once.*

*remain turn feel be*
*prove look run sound*

**ARDILLA INVERSIONES** (IBERICA)
Calle Gerona 46, Barcelona, Spain

Ms May Ling-Wu
Head of Financial Planning
Ardilla Investments (USA)
Stephenson Building
220-228 Colorado Boulevard
Ohio

14th October 19__

Dear Ms Ling-Wu

Thank you for your letter of 8th October.

As you know, the prospects for a good return on investments in Spanish companies have ________ sour. There is a lot of instability about as a consequence of changes in exchange rates and a general loss of confidence. Share prices have ________ wild, with some companies showing large gains and others large falls.

On the telephone yesterday you ________ surprised when I told you that I didn't ________ confident. My feelings last week have ________ right. Things ________ bad just now so probably our analysis will ________ pessimistic. Even the larger investment houses ________ very sceptical about prospects in the short term.

I will contact you at the end of the week but I don't expect prospects to improve until interest rates fall.

Regards

*Maria Isabel Vasquez*

Maria Isabel Vasquez
Investments Consultant

## Transfer

*What is the present economic state of a country you know well? Write five sentences on the present outlook.*

*Example:*
The economy looks strong just now.

# UNIT 31

## HAVE, HAVE GOT and GET

**See also Unit 5 – The present perfect simple**
**Unit 6 – The present perfect continuous**
**Unit 7 – The past perfect**

### A *Sample sentences*

- We didn't have enough time to check the figures thoroughly.
- We have now got a very good team working on the problem.
- We got the results of the survey yesterday. When can you get the next results to us?

### B *Form*

| | V1 | V2 | V3 |
|---|---|---|---|
| | **have** | **had** | **had** |
| **Negative** | don't/doesn't have | didn't have | hasn't/haven't had |
| **Question** | do/does subject have? | did subject have? | have/has subject had? |
| | **get** | **got** | **got** |
| **Negative** | don't/doesn't get | didn't get | hasn't/haven't got |
| **Question** | do/does subject get? | did subject get? | have/has subject got? |

1 **Have** is both a full verb and an auxiliary. (For the forms of the auxiliary see Unit 5.) The negative and question forms of the full verb **have** follow the normal patterns: see the table above.

2 **Get** is a full verb. The negative and question forms follow the normal patterns, so the form **have got** is in effect the present perfect of **get**.

### C *Uses*

1 **Have**. We use the appropriate forms of **do** and **did** in negatives and questions.
We don't have a representative in East Europe.
(*not*: We haven't a representative in East Europe.)

Do you have an agent in Spain?
(*not*: Have you an agent in Spain?)

We didn't have a chance to discuss the price.
(*not*: We hadn't a chance to discuss the price.)

Did you have a chance to discuss delivery?
(*not*: Had you a chance to discuss delivery?)

2 **Get**. In the present, past and past perfect, the main meaning of **get** is 'receive' or 'obtain'.
A: How often do we get a statement from the bank?
B: We get one each week.
A: And when did we get our last statement?
B: We got one on Monday. At that time, we had just got a new loan.

The present perfect **have got** means 'have', i.e. with a present meaning:
We have got a very good team working in the production department.
Have they got their new financial product out yet?

*cf.* Did they get their last financial product out in time?
(*not*: Had they got their last financial product?)

# HAVE, HAVE GOT and GET

## Exercise 1

*Write sentences based on the following prompts.*

1 The company/get/new director/next month. (positive)
2 I/get/your letter/yesterday. (positive)
3 I/just/finish/report. (positive)
4 The government/get/a workable economic plan. (negative)
5 Our competitors/have/good products/at present. (negative)
6 You/get/my letter/yet? (interrogative)
7 TS Corporation/have/plants in Korea? (interrogative)

## Exercise 2

*Some of the sentences below contain mistakes. Underline them and correct them.*

1 We have gotten a good deal from the negotiations.
2 Parlour Smith had major losses last year.
3 They hadn't a good management organisation.
4 Had they the same director then as now?
5 We've got a new policy on sales discounts.
6 Had you got any benefit from the training course you did last week?
7 Have you an agent in Morocco?
8 I got your letter this morning.

## Exercise 3

*You have heard that a company called Harrow sells automotive parts in Japan. You telephone Harrow at their London office to ask about their operations in Asia.*

*Reconstruct the dialogue based on the following prompts.*

You
Harrow (London)
Harrow/manufacturing plant/Japan?
No
From where/Japanese sales reps/get/Harrow goods?
Korea. We/have/plant in Seoul
Harrow/agents/Japan?
Yes/agents.
No sole distributor/Japan
Thank you. Goodbye


## Transfer

*Describe the production and distribution network of any company you know.*

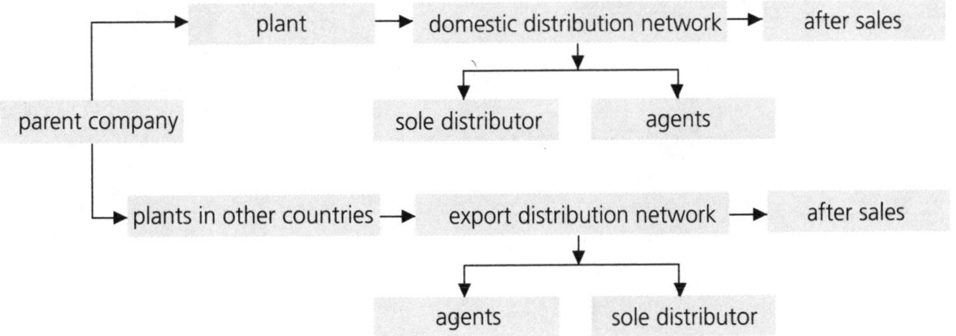


*Begin, for example, as follows:*

*'ABC has a plant in __________. It has a domestic distribution network …' etc.*

# UNIT 32

## MAKE versus DO

*See also* Unit 16 – Verb + object + infinitive

### A *Sample sentences*

- I think you have made a mistake in invoice number 25789.
- This press report has done a lot of damage to our reputation.
- A: What are you doing?
  B: You know we are making an offer for the old stock? Well, I'm doing the calculations.

### B *Form*

| V1 | V2 | V3 |
|---|---|---|
| make<br>do | made<br>did | made<br>done |

### C *Uses*

There are no clear rules about the meanings of **make** and **do**. Generally, we use **make** when there is an end product, e.g. make a profit, make a mistake; and we use **do** when the activity is an end in itself, e.g. do business, do a job.

Below is a list of common combinations:

**do**
*the accounts/budget/forecast   business   damage*
*an exercise   a favour   good   a job*
*repairs   a service   work   wrong*

**make**
*an apology   an appointment   arrangements   a budget/forecast*
*certain   a choice   a complaint   a decision*
*an effort   an enquiry   an excuse   friends (with)*
*a loss   a mistake   money   an offer*
*a profit   progress   a report   sure*
*a trip   (someone) welcome   work (for others)*

***Notes***
Notice the difference between these sentences:
We do all the forecasts in November. (= do the activity)
I am going to make a forecast at the next meeting. (= present the end-product)

## Exercise 1

*Which of these are correct?*

1 The Chairman made a long speech.
2 He said the company did a good profit in the year.
3 He said the company would remain independent, though a large competitor had made an offer to buy a 25 per cent stake in the company.
4 The shareholders could do a choice between independence and prosperity or the uncertainty of being taken over by a large multinational.
5 The Chairman said that those who recommended selling shares were making a big mistake.
6 He believed that independently the company could still make progress.
7 I did a trip in South America and was made welcome everywhere I went.
8 They made the repairs without doing any complaints.

## Exercise 2

*Opposite is a list of nouns each of which can be used with **make** or **do**. Decide which can be used with **make**, and which with **do**.*

an exercise  a favour  a speech  a plan
progress  money  damage  a report
an appointment  a profit  a complaint  a job

## Exercise 3

**Memo**

To: AS
From: HT
We have to make a choice between two market research organisations, Arrow and Bow. Bow have made us an offer but they are very expensive. Arrow do very good work and are cheaper. I will make an effort to visit them but I haven't made an appointment yet. Could you do me a favour and tell me if you know any reason why we shouldn't use Arrow? We don't want to make any mistakes on this.

Thanks.

*Look at the internal memo opposite then answer the questions which follow.*

1 What is the choice HT has to make?
2 Has Bow made an offer?
3 What does HT know about Arrow?
4 What must HT do before she visits Arrow?
5 What does HT want AS to do?

## Exercise 4

*Here is a letter from a Production Manager to a colleague in a subsidiary of a synthetic sports surfaces manufacturing company. The company is developing a new kind of surface for tennis courts but is having problems.*

*Fill in the spaces in the letter with an appropriate form of **make** or **do**.*

**MONDO INTERNATIONAL**

**Am Eichenwald 270**
**D-8902 Kassel**
**Germany**

Mondo Sport Surfaces
1200 Laird Boulevard
Washington DC
38632 USA
12 May 19__

Dear Bernadette,

Re: Tennis SSR567 Project

Further to my telephone call last week, there is some more news I have to tell you.

We ________ a mistake in the initial design stage. We need to ________ some more research on the effects of high temperatures on the surface areas. Please ________ arrangements for a new test in the Schuster Laboratories. I have ________ enquiries about exactly what we need to ________ and Uli and Rosa are going to contact me as soon as they ________ a decision on the tests.

Please ________ sure Gerd knows about the delay and tell him we'll ________ our best to resolve the problem as soon as possible.

Regards,

*Marcus Pressman*

Marcus Pressman
Assistant Director of Production

## Transfer

*Have you made any trips, appointments, presentations or important decisions lately?*
*Have you made any mistakes or made any excuses?*
*Have you done anyone a favour or done any damage to anything?*
*Have you done any good recently?*

# UNIT 33

## VERB + PREPOSITION

*See also* Unit 13 – Verb ...ing
Unit 26 – Verbs of speaking

### A Sample sentences

- We agree with you entirely on the need for additional commitment.
- The whole future of this operation depends on a highly skilled workforce.
- We look forward to hearing the details of your forthcoming visit.
- We have already paid for the services of a tax consultant.

### B Form

Prepositional verb phrases take two forms:

1 verb + preposition + prepositional object
We apologise for any inconvenience caused by the delay.

2 verb + preposition + V1 *...ing*
They succeeded in boosting pre-tax profits.

***Note***
Where a preposition is followed by a verb, the verb form is always V1 *...ing*.

### C Uses

For a list of the more common prepositional verbs, see Appendix 1.

***Note***
We do not use a preposition after these verbs:

| | |
|---|---|
| **answer:** | I'd prefer to answer that question/you at the end of my talk. |
| **ask:** | Excuse me. I'd like to ask you a question, please.<br>*cf*: I'd like to ask you for some more information. ('you' = indirect object; 'ask for' = prepositional verb) |
| **call/phone/ring:** | Please could you call/phone/ring me back later. |
| **discuss:** | We can discuss this matter tomorrow. |
| **enter:** | Don't enter this area without prior authorisation. |
| **meet:** | We are to meet a delegation from China. (BrE)<br>We are to meet with a delegation from China. (AmE) |
| **reach:** | We eventually reached the hotel at 2 o'clock in the morning. |
| **suit:** | Does a meeting on Tuesday suit you? |
| **tell:** | I told them that their tender was successful. |

# VERB + PREPOSITION

## Exercise 1

*Fill in the missing prepositions.*

**1** to agree ________ someone
**2** to allow ________ something
**3** to apologise ________ something
**4** to consist ________ something
**5** to hear ________ something
**6** to look ________ something
**7** to refer ________ someone
**8** to rely ________ someone
**9** to wait ________ someone
**10** to agree ________ something
**11** to apply ________ something
**12** to approve ________ something
**13** to depend ________ something
**14** to insist ________ something

## Exercise 2

*Two managers are discussing a strike by lorry drivers working for road haulage companies. Complete the spaces in the dialogue by selecting an appropriate form of the correct verb from those given here. The first two have been done for you.*

hope for agree to hear about
insist on amount to
allow for depend on wait for
think about rely on

A: Have you heard about (1) the road transport strike?

B: Yes, It's terrible. We rely on (2) the drivers for all our components.

A: We should ________ (3) using our own drivers.

B: That ________ (4) whether they would be happy to drive during a strike.

A: We can ________ (5) them meeting their contractual obligations!

B: Yes, but we have to ________ (6) the problems they could meet on the roads.

A: That ________ (7) supporting the strike!

B: Perhaps. Anyway, we should have a meeting with our drivers and ________ (8) a simple solution.

A: Yes, they might ________ (9) move our components.

B: If not, we'll have to ________ (10) the end of the strike.

## Transfer

*Think of your own family or the place where you work or where you study, or your country. Write six sentences with verb + preposition combinations.*

# UNIT 34

## VERB + OBJECT + PREPOSITION

*See also* Unit 13 – Verb ...ing
Unit 16 – Verb + object + infinitive
Unit 26 – Verbs of speaking

### A *Sample sentences*

- First of all, let me describe the main parts of the system to you.
- They explained the operation of the software to the audience and then demonstrated it.
- Obviously I prefer the new model to the old one.
- They have spent a fortune on developing a very safe working environment.

### B *Form*

Object + prepositional verb phrases take two forms:

1 Verb + object + preposition + prepositional object
protect us from unfair competition

2 Verb + object + preposition + V1 ...*ing*
prevent us from entering the Japanese market

***Note***
Where a preposition is followed by a verb, the verb form is always V1 ...*ing*.

### C *Uses*

For a list of the more common examples of object + prepositional verb, see Appendix 2.

***Notes***

1 The preposition **from** is used after 'disabling' verbs such as:
*prohibit restrain forbid prevent ban veto stop*
They prevented us from exporting the goods.

2 The 'enabling' verbs, on the other hand, take an object + infinitive. Enabling verbs are:
*allow authorise help permit enable encourage*
They helped us to export the goods.

# VERB + OBJECT + PREPOSITION

## Exercise 1

*Below are six examples of the construction verb + object + preposition. They have been mixed up. Rearrange and add to them to create six correct sentences. The first has been done for you.*

| | | | |
|---|---|---|---|
| accused | our competitors | into | the eventual users |
| spend | *me* | with | investment |
| prevent | product A | on | two parts |
| divide | large sums | to | stealing |
| compare | the talk | from | product B |
| explain | the software | *of* | gaining an advantage |

1 *He accused me of stealing*
2 *I want to …*
3 *Let me …*
4 *They'll …*
5 *We …*
6 *We must …*

## Exercise 2

*The extract opposite is from a letter in which a company is unhappy about the quality of service provided by an electrical components manufacturer. Fill in the spaces with suitable words from those given here.*

| Object | Preposition |
|---|---|
| the matter | to |
| you | to |
| the installation | with |
| us | to |
| the H50 | of |

We regret that we need to remind ________ ________ the terms of the contract when you supplied the goods. According to Article 31 Paragraph 4, you would provide ________ ________ full instructions on the installation of the H50. Your representative, Mr Yogi, has consistently failed to explain ________ ________ our technicians.
Six weeks ago we preferred ________ ________ rival products, but the service you have provided is lamentable. If this problem is not resolved immediately and to our total satisfaction, we will have to refer ________ ________ our lawyers.

## Exercise 3

*Read the following dialogue.*

AC: I've compared the Ndlovu products with Rosario's and have reached a clear decision. I prefer the Ndlovu ones. However, they are more expensive.
BR: So, you'll have to convince me of the benefits.
AC: Ndlovu is better – I think by 20 per cent.
BR: Could you remind me of the cost difference?
AC: $23 per unit.
BR: Hmmm. We're spending a lot of money on this so the decision is very important. Can you tell me about the benefits of the Ndlovu product?
AC: I think it's a better design – it'll be easier to use.
BR: Okay, if you prefer Ndlovu to the others that's okay. Will you tell Pat about this?
AC: Sure, I'll send a memo right away.

*Now write the short memo to Pat, telling her of the decision reached.*

**Memo**

**To:** Pat
**From:** AC

## Transfer

*When did you last remind someone of something? What was it?*
*When did you last accuse someone of something? What was it?*
*When did you last provide someone with something? What was it?*
*When did you last tell someone about something? What was it?*
*When did you last interest someone in something? What was it?*
*When did you last convince someone of something? What was it?*

# UNIT 35

## VERB + ADVERB (PHRASAL VERB)

### A Sample sentences

- All exporters must fill in this form in duplicate and send it to the address shown below.
- They put on an excellent buffet supper after the presentation.
- We have worked very hard to speed up delivery; we hope you will make the same effort for payments.
- We regret to inform you that we have had to turn down your very generous offer.
- Please could you turn up early at the stand? We will need to make sure that the samples are all there.

### B Form

Verb + adverb phrases are also called *phrasal verbs.* They consist of:

| verb + | adverb | (+ object) + | rest of sentence |
|---|---|---|---|
| fill | in | this form | in duplicate |
| turn | up | | early at the stand |

The following alternative word order is also possible:

| verb + | adverb + | object |
|---|---|---|
| fill | in | the form |

| verb + | object + | adverb |
|---|---|---|
| fill | the form | in |

| verb + | object pronoun + | adverb |
|---|---|---|
| fill | it | in |

(*not*: fill in it)

Common adverbs used in phrasal verbs are:

*about along away back down forward in*
*off on out over round through up*

### C Uses

Some phrasal verbs keep the individual meanings of the verb and the adverb:
I've brought back the plans. Would you like to see them?

Other phrasal verbs have a different meaning from the individual parts:
He made up a wonderful story about his adventures in Rotaronga. (make up = invent)

In style most phrasal verbs are informal, although this does not mean they are uncommon.

For a list of the more common phrasal verbs, see Appendix 3.

## VERB + ADVERB (PHRASAL VERB)

### Exercise 1

*Match the verbs on the left with a phrasal verb on the right which means the same.*

| | |
|---|---|
| arrive | call off |
| cause | send back |
| discover | turn up |
| stop working | bring about |
| close (a factory) | find out |
| abandon (a meeting) | shut down |
| complete (a form) | break down |
| reject (goods received) | fill in |

### Exercise 2

*Read the formal report. In the dialogue which follows, two people discuss the report.*

*Fill in the spaces with phrasal verbs which mean the same as the non-phrasal verbs in the report.*

The pump stopped working and so the supervisor stopped production. Maintenance staff examined the whole pump assembly and discovered that the flow of liquid into the pump was faster than normal. This may have caused excessive pressure in the pump assembly.

Tomas: What happened?

Janet: First the pump __________ __________ and so the supervisor __________ __________ production.

Tomas: Then what?

Janet: We __________ __________ the pump assembly and saw that the flow into the pump was too fast.

Tomas: And did that __________ __________ a pressure build-up?

Janet: Well, I think so, yes.

### Exercise 3

*Here is an extract from a telephone conversation.*

Jean: Oh, tell Eva that if she comes along next week I'll be pleased to look over the results with her. It doesn't matter when, she can just turn up any day. Oh, and tell her Tom is going to come along tomorrow. Also, tell her next Monday's sales meeting has been called off.

*Write a brief fax to Eva giving her the required information from this extract. Use non-phrasal verbs.*

**Fax message**

KronQvist Pyrolavagen 28
Lidingo Sweden
Telephone: 46 87 465873
Fax: 46 87 465877

To: 33 (1) 43245678
Attention: Eva von Heijne
From:

Regards

### Transfer

*Answer the following questions using phrasal verbs in your answer instead of the underlined non-phrasal verbs. The first has been done for you.*

1 When did you <u>take possession</u> of the house you now live in?
*I moved in to my present house in January of last year.*

2 When was the last time you <u>invented</u> an excuse for not doing something?
3 When was the last time someone <u>arrived</u> unexpectedly to see you?
4 Give an example of something surprising that you <u>discovered</u> recently.
5 Have you ever <u>rejected</u> an offer of work?

# UNIT 36

## SENTENCE TYPES – SIMPLE and COMPLEX

### A *Sample sentences*

- ◆ Managers plan activities.
- ◆ Managers plan activities but most also play a personnel role.
- ◆ All managers are involved in personnel matters because they must ensure that each team member operates efficiently.

### B *Form*

A simple sentence comprises just one clause, i.e. with one verb phrase:
Managers plan activities.

A complex sentence comprises more than one clause, i.e. with more than one verb phrase. We connect the clauses by *coordination, subordination* or *'general purpose' connectors*.
Managers plan activities but must also play a personnel role. (coordination with **but**)
All managers are involved in personnel matters because they must ensure that each team member operates efficiently. (subordination with **because**)
She works for Pharmacon, which makes chemical products. (connection with **which**)

### C *Uses*

1 A simple sentence can be a statement, a question, a command or an exclamation:
Julie leads the production department. (statement)
Who leads the production department? (question)
Don't sign the contract for the moment. (command)
What a ridiculous remark he made! (exclamation)

2 We can use coordination to connect clauses with the coordinating conjunctions **and, or** or **but:**
You can book the ticket now and collect it this afternoon.

3 We can use subordination to connect clauses with subordinating conjunctions, e.g. **when, though, because**:
I'm afraid you won't get the ticket tomorrow because there is a postal strike.

***Notes***

1 We can use a simple statement or question in a presentation to get the audience's attention:
We are on the right track.
When will the date be fixed?

2 Coordination is often more vague, less emphatic than subordination:
We will review our recruitment policy next year. We hope to make a clear decision and implement it by the middle of June and should see the results by the end of the year.
*cf.* We will review our recruitment policy next year. At that time we hope to make a clear decision which we can implement by the middle of June. Therefore we should see results by the end of the year.

Subordination reduces the subordinated clause to a less important role, and thereby shows the relative importance of the two pieces of information.

3 Relative pronoun connectors (**who** and **which**) have an unemphatic connecting effect, sometimes similar to **and**:
They have given the job to Kim, who will be very efficient, I am sure.
They have given the job to Kim, and he will be very efficient, I am sure.

4 After a coordinating conjunction, we can omit the following sentence elements if they are the same as in the main clause. We can omit:
**a** the subject **b** the auxiliary or modal verb **c** the **to** from the infinitive.

We can send your order by post or deliver it ourselves. (**we can** is omitted)
We would like to make a small donation or show our appreciation in some way. (**to** is omitted)

# SENTENCE TYPES – SIMPLE and COMPLEX

## Exercise 1

*Read the advertisement for a clothing manufacturer.*

*There are eight sentences in the advertisement. Classify them according to the following sentence types.*

**A** Simple statement sentence
**B** Simple interrogative sentence
**C** Simple negative sentence
**D** Simple exclamative sentence
**E** Complex sentence with subordinate clause
**F** Complex sentence with relative clause

**_Fornaro_ – Classic Italian Clothes for Men**

***Fornaro*** produces classic menswear. The company, which was formed in 1956, has a growing reputation for high quality suits. Although based in Milan, ***Fornaro*** has production plants in Rome and Florence. ***Fornaro*** products are not only sold in Italy. You can find them throughout Europe. Are you looking for style, quality and classic appeal? Look no further! ***Fornaro*** suits you.

## Exercise 2

*Below are pairs of simple sentences. Join them together to form complex sentences using the method indicated in brackets.*

1 We are reorganising the department. We are recruiting new staff. (coordination)
2 We are advertising for a new computer analyst. Irene has retired. (subordination)
3 The position is at supervisory level. The position carries a high salary. (relative pronoun)
4 We need a young person. We need a skilled programmer. (relative pronoun)
5 We will advertise in various countries. We will advertise in specialist journals. (coordination)
6 We need someone with experience. We don't need a complete expert. (subordination)

## Exercise 3

1 *Here is some information about a Research Department in a small telecommunications company. The information is presented first in a paragraph containing five simple sentences. Then in an improved version, the same information is presented in only two complex sentences, but the paragraph is incomplete. Complete this version by putting one word in each space.*

We need to increase the quality of our research. Increasing the quality of our research will be expensive. Our present research is on a new pocket-sized communications device. The research we are presently engaged in is potentially very exciting. A major technological advance is possible.

*We need to increase the quality of our research __________ will be expensive. Our present research, __________ __________ __________ a new pocket-sized communications device, __________ potentially very exciting __________ a major technological advance is possible.*

2 *Now look at the paragraph opposite in which an employee talks about her company. How many sentences are there? Are they simple or complex?*

*Below is the same paragraph, rewritten using complex sentences. Complete it by filling in one word for each space.*

'I work for ABC. ABC makes automobile parts. The parts we make are mechanical. We also make electrical parts. We sell parts throughout Europe. We also sell parts in Asia. We do not sell in America. Our biggest customers are Japanese. Our Japanese customers are some of the best known car manufacturers in the world.'

*'I work for ABC __________ makes mechanical __________ electrical parts for automobiles. We sell throughout Europe __________ Asia, __________ not in America. Our biggest customers, __________ __________ Japanese, __________ some of the best known car manufacturers in the world.'*

## Transfer

*Write a similar paragraph about a company that you know well. Include complex sentences.*

# UNIT 37

## CONNECTING IDEAS

***See also* Unit 74 – Connecting and sequencing ideas**

### A *Sample sentences*

- The product was launched ten years ago, at a time when competition was fierce. Therefore it was difficult for us to get the commitment of all our senior management. In addition, bank interest rates made it hard for us to get the necessary financial backing, especially since they were very high initially.

### B *Form*

There are four main ways of connecting clauses:

1 Coordination with **and, or** or **but** (see Unit 36).
2 Subordination with a subordinating conjunction, e.g. **when, though, because** (see Unit 38).
3 'General purpose' connectors with **who** and **which** (see Unit 42).
4 Adverbial connectors, e.g. **so, yet, then.**

The clauses are separated by either a full stop (.), comma (,) or a semi-colon (;) and then connected by an adverbial connector:
... at a time when competition was fierce. *Therefore* it was difficult for us to get the commitment of all our senior management. *In addition*, bank interest rates made it hard for us to get the necessary financial backing, *especially* since they were very high initially.

### C *Uses*

We can use the three connecting methods to express the same sentences and ideas. The effect, however, is different.
They only opened up three months ago *but* they've gone bankrupt already. (coordinated clauses are given equal or similar importance)
*Although* they only opened up three months ago, they've gone bankrupt already. (subordinated clause is reduced to a less important role)
They only opened up three months ago; *however*, they've gone bankrupt already. (typical in longer stretches of language to indicate the relationships between sentences and ideas)

Below are some of the more common adverbial connectors:

| | | | | |
|---|---|---|---|---|
| **Cause** | therefore | so | | |
| **Contrast** | yet | however | | |
| **Condition** | then | in that case | | |
| **Comparison** | similarly | in the same way | | |
| **Concession** | anyway | at any rate | | |
| **Contradiction** | in fact | actually | as a matter of fact | |
| **Alternation** | instead | alternatively | | |
| **Addition** | also | in addition | too | |
| **Summary** | to sum up | overall | in brief/short | |
| **Conclusion** | in conclusion | finally | lastly | |
| **Equivalence** | in other words | that means | namely | |
| **Inclusion** | for example | for instance | such as | as follows |
| **Highlight** | in particular | especially | | |
| **Generalisation** | usually/normally | as a rule | in general | |
| **Stating the obvious** | obviously | naturally | of course | |

## Exercise 1

*Below are sixteen common adverbial connectors. The list contains eight pairs of connectors with a similar meaning. Identify the eight pairs. The first has been done for you.*

| | | | |
|---|---|---|---|
| in the same way (1) | to sum up | too | finally |
| alternatively | also | yet | similarly (1) |
| naturally | however | lastly | as a rule |
| of course | instead | usually | in short |

## Exercise 2

*The extract below is from a presentation in which a manager explains changes in company organisation. Complete the spaces with a word or phrase from the box.*

| | | | |
|---|---|---|---|
| naturally | and | in general | furthermore |
| for example | in addition | especially | therefore |
| but | so | | |

In recent years the company has expanded ________ the workload for the management has increased. ________, we have decided to reorganise our management structure. This picture shows the new organisation.

*Fig. 1 New Management Structure*

We plan to divide the present Administration Department into two, creating a new Finance Department and a Human Resources Department. ________, the Sales & Marketing Department will be divided into two. ________, a new Management Services Department will be created. We believe communication channels within the company will be simplified, ________ decision-making will be more streamlined. ________, decisions which solely affect personnel will now be taken at the level of Human Resources. ________, the principle is that decisions should be taken at the lowest practicable level, ________ those everyday decisions which will not affect the whole organisation. ________, the changes will take some time to be fully understood, ________ overall everyone should notice immediate benefits.

## Exercise 3

*Connect the ideas in the pairs of sentences below using the method shown in brackets.*

1 We have an important domestic market. We are also an exporting company. (coordination)
  We have an important domestic market but we are also an exporting company.
2 We sell our goods abroad. We have to set prices with the exchange rates in mind. (cause and stating the obvious)
3 Fluctuation in exchange rates causes instability. It makes forecasting more difficult. (addition)
4 We prefer a stable exchange environment. We have to accept instability. (subordination)
5 Our best products are several years old. The F23 was launched in 1986. (inclusion)
6 We need to expand sales abroad. We need more sales in America. (highlight)
7 Sales in leisure products have increased. We expect a 25 per cent rise during the summer. (generalisation)

## Transfer

*Write sentences about a subject or company you know well. Include adverbial connectors with the following meanings:*

1 highlight
2 generalisation
3 contradiction
4 contrast
5 comparison
6 conclusion

# UNIT 38

## SUBORDINATE CLAUSES

### A Sample sentences

◆ At the AGM the chairman said that he was satisfied with the progress made. After he had presented the results, he invited comments and questions from the audience so that the shareholders could ask for whatever other information they wanted. Although the results were good, many shareholders felt that the company could have achieved better results.

### B Form

A subordinate clause depends on a main clause – it cannot stand by itself as a sentence.

| *subordinate clause* | *main clause* |
|---|---|
| After he had presented the results, | he invited comments and questions from the audience. |

1 A subordinate clause starts with one of the following:

**a** **that**
The chairman said that he was satisfied with the progress made.

**b** a subordinating conjunction
Although the results were good, many shareholders felt that the company could have achieved better results.

**c** a **wh**-word
We can't predict when the money markets will react to the news.

**d** an infinitive + **to**
We went there to hear the results.

**e** a verb *...ing*
While listening to the presentation, the audience asked some difficult questions.

**f** a verb *...ed*
Based in the UK, the company has already moved into Europe.

**g** inversion
Should you wish to claim a refund, you must bring all the documents. (see Unit 11)

2 A subordinate clause contains:

**a** a finite verb in the active or passive:
The chairman said that he was satisfied with the progress made.

**b** a non-finite verb, i.e. infinitive, verb *...ing* or verb *...ed*:
We went there to hear the results.

***Notes***

1 The use of the subjunctive verb forms is possible in **that** clauses after the following:
*demand require insist suggest be necessary/obligatory*
They demanded that he settle the bill immediately.
We suggest that you all be there at least ten minutes before your interview.

The subjunctive has the form of V1 in all persons. We use the subjunctive mainly in formal style; in informal style we use **should** + infinitive:
We suggest that you should all be there at least ten minutes before your interview.

The subjunctive is more widely used in American English.

2 The **were** subjunctive in clauses of condition and contrast is also used:
If I were you, I wouldn't ask for a rise at the moment.

## C Uses

Below are the main types of subordinate clauses.

1 **Cause or reason:**
The company opened *because they saw a gap in the market.*

2 **Condition:**
*If they had invested more in R & D*, they could have developed a better product.
(see Unit 10)

3 **Contrast:**
*Even though their resources were limited*, their results were excellent.
(see Units 43 and 79)

4 **Purpose:**
They moved to a greenfield site *so that they would have room to expand.*

5 **Result:**
The company had invested enough money *so (that) they could cover their bad debts.*

Note that this is different from the adverbial connector of reason **so**:
The Finance Manager had earned enough money; *so he could cover their bad debts.*
(see Units 44 and 85)

6 **Time:**
We left *after the deal was rejected.*
(see Unit 46)

7 **Reported speech:**
She replied *that the offer was not really attractive.*
(see Units 39 and 40)

8 **Reported questions:**
Their accountant wanted to know *why the bills had not been paid.*
(see Unit 40)

9 **Relative clauses:**
First she answered the questions *which had been uppermost in our minds.*
(see Unit 42)

# TASKS 38

## SUBORDINATE CLAUSES

### Exercise 1

*Underline the subordinate clauses in the following sentences and then classify them in the table below. There is one of each type.*

1 The committee met to discuss a river pollution problem.
2 If the pollution was caused by local industries, they would have to pay compensation.
3 The pollution concerned chemicals which had leaked into the river.
4 The problem was noticed when dead fish were found in the river.
5 Although companies had strict regulations on the disposal of chemicals, mistakes occurred.
6 The enquiry asked what training workers had been given.
7 The Manager said her company had done everything possible to avoid the leakage of chemicals into the river.

| Reported question | Condition | Time | Relative clause | Contrast | Purpose | Reported speech |
|---|---|---|---|---|---|---|
| | | | | | | |

### Exercise 2

*Match the clause on the left with an appropriate clause on the right to create a meaningful text. The first one has been done for you.*

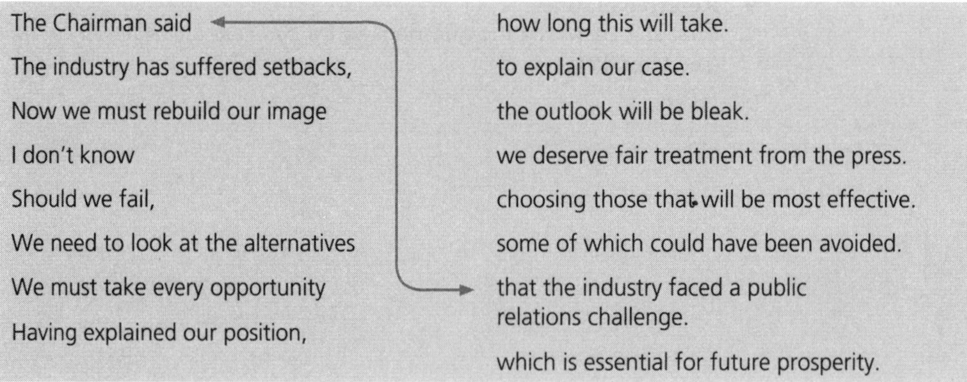

| | |
|---|---|
| The Chairman said | how long this will take. |
| The industry has suffered setbacks, | to explain our case. |
| Now we must rebuild our image | the outlook will be bleak. |
| I don't know | we deserve fair treatment from the press. |
| Should we fail, | choosing those that will be most effective. |
| We need to look at the alternatives | some of which could have been avoided. |
| We must take every opportunity | that the industry faced a public relations challenge. |
| Having explained our position, | which is essential for future prosperity. |

### Exercise 3

*Provide subordinate clauses to combine with the given main clause. Use the type of subordinate clause indicated by the prompt in brackets. The first has been done for you.*

1 The press were critical of the company
(cause or reason) → staff training had not improved
*The press were critical of the company because staff training had not improved.*

2 The company organised a press conference
(purpose) → answer criticisms

3 The chairman said
(reported speech ) → safety record relatively good

**4** The Health & Safety Executive supported the company
(time) → they investigated safety procedures

**5** Every precaution had been taken
(result) → management confident

**6** The press wrote articles
(relative clause) → exaggerated problems

7 ... accidents can still happen.
(contrast) → company carries out regular checks

## *Transfer*

*Write three sentences about the political or economic situation in your country. Include different kinds of subordinate clause.*

*Example:*

Although the government tries to improve health care, there are many problems. They build more hospitals to treat more patients. If the government spent more on health education, the cost of treating people would fall.

# UNIT 39

## REPORTED SPEECH (1)

*See also* **Unit 26 – Verbs of speaking**
**Unit 27 – Verbs of reporting**
**Unit 40 – Reported speech (2)**
**Unit 90 – Requesting information and action**

### A *Sample sentences*

- They say that we will receive the confirmation next week.
- She mentioned that the date of the next meeting hasn't been fixed yet.
- He promised that the conference would be ready for us when we arrived.

### B *Form*

Reported speech takes two forms:

1 A main clause with a verb of speaking/asking + a subordinate clause:

| *main clause* | *subordinate clause* |
|---|---|
| They say | that we will receive the confirmation next week. |

2 A main clause with a verb of speaking/asking + an infinitive with **to** (see Unit 40):
They asked us to send confirmation as soon as possible.

Indirect speech is derived from direct speech:
He said, 'We have signed the contract.' (direct speech)
He said that they had signed the contract. (indirect speech)

The basic rule to determine the tense of the verb in the subordinate clause is as follows:

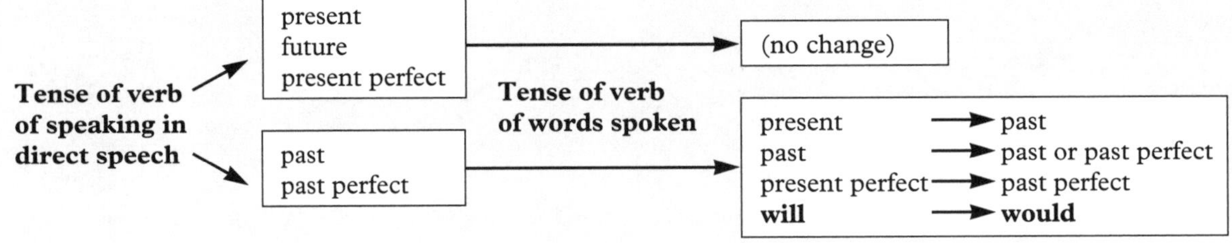


| *Direct speech* | *Indirect speech* |
|---|---|
| She says, 'We have a deal.' | She says (that) we have a deal. |
| She said, 'We have a deal.' | She said (that) we had a deal. |
| She said, 'I have made a deal.' | She said that she had made a deal. |
| She said, 'I will confirm the deal next week.' | She said that she would confirm the deal the following week. |

Other changes are to the pronouns and the time adverbials.

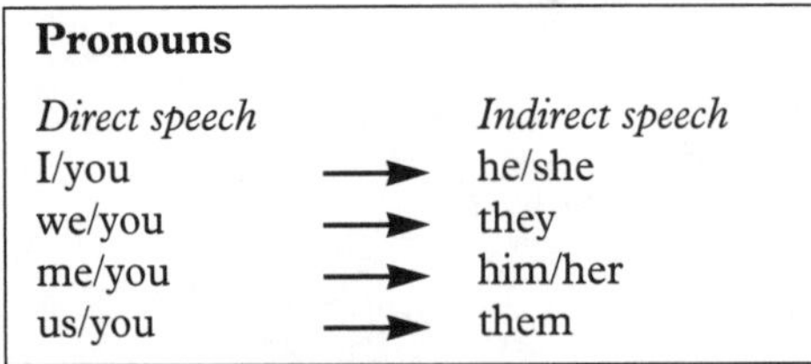

**Pronouns**

| *Direct speech* | | *Indirect speech* |
|---|---|---|
| I/you | → | he/she |
| we/you | → | they |
| me/you | → | him/her |
| us/you | → | them |

**Time adverbials**

| *Direct speech* | | *Indirect speech* |
|---|---|---|
| yesterday | → | the day before/the previous day |
| today | → | that day |
| tomorrow | → | the day after/the following day |
| last … | → | the previous … |
| next … | → | the following … |
| this … | → | that … |

***Note***
The tense of the words spoken does not change where the words spoken are still true:
He said, 'A statement will be made in the press.'
He said a statement will be made in next week's newspaper. (The newspaper hasn't been printed yet.)

### C *Uses*

A list of common verbs of speaking to introduce reported statements is given in Appendix 4.

# REPORTED SPEECH (1)

## Exercise 1

*Below is an extract from a newspaper report on a political meeting. Complete the spaces with an appropriate form of one of the verbs from the box.*

ask warn believe say remind

The Minister ________ the audience that 20 years ago things were very different. He ________ the time had come to face realities and he ________ we had to choose between cooperation or isolation. He ________ that major problems would arise if we made the wrong choice and ________ if we wanted to be an isolated and friendless country.

## Exercise 2

*Here is an interview between a journalist and a Finance Minister. Complete the newspaper report which follows by adding an appropriate verb.*

rise predict continue ask change say work

J: Has the policy of the government changed?
M: No, we are working towards increasing the quality of services and making the economy strong.
J: What do you predict as a level of inflation over the next 12 months?
M: Inflation will continue at present levels – about 2.5 per cent.
J: Are you confident that economic growth will remain strong?
M: Economic growth is now at 2 per cent and should rise to 4 per cent over the coming year.

________ if the policy of the government ________, the Minister ________ the government ________ towards increasing the quality of services and making the economy strong. He ________ that inflation ________ at present levels – around 2.5 per cent – and economic growth, now at 2 per cent, ________ to 4 per cent.

## Exercise 3

*Here is an extract from a telephone conversation between a fashion designer, Marianne, and a clothes manufacturer, Juan.*

Marianne: Did you get the photographs I sent?
Juan: Yes they were really good. I liked them a lot. Now – when are you coming to Milan?
Marianne: Soon, next month maybe, I'll come at the end of the month.
Juan: And will you bring the new designs?
Marianne: Of course! Not only the designs, I'll bring the clothes. They're already made and you can see them whenever you like.
Juan: I know Rina wants to see them. I'll tell her you're coming next month.
Marianne: Fine. Oh, by the way, Rina still owes me some money, you know. I think she has probably forgotten. She said the money would be in my bank last Tuesday and it hasn't arrived yet.
Juan: Okay, I'll tell her. That's all, isn't it?
Marianne: Yeah, I think so. Can you ask Rina to call me? I'll be in all day Friday.
Juan: Okay, I'll tell her. Bye for now.

MODA SPECIALE
Via Vittorio Emanuele 11 200
34000 Milano
Telefono 39 (2) 56567888
Fax 39 (2) 56785490

Ref: JS/23/04

Dear Rina

I spoke to Marianne yesterday. I told her ________ the photographs. She said ________ to Milan at the end of next month. She also said ________ the designs and the finished clothes. She ________ me to remind you that ________. She said you ________ the money ________ in her bank last Tuesday but ________ arrived.

Finally, she ________ if you ________ call her. She said ________ Friday.

Ciao

*Juan*
Juan

*Write a brief letter to Rina telling her the details of this conversation. Use the above as an outline.*

# UNIT 40

## REPORTED SPEECH (2)

*See also* **Unit 26 – Verbs of speaking**
**Unit 27 – Verbs of reporting**
**Unit 39 – Reported speech (1)**
**Unit 90 – Requesting information and action**

### A *Sample sentences*

- I warned them not to put up their prices by more than the annual rate of inflation.
- The bank told the company to suspend its operations until a full investigation could be completed.
- The suppliers asked the purchasing director to give them a little more time to reconsider their prices.

### B *Form*

See Unit 39.

### C *Uses*

In addition to reported statements, there are the following types of reported speech:

1 **Reported commands:**
She told them to check the goods thoroughly before accepting them.
The court ordered them to pay all their debts before 1 January.
He demanded that the faulty goods be collected as soon as possible. (subjunctive)

A list of common verbs of commanding is given in Appendix 5.

2 **Reported requests:**
He asked the manager to accept his resignation.

A list of common verbs of requesting is given in Appendix 5.

3 **Reported questions:**
There are two types of direct questions (see Unit 41):
– **wh**-questions, e.g. When exactly will you be in Switzerland?
– **yes/no** questions, e.g. Does your company provide investment advice?

In reported **wh**-questions, we use the **wh**-question word:
He asked *when* exactly I would be in Switzerland.
In reported **yes/no** questions, we use **if** or **whether**:
She asked if/whether our company provided investment advice.

A list of common verbs of questioning is given in Appendix 5.

4 **Other reported forms:**
I warned them not to put up their prices by more than the annual rate of inflation.
They cautioned him not to make a statement before he had consulted his lawyer.

A list of other verbs of reporting is given in Appendix 5.

# REPORTED SPEECH (2)

## Exercise 1

*Underline the verbs of speaking in the following text and classify them as:*
– verbs of speaking
– verbs of commanding
– verbs of requesting
– verbs of questioning

The senior management all agreed that the company had to take swift measures to capitalise on the situation. First of all they invited their accountants to review their finances as quickly as possible. Naturally, they asked if the situation was as they saw it. Then they commented on the situation to the press. Having convened an extraordinary meeting of the shareholders, they told them to be prepared for a statement. The shareholders also inquired about the truth of the details in the press. The directors invited them to look closely at the options and urged them to wait a little while before making a decision. Finally they instructed the press to write up a full report about the proposed takeover.

## Exercise 2

*Are the following sentences right or wrong? If wrong, correct them.*

1 The company has told to adopt Vision 2000 as our aim for the next five years.

2 Vision 2000 urges that we adopt a range of internal measures to improve productivity and quality throughout the company.

3 Individual managers are asked to implement Vision 2000 in their own departments.

4 Having presented the policy in outline, managers have asked their teams what training would they like.

5 Most teams have asked to not have theoretical training courses.

6 In fact they have all suggested to have project groups to explore the best way to implement Vision 2000.

## Exercise 3

*Report the following exchange between a training manager and a personnel manager. You need to choose an appropriate verb of speaking to introduce each sentence. The first sentence has been done for you.*

PM: When will the new training programme be introduced?
TM: I don't know. But we have approached a number of outside training organisations.
PM: Could I see the list of suppliers?
TM: Yes, I'll let you see the details.
PM: Why don't we make a final decision together?
TM: Well, I prefer to make the final decision myself.

*The Personnel Manager asked when the new training would be introduced ...*

## Transfer

*Write a report of a face-to-face conversation that you have had with someone in your company.*

# UNIT 41

## QUESTIONS

*See also* Unit 39 – Reported speech (1)
Unit 40 – Reported speech (2)
Unit 90 – Requesting information and action

### A *Sample sentences*

A: Who approved this order?
B: I'm afraid I really have no idea.
A: It was Jim, wasn't it?
B: Jim, you approved this order?
C: Yes, I did. Why? Is there a problem?
A: Yes, half of the goods haven't been delivered.
C: Yes, I know. But could you just look at the accompanying note?
It explains everything.

### B *Form*

There are three forms of question:
- *direct* questions
- *indirect* questions
- *statement* questions (+ question tag)

1 **Direct questions**

There are two types of direct questions:
- **wh**-questions, which start with a **wh**-question word (including **how**):
  Who approved this order?
- **yes/no** questions, where the answer is **yes** or **no**:
  Is there a problem? – Yes.

Note that alternative questions have the same form as **yes/no** questions:
Did Helen or Peter check the balance? – Peter.

The basic rules to form a question are shown in the flowchart below.

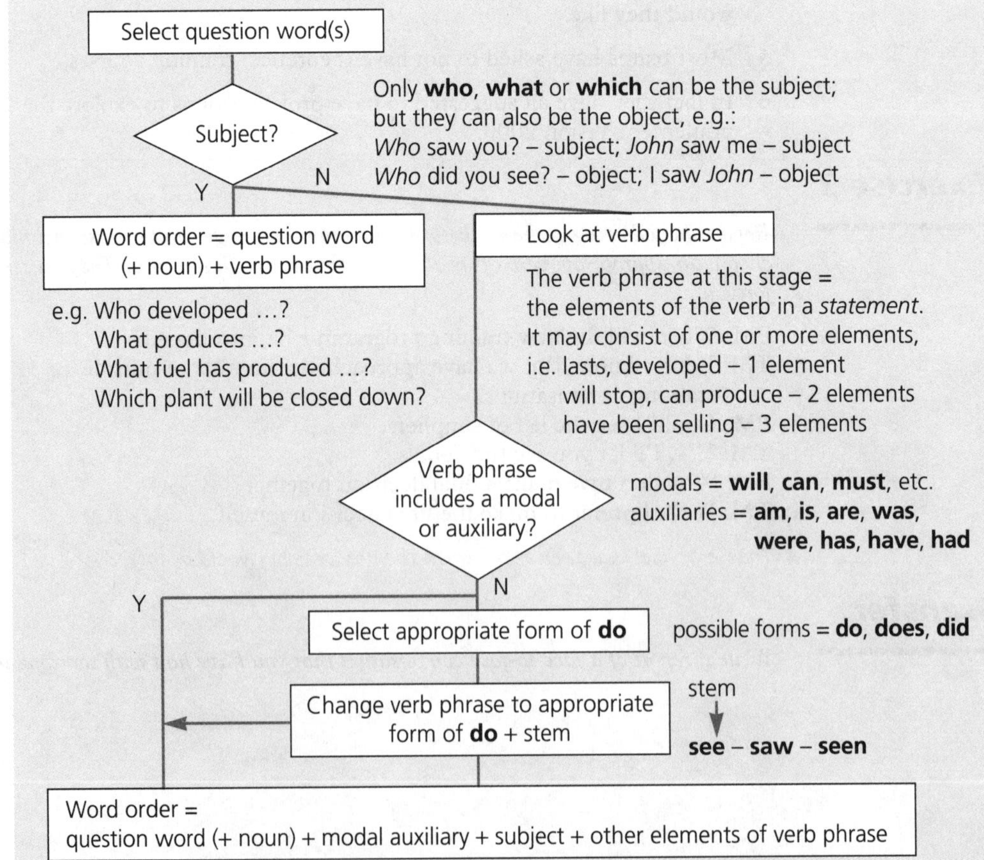

2 **Indirect questions**
Indirect questions comprise:
– a question word (**wh-**, **if** or **whether**)
– a clause with the verb in statement word order:
I don't know which results you are talking about. (*not*: are you talking about)
But could you tell me where I can find the manual? (*not*: can I find)

3 **Statement questions**
There are two types of statement questions:
– a statement with rising intonation:
Jim, you approved this order?
– a statement + question tag:
Jim, you approved this order, didn't you?
Jim, you didn't approve this order, did you?

## C Uses

1 **Direct questions**
Below are the main **wh**-questions according to question word:

**a** Asking about people – **who, whom**:
Who approved this order? (**who** asks about the subject.)
Who(m) are you going to visit in Japan? (In normal speech we use **who** to ask about the object as well; in formal speech and writing we use **whom**.)
Who(m) did you place the order with? (In normal speech we use **who** to ask about the prepositional object; in formal speech and writing we use **whom**.)
With whom did you go to France? (**whom** asks about the prepositional object. This structure is more formal than the previous one.)

**b** Asking about things – **which, what**:
Which agency are we going to use? (**which** + noun asks about the subject.)
What did you decide in the last meeting? (**what** asks about the object.)

**c** Asking about the time – **when, (at) what time**:
When do you plan to be in Paris?
(At) what time/when did you leave the office? (specific clock time)

**d** Asking about the place – **where**:
Where did you hold the conference last year?

**e** Asking for the reason – **why**:
Why are you so concerned about the quality?

**f** Asking about the length of time – **how long**:
How long have you been based in Tokyo?
How long does it take you to get home in the evening? (*not*: How long time?)
(**How long** refers to time or dimension; see below.)

**g** Asking about the distance – **how far**:
How far do you have to travel each day?

**h** Asking about the frequency – **how often**:
How often do you travel abroad?

**i** Asking about the manner – **how**:
How are you going to persuade your staff to accept the new contracts?

**j** Asking about quantity and amount – **how many, how much**:
How many subsidiaries will participate? (asking about the subject)
How many subsidiaries do you have in Europe? (asking about the object)
How much did you pay for the address list? (*not*: How much money?)

**k** Asking about dimensions and specifications – **how long/small,** etc.
How big/long/wide/deep/high will the cabinet be?
How small will the miniature version be?

# UNIT 41 QUESTIONS

**2 Indirect questions**
We use indirect questions in:
- Reported questions (see Unit 40):
  She asked which order Jim had approved.
- Polite requests (see Unit 90):
  Could you tell me which order you approved?

**3 Statement questions** (+ **question tag**)
We use these to ask for confirmation.
- Asking for confirmation of a positive statement:
  Jim, you approved this order?
  Jim, you approved this order, didn't you?
- Asking for confirmation of a negative statement:
  Jim, you didn't approve this order?
  Jim, you didn't approve this order, did you?

## Exercise 1

*Read the following list of questions. Classify them according to the question types.*

1 Are you agents for Fischer equipment?
2 Where can I find this type of product?
3 You're not serious?
4 Fischer are market leaders, aren't they?
5 So you believe they're expensive?
6 Do you think there are better goods available?
7 Can you tell me how reliable they are?

**A** Direct **yes/no** questions
**B** Direct **wh**-questions
**C** Indirect questions
**D** Statement questions with rising intonation
**E** Statement questions + tag

## Exercise 2

*The FUB Group is a drug research body. The group has worked for ten years and has massively exceeded its budget. A journalist asks a leading figure in the group some questions.*

*Are the questions correctly formed or not? If wrong, write the corrections.*

Q: How long time have you been working on the research?
A: Ten years.
Q: Could you tell me who were the main partners in the project?
A: FRS, UBDuss A. G., and Bokal.
Q: And you didn't plan to spend so much money, didn't you?
A: Of course we didn't.
Q: You say the forecasts were inaccurate. Who did resign after these forecasts?
A: Karl Drew resigned.
Q: Was that a correct decision?
A: I don't know – it was his decision.

## Exercise 3

*Explo Corporation is an Australian oil company based in Sydney. One of their technical managers calls Bruck Engineering in Singapore for some information.*

*In the dialogue below the questions are incomplete. Write the complete questions.*

Explo: __________ (1) me something about your company?

Bruck: Yes, we're market leaders for joints for the pipeline business.

Explo: And where __________ (2) ?

Bruck: Our manufacturing base is in Singapore but we have a distribution and sales network throughout Australasia.

Explo: Can I ask __________ (3) ?

Bruck: Yes, we have an agent in Sydney.

Explo: What __________ (4) agent's name?

Bruck: Wall & Martin Joints Ltd.

Explo: I see. And they __________ (5) Sydney?

Bruck: That's right.

Explo: And suppose I wanted to buy direct from you, the manufacturer?

Bruck: No, sorry, you couldn't do that.

Explo: I have to __________ (6) ?

Bruck: Yes, you do.

Explo: And Wall & Martin are the only agents in Sydney, __________ (7) ?

Bruck: They are.

Explo: How __________ (8) Wall & Martin?

Bruck: You should write directly to them.

## Transfer

*Think of a situation where you might telephone an organisation and request information. Write examples of questions you might ask. Use a variety of question forms and different **wh**- words.*

# UNIT 42

## RELATIVE CLAUSES

### A Sample sentences

- The machine which produced this printout has been withdrawn.
- The INJ300, which produced reasonable copy quality, has been replaced by the INJ400.
- Pat Smith, who heads the Administration Department, will meet you on your next visit.
- The only person who can give you the information is out of the office at the moment.
- Last year we sold the site where we started up our company.
- I'm afraid we can't relax our payment terms at a time when others are tightening theirs.

### B Form

There are two types of relative clause:
- defining relative clauses
- non-defining relative clauses

We can distinguish them by the punctuation. Non-defining clauses are enclosed by commas; defining clauses are not.
The machine which produced this printout has been withdrawn. (defining: no commas)
Pat Smith, who heads the Administration Department, will meet you on your next visit. (non-defining: commas)

### C Uses

| | **Defining and non-defining** Personal | Non-personal | **Defining only** Personal and non-personal |
|---|---|---|---|
| subjective | who | which | that |
| objective | who(m) | which | that, zero (no pronoun) |
| genitive | whose | of which/whose | |
| locative | | where | |
| temporal | | when | |

Relative clauses are subordinate clauses (see Unit 38) which provide information about a noun or noun phrase. There are two types of relative clauses: defining and non-defining.

**Defining relative clauses** provide essential information which restricts or clarifies the meaning of the preceding noun or noun phrase by specifying its meaning more clearly.
The only person *who can give you the information* is out of the office at the moment.
The clause 'who can give you the information' identifies the person; without this essential information, the sentence has a very different meaning.

**Non-defining relative clauses** provide additional, non-essential information.
The INJ300, *which produced reasonable copy quality*, has been replaced by the INJ400.
The clause 'which produced reasonable copy quality' provides additional, non-essential information; without this information the basic meaning of the sentence remains the same.

1 **Talking about people (personal):**
The person who/that prepared that report no longer works for us. (subjective – defining)
Carla Jensen, who prepared that report, no longer works for us. (subjective – non-defining)
I've spoken to the workers who(m)/that/zero (no pronoun) we are going to lay off. (objective – defining)
I've spoken to Andrew Green, who(m) we are going to lay off. (objective – non-defining)
Andrew Green, with whom I discussed the layoff yesterday, has agreed to leave. (objective after preposition – non-defining)
The workers with whom I discussed the layoff have agreed to leave. (objective after preposition – defining)

I'd also like to acknowledge a man whose efforts have helped this company over the years. (genitive – defining)
Let's not forget Margaret Davies, whose company had been a regular supplier. (genitive – non-defining)

2 **Talking about things** (**non-personal**):
We have just seen a machine which/that can fill 200 bottles a minute. (subjective – defining)
I'm afraid that the INJ200, which produced reasonable copy quality, has been withdrawn. (subjective – non-defining)
We are not interested in machines which/that/zero (no pronoun) we can't maintain ourselves. (objective – defining)
We think that the INJ300, which you demonstrated a couple of weeks ago, meets our needs. (objective – non-defining)
We cannot deal with companies whose offices/the offices of which are not in the UK. (genitive – defining)
And finally we have the INJ300, whose speed/the speed of which is much higher than the INJ200. (genitive – non-defining)

3 **Talking about places** (**locative**):
We went to a workshop where the whole process is automated. (defining)
The workshop, where we saw the robot, doesn't have a single operator. (non-defining)

4 **Talking about the time** (**temporal**):
I'm afraid I won't be around when the party takes place. (defining)
On December 21, when the party takes place, I shall be out of the country. (non-defining)

***Notes***

1 The relative pronoun after **the reason**:
I have read the reasons *why/that* the delivery was delayed but I find them hard to believe.
The reason *that/why* we are so disappointed is that we had always relied on your prompt service. (*not*: the reason because)

2 The relative pronoun after **all**, **each**, **every** and compounds:
We have rejected all the offers (*that*) we have received.
We have tried everything (*that*) we could.
Each hotel (*that*) we tried gave us the same response.

# TASKS 42

## RELATIVE CLAUSES

### Exercise 1

*Underline the relative clauses in the following extract and write defining (D) or non-defining (ND) by each one.*

Many pharmaceutical companies, which are among the world's largest, invest millions in research into heart disease and conditions which typically relate to the process of ageing. These areas, where research costs are phenomenally high, also offer the greatest potential. Research on curative drugs may be less expensive but the rewards are less because the patients, who will get better, will not need the treatment for years and years. On the other hand, conditions like Alzheimer's disease, heart disease or arthritis, which last for years, could involve long periods of treatment. It is these areas, therefore, which offer the best potential for high profits. A further point is that such research is intended to produce drugs which will be marketed in the richest countries where profit will be highest.

### Exercise 2

*Below are six extracts from a report on a meeting between the Chief Executive of a chemical company and an environmentalist group. Convert each extract into a single sentence by using a relative clause. The first has been done for you.*

1 The Chief Executive looked confident. He spoke for 20 minutes.
The Chief Executive, who looked confident, spoke for 20 minutes.

2 He said the environment was everyone's responsibility. It is a key issue.
3 Lockville is now a beauty spot. There used to be a chemical plant there.
4 We made mistakes in the past. We knew less than we know now.
5 The captains of industry have major responsibilities. We depend on them.
6 The industries produce the products. We criticise the industries. We buy the products.

### Exercise 3

*Combine the prompts below to write sentences in which the information in brackets is given in relative clauses.*

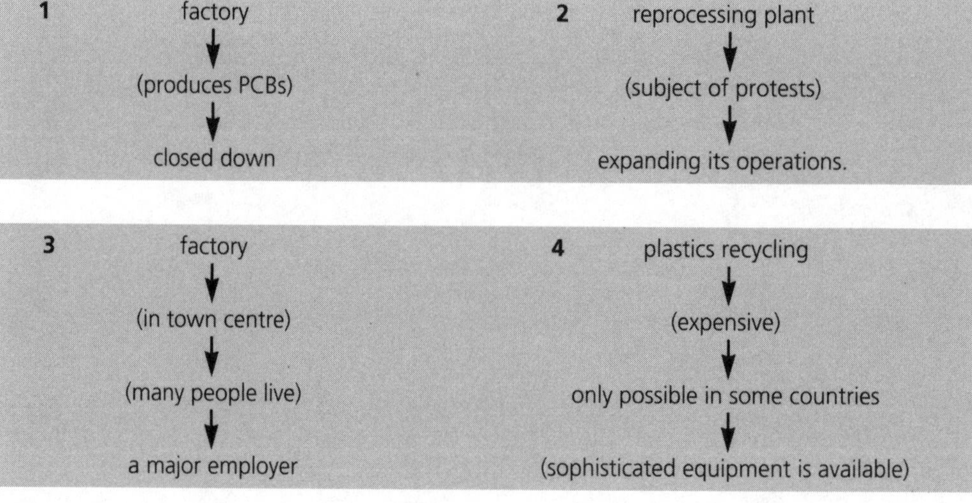

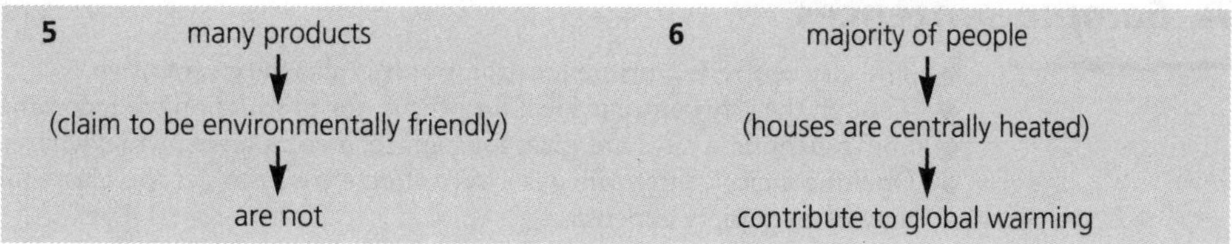


## Transfer

***Write a series of sentences about entertainment and social life in your area. Include various relative clauses.***

*Examples:*

*There are many cinemas where you can see films in the original version.*
*The best theatre, which is in the town centre, is 200 years old.*
*The owner of the club in the town centre, whose wife is a dancer, is Ukrainian.*

# UNIT 43

## CLAUSES of CONTRAST

*See also* **Unit 79 – Contrasting ideas**
**Unit 80 – Comparing ideas**

### A *Sample sentences*

- The city centre is a prime location but it is also very expensive.
- Though the city centre is ideal for offices, for production we recommend a greenfield site.
- Some greenfield sites are ideal for high-tech companies, while/whereas others aren't.
- Opening a city centre office is a very effective way to get top class staff, even though it may be extremely expensive.

### B *Form*

Clauses of contrast are subordinate clauses (see Unit 38) which provide information which contrasts with the main clause. Clauses of contrast start with either the coordinating conjunction **but** (see Unit 37) or a subordinating conjunction (see Unit 38). The main subordinating conjunctions are:

*though    although    even though    while    whereas*

1 Coordination is more vague and less emphatic than subordination:
The city centre is a prime location but it is also very expensive.

2 Subordination reduces the subordinated clause to a less important role:
Though the city centre is ideal for offices, for production we recommend a greenfield site.

We can only use **while** and **whereas** to contrast equivalent ideas:
While greenfield sites are ideal for high-tech companies, they are less suited to heavy industries.
(*not*: While greenfield sites are ideal for high-tech companies, we decided to relocate to an industrial area.)

### C *Uses*

Clauses of contrast present a situation which is unexpected or surprising in view of the information in the main clause.

1 Contrast with **but**:
The city centre is a prime location but it is also very expensive.
A greenfield site offers many attractions but can also present a number of problems.

2 Contrast with **though**, **although** and **even though**:
Although we have investigated a number of sites, we haven't made a decision yet.
**Even though** is more emphatic than **though** or **although**:
Opening a city centre office is a very effective way to get top class staff, even though it may be extremely expensive.

3 Contrast with **while** and **whereas** to contrast equivalent ideas:
While greenfield sites are ideal for high-tech companies, they are less suited to heavy industries.

***Notes***

1 Subordinate clauses with **though**, **although** and **even though** can come before or after the main clause:
Though the city centre is ideal for offices, for production we recommend a greenfield site.
We recommend a greenfield site for production, though the city centre is ideal for offices.

2 Subordinate clauses with **while** and **whereas** can come before or after the main clause and, if totally parallel in construction, can be reversed:
Hi-tech firms can operate almost anywhere, while industrial companies need access to suppliers.
While hi-tech firms can operate almost anywhere, industrial companies need access to suppliers.
Industrial companies need access to suppliers, while hi-tech firms can operate almost anywhere.
While industrial companies need access to suppliers, hi-tech firms can operate almost anywhere.

# CLAUSES of CONTRAST

## Exercise 1

*Read the conversation below. First mark the coordinating conjunctions (CC) and the subordinating conjunctions (SC). Then underline the clauses of contrast.*

John: If we discuss ways to reduce costs, one area we should think about is packaging.
Janina: Well, though packaging is expensive, it can help promote the product. Good packaging also reduces problems in transit.
John: Yes, of course, but we have to cut the costs. Even though we use our own designers, the costs are very high.
Janina: Although it's an expensive part of the production, it is very difficult to reduce costs.
John: While we agree that it's expensive, we don't seem to be able to decide how to reduce the expense!
Janina: I see packaging as part of public relations, whereas I think you are looking at it only in terms of packing the product!

## Exercise 2

*Combine the following pairs of sentences using the conjunctions given.*

1 The market has probably passed its peak.
Computer sales are still very high. (although)

2 Costs have come down.
The advances in computer technology have been considerable. (though)

3 More people own computers.
The number of manufacturers has gone down. (while)

4 Machines are more reliable.
They are more complex. (but)

5 Computing capability has increased.
The physical size of the equipment has diminished. (whereas)

6 Users experience difficulties with compatibility.
A lot of money has been spent on this problem. (even though)

## Exercise 3

*Complete the following short text on the computer software market by adding suitable conjunctions.*

__________ there are millions of different software programs available, only a few become internationally successful. The best become standards which others follow, __________ the originals do not always benefit from this. Of course, different programs work with different operating systems, __________ there are many more programs than operating systems.
__________ the industry is very competitive, it is dominated by a few big software producers. Many of these are closely connected with the major computer manufacturers, __________ there are also many independent software houses. Also, producing new software is not necessarily expensive, __________ innovations in computer hardware certainly involve massive costs.

## Transfer

*Think about changes in the place where you work. Write five sentences containing clauses of contrast.*

# UNIT 44

## CLAUSES of CAUSE or REASON

*See also* **Unit 85 – Cause and effect**

### A *Sample sentences*

- As these chemicals are toxic, they should be locked away when not in use.
- Since we want to reduce health risks, all screens should be fitted with filters.
- We will look at the interior first because this is the highest priority.

### B *Form*

Clauses of cause or reason are subordinate clauses (see Unit 38) which explain the information in the main clause.

Clauses of cause or reason start with a subordinating conjunction (see Unit 38). The main subordinating conjunctions are:
*because as since*

### C *Uses*

Clauses of cause or reason answer the question 'why?'; they present the reason for the information in the main clause.
A: Why should these materials be locked away?
B: Because they are extremely toxic.

**Because, as** and **since** have the same meaning and take the same construction.
Because/as/since our environment is important to us, we intend to introduce a scheme to encourage workers to take more care of it.

***Notes***
After **because** we need a finite verb; after **because of** we need a noun phrase:
Because the damage is severe, we will have to pay compensation.
Because of the severe damage, we will have to pay compensation.
(*not*: Because the severe damage, we will have to pay compensation.)

# CLAUSES of CAUSE or REASON

## Exercise 1

*Below is part of a letter from an oil company offering an applicant a research position.*

*Link the main clause on the left with a phrase or clause of cause or reason on the right and add a suitable connector. The first has been done for you.*

| | |
|---|---|
| We are offering you the job since | we need someone with post-graduate qualifications |
| You are especially suitable ________ | you are in work just now |
| Your academic record is ideal ________ | you are the most experienced candidate |
| We need you to start as soon as possible ________ | you want the job |
| We understand that an immediate start is a problem ________ | your work in the oil sector |
| You need to tell your present employer today ________ | this sort of thing happens all the time |
| Just say you have to leave ________ | we are beginning a new research project this month |
| I'm sure it will not be a problem ________ | this offer |

## Exercise 2

*Look at the following pictures. Each shows an alternative distribution system. Write two sentences, one explaining an advantage, the other a disadvantage, of each system. Your sentences should contain a main clause and a clause of cause or reason.*

Advantage: direct supply to customers/no intermediate stage.
Disadvantage: difficult to meet sudden orders for large quantities/very small stock.

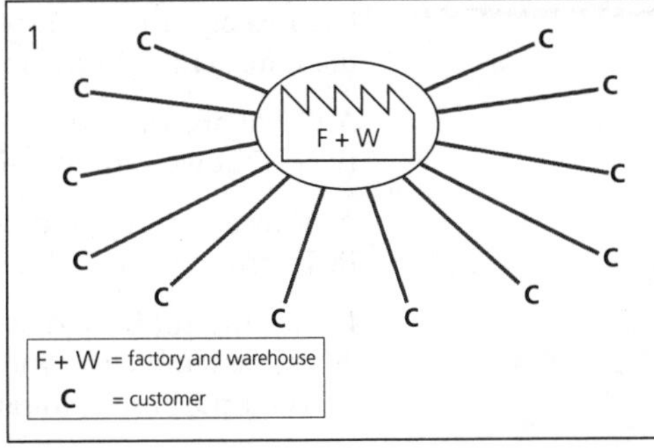


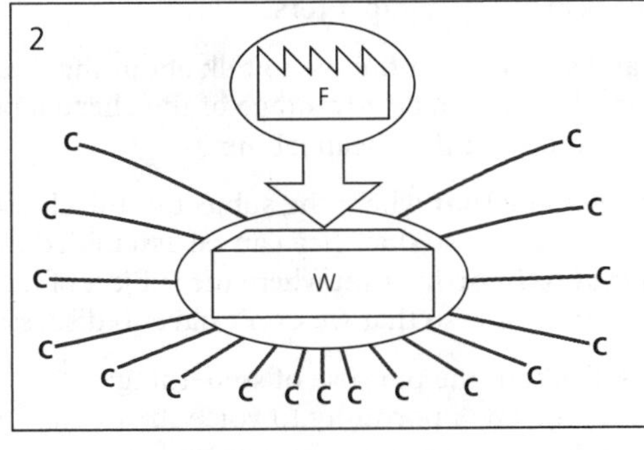


Advantage: Immediate response to large orders/ distribution handled from central warehouse.
Disadvantage: Increased storage costs/more goods held in stock.

## Transfer

*Write six sentences to describe changes that have been made in your organisation. In each sentence describe the change and justify it by using a clause of cause or reason.*

*Example:*
We promoted the Sales Manager because she had performed very well.

# UNIT 45

## CLAUSES of PURPOSE

***See also* Unit 14 – Infinitive**

### A *Sample sentences*

- We are going to move to the north (in order) to take advantage of tax incentives.
- We are going to install a robotic assembly line so as to streamline production.
- We are going to review our pay scales so that they correspond with local levels.
- We are going to automate much of the production in order that we might save on costs.

### B *Form*

Clauses of purpose are subordinate clauses (see Unit 38).

Clauses of purpose consist of:

1 a subordinating conjunction followed by a finite verb (see Unit 38):
We are going to review our pay scales so that they correspond with local levels.

2 infinitive + **to** (see Unit 38):
We are going to move to the north (in order) to take advantage of tax incentives.

3 **for** + noun followed by an infinitive + **to**:
For costs to be reduced, we need to carry out a local survey. (= So that costs can be reduced, we need to carry out a local survey)

The main subordinating conjunctions are:
*so that* *that* *in order that*

Before the infinitive + **to** we can put:
*in order (to)* *so as (to)*

Note the negative forms:
So as not to break the law, we are going to check the labour legislation.
In order not to fall behind our competitors, we need to upgrade our production facilities.

### C *Uses*

Clauses of purpose answer the question 'why?' or 'what …for?'; they present the purpose of the information in the main clause.

A: What are we moving to the north for?
B: So that we can take advantage of tax incentives.

A. Why are we upgrading our production facilities?
B: In order not to fall further behind our competitors.

1 We use **to, in order to** and **so as to** + infinitive to talk about the doer's purpose:
We assemble the goods in Taiwan to take advantage of the cheap labour.
(Our purpose is to take advantage of the cheap labour.)

2 We use **that, so that** or **in order that** where the subject of the clauses is different:
We send the components to Taiwan so that they can be assembled more cheaply.
We can also use **that, so that** or **in order that** where the subject of the clauses is the same:
We are dealing with this matter now so that we don't have to discuss it later.

3 We use **to** + infinitive to talk about the purpose of something:
The meeting is to give everyone an opportunity to voice their opinions.
When we are talking about the purpose of equipment we can say:
The moving arm is to paint the arms and legs of the chair.
The moving arm is for painting the arms and legs of the chair. (**for** + verb *…ing*)

***Notes:***
The following sentences are wrong:
We moved to the north *for* save money. (to save)
We moved to the north *for* to save money. (to save)
We moved to the north *for* saving money. (to save)

# 45 TASKS

## CLAUSES of PURPOSE

### Exercise 1

*Complete the following text by adding appropriate words or phrases from the box opposite.*

| so as not to | in order that | so that | in order to | for |
|---|---|---|---|---|

1 __________ a new building to be a success it has to be the right design.

2 __________ understand design objectives it is necessary to consider the ultimate function.

3 We have chosen the best architects __________ we can be sure of good results.

4 They are preparing sketches __________ we can consider their basic ideas.

5 The architects explained some principles about materials __________ leave us confused.

### Exercise 2

*Read the following exchanges and then write a single sentence containing a clause of purpose. Use each of the phrases from the box once.*

| so that | in order to | so as to | in order that | to |
|---|---|---|---|---|

1 A: Why are the distribution channels being changed?
B: To avoid delays at the ports.

2 A: Why do we need to spend so much money?
B: To guarantee a top quality product.

3 A: Why is it necessary to book in advance?
B: We won't need to worry about space on the ship.

4 A: Why will costs have to be reduced?
B: Then we can have increased profitability.

5 A: What is the red switch for?
B: It switches off the motor in an emergency.

### Exercise 3

*Study the flow chart below showing the main areas in a small chocolate factory. Then complete the text to explain the function of the four departments. Use each phrase in the box once to begin each clause of purpose.*

| to | for | in order to | in order that |
|---|---|---|---|

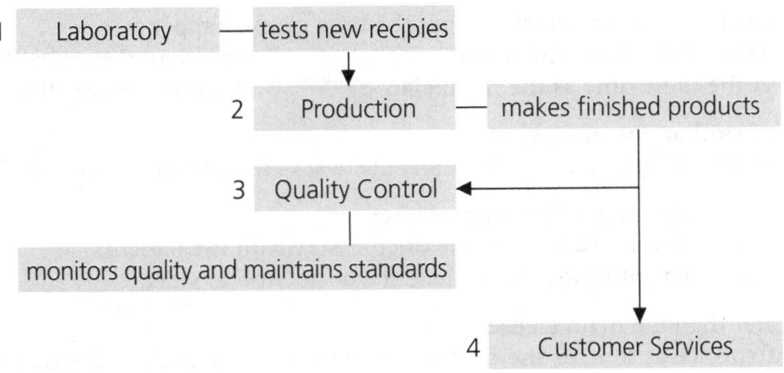


The laboratory is __________. Then there is a Production Department __________. Next we have a Quality Control Department __________ standards. Finally there is a Customer Services Department __________.

### Transfer

*Write four sentences each containing a clause of purpose describing the functions of any organisation you know well.*

# UNIT 46

## CLAUSES of TIME

*See also* Unit 68 – Numerals
Unit 69 – Time (1)
Unit 70 – Time (2)

### A *Sample sentences*

- When an accident happens, you need to call the doctor.
- Having called the doctor, don't leave the patient unattended.
- While waiting for medical help, don't give the patient any medicine.
- Once reported, all serious accidents must be recorded in the accident log.
- After recording the accident, you will be contacted by an accident investigator.

### B *Form*

Clauses of time are subordinate clauses (see Unit 38). Clauses of time comprise:

1 a subordinating conjunction followed by a finite verb (see Unit 38):
When an accident happens, you will need to call the doctor.

2 a subordinating conjunction followed by a non-finite verb (see Unit 38):
After recording the accident, you will be contacted by an accident investigator.

3 a non-finite verb *...ing* or verb *...ed* (see Unit 38):
Once reported, all serious accidents must be recorded in the accident log.

We use the following subordinating conjunctions with finite verbs:
*after as before once since till until when(ever)*
*while/whilst now (that) as long as as soon as*
After you have reported the accident, stay with the patient.

We use the following subordinating conjunctions with verb *...ing*:
*after before since until when(ever) while*
Before leaving the patient, make sure which family members should be informed.

We use the following subordinating conjunctions with verb *...ed*:
*once until when(ever) while*
Once reported, all serious accidents must be recorded in the accident log.

### C *Uses*

Clauses of time ask the question 'when?'; they present the time of the information in the main clause.
A: When do you need to call the doctor?
B: After an accident has happened.

We use clauses of time to show that the time clause happens:
- earlier than the main clause
- at the same time as the main clause
- later than the main clause
- at a non-specific time

1 Earlier than the main clause:
Before calling/you call the doctor, make sure the patient is comfortable.

2 At the same time as the main clause:
While (you are) waiting for the doctor, stay with the patient.
I have been with the patient since the accident happened.

3 Later than the main clause:
After/once/as soon as the doctor has arrived, you may leave the patient.
(After) having reported the accident, don't forget to record it in the log.

4 At a non-specific time:
Always contact the doctor whenever you are in doubt.

***Note***
We use the present or present perfect with **before, after, once, until** and **when(ever)** for future reference:
We will discuss the matter before the inspector visits us. (*not*: will visit)
We will discuss the matter again after the inspector has visited us. (*not*: will visit)

# CLAUSES of TIME

## Exercise 1

*Match the clause of time on the left with a suitable main clause on the right. Then classify the clauses of time according to the table below.*

| | |
|---|---|
| After deciding we could not work alone, | we're now looking ahead to the next one. |
| Once they had studied the product and the market, | we had disagreements. |
| Before agreeing to their proposals, | we had many doubts. |
| While studying the advertising plans, | we studied them very closely. |
| Once understood, | we are delighted with the agency. |
| Whenever we discussed the product launch | they designed a marketing concept. |
| Having seen the success of the launch, | they seemed okay. |
| The campaign finished, | we commissioned an agency to produce an advertising campaign. |

| Subordinate conjunction + finite verb | Subordinate conjunction + non-finite verb *...ing* | Subordinate conjunction + non-finite verb *...ed* | Non-finite verb *...ing* or verb *...ed* |
|---|---|---|---|
| | | | |

## Exercise 2

*Classify the following sentences according to the relationship between the main clause and the time clause. Say whether the time clause occurred:*

– earlier than the main clause (E)
– at the same time as the main clause (=)
– later than the main clause (L)
– at a non-specific time (?)

**1** *After experiencing a period of instability, the company recruited a new Finance Manager.* ☐
**2** *Since she arrived, the company has gone from strength to strength.* ☐
**3** *Whenever she sees problems she has an innovative solution.* ☐
**4** *As soon as she decides on a change, it is readily absorbed by her colleagues* ☐
**5** *Until the department was reorganised, there were repeated problems.* ☐
**6** *Since she has worked for the company, there has been a period of unprecedented expansion.* ☐

## Exercise 3

*The sentences of the text below are in the wrong order. Rewrite them in the correct order.*

**a** When we read it we were very optimistic.
**b** Once we had agreed we needed an advertising campaign, we contacted an agency.
**c** As soon as they had finished this, they began work on a marketing concept for the product.
**d** Until they produced their report, we had not imagined the market was so large.
**e** After explaining the nature of the product, the agency began to study the potential market.

## Transfer

*Think of the economic situation in a country you know well.*

*Write five sentences explaining recent actions by the government. Use time clauses beginning with the following conjunctions.*

*once until before*
*as soon as while after*
*now (that) since*

# UNIT 47

## -ING and -ED CLAUSES

*See also* **Unit 13 – Verb ...ing**

## A *Sample sentences*

- Having spent four years in personnel management, I feel well qualified for the job.
- Considering the results this year, I feel that we should bring forward the investment.
- Given his talent and ability, he should go far.
- If well maintained, this machine should give you years of trouble-free service.

## B *Form*

**-ing** and **-ed** clauses are non-finite subordinate clauses (see Unit 38).

1 We can put a subordinating conjunction before the clause (see Unit 38):
(If) well maintained, this machine should give you years of trouble-free service.

2 We assume that the subject of the subordinate clause is the same as the subject of the main clause:
Designed by a top class international team, this product must be a winner.

***Note:*** This rule is often broken:
Since moving to the UK, their production has dropped.

## C *Uses*

**-ing** and **-ed** clauses (without a subordinating conjunction) can be interpreted in different ways.

Supported by the latest software, this machine is what every manager needs.

This can mean *if* it is supported, *when* it is supported or *because* it is supported. So, we often include the subordinating conjunction to make the meaning clear.

1 Condition (see Unit 10):
If linked to a colour monitor, this laptop can be used as a desktop model.

2 Contrast (see Unit 43):
Although pleased with the results, we still have a long way to go.

3 Cause or reason (see Unit 44):
Having improved quality, we noticed a sharp increase in orders.

4 Time (see Unit 46):
Until registered, a company may not start trading.

5 Manner:
By increasing direct sales, companies can cut out the middle men.

***Note***

The following phrases are used in speech to contradict a previous statement:
*that said*   *having said that*

The latest survey shows economic recovery well on the way. That said, there are still many companies going into liquidation every week.

Economic statistics can often be dangerous instruments. Having said that, our forecasts have proved to be very accurate.

## Exercise 1

*Classify the six sentences below according to the following uses of the* **-ed** *or* **-ing** *clause.*

| Condition | Contrast | Cause or reason | Time | Manner |
|---|---|---|---|---|
| | | | | |

1 Despite having innovative and stylish design, Alvo cars do not reach a wide market.
2 Although they have performed well in rally sport, the cars are not known for their reliability.
3 Having won fame in the domestic market, the company pushed for sales in the United States.
4 If well received there, then the car would genuinely make an international impact.
5 Experiencing continual technical problems, the car failed to convince.
6 However, through improved quality control, the company has improved its reputation.

## Exercise 2

*A company noticed a gap in the market and began to develop an innovative cooking system which uses only 20 per cent as much heat as conventional cooking methods. The flow chart below shows the stages in the development of the product.*

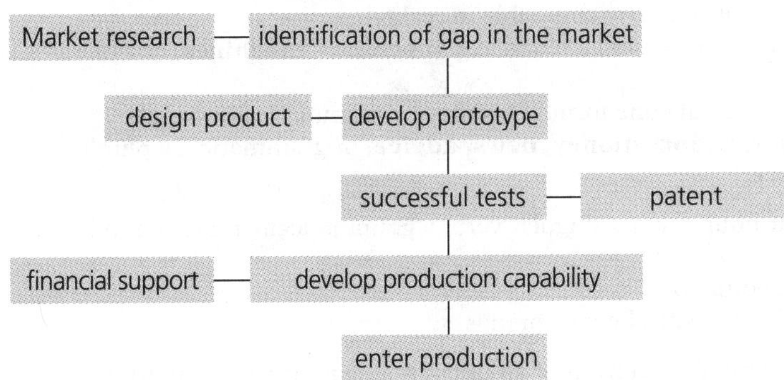


*Use the flow chart to complete the description below. Use the correct non-finite form of the verbs in the box below, to show the sequence of events, reason for events, etc.*

| design set up obtain develop carry out complete |
|---|

__________ some market research SALLO identified a gap in the market. __________ a product, they developed a prototype. __________ successful tests, SALLO received a patent. The company looked for financial support. __________ that, the company developed the production capability. __________ the necessary production facilities, the company entered production. __________ in only 12 months, the SALLO product could revolutionise cooking.

## Exercise 3

*The following sentences are ambiguous. Rewrite them in order to remove the ambiguity and offer two possible interpretations. The first has been done for you.*

1 Developing the product, we are optimistic.
 **a** If we develop the product we will be optimistic.
 **b** Now we are developing the product and we are optimistic.
2 With our software installed, you have more computing power.
3 Calling our service team, your satisfaction is guaranteed.
4 Stored in the warehouse, goods deteriorate.
5 Cutting the workforce, the company improves its profitability.

## Transfer

*Make five sentences containing* **-ed** *or* **-ing** *clauses about a product you know and like.*

***Example:*** Made in Taiwan, my ABC is excellent quality.

# UNIT 48

## NOUNS

*See also* Unit 58 – Articles
Unit 68 – Numerals

### A *Sample sentences*

- ◆ ABC have their headquarters in the Hague.
- ◆ The equipment is very simple to install.
- ◆ The machines will be in operation next week.
- ◆ Your board are expected to make a decision at the next meeting.

### B *Form*

We can classify nouns as shown in the following chart.

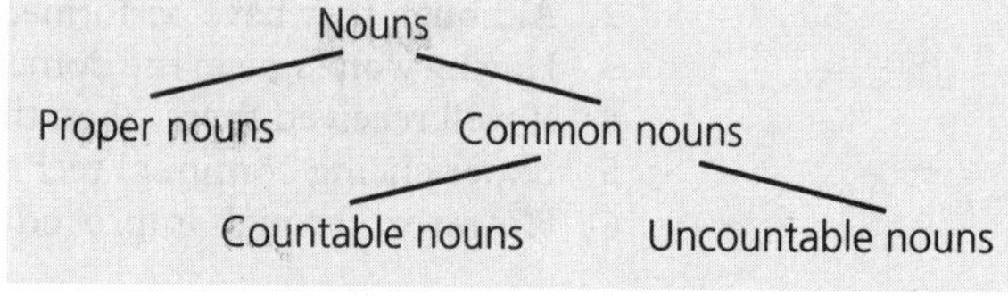


1 **Proper nouns** are names and are written with a capital letter:
Susan Smith, Great Britain, General Electric

In exceptional cases they take **the**:
the Hague, the USA, the Bank of England (see below).

2 **Common nouns** can be divided into *countable* and *uncountable*. This distinction is a grammatical distinction, not a real-world distinction, e.g. **money** is grammatically uncountable (see below), but is clearly countable in reality!

**a** Countable nouns have a singular and a plural, e.g. **machine** – **machines**, or a plural only, e.g. **people**.

**b** Uncountable nouns have only one form. This may be grammatically singular, e.g. **equipment, information, money, news, advice**, or grammatically plural, e.g. **personnel, police**.

A grammatically singular noun takes a singular verb; a grammatically plural noun takes a plural verb.
The information is in the brochure.
The personnel are very happy with the new premises.

You cannot put **a/an** or a number in front of an uncountable noun. You cannot say *an equipment*, *an information*, *a news* etc; you can say *a piece of equipment*, *an item of information/news*.

***Note***
Singular countable nouns normally take a singular verb:
The machine is operating.
Sometimes, however, a singular countable noun can take a plural verb when the noun refers to 'more than one person':
The board are discussing that question now. (board = more than one person)

### C *Uses*

1 Proper nouns refer to unique people or objects, i.e. **Norway** refers to one country and **Susan Smith** (in a given conversation) refers to one person. The following proper nouns take the definite article:

**a** Plural names:
the Netherlands    the Midlands    the Alps    the Thomsons (the Thomson family)

**b** Public institutions and facilities:
the Hilton    the Odeon (cinema)    the British Museum

**c** Newspapers:
*The Times*    the *Daily Express*

2 Common nouns:
Most common nouns are countable. They can take an indefinite or definite article, or no article at all. (See also Unit 58.)
We have negotiated a bank loan.
We have renegotiated the bank loan.
At the moment it is difficult to get bank loans.

For a list of uncountable common nouns and other exceptions, see Appendix 6.

## Exercise 1

*Underline the mistakes in the following sentences and correct them. Some sentences have more than one mistake.*

1 The informations you need are in the post.
2 There's three thousand people coming to visit the exhibition.
3 Alison and Sara read the *Times*.
4 When I go to The Hague I stay in Hilton Hotel.
5 The headquarter is in United States.
6 We have had a lot of troubles with the machinery.
7 Woodpohl makes top quality furnitures.
8 Twelve persons work in my section.
9 This is an expensive equipment.
10 The import agency gave wrong advices.

## Exercise 2

*Identify the countable (C) and uncountable (U) nouns in the list below and write C or U in the boxes.*

*money* ☐ *cheque* ☐ *profit* ☐ *debt* ☐ *assets* ☐

*machinery* ☐ *machine* ☐ *plant* ☐ *production* ☐ *product* ☐

*supervisor* ☐ *foreman* ☐ *chargehand* ☐ *worker* ☐

*furniture* ☐ *news* ☐ *spokesman* ☐ *mathematics* ☐

## Exercise 3

*Make sentences using the prompts below. The first has been done for you.*

1 premises/build/1988.
The premises were built in 1988.
2 Economics/be/interesting
3 What/be/trouble/with/equipment?
4 Where/be/headquarters?
5 University/receive/funds/from/government.
6 Funds/be/insufficient.
7 United States/consist of/50 states.
8 Your/advice/last week/be/good

## Transfer

*Make a list of 12 uncountable nouns. Most of these will be grammatically singular, e.g.* ***information****. Identify any that are not.*

# UNIT 49

## NOUN COMPOUNDS

*See also* Unit 48 – Nouns

### A *Sample sentences*

- The market survey has produced some very interesting results.
- We expect to appoint a new sales manager next year.
- Taxpayers are absolutely horrified by the new tax rates.
- The legislation deals very harshly with law-breakers.

### B *Form*

A noun compound comprises two or more nouns which are combined together into a phrase. A noun compound comprises:

one or more modifying nouns + a head noun

The modifying noun acts like an adjective and gives more information about the head noun.

A: We have carried out a survey. (head noun)
B: What type of survey?
A: A market survey. (modifying noun)

1 The modifying noun, like an adjective, comes before the head noun:

research study (= a study by research)
market research (= research into the market)

2 The modifying noun, like an adjective, remains in the singular:

newspaper publisher (= a publisher of newspapers)
taxpayer (= a person who pays taxes)
*cf.* sales manager (= the manager responsible for sales; *not*: the manager responsible for sale)

3 There are no fixed rules about writing compounds:

conversion process (two separate words)
law-breaker (hyphenated)
timescale (one word)

As language changes, there is a tendency for new compounds to be formed and for familiar compounds to be written as one word. The following are all possible:

work force work-force workforce

### C *Uses*

1 Noun compounds are shorter and more convenient than noun phrases:

a taxpayer *versus* a payer of taxes

2 Noun compounds are more concise – and therefore have greater impact – than noun phrases:

a product design brief *versus* a brief for the design of a product

3 Noun compounds can be ambiguous:

criminal lawyer (a specialist in criminal law or a lawyer who is a criminal)

4 Noun compounds can become too long and difficult to understand:

quality control management development officer (= officer for the development of management in the control of quality)

It is easier and more comprehensible to say:

the management development officer responsible for quality control

## Exercise 1

*Read this short newspaper report and underline all examples of noun compounds.*

**Alpo wins Jordan order**

Alpo Holdings has boosted its drive into automobile markets with a $47.5m sales contract to build 2,000 bus bodies for the Jordanian government.

The order equates to 46 per cent of Alpo's bus parts turnover and is backed by a cash deposit and a $37m OECD-supported buyer credit.

## Exercise 2

*Rewrite the following phrases as noun compounds.*

a concession on taxes
a machine which is a tool
a holiday which lasts ten days
a report on an accident
a court of law
a licence to export

## Exercise 3

*You work for Arrow and you have to arrange insurance for the plant. Opposite is a letter to an insurance company requesting a visit and a quote for insurance. Using words from the box, fill in the spaces with appropriate noun compounds.*

*administration park despatch loading production storage*

**▲RROW Ltd**
Widford Hall Lane
Croydon
Surrey CR5 6TT

Silver Moon Insurance Company
440-442 Parliament Street
York YO1 42BU

Ref: LRBE/SS

6th June 19..

Dear Sir

Re: Insurance quotation

We are in the process of reviewing our insurance cover and would be interested in receiving a quotation from you. Please contact us in order to arrange a visit to our plant.

The plant consists of a car ________, the ________ facilities, a ________ bay and a ________ area. There is also a ________ depot, an ________ block and a canteen.

The total area covered is 1202m$^2$.

I look forward to hearing from you so we can arrange a visit.

Yours faithfully

## Exercise 4

*Below are seven newspaper headlines. Break the noun compounds into longer phrases which could be the opening lines for each report. The first has been done for you.*

1 **Government policy crisis**
There is a crisis in government policy ...

2 **Poisonous chemicals disaster**

3 **North Sea oil rig accident**

4 **Air speed record**

5 **Airport congestion problem**

6 **Chemicals industry results disaster**

7 **GAS POLLUTION ROW**

## Transfer

*How many noun compounds can you make with* ***sales****?*

*Examples:* sales figures    company sales

# UNIT 50

## GENITIVE FORMS

*See also* Unit 48 –Nouns
Unit 59 – Pronouns

### A Sample sentences

- ◆ The company's acquisition astonished everybody in the city.
- ◆ We need to build up stronger links with Rotaronga's trading partners.
- ◆ If the lid of the machine is left open, the optics will burn out.
- ◆ Today's rise in share prices has amazed everyone.
- ◆ President Clinton's election was widely forecast by the polls.

### B Form

The genitive is written with an apostrophe (+ **s** if the noun is singular) or with the preposition **of**:
this year's results (= the results of this year)
the last two quarters' results (= the results of the last two quarters)
the development of a new distribution network
the prices of all new products

### C Uses

1 We typically use the genitive with **'s or s'** with the following nouns:

**a** human nouns:
President Clinton's election

**b** animal nouns:
the lion's share

**c** time nouns:
the last two quarters' results

**d** location nouns:
Rotaronga's trading partners    the country's development

**e** organisation nouns, where an organisation is a group of people:
the government's decision    the board's reaction

2 We use the genitive with **of** with things:
the lid of the machine (*not*: the machine's lid)
the development of management science

3 We can use either the apostrophe form or the **of** form with organisation nouns:
the company's results *or* the results of the company
the meeting's decision *or* the decision of the meeting.

## Exercise 1

*Underline examples of the genitive forms in the advertisement below.*

**TT SOFT**

***Tomorrow's software at today's prices!***

Telephone our sales staff and place your order today.
We are the country's top suppliers of all types of business applications software ranging from the very latest word processing and graphics packages to sophisticated special applications.
Your future's better with us!

**Look at these phenomenal savings!**

In a special deal for TT SOFT, Bell has slashed 50 per cent off its desktop packaging program Bell Desk 500.

Trumpet's world-beating spreadsheet at $100!!

A state of the art publishing program for $150!!

**Meet your needs!**
**Meet the needs of your computer!!**
**Meet us with a telephone call on FREEPHONE 505050 NOW!!!**

## Exercise 2

*Each of the sentences below contains a genitive using* ***of****. If it is grammatically correct to do so, change it to a construction with an apostrophe.*

1 The results of the pharmaceutical group Physic are encouraging.
2 Turnover for the first two quarters has shown a 20 per cent rise.
3 The workforce of the company will benefit.
4 All the pay packets of the employees will include a bonus.
5 A meeting of the shareholders scheduled for the end of September will be a cheerful affair.
6 The Chairman of the Board celebrates ten years in that role.
7 Profits for each year of his tenure have increased well above the industry average.

## Exercise 3

*Dolcetto International is being investigated by the Serious Fraud Office, a special police unit. The following is an extract from a newspaper report. Improve some of the sentences by changing the genitive forms.*

The Board's decision to raise the dividend was against the advice of the auditor. Now the companies' shares have been suspended and its AGM has been postponed. The director's passports have been confiscated by the judicial authorities. A spokesman for Mr Sherlock Holmes, the Managing Director, said Mr Holmes had no comment to make. Mr Holmes's wife, also a Board's member, said the investigation was 'a disgrace'.

Meanwhile, the employees of the company reported for work as usual. A worker's representative said her colleagues were worried about their jobs.

## Transfer

*Look through any document or newspaper and underline the first ten genitive forms you find.*

# UNIT 51

## ADJECTIVES versus ADVERBS

*See also* Unit 24 – **Be** (1)
Unit 25 – **Be** (2)
Unit 28 – Verbs of the senses
Unit 30 – Verbs + adjectives

### A Sample sentences

- She speaks fluent English and she speaks French and Spanish fluently, too.
- We can offer you a permanent software solution.
- We can mend this equipment permanently or just fix it for now.

### B Form

1 Many adjectives are derived from nouns or verbs. For the most common adjective derivations, see Appendix 7.

2 Other adjectives, especially one- or two-syllable adjectives, do not have a suffix:
*good bad young old big small*

3 Most adverbs are derived from adjectives by adding **-ly**; adjectives ending in **-ic** add **-ally**:
*definite – definitely useful – usefully productive – productively*
*dramatic – dramatically systematic – systematically*
But: *public – publicly*

***Notes***

1 Some adjectives end in **-ly**:
*lively lovely friendly lonely*

2 Some adjectives have the same form as adverbs:
*early late straight hard short long fast*
I intend to take the early flight to Paris so that I can arrive early at your office.

3 Some adverbs ending in **-ly** have a different meaning from the adjective without **-ly**:
He is a hard worker. He works hard.
*But*: He hardly works. (= almost not at all)

4 Irregular forms: *good – well*

### C Uses

We use **adjectives** in the following instances:

1 To give more information about nouns:
The *economic* situation has changed.
Which situation? The economic situation.

2 After the verb **be** (see Unit 24):
They were *angry* about the breakdown. (adjective + preposition)
They were *angry* that the machine had broken down. (adjective + **that**-clause)
They were *angry* to hear about the breakdown. (adjective + **to** + infinitive)

3 After verbs of the senses (see Unit 28):
The new furniture looks very *nice*.

4 After linking copular verbs (see Unit 30):
Profits have remained *stable* this year.

We use **adverbs** in the following instances:

1 To give more information about a verb:
Our costs have risen *slightly*.
How did they rise? Slightly

2 To give more information about an adjective:
We have had an *extremely* good year.
How good? Extremely good

3 To give more information about an adverb:
They responded to our call *really* quickly.
How quickly? Really quickly

4 To give more information about a sentence:
*Firstly*, let's look at last year's results.

***Note***

Be careful of the difference in meaning between these adjectives and adverbs:

*economic* (in the economy) — *economical* (money-saving)
*interesting* (to someone) — *interested* (in something)
*late* (not early; adj.) — *lately* (recently; adv.)
*short* (not long; adj.) — *shortly* (soon; adv.)
*present* (current; adj.) — *presently* (soon; adv.)

## ADJECTIVES versus ADVERBS

### Exercise 1

*Give the corresponding adverbs for the following adjectives.*

1 reliable
2 necessary
3 erratic
4 slow
5 late
6 traditional
7 competent
8 excellent

### Exercise 2

*Each of these sentences contains a mistake. Correct them.*

1 The economical arguments for reducing the investment are very strong.
2 The plane arrived lately so I missed the start of the meeting.
3 I am not interesting in seeing the museums.
4 My last job was in software programming but actually I work in quality control.
5 Reducing R & D spending is not economic in the long term.
6 The Director is in hospital because she has been working too hardly.

### Exercise 3

*Circle the correct word from the choices given in the sentences below.*

1 The profit forecast is **real/really** good.
2 **Poor/poorly** sales were caused by a drop in confidence.
3 The **presently/present** board has insufficient experience.
4 We are very **interesting/ interested** in your proposal.
5 The President sounded **optimistic/optimistically** about the prospects for growth.
6 He spoke **enthusiastic/enthusiastically** about the new products.

### Exercise 4

*Read the following extract from a sales manager's presentation on the sales of two ranges of personal computers over five years. He is describing the graph. Use adjectives or adverbs from the box to fill in the spaces.*

*clearly important gradual considerable faster naturally dramatically firstly greater*

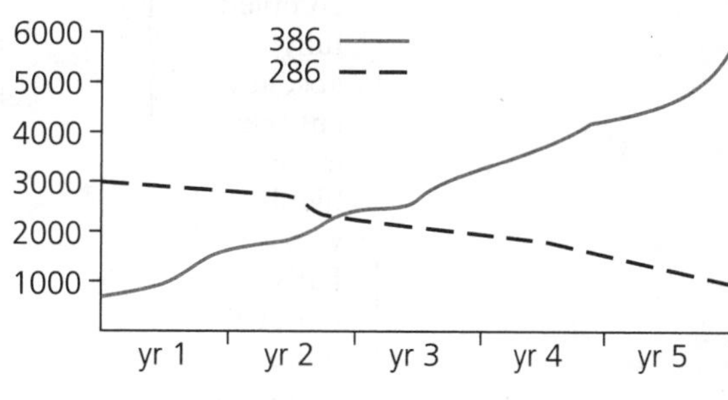


*__________, I'd like you to look at the graph here which compares the sales of the 386 models with the 286s over five years. __________ there has been a __________ change with the consumer showing __________ taste for 386 machines. The __________ decline in the popularity of the 286 reflects the complexity and range of software and the fact that users need to have __________ operating machines. As for the 386, sales have indeed increased __________. In response to these __________ changes, we have __________ concentrated our efforts on developing improved 386 models.*

### Transfer

*Write a short paragraph describing changes in a market that you are familiar with. Include various adjectives and adverbs.*

# UNIT 52

## ADJECTIVE MODIFICATION with ADVERBS

*See also* Unit 51 – Adjectives versus adverbs
Unit 75 – Describing trends
Unit 77 – Asserting and downtoning information

### A *Sample sentences*

- The project group has carried out an extremely thorough study.
- I'm afraid that the results are completely useless.
- It is highly probable that we will move into the perfume sector next year.
- The results of the study show that the product is commercially viable.

### B *Form*

Most adverbs are derived from adjectives by adding **-ly**; adjectives ending in **-ic** add **-ally**:
*definite – definitely* *useful – usefully* *productive – productively*
*dramatic – dramatically* *systematic – systematically*
But: *public – publicly*

### C *Uses*

Adverbs modify adjectives in two ways:
– by intensifying their meaning, e.g. an *extremely* good year, *reasonably* good results
– by indicating a point of view, e.g. *technically* possible (= possible from a technical point of view)

1 Intensifying adverbs:
They have carried out an *extremely* thorough study.
How thorough? Extremely thorough.

We can classify intensifying adverbs on a scale from 'totally' to 'moderately', where 'totally' intensifies the adjective to a high degree and 'moderately' intensifies the adjective to a moderate degree.

wholly
totally
completely
fully
absolutely
entirely
extremely
highly
very
fairly
reasonably
quite
moderately

2 Point of view adverbs:
The product is *technically* viable.
Viable from which point of view? From a technical point of view. (i.e. technically viable)

***Notes***

1 **Real** versus **really**:
I was real interested in the job. (AmE – informal)
I was really interested in the job. (BrE and AmE)

2 The position of **quite**:
Quite an important person
Quite a big company.

# 52 TASKS

## ADJECTIVE MODIFICATION with ADVERBS

### Exercise 1

*Which pairs of words in the following list have similar meanings?*

entirely quite highly reasonably extremely totally

### Exercise 2

*Complete the following exchanges by adding an appropriate adverb from the box in the spaces.*

moderately wholly fairly
very extremely

1 A: It was a good year.
B: How good?
A: __________ good. As good as we could expect.

2 A: There was a small fall in output in the first quarter of the year.
B: How small?
A: __________ small – only about 5 per cent.

3 A: The exhibition was successful.
B: How successful?
A: __________ successful – we met very many prospective customers.

4 A: The report was critical.
B: How critical?
A: __________ critical. They condemned everything about the plant.

### Exercise 3

*Change the sentences below so that the underlined adjective is replaced by its corresponding adverb. The first has been done for you.*

1 From a commercial point of view the decision was clever.
It was a commercially clever decision.

2 From an economic perspective the policy was catastrophic.
The policy ______________________________

3 In theory the design was innovative.
______________________ the design ______________________

4 But to be frank, it was wrong.
But ______________________ it ______________________

5 From a logical point of view your argument is unsustainable.
Your argument ______________________________

6 From an academic standpoint you are right.
You are ______________________________

### Transfer

*Write six sentences about your country's economy. Include the following adjectives with adverbs which modify them.*

strong weak independent
optimistic pessimistic well-organised

*Example:*
Taiwan has a particularly strong economy.

# UNIT 53

## COMPARISON of ADJECTIVES

*See also* Unit 51 – Adjectives versus adverbs
Unit 52 – Adjective modification with adverbs

### A *Sample sentences*

- We can certainly offer lower prices than any other local supplier.
- They have the most expensive products on the market.
- If you have any further questions, please contact me.
- If any company can provide more attractive terms, we will match them on the spot.

### B *Form*

The comparative form adds **-er** and the superlative form is made by using **the** and adding **-est**.

1 Adjectives with one syllable:

| | | |
|---|---|---|
| *long* | *longer* | *the longest* |
| *big* | *bigger* | *the biggest* |
| *low* | *lower* | *the lowest* |
| *late* | *later* | *the latest* |

2 Two-syllable adjectives ending in **-y**, **-ow**, and **-le**:

| | | |
|---|---|---|
| *easy* | *easier* | *the easiest* |
| *narrow* | *narrower* | *the narrowest* |
| *simple* | *simpler* | *the simplest* |

3 Other two-syllable adjectives and longer adjectives:

| | | |
|---|---|---|
| *reliable* | *more reliable* | *the most reliable* |
| *expensive* | *more expensive* | *the most expensive* |

Longer adjectives use **more** in the comparative and **the most** in the superlative.

4 Irregular adjectives:

| | | | | | | | | |
|---|---|---|---|---|---|---|---|---|
| *good* | *better* | *best* | *little* | *less* | *least* | *bad* | *worse* | *worst* |
| *much* | *more* | *most* | *far* | *farther/further* | *farthest/furthest* | | | |

### C *Uses*

1 Comparison of objects:
- To compare two objects:
  Our prices are lower than theirs.
- To compare more than two objects:
  Our prices are the lowest. (of all the prices)
- To compare an object and a definite standard:
  Our quality is already high, but we must make it still higher.
- To show that one comparison depends on another. We can use **the** + comparative adjective … **the** + comparative adjective:
  The faster we can improve quality, the more profitable we will become.
  (i.e. If we can improve quality, we will become more profitable.)

2 Modification of comparison. We can use an adverb before a comparative adjective to indicate the degree of comparison:
Our prices are *much* lower than theirs.

far
much
substantially
considerably
significantly
moderately
somewhat
slightly
a little

***Note***
You cannot say: 'Rossomon are more bigger than Matushi.' (bigger)

# 53 TASKS

## COMPARISON of ADJECTIVES

### Exercise 1

*Complete the following table.*

| | | |
|---|---|---|
| slow | ________ | ________ |
| ________ | more difficult | ________ |
| modern | ________ | ________ |
| ________ | ________ | the easiest |
| capable | ________ | ________ |
| ________ | drier | ________ |
| quick | ________ | ________ |
| ________ | ________ | the worst |
| far | ________ | ________ |
| ________ | more | ________ |
| a little | ________ | ________ |
| ________ | ________ | the most advanced |

### Exercise 2

*Read the two descriptions of computer systems. Write five sentences which explain differences between the two machines.*

*Example:*
The Carro XT has a more powerful processor.

**The Carro XS 386 X**
20 MHz Processor
2 MB RAM memory – expandable to 32 MB
20 MHz high speed processor
1.44 MB 3.5″ floppy disk drive
14″ super VGA 1024 x 768 colour monitor
3 years on-site warranty plan
Price £749

**The Carro XT 486 X**
33 MHz Processor
4 MB RAM memory – expandable to 64 MB
33 MHz processor – ultra high speed
1.44 MB 3.5″ floppy disk drive
17″ super VGA 1280 x 1024 colour monitor
4 years on-site warranty plan
Price £1149

### Exercise 3

*Use the graph below to compare the effects on the environment of four different means of transport. Write sentences which compare the $CO_2$ pollution levels of planes, taxis, cars and buses, using different forms of the following adjectives.*

clean dirty much little

*Example:*
Cars are more polluting than taxis.

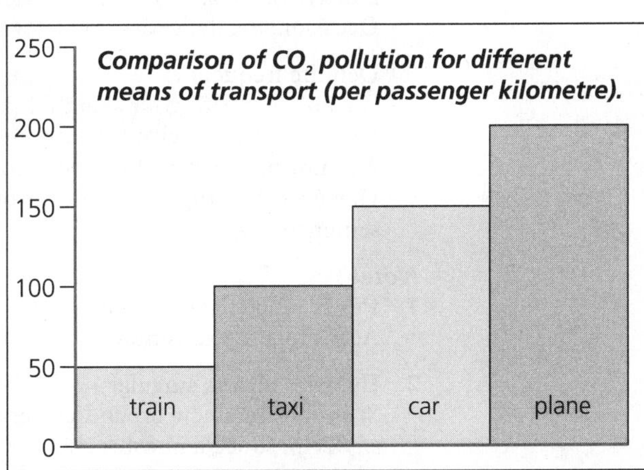


### Transfer

*Compare your country and two other countries that you know well. Write at least six sentences.*
*Or*
*Compare a product you know well with two other similar products from different manufacturers. Write at least six sentences.*

# UNIT 54

# EXPRESSIONS of FREQUENCY

***See also*** **Unit 2 – The present simple**
**Unit 51 – Adjectives versus adverbs**
**Unit 66 – Each and every**

## A *Sample sentences*

- For peace of mind, always let FHG deliver your most important parcels.
- We can usually guarantee a next day service to any city on the mainland.
- Our engineers will visit your office once a month to check the equipment.
- We rarely have any complaints, but we will look into the matter immediately.

## B *Form*

We can divide expressions of frequency into *indefinite* frequency and *definite* frequency.

1 We can classify expressions of indefinite frequency on a scale from 'always' to 'never', where 'always' = 100 per cent and 'never' = 0 per cent. These numbers are only a general indication, not exact values.

| | |
|---|---|
| 100% | always |
| 95% | nearly always/almost always |
| 90% | usually/normally/generally/regularly |
| 75% | often/frequently |
| 50% | sometimes |
| 40% | occasionally |
| 25% | rarely/seldom |
| 10% | hardly ever/scarcely ever |
| 0% | never |

2 If we want to be more precise, we can use one of the following types of expressions:
**a** once/twice/three times a day/week/month/year
**b** every hour/day/week/month/year
**c** hourly/daily/weekly/monthly/quarterly/annually/yearly

***Note***
**Hourly**, **daily**, **weekly**, **monthly**, **quarterly**, **yearly** are both adjectives and adverbs; **annually** is only an adverb (adjective = **annual**).
We review the figures monthly. (adverb)
We have a monthly review of the figures. (adjective)

## C *Uses*

1 **Questions about frequency:**
How often do you travel to Europe?

2 **Statements about frequency:**
Indefinite frequency:
We usually deliver next day. (normal position for adverbs of frequency is before the verb)
I am rarely at the office after 7 in the evening. (adverb of frequency after the verb **be**)

For emphasis the following adverbs can be put at the beginning of the sentence:
*usually normally generally regularly often frequently sometimes occasionally*
Occasionally, deliveries are delayed for technical reasons.

Definite frequency:
We hold a meeting for shareholders once a year.
Once a week I receive a printout of all transactions.
The normal position for expressions of definite frequency is at the end of the sentence. However, for emphasis the expression of frequency can be put at the beginning of the sentence.

***Notes***
1 **Per** is official and formal:
According to the contract we should receive one statement per month.

2 **Every** is always singular:
We produce a new brochure every year. (*not*: every years)
*cf.* We produce a new brochure every six months. (= every period of six months)

# EXPRESSIONS of FREQUENCY

## Exercise 1

*Two sales representatives meet in a hotel. They have very different ways of doing business. Complete the conversation using frequency expressions from the box so that Kerry always has quite the opposite way of doing things! Use each expression once.*

| seldom | hardly ever | nearly always | never | normally | always | sometimes |
|---|---|---|---|---|---|---|

Lee: I always fly here.

Kerry: Do you? I __________ fly. I __________ come by car.

Lee: By car? How awful! What about this place? I rarely stay in this hotel. Do you often come here?

Kerry: I __________ stay here, though __________ I stay at the place opposite.

Lee: I see. What about your customers – is this a good place for you to meet them? Do you do much business here? I think it's terrible. I __________ sell anything!

Kerry: Really? No, I think it's great. I __________ sell quite a lot here. I've several good customers here.

Lee: Fancy a drink?

Kerry: Thanks, I'll have an orange juice.

Lee: Orange? I __________ drink orange. I prefer apple juice.

## Exercise 2

*Complete the following sentences by putting a frequency expression in each space.*

1 I __________ walk to work, I __________ go by car. I __________ take the bus.
2 I __________ travel abroad. When I travel abroad I __________ stay in a hotel.
3 If I go a long way I __________ fly. When I arrive at the airport I __________ take a taxi to my hotel. I __________ hire a car.
4 We have a regular meeting with the Director of the Department every __________.
5 We __________ phone our most important customers.

## Exercise 3

*Complete the following sentences with an expression of definite frequency based on the frequency given in brackets.*

1 We hold our shareholders' meeting __________. (December)
2 I meet my deputy __________ __________ __________. (Monday and Thursday)
3 I send a report to Head Office __________ __________ __________. (January, March, May, July, September etc.)
4 I telephone our agents __________. (Monday, Tuesday, Wednesday, Thursday etc.)
5 We publish a profit and loss account __________ __________ (July and January)
6 We produce detailed sales results __________. (April, July, October, January)
7 I meet the Managing Director every __________. (week 1, 3, 5, 7, 9, 11, 13, etc.)

## Transfer

*Write six sentences describing things that you do or don't do and indicate how often you do them by including frequency expressions.*

# UNIT 55 DEGREE with VERY, TOO and ENOUGH

*See also* Unit 52 –
Adjective modification with adverbs

## A Sample sentences

- Our Money Map can identify investment opportunities very quickly.
- This investment is very suitable for clients looking for a secure investment.
- Too many people do not have adequate insurance.
- If you don't have enough time now, you can take a couple of samples with you.
- We need better protection; at present we don't feel secure enough.

## B Form

**Very**, **too** and **enough** are adverbs (see Unit 51).

**Very** and **too** come before the adjective or adverb:
Our Money Map can identify investment opportunities very quickly.
That level of return on investment is too good to be true.

The adverb **enough** comes after the adjective or adverb:
The current supplier is not reliable enough.

The determiner **enough** comes before the noun:
We have enough offers to make a decision soon.

## C Uses

1 **Very** is a degree adverb; it intensifies the meaning of an adjective or adverb:
This machine can provide a very fast response.
We can respond to orders very quickly.

2 The adverbs **too** and **enough** have related meanings. **Too** means 'more than enough' or 'more than acceptable':
Our present office is too big. (i.e. it is not acceptable)

**Enough** means that something is acceptable:
Our present office is big enough. (i.e. it is acceptable)

Compare **too** and **enough** in following sentences:
The present office is too small.
The present office is not big enough.

**Too small** means 'too small for us to work in'; **not big enough** means 'not big enough for us to work in'; therefore **too** and **enough** function by reference to a level, a person and an activity:

| *level* | *person* | *activity* |
|---|---|---|
| This office is too small | for us | to work in |

Often we do not mention the person and the activity because they are obvious from the context:
Your prices are too high. (for us to buy)

3 The determiner **enough** also refers to a level:
We have enough offers.

As with the adverb **enough**, often we do not mention the person and the activity:
We have enough offers. (to make a decision)

# DEGREE with VERY, TOO and ENOUGH

## Exercise 1

*Decide if the following sentences are both grammatically and logically correct. If wrong, correct them.*

1 The price is too high but I can still afford it.
2 We don't have people enough to meet the order.
3 It doesn't cost very money.
4 The plant at Lagos is very large. In fact, it is too big.
5 We sold very few products. In fact, we sold enough.
6 The country is very small and it has a very large population. It is enough heavily populated.

## Exercise 2

*Below is an extract from a letter from a printing firm to a dissatisfied customer. Fill in the spaces with **very, too** or **enough**.*

*We were ________ sorry to hear that you are not satisfied with the printing work which we sent last week and in particular that the colour red is ________ strong. We checked the work ________ carefully before it was despatched and we felt that it was good ________ to meet our ________ high standards. However, since you are not happy, our representative will visit you on Friday to discuss the problem. We understand your need is urgent so I hope this is soon ________ to fit in with your schedule. If it is ________ late please telephone us.*

## Exercise 3

*Complete the sentences below by using a construction with **very, too** or **enough**. The first has been done for you.*

1 *The delivery time is too long. In other words it is not* short enough for us.
2 *The service you provide is too slow for us. In other words it is not* ________
3 *The quality of the workmanship is disappointing. In fact it is not* ________
4 *The report is not long enough. In other words it is* ________
5 *The conference is not early enough in the year. In other words it is* ________
6 *The registration fee is very expensive. In fact it is* ________
7 *The venue is far away. In fact it is* ________

## Transfer

*Describe the business and economic environment in your country using **very, too** and **enough** in at least five sentences.*

*Examples:*
It is easy enough to conduct business here but taxes are too high.
It is very difficult to invest large quantities of the national currency in other countries.

# UNIT 56

## SO versus SUCH

*See also* Unit 38 – Subordinate clauses
Unit 45 – Clauses of purpose
Unit 74 – Connecting and sequencing ideas

### A *Sample sentences*

- The hotel was so noisy that we had to move.
- Suddenly there was such a loud noise in the conference hall that many people ran out.

### B *Form*

We use **so** before an adjective or an adverb:
The hotel was *so noisy* that I left at once.
He spoke *so quietly* that I couldn't hear what he said.

We use **such** before (an adjective +) a noun:
There was *such a* (*loud*) noise that he ran to investigate.

Note the position of **such**:
such an (efficient) machine (before the indefinite article with countable singular nouns)
such (efficient) machines (with countable plural nouns)
such (efficient) machinery (with uncountable nouns)

### C *Uses*

1 As adverbs of degree (see Unit 55):
The hotel was so noisy that we couldn't sleep. (= the hotel was too noisy for us to sleep or the hotel was not quiet enough for us to sleep)

2 To indicate the result:
The hotel was so noisy that we had to leave. (with the result that we had to leave)

3 To add emphasis:
The food was so delicious!
They gave us such a warm reception!

4 In negative comparisons:
Our fuel consumption is not so high as I thought. (or not as high as)

5 Phrases with **so,** such as **so long as, (in) so far as, so far**:
So long as their policy does not change, we can't do business with them. (condition concerned with time)
Their offer is attractive – (in) so far as it goes. (extent)
We have received three offers so far. (up to now)

## Exercise 1

*Complete the following sentences by adding **so** or **such**.*

1 *The work was __________ bad that we refused to pay.*
2 *The payment was __________ late that we contacted our lawyers.*
3 *After __________ a long time we had given up hope of payment.*
4 *It was __________ a large debt that we had to try to recover it.*
5 *__________ expensive items cost a lot to repair.*
6 *Costs increased __________ rapidly that we abandoned the research.*

## Exercise 2

*Read the phrases on the left and find the correct ending from the alternatives on the right to make seven meaningful sentences. The first has been done for you.*

| | |
|---|---|
| The work is so bad that | are very valuable. |
| We are so late that | operating it is easy. |
| It is such a good design that | the meeting will be over. |
| With such good progress | it will have to be re-done. |
| Such material | we accepted his idea. |
| Such customers | we will finish early. |
| He argued so convincingly that | can be recycled easily. |

## Exercise 3

*Rewrite the following sentences using the words given in brackets. Sometimes only a small change is necessary. Do not change the original meaning. The first has been done for you.*

1 The very high quality justifies the price. (such/justifies the price)
Such high quality justifies the price.
2 The project has gone well until now. (so far)
3 If the weather remains good, the building work will be completed before Christmas. (so long)
4 I was surprised by the excellent performance. (such/surprised me)
5 The engine was not as noisy as I had expected. (so)
6 The service we received was not good enough for us to continue with that supplier. (so bad/changed)

## Transfer

*Write five sentences about the quality of service you received from an institution or company recently. Use **so** and **such** in your sentences.*

# UNIT 57

## ALREADY, YET, AGAIN and STILL

*See also* Unit 5 – The present perfect simple

### A *Sample sentences*

- We have made the leasing arrangements already.
- Have you signed the contract yet?
- We will look at our software requirements again next year.
- We still haven't made a decision about the brochure, but we are going to discuss it again soon.

### B *Form*

**Already**, **yet**, **again** and **still** are adverbs of time.

1 We can put **already** at the end of the sentence:
We have made the leasing arrangements already.

Note the other possible positions:
The leasing arrangements are already complete. (after **be**)
The agreement has already been signed. (after the first modal or auxiliary)
They already invest heavily in the technology programme. (before the main verb)

2 **Yet** usually comes at the end of the sentence:
A: Have you signed the contract yet?
B: Yes, but I haven't sent it back yet.

3 **Again** usually comes near the end of the sentence:
We will look at our software requirements again next year.

4 **Still** is used as follows:
That matter is still under discussion. (after **be**)
That matter is still being discussed. (after the first modal or auxiliary)
We still intend to invest in the technology programme. (before the main verb)

### C *Uses*

1 **Already** means 'by this/that time'; we use it in positive statements:
We have made the leasing arrangements already. (by this time, i.e. by now)

2 **Yet** means 'by now'; we normally use it in negative statements and questions:
A: Have you received the contract yet? (by now)
B: No. I was told yesterday that it hadn't been checked yet. (by that time, i.e. yesterday)

3 **Still** means 'up to this/that time':
They are still using the old pump. (up to this time)
= They haven't stopped using the old pump yet. (by now)
Last month I was still trying to find a suitable supplier. (up to that time)
= I hadn't found a suitable supplier yet. (by then)

4 **Again** means 'another time' or 'as before':
We have asked for the same discount again. (another time or as before)

***Notes***

1 Tenses with **already** and **yet**:
We have already investigated the cause of the problem. (present perfect in BrE)
We haven't investigated the cause of the problem yet. (present perfect in BrE)
We already investigated the cause of the problem. (past simple in AmE)
We didn't investigate the cause of the problem yet. (past simple in AmE)

2 Notice the link between **yet** and **still**:
A: Have you completed the study *yet*, or are you *still* working on it?
B: Yes, last week. But I was told yesterday that the draft hadn't been checked *yet* and that we are *still* waiting for the expert's opinion.

# ALREADY, YET, AGAIN and STILL

## Exercise 1

*Below is the text of an internal phone call between two sales people in an engineering firm. They are discussing a problem with an export licence. Use **already, yet, again** and **still** to complete the spaces.*

*A: I'm afraid we __________ haven't received authority to export the goods.*

*B: Has the Trade Department contacted you __________?*

*A: No, not __________. I'll telephone them __________ to see why there's such a delay.*

*B: Okay. Our customers have __________ complained about the delay and I __________ can't give them a delivery date.*

*A: I know. I'll call you __________ this afternoon.*

## Exercise 2

*Read the following sentences and place an arrow (↑) in the place where the word in brackets can be placed. If two places are possible, put in a second arrow.*

| | | |
|---|---|---|
| 1 | She has arrived. | (already) |
| 2 | She has not arrived. | (still) |
| 3 | Has she arrived? | (yet) |
| 4 | She has not arrived. | (yet) |
| 5 | I'll telephone his office. | (again) |
| 6 | We hope to see Eddie Roberts soon. | (again) |
| 7 | We are developing a new system. | (again) |
| 8 | We use an American consultant. | (still) |

## Exercise 3

*Look at the figures below and complete the sentences with appropriate words. Include **already, yet, again** or **still** in your answers.*

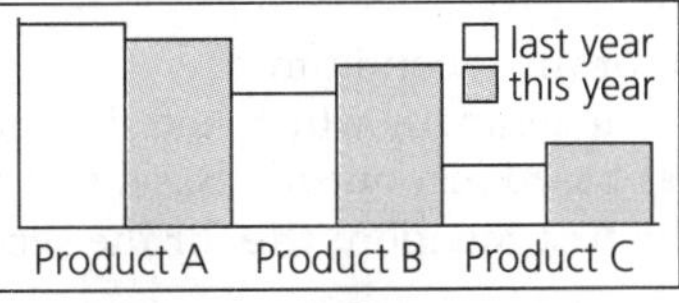


**Comparison of sales of Products A, B and C last year and this year.**

1 *A is __________ the top selling product.*

2 *Sales for C are __________ __________ __________.*

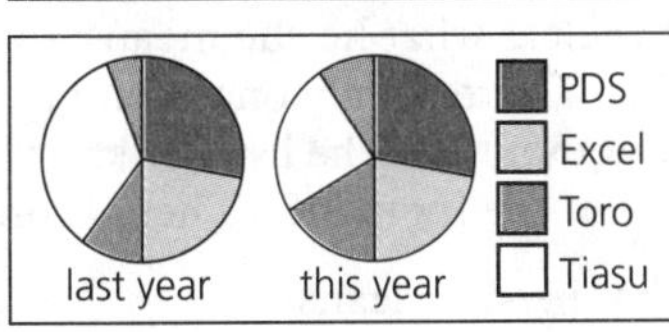


**Market share of market leaders (last year and this year).**

3 *The PDS market share __________ __________ 28 per cent.*

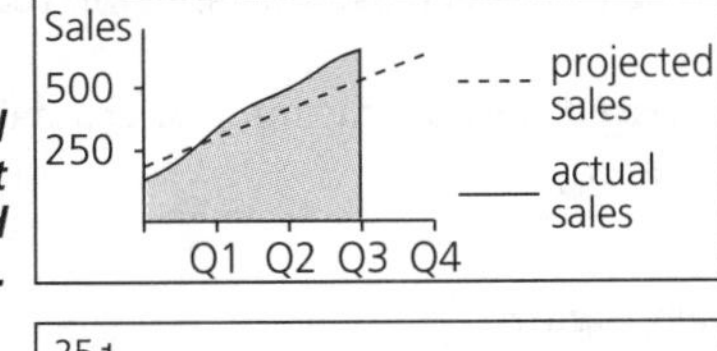


**Projected and actual sales for current year at end of third quarter (93).**

4 *At the end of the third quarter we __________ __________ __________ the target for the end of the year.*

25
20
15
10
5
1 2 3 4 5

**Sales development for Haracel (years 1–3).**

5 *Sales __________ not __________ 20,000 units __________.*

## Transfer

*Think of any plans that a company you know well or your government has followed in recent months. Write five sentences describing the progress of these plans. Use **already, yet, again** and **still.***

# UNIT 58

## ARTICLES

*See also* Unit 48 – Nouns
Unit 61 – **Some, any and related words (1)**

## A *Sample sentences*

- A bank is an institution which offers financial services.
- You can receive product information from our Customer Services Department.
- Associated Industries can supply the machinery and equipment you need.

## B *Form*

There are three forms of the article:

**a**(**n**) – the indefinite article
**the** – the definite article
0 – the zero article

## C *Uses*

1 We use the *indefinite article* with singular countable nouns (see Unit 48), when we introduce a word or idea for the first time:
A charity is not an institution which can make a profit.

2 We use the *zero article* with uncountable nouns and most proper nouns (see Unit 48), when we introduce a word or idea for the first time:
This accommodation includes fixed furniture and fittings. (*not*: an accommodation, a furniture)
*cf.* The tenant shall be responsible for maintaining the accommodation. (specific accommodation)

Paul Berisford is in charge of plant and equipment. (*not:* the Paul Berisford, a Paul Berisford)

We also use the zero article with plural countable nouns (see Unit 48), when we are speaking generally:
Shareholders are invited to the annual general meeting.
*cf.* The shareholders were invited to the meeting. (specific shareholders)

3 We use the *definite article* in the following cases:

**a** When we mention a word or idea for the second time:
While I was in Switzerland I visited *a* company which had designed *an* innovative kitchen product. *The* company was based just outside Basel and *the* product was called Kitchen Magician. (**a** for the first mention; **the** for the second.)

**b** When the speaker presumes that it is clear what he/she means:
There are four points on the agenda. (There is only one agenda.)
I'll leave the instructions next to the computer. (The listener knows which instructions.)
The economy is in a very poor shape at the moment. (There is only one economy.)

**c** When the speaker makes it clear what he/she means:
The recommendations in your report were very useful. (specific recommendations, i.e. in your report)
The market analysis which you prepared omits a number of crucial points. (specific market analysis, i.e. which you prepared)

**d** When we talk about institutions:
Did you see the news on the TV last night?
There was an interesting article about our competitors in the newspaper.

**e** We can use **the** with some nationality words:
A recent survey showed that the French admire hard work, the Germans are competitive and ambitious, and the British prefer to work in the security of a group.

***Note***
We do not use an article with the names of meals, or with the institutions and other common words listed in Appendix 8.

## Exercise 1

*Read the following sentences, where each article or the absence of the article is numbered. Then place each number in the table according to the particular use of each article.*

**a** Harris and Co[1] make car components[2]. The[3] company has an[4] agent in Paris.
**b** A[5] long delay occurred when a[6] document was lost. The[7] delay almost resulted in the[8] customer cancelling the[9] order. An[10] internal enquiry found that a[11] computer error caused the[12] problem.
**c** Information[13] on the[14] history of Alba[15] can be found at the[16] Tourist Office.

| Zero article proper name | Indefinite article countable, first mention | Definite article second or subsequent mention |
|---|---|---|
| | | |
| **Zero article plural countable nouns, general meaning** | **Definite article a specific meaning is clear** | **Zero article uncountable, first mention** |
| | | |

## Exercise 2

*Add articles where necessary in the following sentences.*

**1** ________ *University of Leeds is one of* ________ *biggest in England. It is also* ________ *important centre for medical studies.*

**2** *Butter is* ________ *major agricultural product in* ________ *European Union. Another is rape seed oil. Most of* ________ *butter is consumed by EU countries.*

**3** ________ *Super Motor Company makes* ________ *range of high-performance cars, including* ________ *luxurious Grosso 55XT. This is* ________ *perfect example of* ________ *modern automotive engineering.*

## Exercise 3

*Here is a text adapted from an advertisement produced by the Bahrain Tourism Board. If appropriate, add an article* ***a***, ***an***, *or* ***the*** *in the spaces in the text. If the zero article is required, leave the space blank.*

**Make ________ right connections in Dubai – ________ business centre of ________ Middle East**

When it comes to selecting ________ base for your regional headquarters, Dubai is ________ logical choice. ________ city has become ________ region's leading centre for ________ trade, ________ transport and ________ distribution, ________ industry, ________ conferences and ________ exhibitions. For good reason. Dubai encourages ________ enterprise. ________ state-of-the-art telecommunications system puts you in instant touch with ________ world. ________ 60 international airlines link Dubai with over 100 cities worldwide. And ________ city boasts sophisticated ________ banking, ________ finance and ________ other services, as well as world-class office accommodation. And ________ lifestyle is great too!

## Transfer

*Select any two paragraphs from an English newspaper or magazine. Underline the articles and classify their uses as in Exercise 1.*

# UNIT 59

## PRONOUNS

### A *Sample sentences*

- ◆ They gave us a comprehensive explanation of their network.
- ◆ I think it was useful to exchange views; for us to hear yours and for you to hear ours.
- ◆ Please give my regards to Pierre and tell him I hope to see him myself next year.

### B *Form*

We can divide pronouns into three types: *personal*, *reflexive* and *possessive*.

| | Personal | | Reflexive | Possessive | |
|---|---|---|---|---|---|
| | **subject** | **object** | | **determiner** | **pronoun** |
| 1st person sing. | I | me | myself | my | mine |
| pl. | we | us | ourselves | our | ours |
| 2nd person sing. | you | you | yourself | your | yours |
| pl. | you | you | yourselves | your | yours |
| 3rd person sing. masc. | he | him | himself | his | his |
| fem. | she | her | herself | her | hers |
| non-personal | it | it | itself | its | its |
| pl. | they | them | themselves | their | theirs |

### C *Uses*

1 Personal pronouns:
*They* gave *us* a comprehensive explanation of their network.
Please contact *me* next week. (me = the person)
Please contact *us* next week. (us = the company)

2 Reflexive pronouns:
We use a reflexive pronoun when the object is the same as the subject:
First *I*'d like to introduce *myself*; then I'd like *you* to say a few words about *yourselves*.
*We* should ask *ourselves* how we managed to get into the mess.

3 Possessive pronouns:
A: *Our* company has *its* brochures printed by a company in Manchester. How about *yours*? (yours = your organisation)
B: *Ours* are printed locally. (ours = our organisation)

***Notes***

1 When using personal pronouns you usually mention yourself last:
My colleagues and I would like to offer you this small gift. (*not*: I and my colleagues)
My advice is that one should always listen carefully before one speaks. (one = indefinite pronoun, i.e. a person)

2 Reflexive pronouns:
I did it myself. (I did it; not anybody else)
I did it by myself. (without anyone else's help)

3 Personal pronouns with **own** add emphasis:
We use our own components in the manufacturing process. (rather than anyone else's components)

## Exercise 1

*Replace the underlined words below with appropriate pronouns.*

1 Paul designed the system without any help.

2 Jane is my boss. My boss and I have worked together for years.

3 I understand that your company has an office in Buenos Aires. Our company has one there too. Our office is in the south of the city. Where is your office?

4 Mary called in. Mary left a package for John. Can you take the package to John?

5 Hernandez and Fernandez make life difficult for Hernandez and Fernandez.

## Exercise 2

*Replace the underlined words with an appropriate pronoun in the following sentences.*

1 Oh, Mr Beard! Mrs Ford phoned. Mrs Ford asked me to ask Mr Beard to phone Mrs Ford back as soon as Mr Beard can.

2 JJD make plastic joints. JJD have supplied our company, Thomson Boro Ltd, for years. JJD have always provided Thomson Boro Ltd with good service but a recent supply was very poor quality. I telephoned their sales rep. I told their sales rep about the problem and the sales rep said the problem would be resolved easily.

3 The suppliers phoned a moment ago. The suppliers said the goods were damaged in transit and that the responsibility is not the suppliers'. The suppliers are sending one of their representatives here tomorrow to discuss the problem. In any case, the goods are useless. We must not pay for the goods.

## Exercise 3

*The text below is part of an advertisement for an electronic components manufacturer. Underline the pronouns in the text and then label them as personal subject (PS), personal object (PO), reflexive (R) or possessive (P). Do not underline any possessive determiners.*

Our products are sold throughout the world. We export to more than 30 countries. We have a network of agents and technicians based in service centres in 15 countries. We pride ourselves on the excellence of our after-sales service. Your needs are also ours and so we guarantee to provide you with the best service in the sector. We make the products and you use them.

Hambro – do yourself a favour!

Hambro – you call us – we serve you!

Hambro products – they work for you!

## Transfer

*Write five sentences about your company or some place you know well. Use examples of different types of pronouns.*

# UNIT 60

## DEMONSTRATIVES

### A Sample sentences

- A: Is that the service department?
  B: No, this is the technical department.
- Did you understand those figures? I really can't see how she got these results.
- So those are our objectives and that concludes my short talk.

### B Form

Demonstratives are words which point to something in the context – something near or something distant. They can be pronouns (see Unit 59) or determiners.

These are the forms of the demonstratives:

| | Singular | Plural |
|---|---|---|
| Near reference | **this** | **these** |
| Distant reference | **that** | **those** |

### C Uses

1 The demonstratives **this** and **that** can point *backwards* to something we mentioned earlier:
We planned the campaign very carefully and this/that was a great success. (pronoun)
We launched the RD 4500 in January. This/that product has proved very popular at the top end of the market. (determiner)

2 The demonstrative **this** can point *forwards* to something we are going to mention later:
This is the way that we plan to proceed. (pronoun) First we will reduce all unnecessary costs. By unnecessary costs I mean these types of items: inventory, labour and other non-fixed overheads. (determiner)

3 The demonstratives **this** and **that** can point to something in the real world, i.e. outside the language:
I'd like to draw your attention to two sets of figures. These (here) show the present situation; and those (there) refer to last year.

***Notes***

1 We use **that** and **those** before a relative clause:
Those who have already applied for shares will have to declare their interest.

2 In colloquial speech we use the forward-pointing **this** to introduce a subject that we are going to describe more fully afterwards:
So, we went into this bar in Barcelona, and you wouldn't believe what we saw.

## Exercise 1

*Identify examples of demonstratives in the following extract from a conversation and classify them according to the uses listed below:*

1 Pointing backwards (B)
2 Pointing forwards (F)
3 Referring to something in the real world (RW)
4 Introducing a relative clause (RC)
5 Colloquial speech (CS)

'The company sent us a letter. That was the first indication that they were interested in the proposal. We read this with much interest because they were offering us something we had asked for: a 50 per cent share in royalties on all the products they made, obviously meaning all those we agreed to let them make. This is it – here – read it. And then can you put it on that file over there? I need to show it to that consultant fellow who's coming in later. Now look … I want to say this. We should not necessarily accept what is on offer. Accepting it straight away … that would be a mistake.'

## Exercise 2

*Read the extracts from two job vacancy announcements. Circle the demonstratives in each one, then link them to the phrases that they refer to. The first has been done as an example.*

**Editor/Eastern Europe**

This is an opportunity to work in a research organisation publishing economic surveys on Eastern Europe. This is a new position created to meet growing demand for products in this area.

Those applicants with a good economics degree, experience in publishing and a good knowledge of the region should write with a concise CV to Steven Wright, Personnel Officer, PO Box 456, London SE22 5RF.

**Could you help to influence economic policy in London or Brussels?**

Government Economic Service offers the chance to work at the heart of economic decision-making in this country.

GES staff provide specialist advice to most government departments. To this end we put both micro and macro economic principles into practice, balancing industry specific principles against those which affect the whole economy. We offer preparation for European Commission recruitment competitions. In order to qualify for these competitions you should have post-graduate experience in economic research, well-developed communication and analytical skills, problem-solving abilities and a serious motivation towards a career in the European Community.

If you possess these qualities send for further information and an application form to Steven Wright, Personnel Officer, PO Box 456, London SE22 5RF.

## Exercise 3

*Monica Schmidt has some money to invest and so she has a meeting with a financial advisor, Corina Lopez, at her bank. Below is part of their conversation together with two tables that Corina used to illustrate what she was saying. Fill in the blanks with demonstratives.*

Calculation of interest income

$$\text{Interest income} = \frac{\text{Investment} \times \text{Annual interest rate in \%} \times \text{Running period in days}}{100 \times 360}$$

Example: Fr. 100,000 invested for 3 months at 7.5%.

$$\text{Interest income} = \frac{100{,}000 \times 7.5\ \% \times (3 \times 30)}{100 \times 360} = \text{Fr. } 1875$$

*MS: What are ________ two tables?*

*CL: Good question, now let's look at them. ________ one shows how we calculate investment income, while ________ shows an example.*

*MS: I see. Could you explain them?*

*CL: Of course. The basic calculation is like ________ . The investment multiplied by interest rate multiplied by running period in days – all ________ over 100 x 360.*

*MS: I see. And in ________ example, it's for ________ much – 100,000 francs?*

*CL: Yes, the interest rate – ________ 's 7.5 per cent, the time is three months, ________ 's 3 times 30. If you finish the calculation you have ________ much: 1875 francs.*

# UNIT 61

## SOME, ANY and RELATED WORDS (1)

*See also* Unit 62 – **Some, any and related words (2)**

### A *Sample sentences*

- Unfortunately we don't have any spare parts for some of the old models.
- If you can't supply us with any parts, please give us the name of someone who can.
- I'm afraid we can't do anything about it at the moment.
- You can get that information from any of our branch offices.

### B *Form*

| **some** words<br>Positive statements | **any** words<br>Negative statements | Questions |
|---|---|---|
| *Determiner*<br>I need **some** advice | I **don't** need **any** advice | Do you need **any** advice? |
| *Pronoun*<br>I need **some** of the documents | I **don't** need **any** of the documents | Do you need **any** of the documents? |
| *Pronoun*<br>I spoke to **someone** yesterday<br>I'd like to ask **something** | I **didn't** speak to **anyone** yesterday<br>I **don't** want to ask **anything** | Did you speak to **anyone** yesterday?<br>Would you like to ask **anything**? |

***Note***
**Somebody** = **someone**; similarly, **anybody** = **anyone**.

### C *Uses*

1 Uses of **some** and compounds. **Some** is a determiner and a pronoun; **someone** and **something** are pronouns. We use **some** words in:

**a** Positive statements:
I have some samples in my briefcase. (determiner + plural countable noun)
We received some money from your bank last week. (determiner + uncountable noun)
Some of the older models are more reliable than the newer ones. (pronoun)
There's someone waiting for you in your office. (pronoun)

**b** Polite offers in the question form:
Do you have some other questions? (inviting questions)
Can I offer you some more coffee?
Both **some** and **any** are correct, but **some** is felt to be more polite.

2 Uses of **any** and compounds. The uses of **any** + compounds are parallel to the uses of **some** + compounds above. We use any words in:

**a** Negative statements:
We didn't receive any payments this morning. (determiner + plural countable noun)

**b** Direct questions (see Unit 41):
Does anyone have any comments? (pronoun; determiner + plural countable noun)

**c** **Yes/no** indirect question (see Unit 41):
I wonder if anyone can answer that question.

**d** Conditional clauses (see Unit 10):
If anyone would like to see a demonstration, it can be arranged.

**e** Comparisons after **-er, more** (see Unit 53), **less, as, too** (see Unit 55):
The situation is much more serious than anyone could have imagined.
The breakdown is too complicated for anything to be done about it this evening.

**f** To mean 'every' or 'all' (see Unit 66) – **any** + singular countable noun, or **any** + uncountable noun:
Any sales manager can sell this product (every sales manager or all sales managers)
Any information would be much appreciated. (all information)

***Note***
We do not use **any** (unstressed) with singular countable nouns:
Are there any questions? (*not*: any question)

# SOME, ANY and RELATED WORDS (1)

## Exercise 1

*The following sentences all contain one mistake. Correct them.*

1 I haven't seen some examples yet.
2 There were any questions so the meeting ended.
3 We don't need no help with this.
4 I didn't have problem coming to see you.
5 The meeting was longer than someone would have wanted.

## Exercise 2

*Choose the sentence with the closest meaning (a, b or c) to the one given.*

1 Some companies raise money by issuing shares.
  **a** A number of companies raise money by issuing shares.
  **b** Companies raise money by issuing shares.
  **c** All companies raise money by issuing shares.

2 I spoke to someone yesterday about investing in shares.
  **a** I spoke to some people yesterday about investing in shares.
  **b** I spoke to a person yesterday about investing in shares.
  **c** I spoke to some person yesterday about investing in shares.

3 I don't think just anyone can answer this question.
  **a** I don't need anyone special to answer this question.
  **b** I need some special people to answer this question.
  **c** I need someone special to answer this question.

4 Any of the goods in this section are available within two weeks.
  **a** Some of the goods in this section are available within two weeks.
  **b** All of the goods in this section are available within two weeks.
  **c** Most of the goods in this section are available within two weeks.

## Exercise 3

*The following is an extract from a telephone conversation between a computer user and the Customer Service Centre of a major software manufacturer. Fill in the spaces with a suitable word from the box.*

| *someone any some anyone anything some something* |
|---|

*Customer: I'd like __________ information about upgrading software please. I understand that last month you were offering Grapho 5.1 free of charge to users who had bought 5.0 in January or February. I bought mine in January but I haven't received __________ information and now the free offer is closed.*

*CSC: Yes, I'm sorry, that's correct. __________ who was a registered user should have received news of the offer.*

*Customer: I didn't receive __________*

*CSC: I'm sorry about that. Have you been receiving our regular newsletter since you bought your Grapho software? There's always __________ in there about offers.*

*Customer: No, I haven't.*

*CSC: Hold on please, there's __________ here I can ask about this ...*

## Transfer

*Think of a situation where you have had to complain about some aspect of service. Write examples of the kinds of things you say in this situation. Use examples of* ***some*** *and* ***any*** *words.*

# UNIT 62

## SOME, ANY and RELATED WORDS (2)

*See also* **Unit 61 – Some, any and related words (1)**

### A *Sample sentences*

- There must be a piece of software somewhere which can convert these files.
- After their poor service we won't ever deal with them again.
- Do you ever read the financial reports published by Rice Brooker?

### B *Form*

| **some** words | **any** words | | **no** words |
|---|---|---|---|
| Positive statements | Negative statements | Questions | Negative statements |
| *Determiner*<br>I have **some** information | I **don't** have **any** information | Do you have **any** information? | I have **no** information |
| *Pronoun*<br>I need **some** of the documents<br>I told **someone** in head office<br>I'd like to say **something** | I **don't** need **any** of the documents<br>I **didn't** tell **anyone** in head office<br>I **don't** want to say **anything** | Do you need **any** of the documents?<br>Did you tell **anyone** in head office?<br>Would you like to say **anything**? | I need **none** of the documents<br>I told **no-one** in head office<br>I would like to say **nothing** |
| *Place adverb*<br>I've seen him **somewhere** | I **haven't** seen him **anywhere** | Have you seen him **anywhere**? | I have seen him **nowhere** |
| *Time-when adverb*<br>I'll see him again **some time** | I **won't ever** see him again | Will I **ever** see him again? | I will **never** see him again |
| *Time-frequency adverb*<br>I **sometimes** go to the USA | I **don't ever** go to the USA | Do you **ever** go to the USA? | I **never** go to the USA |
| *Degree adverb*<br>I was **somewhat** surprised | I **wasn't at all** surprised | Were you **at all** surprised? | I was **not at all** surprised |

### C *Uses*

1 Uses of **some** and **some** words:
**Some** is a determiner and a pronoun; **someone** and **something** are pronouns; and other **some** compounds are adverbs:
The bank interest must be somewhere on the profit and loss account. (adverb)
We sometimes hold our annual partners' meeting in London. (adverb)

2 Uses of **any** and **any** words:
Has anyone here ever stayed in the Cairo Hilton?
I'm afraid that I can't find your CV anywhere.

3 Uses of **no** and **no** words:
There are no overhead transparencies left in the box. (determiner + plural countable noun)
I have absolutely no idea why we continue to rent equipment from them. (determiner + uncountable noun)
Why has none of this information appeared in the report? (pronoun)
I was not at all surprised at the news of the takeover. (adverb)

***Note***
**Some time** (two words) is a time-when adverb; **sometimes** (one word) is a time-frequency adverb:
We visited them some time last year. We visit them sometimes.

# SOME, ANY and RELATED WORDS (2)

## Exercise 1

*Are the following sentences right or wrong? If wrong, make the necessary correction.*

1 I sometime give presentations to other companies.
2 If there is anything I can do to help, please contact me.
3 I was something impressed by her performance.
4 I'm afraid I don't have any more information to give you.
5 So, if nobody has some questions, let's move on to the practical demonstration.
6 To be honest, we don't ever exceed our agreed budgets.

## Exercise 2

*Complete the following dialogue with **some, any** or a related word/phrase.*

A: Do you __________ visit the Asian plants?

B: Well, I'm __________ sure what will happen next year, though I am tentatively planning a trip __________ in the autumn.

A: And do you plan to go __________ in particular?

B: Well, I suppose if I go __________, it will be to Korea and Taiwan.

A: Oh, that's interesting. I __________ go out there myself. Usually at very short notice.

B: I see.

A: I must say there is __________ that I dislike more than these hastily arranged trips.

B: I agree. __________ is better than finding yourself in a meeting without __________ of the right papers.

A: Absolutely!

B: Well, I think we should try to do __________ about it.

## Exercise 3

*Below is part of a presentation about software security from an EDP manager to computer operators in a bank. Match the phrase on the left with an appropriate phrase on the right to create complete sentences. Then fill in the spaces with words from the box opposite. The first has been done for you.*

| ever | anyone | anything |
|---|---|---|
| some time | any | somewhere |
| anybody | not at all | no-one |

| | |
|---|---|
| Of course, security in our software | it will just be forgotten. |
| Of course there is | but I'm __________ sure we've solved all the problems. |
| If __________ suspects that | and there'll be no problem. |
| Don't __________ think that | is something we all regard as an important issue |
| It will turn up __________ | __________ information has been lost or changed, the incident must be reported. |
| Does __________ have __________ | __________ here who doesn't understand the critical nature of tight security in banking. |
| __________ ago we had a meeting specifically on this | to say on this? |

# UNIT 63

## QUANTIFIERS (1)

*See also* Units 61 and 62 – **Some, any and related words (1) and (2)**
Unit 64 – **Quantifiers (2)**
Unit 66 – **Each and every**

### A *Sample sentences*

- We have considered all the locations and none is really suitable.
- We feel that many of the candidates had not really read the job requirements.
- We have not got much faith in the system at the moment.
- There are few organisations operating in our market niche and even fewer which we would consider real competitors.
- At present we have no plans for opening an office in the Far East.

### B *Form*

| Countable singular | Countable plural | Uncountable |
|---|---|---|
| all the | all/all (of) the | all/all (of) the |
| | most (of the) | most (of the) |
| | many (of the) | much (of the) |
| a lot of (the) | a lot of (the) | a lot of (the) |
| | lots of (the) | lots of (the) |
| | several (of the) | several (of the) |
| | a few (of the) | a little (of the) |
| | few (of the) | little (of the) |
| no | no | no |

***Notes***

1 **A lot of** and **lots of** are more colloquial than **many** and **much**.

2 The use of the definite article:
All equipment needs replacing. (understood from the context)
All (of) the equipment needs replacing. (specific equipment in the plant or other location)
All equipment is dangerous. (all equipment in the world)

### C *Uses*

1 **Much, many, a lot of** and **lots of** when used in positive statements:
Many of the older products have now been withdrawn.
A lot of the older products have now been withdrawn.

**How much** and **how many** are the question words to ask about quantity:
How much is the hourly rate for consultancy services? (how much = money)
How many consultants will we have to work with?

2 **A few** and **few** versus **a little** and **little**:
We have a few reliable suppliers. (not many but enough)
We have few reliable suppliers. (not many and not enough)
We have little time before the end of the meeting. (not much and not enough)

We often use **a few** and **a little** with **only**:
There are only a few organisations operating in our market niche. (*not*: only few organisations)
*cf.* There are few organisations operating in our market niche. (similar meaning to **only a few**)

3 We often use **very** with **few, little** and **many**:
The plant was not visited by very many people.
We have had very little support from the bank and very few enquiries from our customers.

***Note***
We do not use **the** before **most**:
Most (of the) managers do an orientation course as soon as they join us. (*not*: the most)

## Exercise 1

*Place the following in order from 1 (maximum) to 7 (minimum).*

☐ Several of our products are made from recycled plastic.
☐ None of our products are made from recycled plastic.
☐ Few of our products are made from recycled plastic.
☐ Many of our products are made from recycled plastic.
☐ Most of our products are made from recycled plastic.
☐ A few of our products are made from recycled plastic.
☐ All of our products are made from recycled plastic.

## Exercise 2

*Replace the underlined words with a word or phrase from the box.*

| a few | much | all | no | few | most |
|---|---|---|---|---|---|

1 Not many but some of our clients responded to the survey.
2 The majority of them had some positive comments to make.
3 Not one of our customers thought our products were unreliable.
4 A lot of constructive criticism centred on product distribution and delivery.
5 Not many and not enough customers wanted regular news on our new products and services.
6 Every one of the respondents said our packaging was good.

## Exercise 3

*The Management Communications Consultancy runs intensive training courses. They have carried out a survey of client opinion on their courses. Here is a summary of the results.*

| Summary of results of client opinion on courses | | | |
|---|---|---|---|
| No. of respondents 420 | | | |
| | Very satisfied | Satisfied | Not satisfied |
| Services/products | 75% | 19% | 6% |
| Professionalism | 80% | 18% | 2% |
| Materials | 31% | 54% | 15% |
| Seminar rooms | 10% | 20% | 70% |
| Organisation | 100% | 0% | 0% |
| Value for money | 20% | 80% | 0% |

Make eight sentences based on the above using the quantifiers **all, many, much, several, (a) few, little** and **no**.

*Examples:*
Several respondents were not satisfied with the materials.
A few respondents were not satisfied with our services and products.

## Transfer

Write comments on a company that you know well, or its products. Use the quantifiers **all, many, much, several, (a) few, (a) little** and **no**.

*Example:*
All ABC products are very good – a few are very expensive.

# UNIT 64

## QUANTIFIERS (2)

*See also* Units 61 and 62 – **Some, any and related words (1) and (2)**
Unit 63 – **Quantifiers (1)**
Unit 66 – **Each and every**

### A *Sample sentences*

- There will be an appraisal of the whole department next week and all the staff will be interviewed.
- Each manager and all their deputies will be invited to submit suggestions for the new quality circle.
- Under no circumstances may anyone enter the operating theatre without prior authorisation.

### B *Form*

See Unit 63.

### C *Uses*

1 **All the** versus **the whole**:
**The whole** + singular countable noun is more common than **all the** + singular countable noun:
The whole department will be investigated. (more common)
All the department will be investigated. (less common)

2 **Each/every** versus **all**:
**Each/every** + singular countable noun has the same meaning as **all** + plural countable noun:
Each manager has a personnel role in relation to his or her staff.
All managers have a personnel role in relation to their staff.

3 **No** words:
The determiner **no** is related to the following **no** words – **no-one, nowhere, never, nobody, nothing**:
No-one has contacted us so far. (pronoun)

A: Where have you been?
B: Nowhere interesting. (adverb of place)

You must never reveal any of this information to anyone outside the company. (adverb of time)

If you use **no** or a **no** adverb phrase at the beginning of a sentence, use an inversion construction:
Under no circumstances may anyone enter the operating theatre.
*cf.* No-one may enter the operating theatre under any circumstances.

Never have I visited such a clean plant.
*cf.* I have never visited such a clean plant.

Nowhere else in Europe are conditions as good as here.
*cf.* Conditions are not as good as here anywhere else in Europe.

## Exercise 1

*Underline all the quantifiers in the following advertisement for an insurance broker.*

> Not all clients require the same services. Some need a very personalised approach to their problems with several meetings and a few specialist consultations: others can be handled on a more generalised basis with no fee unless some work is actually carried out. In fact, most of our clients feel that we have the right mix of products for them; and many more join us each year. So we'd like to say that we can do more than please some of the people some of the time; we feel that, all in all, we can satisfy most of the people most of the time.

## Exercise 2

*Again, underline the quantifiers in the text below and then rewrite the sentences with different quantifiers but without changing the meaning.*

> The majority of our competitors have managed to reduce their costs over the last year. Each of them has tried to introduce cost-cutting measures. Of course, not one of these measures has been an absolute success; and a number of them have been a total failure. For example, when Planton tried to save a small amount of money by merging two departments, the results were catastrophic. Not enough people in the new department were happy to work together as a newly-formed team. Finally, Planton had to invest a large sum of money on team-building activities just to solve the new problems which had been created.

## Exercise 3

*Organise the jumbled text below into a paragraph.*

1. There are several reasons, but the simple answer is that they all need to earn an income.
2. At the same time, through their work most of them produce the goods and services needed by the population.
3. Of course, there are a few people who can afford not to work.
4. In this way they are helping to ensure that a high standard of living is maintained for the community as a whole.
5. Every day in Britain more than 24 million people go to work.
6. But why do people work?
7. But for most of them, this is not an end in itself.
8. And, unfortunately, there are some people who can't find work.
9. Some of these people work in offices, but most of them work in factories.
10. With this money they can buy the goods and services that everybody needs.

## Transfer

*Write some sentences about business practice in your country. Write about:*

- business meetings
- timekeeping
- personal contact
- hospitality

*Remember to use as many quantifiers as you can.*

# UNIT 65

## BOTH, EITHER and NEITHER

### A Sample sentences

- Both of the investments are attractive.
- We must either launch the product now or postpone it till the end of next year.
- Neither of the candidates really impressed me.

### B Form

**Both**, **either** and **neither** are determiners, pronouns and conjunctions.
Both candidates impressed me. (determiner)
Neither of the candidates impressed me. (pronoun)
Either we appoint now or we wait till the spring. (conjunction)

1 **Both** takes a plural verb:
Both candidates have now been interviewed. (determiner + plural countable noun)
We interviewed both (of the candidates) on Monday. (pronoun)

2 **Either** and **neither**:
Either solution is acceptable to us. (determiner + singular countable noun)
I'm afraid that neither (of the solutions) is acceptable to us. (pronoun)

### C Uses

**Both**, **either** and **neither** indicate quantities.

1 **Both** indicates a quantity of two:
Both of the investments are attractive (There are two investments.)
We plan both to study the alternatives and to implement one soon. (We have two plans.)

2 **Either** indicates:
**a** one of two possible alternatives:
We can accept either solution. (There are two acceptable solutions.)
We will have to either launch the product now or wait till the spring. (There are two alternative actions.)
**b** addition of negation ('and also not'):
A: I haven't had a single refusal today.
B: No, I haven't either. ('and I also not'; see also **neither** below)

3 **Neither** indicates:
**a** that both options are excluded:
Neither of the candidates really impressed me. (There are two unimpressive candidates.)
Unfortunately neither the documents nor the letters are ready yet. (Both are not ready.)
**b** addition of negation ('and also not'):
A: I haven't had a single refusal today.
B: Neither have I. ('and I also not'; see also **either** above, and inversion below)

***Notes***

1 If you use **neither** or **nor** at the beginning of a sentence or clause, use an inversion construction:
Neither have we broken the law, nor has our local office.

2 If you use the article with **both**, put it after, not before **both**:
Both the solutions are acceptable. (*not*: the both)

3 We can replace **both** with **each** (see Unit 66):
We have summarised both/each of the reports.
Both locations have their advantages./Each location has its advantages.

4 We do not use a negative verb after **neither**:
Neither the documents nor the letters are ready yet. (*not*: are not ready yet)

5 The emphatic use of **both** ... **and**:
One should invest for both the long term and the short term.

## BOTH, EITHER and NEITHER

### Exercise 1

*Write sentences based on the following prompts including the word(s) in brackets. The first has been done for you.*

1 (Both) Jean/Jacques speak English.
Both Jean and Jacques speak English.
2 (Both) Simone speaks Italian/Spanish.
3 (Either … or) We continue/stop investment.
4 (Not only … also) Singapore is a vibrant business centre. It is in the centre of a spectacular economic region.
5 (Neither … nor) We don't sell/don't rent equipment.

### Exercise 2

*Rewrite the following pairs of sentences as single sentences using the words in brackets.*

1 Philip is not the right candidate. Arne is also not suitable. (neither … nor)
2 Marta wrote to me with a good proposal. Juana also sent a good one. (both … and)
3 I criticised the poor quality of the printing. Edith criticised it too. (both … and)
4 I can book the seminar rooms. Alternatively you can do it. (either … or)
5 Akira is a very creative designer. He also works very efficiently. (not only … but also)

### Exercise 3

*Uta and Marina are trying to arrange a time to meet. Look at their diary extracts and then complete the spaces in the extract from their conversation.*

**Marina's diary**

WEEK 33

| | am | | pm | |
|---|---|---|---|---|
| Monday | am | Discuss D45 project | pm | |
| Tuesday | am | | pm | |
| Wednesday | am | Presentation 10.00 | pm | Meet AD 3.00 |
| Thursday | am | Meet Ann 10.30 | pm | |
| Friday | am | | pm | |

**Uta's diary**

WEEK 33

| | am | pm |
|---|---|---|
| Monday | meeting with FDT | |
| Tuesday | training seminar all day | |
| Wednesday | | Paul 2.30 |
| Thursday | Juan 10 | Visit TF |
| Friday | | Leave for Milan 2.00 |

Marina: Can we meet during week 33?

Uta: Yes, I think so. I'm quite busy but I'm sure we'll find a time.

Marina: How about Monday or Tuesday?

Uta: I'm afraid I'm very busy on __________ Monday __________ Tuesday. I could manage __________ Wednesday __________ Friday.

Marina: Let me see. I can manage __________ Wednesday morning __________ Wednesday afternoon. Friday? Yes I can manage __________ the morning __________ the afternoon.

Uta: Friday morning would be okay. Can we say 10 o'clock?

### Transfer

*Write six sentences comparing two similar service companies that you know well, e.g. training or language teaching organisations. Use **both, either** and **neither**.*

# UNIT 66

## EACH and EVERY

***See also*** **Unit 63 – Quantifiers (1)**
**Unit 64 – Quantifiers (2)**
**Unit 65 – Both, either and neither**
**Unit 67 – Compounds with every**

### A *Sample sentences*

- This point comes up on the agenda every few months.
- Each offer must be submitted together with all the supporting documentation.
- On each of the occasions we've planned to meet, something has cropped up.

### B *Form*

**Each** is a determiner and a pronoun; **every** is a determiner:
Each/every company has its own corporate culture. (determiner)
Each of the companies we visited was very different. (pronoun)

1 The determiners **each** and **every** take a singular countable noun and a singular verb.
2 The pronoun **each** takes a singular countable noun and a singular verb.

***Note***
After a plural subject **each** is plural:
The companies each have their own distinctive management style.
*cf.* Each of the companies has its own distinctive management style.

### C *Uses*

1 We use **each** for any number of people/things taken separately (minimum two), when we think about them one at a time:
Each of the departments will receive a copy. (many individual departments)
Each European subsidiary will send a representative. (many individual subsidiaries)
Each of the (two) senior directors will give a short presentation. (two directors)

2 We use **every** for a group of people/things taken separately (minimum three), when we think about them as a whole group:
We will certainly read every page of the report. (all the pages)
Every presentation should have a beginning, a middle and an end. (all presentations)

**Every** + singular noun = **all** + plural noun:
We've checked every figure/all the figures very thoroughly.

3 Expressions of definite frequency (see Unit 54):
 a We can use **each** or **every** with single periods:
 We take a back-up copy each/every hour/morning/afternoon.
 b We use **every** where the period includes a number greater than one:
 The machine should be serviced every three months. (*not*: each three months)
 *cf.* The machine should be serviced every/each month.

 We hold our sales meeting in a different city every two years. (*not*: each two years)
 *cf.* We hold our sales meeting in a different city every/each year

***Notes***
1 After **every**, we can use a plural pronoun to avoid using 'he' or 'she':
Every manager should meet their whole team at least once each week.

2 We do not use **each** or **every** with a negative verb:
None of the banks wanted to see our references. (*not*: each of the banks didn't want)

3 **Every day** (two words) is an adverb; **everyday** (one word) is an adjective:
The first shift starts at 8 o'clock every day.
Accidents are an unfortunate everyday problem.

## EACH and EVERY

### Exercise 1

*How many combinations can you make with **each** and **every** + the following phrases?*

day people of the departments
of the two managers two years equipment

### Exercise 2

*Plural nouns and uncountable nouns cannot be used with **each** and **every**, but they can be used with **all**. Link each phrase on the left containing **all** with a phrase on the right containing **each** or **every** to make six sentences.*

| | |
|---|---|
| We've checked all the facts | each interviewee completed a questionnaire. |
| We've serviced all the equipment, | every building seems to be empty. |
| We've reviewed all the news thoroughly | down to every last coin. |
| We've checked all the premises and | including each device we checked in the summer. |
| We've appraised all the personnel and | down to every last detail. |
| We've counted all the money again | and listened again to every item. |

### Exercise 3

*Complete the following sentences using a phrase with **each** or **every**. The first one has been done for you.*

1. We accept sterling, francs, pesetas etc.; in fact you can pay us in ___every___ European ___currency___.
2. We have tried to get accommodation in all the hotels in Prague but __________ __________ is taken.
3. We have given him a lot of sound advice but __________ __________ falls on deaf ears.
4. I think I left my baggage on the plane; __________ of my two __________ has my name on it.
5. We need to renew a lot of our existing machinery as nearly __________ __________ in the plant is more than 20 years old.
6. It is important to make progress, but we need to take __________ __________ with care.
7. There is so much traffic on the roads that I think it would be a good idea to tax __________ __________ according to its engine size.
8. Overseas travel can be very tedious, especially when __________ __________ involves a weekend away from home.
9. To analyse work, you can take __________ __________ and subdivide it into its constituent parts.

### Transfer

*We can use **each** and **every** in a 'top down' description when we talk about individual parts or items. One example would be when describing an organisation:*

The company is divided into three divisions. Each division is responsible for one product line and each division is headed by a director who has responsibility for the division's activities. Each director reports to …

*Now write about your company in the same way.*

# UNIT 67

## COMPOUNDS with EVERY

*See also* Units 63 and 64 – Quantifiers (1) and (2)
Unit 60 – **Both, either and neither**
Unit 66 – **Each and every**

### A *Sample sentences*

- We have informed everybody about our new address.
- I accept everything that was said in the meeting.
- Every time I make a constructive suggestion, Peter opposes it.

### B *Form*

| | |
|---|---|
| **Personal pronoun** | everyone, everybody |
| **Non-personal pronoun** | everything |
| **Adverb of place** | everywhere |
| **Adverb of frequency** | every time |

### C *Uses*

**Every** compounds:
Everybody (that) I contacted was very positive about the prototype. (*not*: all people what)
Everybody who/that asked for further information has been contacted. (*not*: all people what)
We did everything that was possible to avoid bankruptcy. (*not*: everything what)

We have customers everywhere in Europe.
Our products can be found everywhere (where/that) there are people.

Every time (that) I make a constructive suggestion, Peter opposes it. (*not*: every time when)

***Notes***

1 After **every** compounds, we can use a plural pronoun to avoid using 'he' or 'she':
Everyone who is against this suggestion should give their reasons briefly.

2 **Everyone/everybody/everything** (pronouns) are written as one word; but **every one** (each single one) is written as two:
I have contacted everyone to discuss this matter. (all the people)
Every one of the participants has now given me their replies. (each single one of the participants)

# COMPOUNDS with EVERY

## Exercise 1

*Read the extract below from a promotional leaflet of a textiles company. Identify the seven mistakes and correct them.*

Every products are made using the finest quality woven fabric.

Everything what you see being printed here is based on traditional checked patterns.

Everyone of our fabrics is made using the best quality cloth available.

Almost every time when you visit a top fashion fair in Milan or Paris you will see examples of our fabrics.

Every where we enter competitions we receive some recognition of our high standards.

We can finish everything material in any way you want, including various special effects.

Every dyes we use contain only natural colours.

## Exercise 2

*Fill in the spaces with words from the box.*

| everywhere | each | everyone |
|---|---|---|
| every day | everything | every |

1 __________ in this workshop has done an apprenticeship with an engineering company.
2 More than 400 machine tools are produced here __________ , except Saturday and Sunday.
3 __________ production line runs continuously, for 24 hours.
4 __________ eight hours a supervisor checks the level of output.
5 __________ is maintained by our own team of fitters.
6 All the production is distributed to agents __________ in Europe.

## Exercise 3

*Replace the underlined words in the following sentences with **each**, **every** or a compound with **every**, and make any other necessary changes in the rest of the sentence.*

1 We design <u>every article</u> we make.
2 <u>All the employees</u> here receive a productivity bonus.
3 <u>Every</u> worker is entitled to 30 days' paid holiday.
4 <u>All the</u> decisions are taken by the Board.
5 A new worker is elected to the Board <u>after two years, in other words in 1993, 1995, 1997 etc.</u>
6 <u>In every place</u> you go here you see examples of our company's good organisation.

## Transfer

*Write five sentences, using **each**, **every** or compounds with **every**, about your home town or the place where you live or work.*

*Examples:*

Every apartment in the block where I live has a garage and a balcony.
Everyone who lives here pays for the maintenance of the lift.

# UNIT 68

# NUMERALS

## A Sample sentences

- We have two possible options for next season's fashions: other fabrics or additional styles.
- About a quarter of our present collection is made in France.
- These dresses will retail at about 2,000 French francs each.
- We meet our major customers twice a year – once in Milan and once in Paris.

## B Form

We can divide numerals into *cardinals*, *ordinals*, *fractions and decimals* and *frequency expressions*.

**1 Cardinals**

Here are some examples:

0 – **nought, zero (especially in mathematics and for temperatures), 'oh' (in telephone numbers), nil (in sports)**
100 – **a/one hundred.** We offer a/one hundred different products.
101 – **a/one hundred and one**
1,000 – **a/one thousand.** At present we employ a/one thousand employees. **(*not*: one thousand of)**
1,101 – **one thousand, one hundred and one**
3,000 – **three thousand.** Three thousand garments were on display. **(*not*: three thousands of garments)**
1,000,000 – **a/one million**

**2 Ordinals**

Here are some examples:

1st – **first.** The first of April **(spoken).**
2nd – **second.** This is the second time we have visited Paris.
3rd – **third.** Our third attempt to find an agent was successful.
4th – **fourth.** He is our fourth distributor in as many years **(i.e. in four years).**
21st – **twenty-first.** These products will take us into the twenty-first century.
100th – **(one) hundredth.** Our (one) hundredth trade fair.
101st – **(one) hundred and first**
1000th – **(one) thousandth**
1000000th – **(one) millionth**

Note also:
*next last (an)other additional*
The next/last five years will be/were critical. **(*not*: five next/last years)**
We need another/an additional two weeks to finalise the designs.
We have invited another person. **(One more person has been invited.)**
We have invited five other people. **(other can mean more or different)**
We have invited another five people. **(five more people)**

**3 Fractions and decimals**

Here are some examples:

½ – **(a) half.** Over (a) half (of) our present collection is made in France.
⅓ – **a/one-third.** We can usually offer a discount of one-third off the list price.
⅔ – **two-thirds.** Over two-thirds of our workers live in the village.
¼ – **(a) quarter.** The earliest starting time is (a) quarter past seven.
¾ – **three-quarters.** It takes me three-quarters of an hour to walk to the office.
⅒ – **a/one tenth.** This represents a tenth of our investment.
1½ – **one and a half.** The whole process takes one and a half hours/one hour and a half. **(*not*: one and a half hour)**

2.5 – **two point five**
3.75 – **three point seven five (*not*: seventy-five)**
26.012 – **twenty-six point zero (or 'oh') one two**

**4 Frequency expressions**

*once twice three times four times*
We meet our major customers twice a year.

## C Uses

**1 Dates**

Notice the difference between the written and the spoken forms and between British and American English:

We opened our new office on 5 April 1993 (BrE written) *or* on the fifth of April, nineteen ninety-three *or* on April the fifth, nineteen ninety-three (BrE spoken).

We opened our new office on April 5th 1993 (AmE written) *or* on April fifth, nineteen ninety-three (AmE spoken).

5/4/1993 5 April 1993, i.e. date/month/year (BrE written)
4/5/1993 5 April 1993, i.e. month/date/year (AmE written)

**2 Times**

Notice the written and spoken forms:

The meeting will start at 9.00/9.00 a.m/9 o'clock (written) *or* at nine a.m./9 o'clock (spoken).

The meeting will finish at 4.30 p.m./16.30 (written) *or* at four thirty p.m./half past four/sixteen thirty (spoken).

There will be cocktails for 1½ hours from 5.45/17.45 (written) *or* for one and a half hours/an hour and a half from five forty-five/(a) quarter to six/seventeen forty-five (spoken).

**3 Dimensions and specifications**

Below are some expressions in both the written and spoken forms:

**a** *Money:*

£125 – a/one hundred and twenty-five pounds
$1m – a/one million dollars
DM 1 bn – a/one billion German marks (1 billion=1,000 million)

**b** *Dimensions:*

Distance:
1 mm – a/one millimetre
10 cm – ten centimetres
5 m – five metres
7.5 km – seven point five kilometres
2 m × 5 m – two metres by five metres

Mass:
10 g – ten grams
1,000 kg – a/one thousand kilos/kilograms

Square measure:
100 $cm^2$ – a/one hundred square centimetres
10,000 $m^2$ – ten thousand square metres

Capacity measure:
10 cl – ten centilitres
2 l – two litres

Cubic measure:
1,000 $cm^3$ – a/one thousand cubic centimetres
100 $m^3$ – a/one hundred cubic metres

**c** *Mathematical symbols:*

2 + 2 – two and/plus two
= 4 – is/equals/is equal to four
– 2 – minus/less two
× 6 – times/multiplied by six
÷ 3 – divided by three
/2 – divided by two
( ) – brackets
{ } – braces
[ ] – square brackets
< > – angle brackets

> – is greater than
< – is less than
≡ – is identical with/is equivalent to
≈ – is approximately equal to
$2^2$ – two squared
$2^3$ – two cubed
$2^4$ – two to the power four
$2^n$ – two to the power *n*
$\sqrt{4}$ – the square root of four
$\sqrt[3]{27}$ – the cube root of twenty-seven

# UNIT 68

## NUMERALS

*Notes*

1 **And** in numbers (BrE):
175 – a/one hundred *and* seventy-five (BrE)
175 – a/one hundred seventy-five (AmE)
1005 – a/one thousand *and* five (BrE); a/one thousand five (AmE)

2 Singular and plural forms:
**Hundred, thousand** and **million** need **a** or **one** in the singular:
About a/one hundred people came to the meeting. (*not*: hundred)

**Hundred, thousand** and **million** do not take a plural **-s** in precise numbers or after quantifiers, e.g. **several, a few**:
$500 – five hundred dollars (*not*: five hundreds *or* five hundreds of)
several million pounds (*not*: several millions of pounds)

**Hundred, thousand** and **million** take a plural **-s** when the number is not precise or after **many**:
hundreds of customers
thousands of enquiries
many millions of dollars

3 In approximations we put the smaller number first:
four or five hundred people (*not*: five or four hundred people)

4 **Another** versus **different**
Would you like another glass of wine? (one more glass)
The wine tasted quite different from what I expected. (*not*: quite another)

5 **Next** versus **nearest**
We use **next** to mean 'the nearest in time':
We will display our next collection at the Paris fashion show.

But we say:
In the near future (*not*: in the next future)

We use **nearest** to mean 'the next in distance, time, degree and quality':
Do you know where the nearest chemist is, please? (*not*: next chemist)
The nearest colour to your sample is this one here.

## Exercise 1

*Write how you would say the following numbers.*

| | | |
|---|---|---|
| 1,000,000 | 5,000,000,000 | 4,385,567 |
| US $5.3 m | DM 7.2bn | Yen 5,753 |
| $10.20 | £100 | £3.99 |
| 4.56 | ¼ | ⅞ |
| 3,156 | 3.156 | |
| 26°C | 1250°C | |
| 44.5 kg | 22.47 g | |
| 102 km | 500 m | 225 cm |

## Exercise 2

*Hannah Dobson is a marketing consultant who is out of the office today. Her assistant, Pierre, takes down the following notes from a telephone conversation about a seminar Hannah has to attend in a few weeks' time. Later Hannah telephones Pierre and he gives her the message. Below are his exact words. Fill in the spaces by writing all the numbers as Pierre would* ***say*** *them. The first two are done for you.*

Seminar: Marketing 2000

Dates: 23/05/95 and 22/06/95
Time: 10.30 – 15.00

Room 204
Harrow Conference Centre
189 Beechlands Parade
N10 17EG

Tel: 081 299 5055

Cost: £195 + 17.5% VAT
No. of participants: 80–100

Lunch (1½ hours) served in Black Swan Hotel £17.50

'Hannah? There's an important message about the Marketing Two Thousand conference. It's on the twenty-third of May and on __________. It starts at __________ and finishes at __________. It's in room __________ at the Harrow Conference Centre which is at __________ Beechlands Parade, N __________ EG. The phone number is __________. The cost for each participant is __________ VAT and there will be between __________ and __________ participants. Finally, the lunch, which lasts for __________, will be at the Black Swan Hotel and will cost __________.'

## Exercise 3

*Explain the following information to a colleague. Write down exactly what you say.*

| Forecast sales | Actual sales | % change |
|---|---|---|
| 120,000 units | 103,764 units | –13.53% |
| $1.75m | $1.59m | –9.14% |

The actual sales were __________ units compared with the forecast sales of __________, a percentage difference of __________. In terms of turnover, actual turnover was __________, compared with the forecast turnover of __________, a drop of __________ per cent on the forecast.

## Transfer

*Practise reading numbers from any document you can find, such as product specifications, financial details, economic trends, etc.*

# UNIT 69

## TIME (1)

*See also* Unit 70 – Time (2)

### A *Sample sentences*

- We expect to receive a reply to our request in two weeks.
- The delegation will arrive at our headquarters at 10.30 sharp.
- Our records show that we despatched the goods on 25 July.

### B *Form*

We can divide prepositions of time into:

1 time-when prepositions, which answer the question: 'When did it happen?'
2 time-duration prepositions, which answer the question: 'How long did it last?'

1 **Time-when prepositions (see Unit 70):**
*at in on by during before after between*

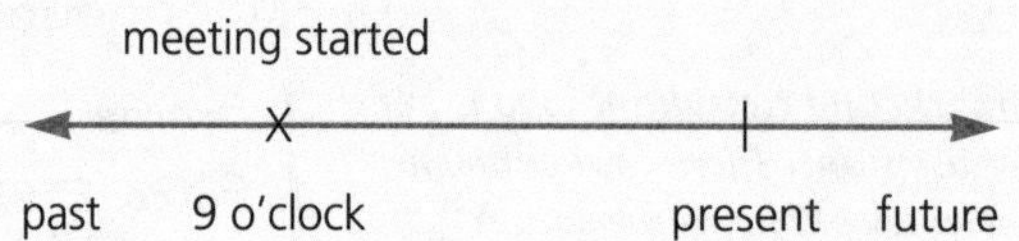


The meeting started at 9 o'clock. (point of time when the meeting started)

2 **Time-duration prepositions (see Unit 70):**
*from … to … up to until till for*

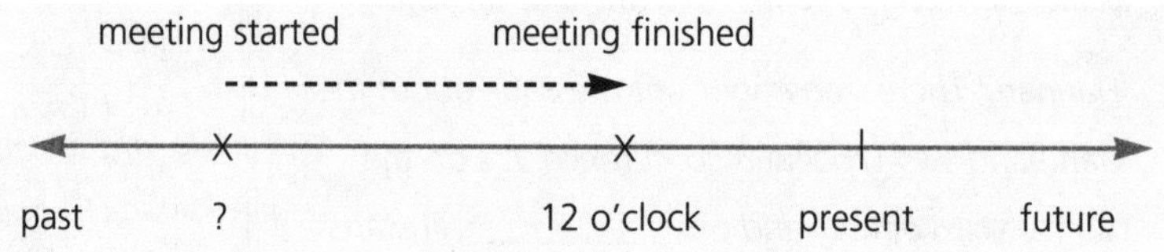


The meeting lasted until 12 o'clock.

### C *Uses*

1 **At, in, on** and **by**:

**At** + clock time
at 6 o'clock
**On** + days of the week
on Monday
on Thursday afternoon
**In** + parts of the day
in the morning/afternoon/evening
*but*: at night

**On** + dates
on 3rd May (spoken: on the third of May)
**In** + months and years
in May
in 1992 (spoken: in nineteen ninety-two)
**By** + a deadline
It must be finished by 1 January. (at the latest)

*Note*: **in time** = in sufficient time with time to spare and **on time** = punctually.

2 **By** and **until/till**:
We use **by** for an action which happens at or before a deadline:
We plan to complete testing by 1 January.

We use **until** or **till** for an action which continues up to a deadline:
We plan to continue testing until/till 1 January.

3 Omission of time preposition:
- **a** before **this, last** and **next** when we use the above words in relation to now:
this evening (not: on this evening); last week (*not*: in last week)
- **b** in phrases beginning with **yesterday** and **tomorrow**:
yesterday afternoon (*not*: in yesterday afternoon); tomorrow morning
- **c** in expressions indicating the time frame:
I travel abroad 60 days a year. (*not*: in a year)
The plane flies at 200 kilometres an hour. (*not*: in an hour)
*but* The equipment can fill 200 bottles (in) an hour.

## Exercise 1

*Underline all the time prepositions and label them TW (time-when) or TD (time-duration).*

The night shift comes on at 10 p.m. and works for eight hours, so the morning shift starts at 8 a.m. Staff work continuously, with no official breaks during the eight hours, but in practice there are opportunities for short breaks during the shift.

During the night most of the work is routine maintenance and only 20 or so workers are on duty. In the morning when the day shift starts we work at 80 per cent of full production capacity. Well, at least we do in the summer and autumn months, up until about the end of November when production is reduced to about 60 per cent.

We don't work on Sundays of course – the factory closes, except in an emergency.

## Exercise 2

*Complete the spaces in the following with an appropriate preposition. If no preposition is needed, leave the space blank.*

1 *The meeting will be held ________ 5th July 1994.*
2 *The project began ________ June.*
3 *We'll have a 20-minute break ________ 4 o'clock.*
4 *The report won't be ready ________ we've collected all the field survey data.*
5 *The work, which has already started, will be finished ________ the end of the week at the latest.*
6 *Make sure you've read the survey before our meeting ________ next week.*
7 *We'll work all day and relax ________ the evening.*

## Exercise 3

*Write an appropriate sentence for each of the following time line diagrams. The first has been done for you.*

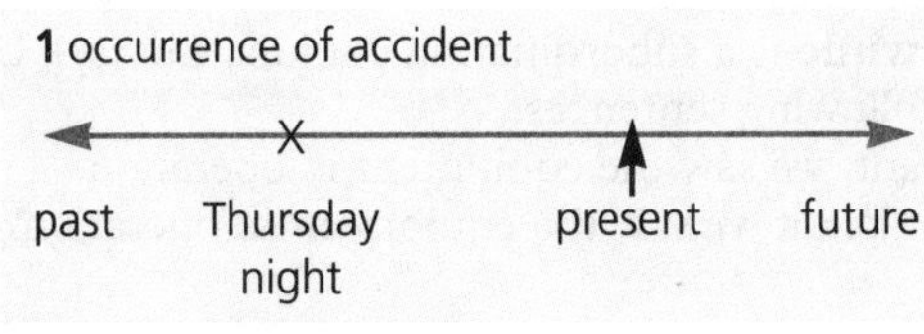


The accident occurred on Thursday night

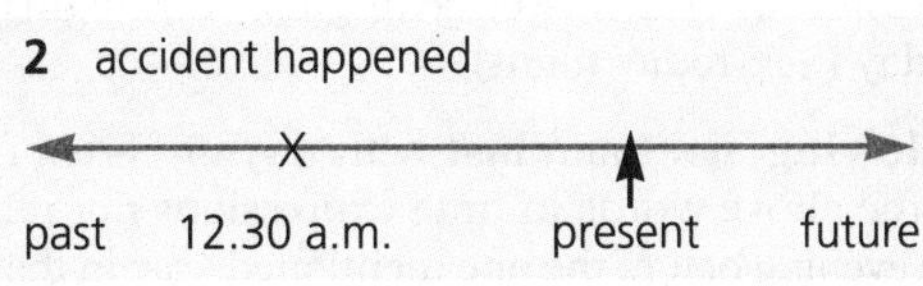


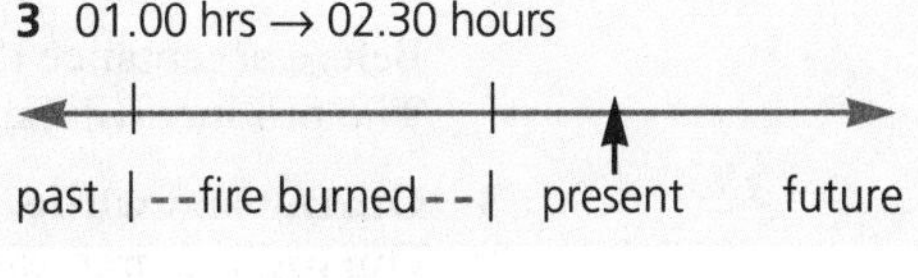


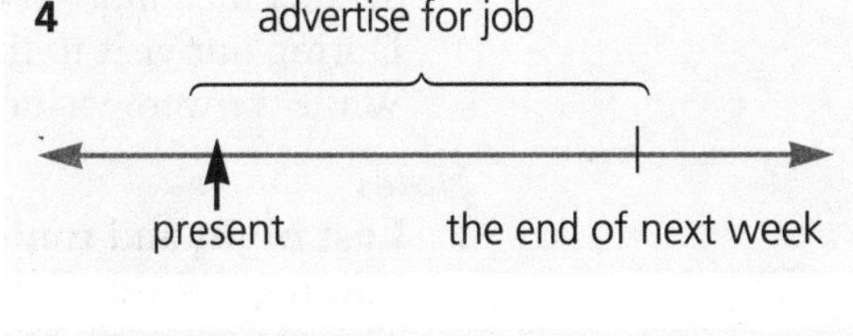


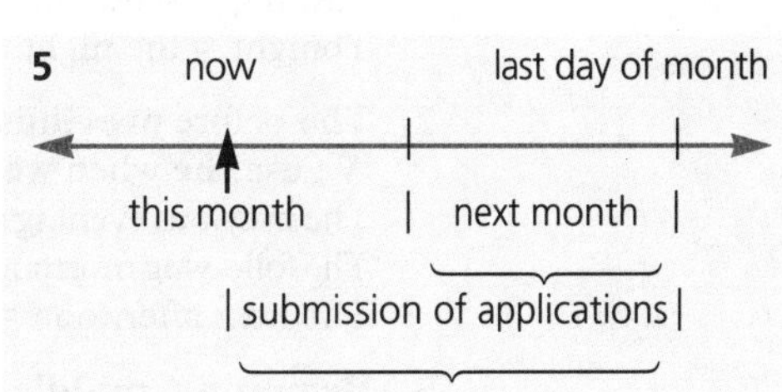


## Transfer

*Describe a typical working day in your company and also any seasonal variation in your company's activities during the year.*

# UNIT 70

## TIME (2)

*See also* Unit 69 – Time (1)

## A *Sample sentences*

- During the last quarter we started to use a new packaging material.
- Next year we are opening a branch office in Minsk.

## B *Form*

See Unit 69.

## C *Uses*

1 **For** and **during**:

The meeting lasted for two hours.
(length of activity)

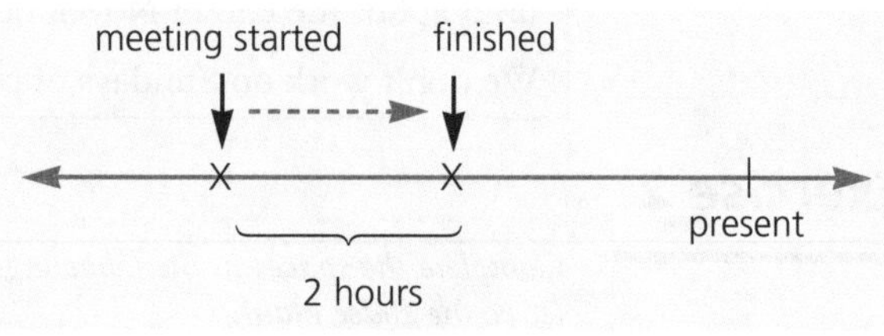


During the meeting we had a short adjournment.
(period within which another activity happened)

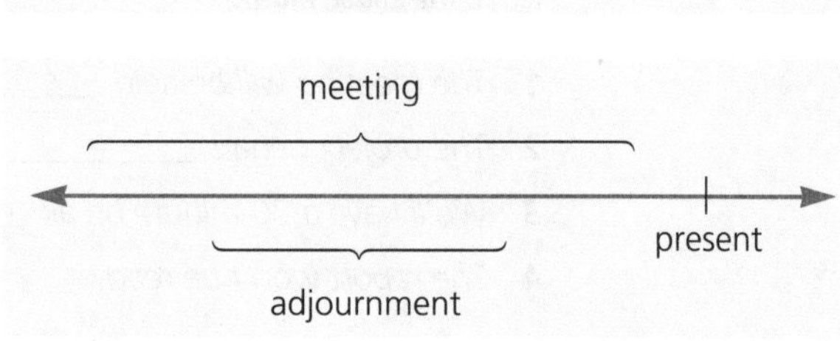


The computer went down during the night.
(period of time providing a time frame when the event happened)

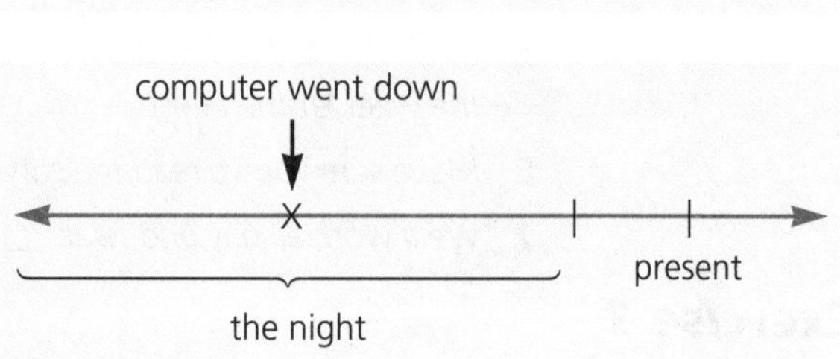


2 **Before** and **after**:

Before acceptance there will be a period of testing.
The product will be maintained by us after signature of the contract.

3 **During** and **while**:
**During** is a preposition; **while** is a subordinating conjunction (see Unit 46). Notice the parallel meanings in the following sentences:
During our visit to the plant, we saw the equipment in operation.
While we were visiting the plant we saw the equipment in operation.

***Notes***

1 **Last night** and **tonight**:
Last night = the night of yesterday (*not*: yesterday night *or* this night)
Tonight = the night of today (*not*: today night)

2 **The** before **previous**, **following**, **next** and **last** with **day** or parts of the day:
We use **the** when we use the above words in time expressions not related to now.
The previous evening = the evening before the one mentioned (*not*: in the previous evening)
The following morning = the morning after the one mentioned (*not*: in the following morning)
The next afternoon = the afternoon after the one mentioned

3 **Beginning**, **middle** and **end**:
At the beginning of the year we commissioned a quality study.
*but*: In the beginning God created the heavens and the earth.
She interrupted us in the middle of the meeting.
At the end of the contract there is a clause you should read.
In the end and after much discussion they agreed to the new terms. (finally)

## Exercise 1

*Are the following sentences right or wrong? If wrong, make the necessary correction.*

1 We finished the project on time; so we had three days to spare.
2 We worked on the study for two weeks.
3 While the two-week period, we had no technical support at all.
4 Before to start on the next study, there will be a short training course.
5 The next year we are sure to see the results of our efforts.
6 The following day they agreed to sign the contract without any conditions.

## Exercise 2

*Put a suitable preposition into the blanks so that your completed sentences are chronologically and grammatically correct. The first one has been done for you.*

1 *We completed the user study in January.* ___After___ *this stage we moved on to the market study.*
2 *Unfortunately the user study overran by one week. The reason was that* _________ *the analysis stage, we encountered some unexpected problems with the data.*
3 *So we finally managed to input all the data* _________ *15 January.*
4 *We continued to receive data output* _________ *another week.*
5 *Naturally we had to verify the results* _________ *we could hand over the results to the client.*
6 *So* _________ *the beginning and the end of the project we needed a total of 8 weeks.*
7 _________ *the beginning of our first meeting, the client told us that time was of the essence;* _________ *the middle I explained about the unexpected problems. So,* _________ *the end I don't think the overrun will be a significant factor.*

## Exercise 3

*Below is an extract from the log of Sygma II, an oil platform in the North Sea. Complete the text by writing suitable prepositions in the gaps.*

_________ the day the sea had been very rough. _________ 16.00 the helicopter arrived bringing the replacement drillers. These were needed as 2 of our crew had gone sick _________ the previous night. The new drillers are to stay with us _________ the end of next week. They have just worked _________ 2 months onshore and are happy to have a change. _________ the evening the sea calmed down and we were able to start working comfortably again. However, just _________ the evening shift started, the computer went down again. The computer technicians were called in and _________ 22.00 they had the computer running again. _________ that, there were no problems _________ the night shift. The morning shift reported for duty _________ time at 06.00.

## Transfer

*Murphy's law states, 'If anything can go wrong, it will.' Write about one such occasion in the form of a log and use as many prepositions of time as possible.*

# UNIT 71

## PLACE

### A *Sample sentences*

- When you arrive, drive into the car park and leave your car in the visitors' parking area.
- First we take the chips from the belt here and put them onto a work bench.
- The waste materials are deposited on this surface here. Finally they are taken to the disposal unit.

### B *Form*

We use a preposition before a noun or noun phrase:
into the parking area
from the belt

We can divide prepositions of place into:
1 place prepositions
2 position prepositions
3 movement prepositions

**1 Place prepositions**
The preposition we use depends on our view of an object. The object may be :

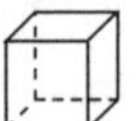
a volume with three dimensions of height, length and width, e.g. a room, a carton

a surface with two dimensions of length and width, e.g. a page, a shelf

an area enclosed by boundaries, e.g. a car park, a garden

a line with one dimension of length, e.g. a conveyor belt, a motorway

a location without any specific dimensions, e.g. a meeting, work

So we have the following prepositions:

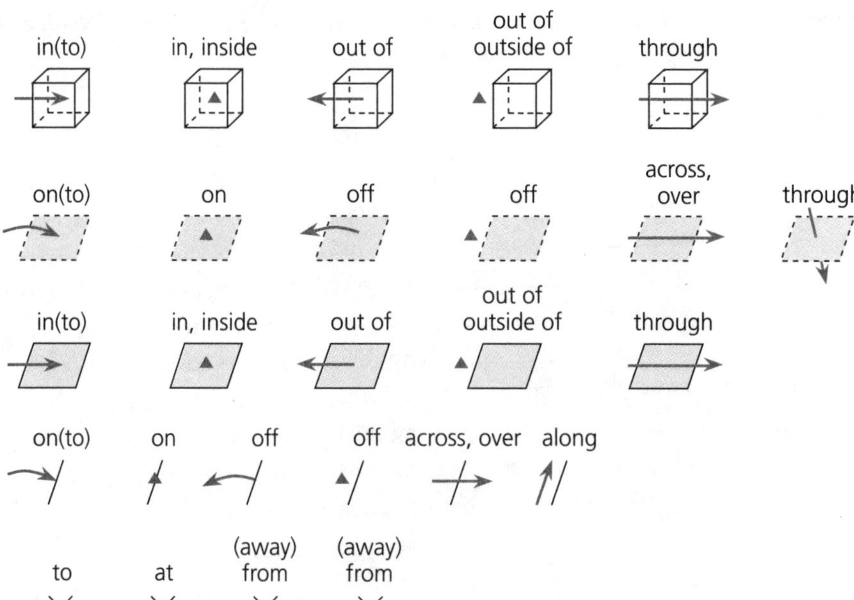

2 **Position prepositions**
These describe the relative position between two objects. The main prepositions are:

| | | | | | |
|---|---|---|---|---|---|
| *above* | *below* | *over* | *under* | *in front of* | *behind* |
| *by* | *beside* | *on top of* | *beneath* | *next to* | |

The warehouse is next to the production area.
The despatch area is behind the visitors' car park.

***Notes***
**Over/under** and **above/below**:
We normally use **over** and **under** to describe a direct vertical relationship:
This new device works equally well under a table or any other piece of furniture.

We use **above** and **below** to say that one object is higher or lower than another:
300 metres below sea level
20 degrees above zero

3 **Movement prepositions**
The main prepositions are:

| | | | | | |
|---|---|---|---|---|---|
| *into* | *out of* | *towards* | *away from* | *along* | *through* |
| *behind* | *in front of* | *along* | *across* | *over* | *onto* |
| *up* | *down* | *around* | *outside* | | |

If you walk along the corridor, you'll come to my office on your left.
Just walk straight into the room.

## C *Uses*

In addition to the above rules, notice the following expressions:

1 With **at**:
At the top/bottom of the next page
At the beginning/end of the contract
At the front/back of the factory
The train arrived at the station twenty minutes late. (arrive **at** a building)
*cf.* We arrived in London just as the results were being announced.
(arrive **in** a country or city)
He was at university until he was 28. (*also*: at school/work)
She started work at 16/at the age of 16.
At last the engineer has found the fault.

2 With **in**:
She is in the UK/in London. (with countries, towns and villages)
He is in hospital for a check-up. (He is a patient.)
*cf.* He is at the hospital. (He is visiting, i.e. not a patient.)
She is in prison/church/school/work. (i.e. institutions)
She is in business/computers/plastics/medicine. (showing type of employment)

3 With **on**:
Take the first turning on the left/right. (*not*: on the left side)
You'll find my office on the ground floor.
The printout is on top of the computer.
London is on the river Thames.

4 **In** versus **into** versus **to**:
We drove in France. (inside France)
We drove into France. (We entered France from another country.)
We drove to France. (France was our destination by car.)

5 **To have been to**:
Have you ever been to the USA? (**have been** + **to** = to have gone and returned from, i.e. Have you ever visited ...?)

# TASKS 71

## PLACE

### Exercise 1

*Complete the spaces in the following conversation using words from the box. You will have to use some of the words more than once.*

| at through over in to from on near along around out of across |
|---|

A: What field of business are you __________ ?

B: Computers.

A: Oh, that's interesting. I have a sister who used to be __________ computing but she's __________ prison now.

B: Prison?

A: Yes – software fraud.

B: Oh dear! Are you American?

A: No, I'm __________ Canada. And you?

B: Florence, Italy.

A: Oh how beautiful. I was there a few years ago with my wife.

B: Really?

A: Yes, we flew __________ London, hired a car __________ the airport, had a look __________ London, took a ferry __________ the Channel, drove __________ France, __________ the Alps …

B: You didn't go __________ Monte Bianco?

A: Mont Blanc? No, we went a longer route, __________ Col di Tenda. Then we drove south __________ Florence. What's the river __________ Florence? I never remember.

B: The Arno.

A: Oh yes, Florence is __________ the Arno.

B: Where did you stay?

A: I don't remember, __________ a hotel. Maybe __________ the Grand Hotel, is that possible?

B: The Grand? No, I don't know that one. Did you go anywhere else __________ Italy?

A: Sure – we went __________ Rome. We walked __________ the Via Appia Antica for six hours! It was wonderful! Then we had to leave. We flew __________ Rome.

B: It sounds a good trip.

A: It was great! Say, have you ever been __________ Canada?

B: Yes I have. I stayed with a friend __________ Vancouver – about 40 miles away.

## Exercise 2

*The text below describes the processing of sugar beet to make sugar and animal feed. Fill the spaces in the text with an appropriate preposition from the box. You may have to use some of the words more than once.*

| out of | outside | onto | into | along | off | in |
|---|---|---|---|---|---|---|

*The beet is taken __________ lorries and stored __________ piles __________ the processing area. The beet is sent __________ a system of channels __________ the processing area. It is shredded and dried __________ a huge cylindrical drier. Dried shreds of beet are packed __________ bags and sold as animal feed. The sacks of animal feed are stored __________ a large warehouse before being loaded __________ lorries for despatch. The main sugar production involves treating the liquid sugar which comes __________ the beet __________ the drying process.*

## Transfer

*Write a short description of a process you are familiar with. Your chosen process could relate to any of the following: production, payment, distribution, research, etc.*

# UNIT 72

## LIKE, AS and SUCH AS

### A Sample sentences

- As I said on the phone, we are looking for agents who can handle our goods.
- She has been employed as a training officer for the last three years.
- We specialise in areas like preparing business plans and raising risk capital.

### B Form

Both **like** and **as** are prepositions. **As** is also a subordinating conjunction (see Unit 38).

### C Uses

Both **as** and **like** mean 'the same as' or 'similar to'.

1 **As**:
She works as a training officer. (That is her real job.)
As I said on the phone, we are looking for agents. (**as** + subject + verb; *not*: **like** + subject + verb)
The prices are as shown in our catalogue. (= those shown in the catalogue)
The documents enclosed are as follows: first the agent's letter to us and second our reply to them. (= those now to be specified)
We use credit cards, such as American Express and Visa. (for example)

2 **Like**:
Her office is so beautifully decorated that it is like a film set. (It is not really a film set.)
We use credit cards like American Express and Visa. (such as)
We specialise in areas like preparing business plans and raising risk capital. (*not*: **to prepare**, because **like** is a preposition and is therefore followed by verb *...ing* – see Unit 13)
We are not like them at all because our customers are small firms. (= similar to; notice the object pronoun after the preposition **like** – see Unit 59)

3 **Like** versus **as**:
After the restructuring we started to operate as a profit centre. (= we became a profit centre)
After the restructuring we started to operate like a profit centre. (but we did not actually become a profit centre)

## Exercise 1

*In the following passage, label the uses of **as** with **C** (for conjunction) or **P** (for preposition).*

As you know, we have an important decision to make. As we plan for the new year, we have to decide if we want to continue advertising through sponsorship, as we did this year, or change our policy. As sponsorship is expensive, to stay with it is not a small decision. On the other hand, other forms of advertising, television as much as printed word advertising, may be less effective. As marketing manager, I do of course have a personal view on this.

## Exercise 2

*The following extract is part of a memo from a marketing manager of a European subsidiary to his Head Office in the United States.*

We use sales staff who work as independent operators. They cooperate with our branches which operate like independent businesses.

The marketing consultant we use works as a freelancer. He recommended advertising in a magazine like *Construction Weekly*.

He wants to see a report such as an annual report. The report I sent yesterday is exactly the same as our weekly sales review.

*Now mark the following as TRUE or FALSE.*

1 Our sales staff are not actually independent operations.
2 Our branches are not really independent, but they work in a way that is similar to independent operations.
3 We use a marketing consultant who is independent from us.
4 He suggested advertising in *Construction Weekly*.
5 He wants to see a report which is similar to an annual report.
6 The report was just like the annual sales review.

## Exercise 3

*Complete the spaces in the following sentences with an appropriate word or words.*

*The Munich Trade Fair was __________ successful __________ in previous years. The last day was __________ a carnival – there was such optimism from everyone involved. A fair always has useful advantages, __________ meeting new customers, seeing competitors' work, meeting friends and of course it gets a lot of publicity. But a lasting benefit is always that a good stand at an international exhibition __________ Munich clearly shows that we are a leading player in the world market. __________ we know, a high profile is essential to maintain our reputation for strength in the market.*

## Transfer

*Write five sentences about yourself including **as, like** or **such as**.*

# PART 2

# FUNCTIONS

# UNIT 73

# CLASSIFYING INFORMATION

## A Sample sentences

- We can divide our services into local, national and international.
- Our forecasts can be classified as long-range or medium-range.
- There are four types of management activity: planning, leading, organising, and controlling.
- We need to look at all the parts of the contract, from the preamble to the arbitration clause.

## B Form

We can classify information according to its *types* and its *parts*.

1 The types:
There are two types of events: those that may happen and those that definitely will happen.
Other nouns with the same meaning:
*sorts varieties kinds*

We can divide our services into local, national and international.
Other verbs with similar meanings:
*classify as split into sort into fall into*

2 The parts:
We need to look at all the parts of the contract.
Other nouns with similar meanings:
*elements stages steps*

The whole manufacturing process consists of four steps.
Other verbs with similar meanings:
*comprise contain involve be divided into*
*be broken down into be made up of*

## C Uses

1 Describing the types:
We can divide business plans into strategic and tactical.
Our range of services falls into three main categories.
The psychoanalyst Jung classified people as thinkers, sensors, intuitors or feelers.

2 Describing the parts:
The raw materials we use consist of both imported and locally produced items.
The locally produced items comprise electrical and mechanical components.
Our operation involves promotion and distribution.

***Notes***

1 The department comprises six teams. (*not:* comprises of)
2 At the moment the department consists of six teams. (*not:* is consisting of)

# CLASSIFYING INFORMATION

## Exercise 1

*Read the paragraph below then complete the labelling of the chart.*

Harland Computer Services (HCS) provides two main services. The first is consultancy, the second is computer software. The consultancy arm of the company is split into two categories: specific task applications (STAs) and system planning (SP). The software production is divided into three separate departments: standard applications (SA), customised solutions (CS) and research and development for innovative software solutions (RDISS).

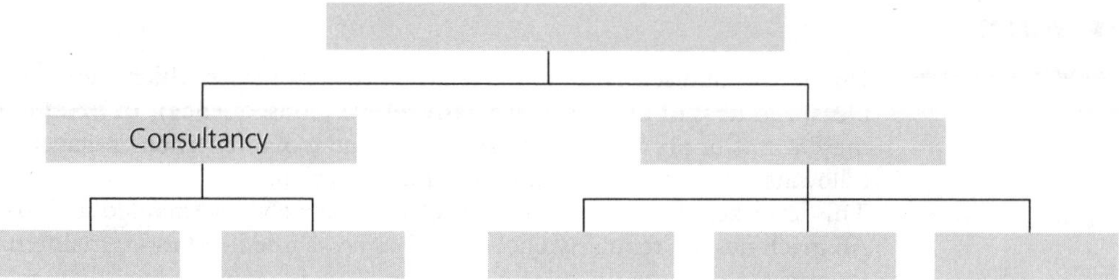


## Exercise 2

*The following sentences contain mistakes. Underline the mistakes and then correct them.*

1 The products can be divided in four types.
2 The market is consisting of four main categories of product.
3 The company's research projects fall in two main kinds.
4 The Communications Department comprises of three different sections.
5 The first stage of the project is broken down by three parts: preliminary enquiries, technical research and scheduling.
6 There are several stage in the project.

## Exercise 3

*Chemco Incorporated is a large industrial group based in Detroit, USA. The main product areas are:*

**a** Chemicals (acids, fluorides, chlorides, etc).
**b** Paints and varnishes (emulsions, oil paints, gloss paints, wood-treating liquids).
**c** Oils (lubricants, engine oils).
**d** Pharmaceuticals (prescription drugs, over-the-counter (OTC) drugs).
**e** Foods (cooking oils, food preservatives, colourings, flavourings).
**f** Fertilisers (nitrogen-based fertilisers, phosphates).

*Use the prompts below to write sentences which classify Chemco products.*

1 Chemco production/be divided into/six areas
2 Paints and Varnishes Division/consist of/types
3 Chemicals Division/split into/kinds
4 Oils Division/comprise/varieties
5 Pharmaceuticals Division/involve/categories
6 Foods Division/contain/types
7 Fertilisers Division/be classified into/sorts

## Transfer

*Describe a basic classification of the products or services of a company that you know well.*

# UNIT 74 CONNECTING and SEQUENCING IDEAS

*See also* **Unit 36 – Sentence types: simple and complex**
**Unit 37 – Connecting ideas**
**Unit 38 – Subordinate clauses**
**Unit 78 – Equating and including ideas**

## A *Sample sentences*

◆ First I'd like to show you round the plant; after that you'll have a chance to see the workshops. In particular, I'd like you to spend some time with the apprentices, which was not in the original programme. Therefore the demonstration of the RD567 will take place a little later than planned.

## B *Form*

Connectors and sequence markers are words or phrases which show the relationship between ideas, e.g. **first of all** (sequence), **therefore** (consequence), **in brief** (summary). We put these words or phrases at or near the beginning of a sentence or clause. They connect the following information with the earlier information:

This lever here has been a little unreliable. *So* we've overhauled it. (cause)
All machines are regularly checked. *However*, some need more maintenance than others. (contrast)
*After* visiting the workshops, there'll be time to talk to the apprentices. (time)
*In brief*, the visit today is intended to give you an overview of our activities and an opportunity to talk to the workers on the shopfloor. (summary of two main points)

We can use connectors and sequence markers to signal different types of relationships between ideas. The main relationships are:

1 time
2 logic (cause, contrast, condition, comparison and concession – see Units 37 and 38)
3 text (addition, summary, paraphrase, example and highlight)

## C *Uses*

Below are the main words and phrases for the above relationships.

1 To signal time relationships:
Beginning
*First first of all initially to start with the first step at the first stage*
*Second secondly the second step at the second stage*
*Third thirdly the third step at the third stage*
*Then after that*
*Next subsequently the next step at the next stage*
*Finally the final step at the final stage*
End

Other language forms:
**before** + verb *...ing* (see Unit 13):
Before visiting the plant, I'll give you a short explanation of what you'll see.
**after** + verb *...ing* (see Unit 13):
After visiting the plant, there'll be time for questions.
**(after) having** + verb *...ed*:
(After) having visited the plant, you'll have a much better idea of our plans.

2 To signal logical relationships:
The main categories are given below and you will find the connectors and sequence markers in Appendix 9.
*cause comparison concession contradiction*
*condition alternation contrast*

3 To signal textual relationships:
The main categories are given below and you will find the connectors and sequence markers in Appendix 9.
*addition summary conclusion equivalence inclusion*
*highlight generalisation stating the obvious*

# CONNECTING and SEQUENCING IDEAS

## Exercise 1

*Classify the words and phrases listed below, depending on their use in connecting and sequencing ideas. Then match them with the following headings. There is one example for each type.*

| | | | |
|---|---|---|---|
| *firstly* | *to sum up* | *notably* | *on the whole* |
| *that's why* | *in that case* | *actually* | *anyway* |
| *in the same way* | *instead* | *in addition* | *lastly* |
| *in other words* | *for instance* | *clearly* | *yet* |

| time relationship | cause | contrast | comparison |
|---|---|---|---|
| | | | |
| **concession** | **contradiction** | **alternation** | **addition** |
| | | | |
| **summary** | **conclusion** | **equivalence** | **inclusion** |
| | | | |
| **highlight** | **generalisation** | **condition** | **stating the obvious** |
| | | | |

## Exercise 2

*Read the following extract from a politician's speech about energy production. Identify and underline 13 examples of connecting ideas or sequencing. Indicate what kinds of relationship are illustrated by each example. Select from the different types listed in the box opposite.*

| | |
|---|---|
| time relationship (TR) | generalisation (GEN) |
| stating the obvious (OBV) | contrast (CONTRA) |
| cause (CAUSE) | condition (COND) |
| contradiction (CONTRAD) | summary (SUM) |
| equivalence (EQUI) | inclusion (INC) |
| highlight (HL) | |

'To begin with we need to consider the long-term implications of the decision to increase our dependence on gas-fired energy production. For example, let us say we do go ahead. In this case we decrease our reliance on coal. As a result we reduce costs because we understand that gas is cheaper than coal. In fact, the case is not proven, especially because we have no way of knowing what the relative costs of coal and gas will be in ten years' time. However, as a rule gas is much cleaner than coal and this is a genuine advantage. As a consequence of these two advantages, gas looks a better option. In other words, it's cheaper and cleaner so it's better. In that case we don't need to hesitate. Naturally, nothing is so simple. In short, cost is an unknown factor. We don't know which would be the most economical choice.'

## Transfer

*Prepare a short presentation of a product or company you know well and include examples of connecting and sequencing ideas. Use the phrases in the box.*

*especially   in conclusion   naturally   then   to sum up   in fact*
*finally   secondly   first of all   as a matter of fact*

# UNIT 75

## DESCRIBING TRENDS

*See also* **Unit 52 – Adjective modification with adverbs**
**Unit 53 – Comparison of adjectives**

### A *Sample sentences*

- Our turnover rose last year, but our profits dropped.
- The banks have raised their interest rates twice this year and this has pushed up the cost of borrowing.
- There has been a slight increase in the value of the dollar, but the pound is down again.

### B *Form*

Trends are changes or movements. These changes are normally in numerical items, e.g. costs, production volumes or unemployment. There are three basic trends.

For each trend there are a number of verbs and nouns to express the movement. We can divide the verbs into *transitive* and *intransitive*. After a transitive verb we must put an object:
The banks have raised their interest rates twice this year.
After an intransitive verb we cannot put a direct object:
Our turnover rose last year, but our profits dropped.

Now let's look at the language of trends in more detail.

1 ↗

| Verbs | | Nouns |
|---|---|---|
| Transitive | Intransitive | |
| increase | increase | increase |
| raise | rise | rise |
| put/push/step up | go/be up | |
| | grow | growth |
| extend | extend | extension |
| expand | expand | expansion |
| | boom | boom (dramatic rise) |

2 

| Verbs | | Nouns |
|---|---|---|
| Transitive | Intransitive | |
| decrease | decrease | decrease |
| | fall | fall |
| drop | drop | drop |
| put/push down | go/be down | |
| | decline | decline |
| cut | | cut |
| reduce | | reduction |
| | collapse | collapse (dramatic fall) |
| | slump | slump (dramatic fall) |

3 

| Verbs | | Nouns |
|---|---|---|
| Transitive | Intransitive | |
| keep/hold … stable/constant | remain stable | stability |
| maintain … (at the same level) | stay constant | |

4 Other expressions

**To stand at:** We use this phrase to focus on a particular point, before we mention the trends of movements:

In the first year sales in our region stood at 109,000 units.

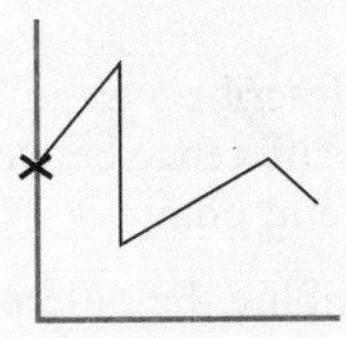

**To reach a peak of**:

In the sixth year sales in our region reached a peak of 24,000 units.

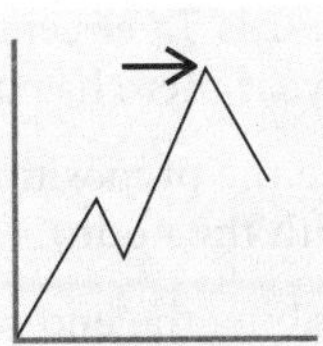

Sometimes we need to give more information about a trend, as follows:
There has been a *slight* increase in the value of the dollar. (the degree of change)
Share prices fell *rapidly* on the London stock exchange today. (the speed of change)
Remember that we modify a noun with an adjective (a *slight* increase); and a verb with an adverb (to increase *slightly*).

Describing the degree of change

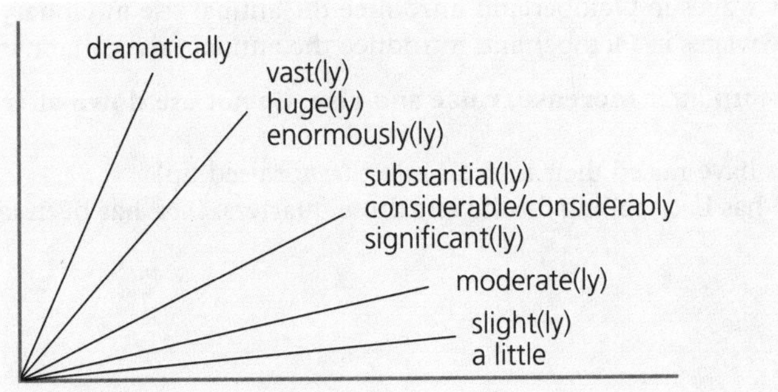


Describing the speed of change

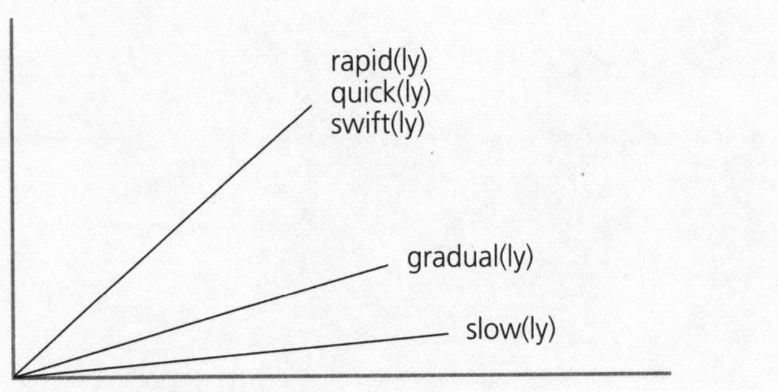


Appendix 10 shows:

- the different types of lines in graphs
- the names for the axes on a graph
- the different types of graphics

## C *Uses*

We can describe a trend by looking at:
- the difference between two levels
- the end point

1 Describing the difference:
This year turnover has increased by 5 per cent. (The difference between this year and last year is 5 per cent)
This year there has been an increase in turnover of 5 per cent.

Notice the prepositions. We use **to increase *by*** (with the verb) and **an increase *of*** (with the noun).

2 Describing the end point:
This year turnover has risen to £3m. (The end result is that turnover is up to £3m.)
This year there has been a rise in turnover to £3m.
Notice the prepositions. We use **to rise *to*** (with the verb) and **a rise *to*** (with the noun).

***Notes***

1 **Rise** and **raise**
(For the use of the verbs, see Unit 29.) Note the following use of the nouns, meaning 'increase in pay':
We review wages in October and introduce the annual rise in January. (BrE)
We review wages in October and introduce the annual raise in January. (AmE)

2 Do not use **up** after **increase**, **raise** and **rise**; do not use **down** after **fall**, **drop** and **decrease**:
The banks have raised their interest rates. (*not*: raised up)
Our GNP has been falling for the last three quarters. (*not*: has been falling down)

## Exercise 1

*The sentences below describe the accompanying graphs. Complete the sentences with the most appropriate of the given alternatives.*

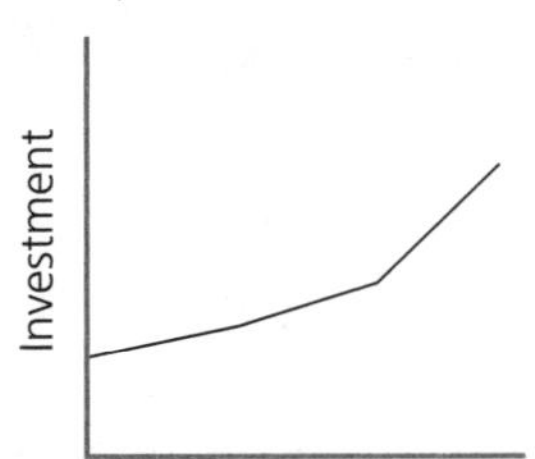


1 Investment shows
 **a** a sharp increase.
 **b** a slight increase.
 **c** a slight fall.

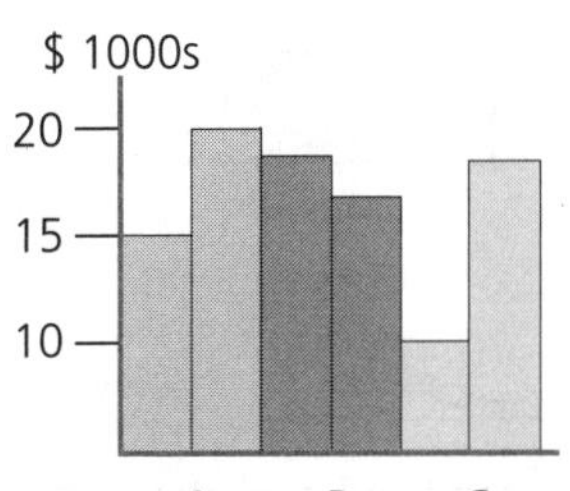


2 Sales of Product A have
 **a** raised by $5000.
 **b** risen by $5000.
 **c** developed by $5000.

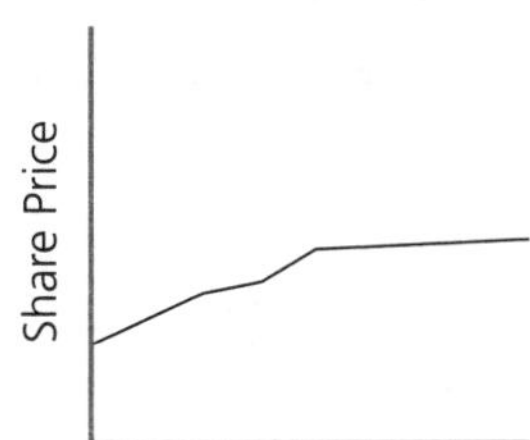


3 After a period of continual increase, the share price
 **a** has remained stable.
 **b** has fallen slightly.
 **c** has expanded.

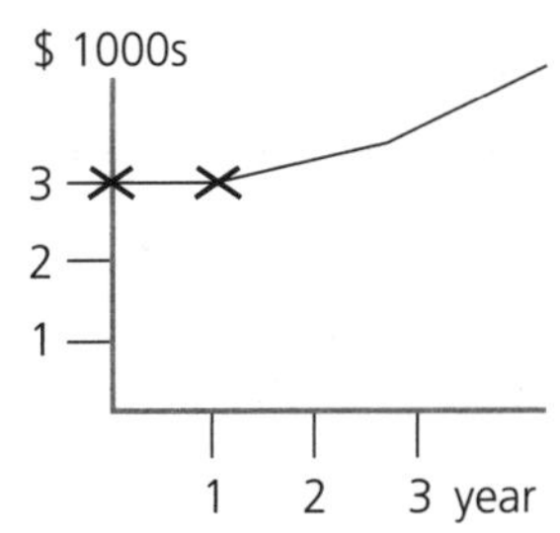


4 In the first year costs
 **a** stood by $3000.
 **b** are standing at $3000.
 **c** stood at $3000.

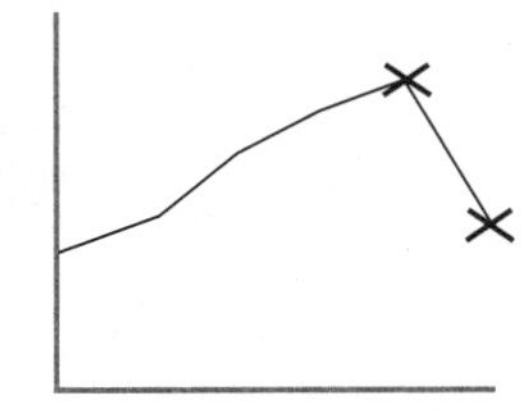

5 The price
 **a** reached a peak and then slumped.
 **b** slumped then reached a peak.
 **c** slumped then grew slowly.

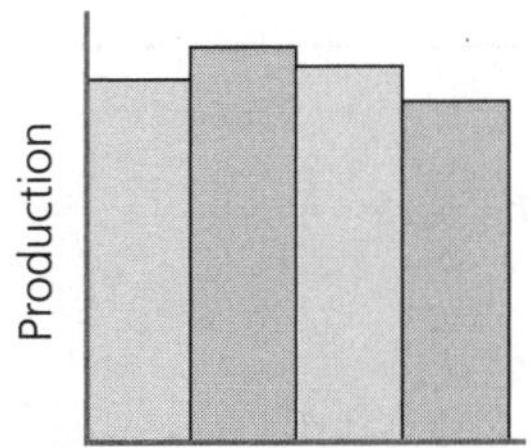


6 The cut in production
 **a** is dramatic
 **b** is very slight.
 **c** is very rapid.

# TASKS 75

## DESCRIBING TRENDS

### Exercise 2

*Match each sentence below to one of the following pictures (a)–(h).*

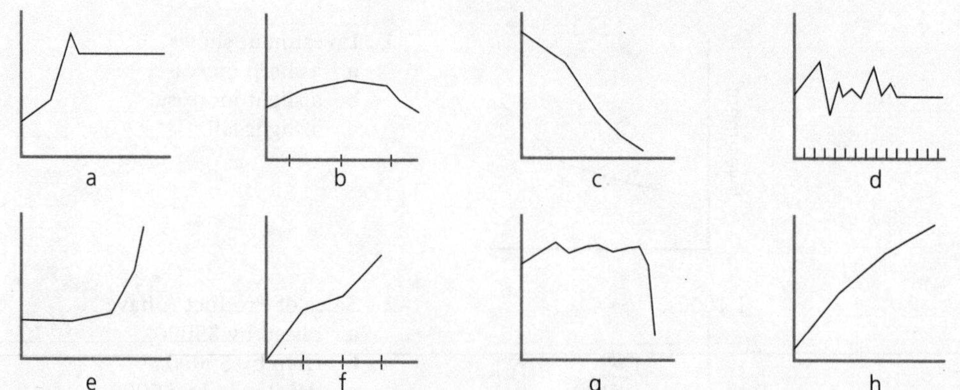


1 The level of investment rose suddenly.

2 Sales of Product A fell slightly in the final quarter.

3 The Research and Development budget has stabilised over the past few years.

4 At the end of the first year sales stood at 50 per cent of the present level.

5 The share price reached a peak before falling a little and then maintaining the same level.

6 There has been a steady increase in costs over several years.

7 The sudden collapse in share prices has surprised everyone.

8 The value of the shares has shown a steady decline.

### Exercise 3

*Look at the graph below then complete the sentences with appropriate words or phrases.*

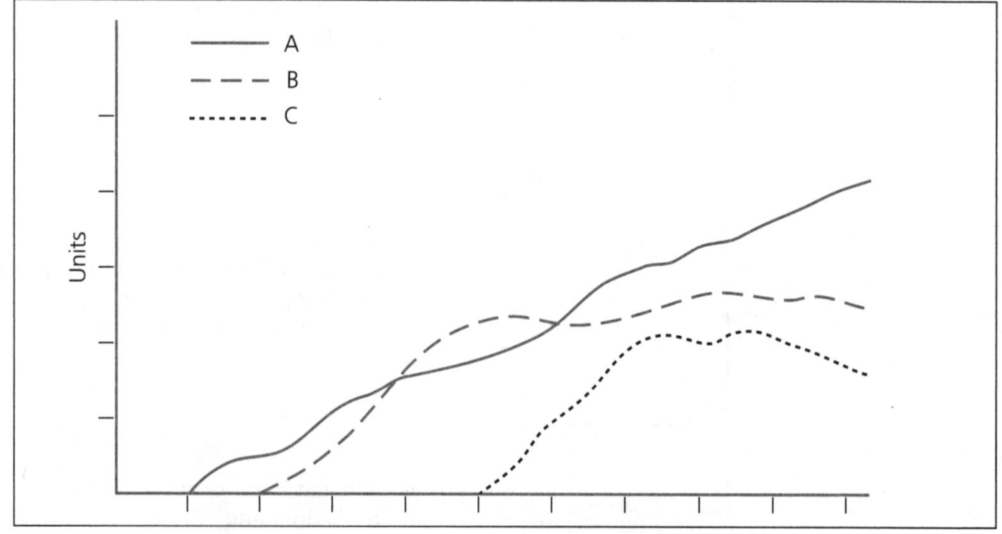


1 *The ________________________ compares the performance of three products, A, B and C.*

2 *The ________________________ shows time over ten years.*

**3** *The* ______________________ *shows the volume of sales in number of units.*

**4** *Product A is represented by the* ______________________.

**5** *The performance of Product B is shown by the* ______________________.

**6** *You can see the performance of Product C in the* ______________________.

**7** *Clearly* ______________________ *is the most successful product.*

**8** *Sales of Product B* ______________________ *in recent years.*

**9** *Sales of Product C* ______________________.

**10** *Product A has shown a* ______________________.

## Transfer

*Draw a graph which shows developing trends. Choose any of the following subjects:*

- company performance
- product sales
- economic trends
- development of tourism, industry or leisure interests

*Then write a short paragraph describing your graph, accounting for its profile.*

# UNIT 76

## DESCRIBING the ORGANISATION

### A Sample sentences

- The company is headed by the Managing Director.
- The Sales Director is supported by a sales team.
- The R & D Department is responsible for new product development.
- The parent company is based in Brussels, with subsidiaries in Frankfurt and Milan.

### B Form and uses

We can describe an organisation in terms of:

- hierarchy
- responsibilities/functions
- titles
- affiliates
- structure

**1 Hierarchy**

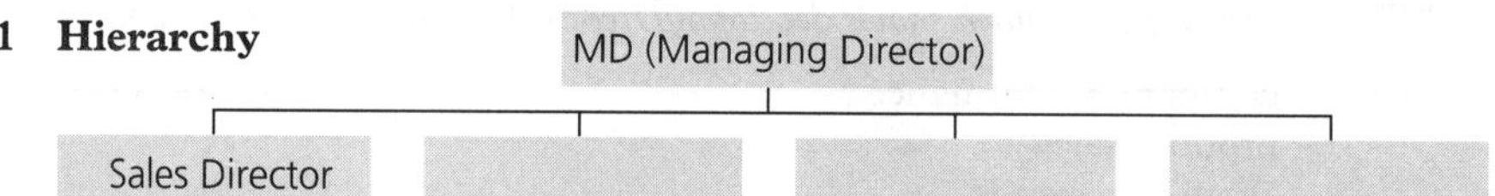


The company *is headed by* the MD.
The Sales Director *reports to* the MD. (*not:* depends on)
The Sales Director *is under* the MD.
The Sales Director *is accountable to* the MD.

The Sales Director *is supported by* a sales team.
The Sales Director *is assisted by* a Sales Assistant.

Sales Director
Sales Team
Sales Assistant

**2 Responsibilities/functions**

The Controller *is responsible for* accounting throughout the company.
The Production Department *takes care of* product manufacturing.
The Factory Manager *is in charge of* plant and equipment.

**3 Titles**

Below are the main managerial titles with common US equivalents in brackets:
*Chairman/Chairperson (President)*
*Managing Director (Chief Executive Officer/Senior Vice-President)*
*Finance Director (Vice-President Finance)*
*Sales Manager (Sales Director)*

***Note:***
The directors and chairman of a company usually sit on the board of directors (executive board).

**4 Affiliates**

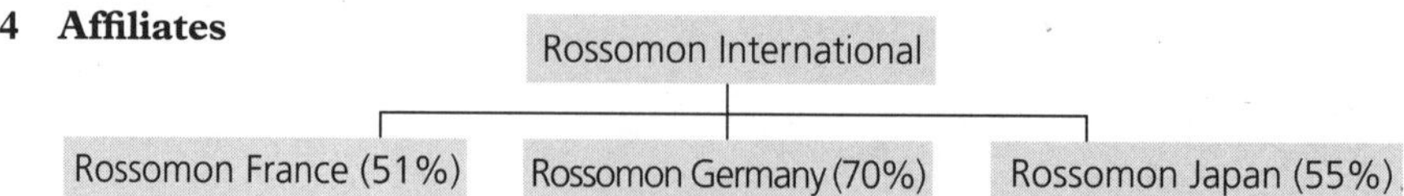


Rossomon International is the *parent company*.
Rossomon France, Rossomon Germany and Rossomon Japan are *subsidiaries* (more than 50 per cent owned by the parent).

**5 Structure**

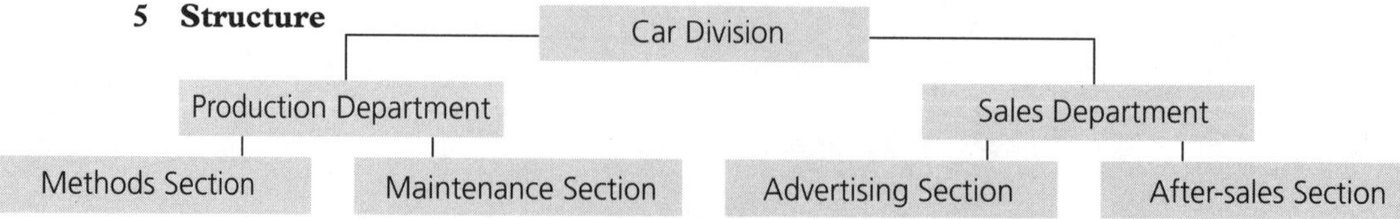

# DESCRIBING the ORGANISATION

## Exercise 1

*This exercise is concerned with describing corporate organisation. Look at the chart below which shows the structure of the DSA Corporation. Then complete the paragraph which follows, using the correct form of the words in the box.*

DSA Corporation (New York)

| Building Materials | | Construction | Civil Engineering |
|---|---|---|---|
| KAF Inc. | Halcon | Conway | RoadCo |

*The DSA Corporation consists of three ______________ , Building Materials, Construction and Civil Engineering. DSA ______________ New York and comprises four ______________ , KAF Inc., Halcon, Conway and RoadCo. Each of these is ______________ a Senior Vice-President who ______________ the ______________ .*

***subsidiary   division   be based in   parent company   be headed by   report to***

## Exercise 2

*This exercise is concerned with describing management hierarchy. The illustration below shows the organisation of KAF Inc. Study the organisation chart, then complete the paragraph which follows, using the correct form of an appropriate word or phrase from the box.*

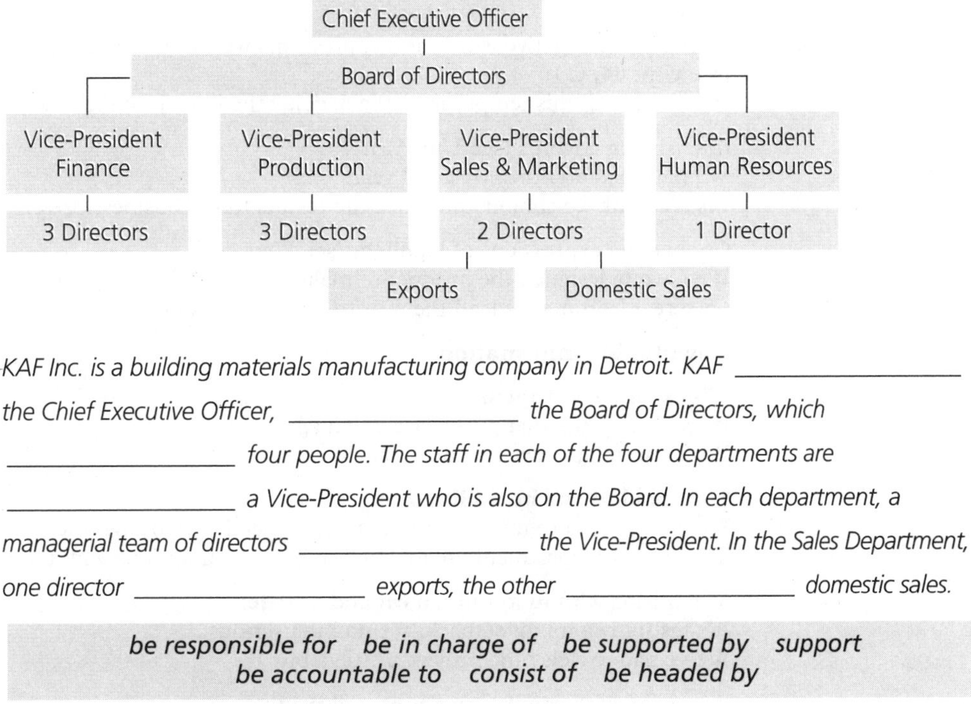


*KAF Inc. is a building materials manufacturing company in Detroit. KAF ______________ the Chief Executive Officer, ______________ the Board of Directors, which ______________ four people. The staff in each of the four departments are ______________ a Vice-President who is also on the Board. In each department, a managerial team of directors ______________ the Vice-President. In the Sales Department, one director ______________ exports, the other ______________ domestic sales.*

***be responsible for   be in charge of   be supported by   support***
***be accountable to   consist of   be headed by***

## Transfer

*Describe the internal hierarchy of your company, beginning with the Managing Director (CEO). Where do you fit into the organisation?*

# UNIT 77

## ASSERTING and DOWNTONING INFORMATION

*See also* **Unit 88 – Scale of likelihood**
**Unit 83 – Asking for and giving opinions**

### A *Sample sentences*

- In no way will this temporary setback delay the launch of the new product.
- It was their negative attitude that upset me most.
- What most annoyed me was the fact that we never started the meetings on time.
- I tend to think that he will lose his job after the merger.
- In a way I have to accept the validity of the points she made.

### B *Form and uses*

We use assertion when we want to emphasise what we are saying. We often do this to influence the attitudes and behaviour of our listeners. Similarly, we use downtoning when we are not certain and want to protect ourselves from our listeners.

**1 Asserting information**

Fronted topic:
Here we move an element – but not the subject – to the front of the sentence and normally stress it in our pronunciation. This carries great emphasis:
Last year's results (stressed) we have already discussed. So let's move on to the forecasts.
Sometimes (stressed) I go down to the plant. But normally I send my deputy.

Cleft sentences:
Here we divide the sentence into two halves – stressing the topic. We can do this in two different ways:
It's the uncertainty that is creating such a bad atmosphere. (**it's** + subject + **that**)
What is creating such a bad atmosphere is the uncertainty. (relative clause + **is** + subject)

Inversion:
After certain negative words and expressions we can use inversion for added emphasis (see Unit 64, C3):
In no way will this temporary setback delay the launch of the new product.

Intensifying adverbs (see Unit 52):
We have had an *extremely* good year.
I *really* think we should announce the results to the business press.

Connecting expressions of highlight (see Unit 74):
We have redesigned the product to make it even easier to operate. *In particular*, the on-screen commands lead the user through every step.

**2 Downtoning information**

With **seem** and **appear**:
It seems/appears that profits are down again.
Profits seem/appear to be down again.

With **tend to** and **be inclined to**:
We always tend to underestimate the time needed to design the prototype.
The R & D Department are inclined to be over-ambitious with their timescales.

Minimising with **just, only, a bit** and **a little**:
It's just/only a minor setback; it's nothing serious.
We've had to delay the project a little/a bit.

Possibility with **maybe, perhaps** and **might**:
Perhaps/maybe we should inform the MD.
We might consider informing the shareholders.

Reservation with **in a way** and **to some/to a certain extent**:
In a way/To a certain extent I have to accept the validity of the points she made.

# ASSERTING and DOWNTONING INFORMATION

## Exercise 1

*Mark the following sentences as assertive (A) or non-assertive (NA). Underline the words which make the sentence either assertive or non-assertive.*

1 I'm inclined to think that the results are satisfactory. ☐
2 I feel that there are one or two small problems here. ☐
3 What we need is a new direction in policy. ☐
4 It could be said that the chances of success are limited. ☐
5 It's important that we conclude these negotiations this week. ☐
6 I tend to think there's likely to be a fall in interest rates soon. ☐
7 I'm sure that there's no point in meeting Mr Roach. ☐

## Exercise 2

*Rewrite the following sentences to include the words or phrase given in brackets.*

1 The price is far too high (inclined to think)
*I'm inclined to think that the price is too high.*
2 I can't go any lower. (tend to feel)
3 The password may not be given to anyone else. (under no circumstances)
4 I think we can expect good sales. (extremely)
5 I believe we can expect very disappointing results. (really)
6 You must look at the alternatives. (perhaps, might)
7 There's a huge difference in our positions on this. (appears)
8 We don't agree with you! (seem)

## Exercise 3

*The flow chart below summarises a negotiation between Bücher, a components supplier, and Halbo, a sales agent. Use it to create a short dialogue. Use non-assertive (NA) or assertive (A) sentences where indicated.*

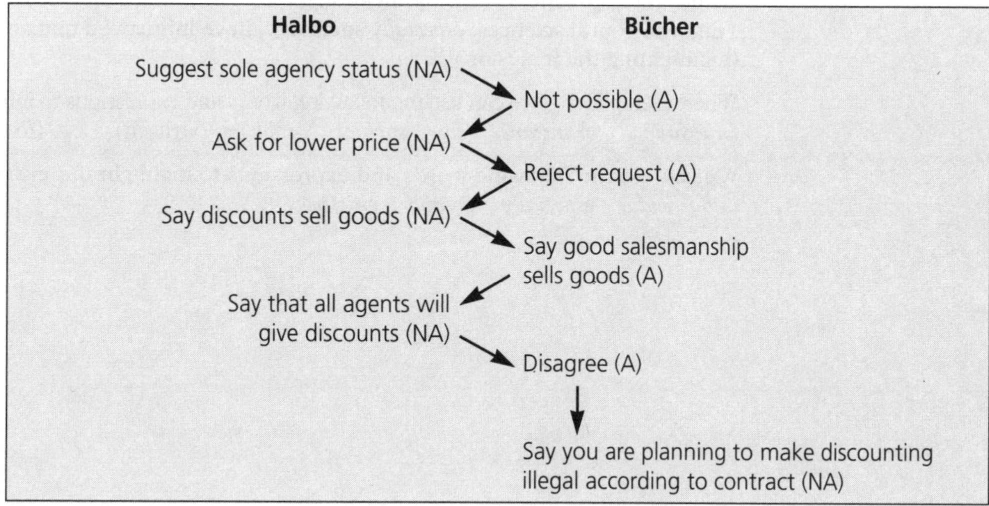


## Transfer

*Imagine you are in negotiation with a business partner, a colleague or a friend. Write a series of non-assertive sentences that you could use in a negotiation on a topic you decide. Then write equivalent assertive phrases.*

# UNIT 78

## EQUATING and INCLUDING IDEAS

***See also* Unit 74 – Connecting and sequencing ideas**

## A *Sample sentences*

◆ The new company motto, namely 'Quality is all', will have profound effects on our working practices. In particular, we will need to look carefully at two areas: in other words, materials receipt and goods despatch.

## B *Form and uses*

If we want to give more information about an item in the text, we can do so by using two types of text connectors: *equivalence* and *inclusion*:
Our new company motto, *namely* 'Quality is all'... (New motto is equivalent to 'Quality is all'.)
We will need to modify working practices, *for example* time-keeping. (Modified working practices include time-keeping.)

1 **Equivalence**
We can show the equivalence of two ideas by *designation* or by *reformulation*. When we use designation, we identify the second idea as equivalent to the first:
Our French partner company, *that is to say* Rossomon France, is sending two delegates.
Our French partner company, Rossomon France, is sending two delegates. (zero marker)

We can use the following words and expressions for designation:
*in other words* *that means* *namely* *that is to say*
Alternatively, we can use a zero marker as in the second example above.

When we use reformulation, we reword the first idea – often to identify it more clearly to the audience:
ESP, *or* English for Specific Purposes, is concerned with training for professionals.
The profit on your property sales, *technically speaking* the equity, is not taxable.

The following words and expressions are examples of reformulation language:
*or (rather)* *(more) simply/to put it simply* *technically (speaking)* *in more technical terms*

2 **Inclusion**
We use inclusion where the first item includes the second:
The behavioural sciences, *such as* psychology and sociology, have influenced management practices. (exemplification)
The behavioural sciences, *especially* sociology, have influenced management practices. (highlighting the inclusion)

When exemplifying, we can use the following words and expressions to introduce our examples:
*for example* *for instance* *say* *such as* *as follows* (written) *e.g.* (formal and written)

We can use the following words and expressions to highlight our examples:
*in particular* *especially* *notably* *chiefly*

# 78 TASKS

## EQUATING AND INCLUDING IDEAS

### Exercise 1

*Underline seven examples of text connectors and classify them in the table which follows the text. Finally, identify one further example of designation, using a zero marker.*

Some of the most important American companies, notably Allen Morland and KRD, are experiencing problems in their home markets. In particular, a growth in competition from S.E. Asian producers is affecting formerly secure positions. The leading producer in Korea, namely Reto Inc, has gained a large market share, 23 per cent. In other words, there are big changes happening in the world market. There is a lot more competition. Technically speaking, we are witnessing a diversification due to increased market penetration by hitherto unknown producers. There are no easy ways to face these changes. There are plenty of inappropriate short-term solutions, such as governments erecting trade barriers, for example.

| Highlighting example (3) | Introducing example (1) | Reformulation (1) | Designation (2) |
|---|---|---|---|
| | | | |

### Exercise 2

*Complete the spaces in the following press release with an appropriate text connector from the box.*

(zero marker)
notably
in particular
namely
in other words
for example

*A major international airline, ______________ World Air, has recommended immediate checks on part of the hydraulic system of a popular aeroplane, ______________ the AD780. The centre of concern is the actuating cylinders, ______________ , the device in the hydraulic system which expands or contracts when pressure is applied. The warning comes after three critical reports, including, ______________, last week's ICAO survey of 700 transatlantic airliners, ______________ several AD780s. The report from ICAO noted, ______________, concern over the hydraulics in several planes.*

### Exercise 3

*Complete the following medical report by adding a text connector where appropriate. In one case use the zero marker.*

*The patient has a bad sore throat, or ___________ he has inflammation of the pharynx. He also has chronic sinusitis, ___________ he has a bad sinus problem. He needs a course of antibiotics, ___________ penicillin. He should also have a long rest, and ___________ give up singing in a rock band. If the problem does not improve, he should see the consultant, ___________ Doctor Battiato, who is an expert in these acute throat disorders. Problems of this nature seem to have become more common, ___________ in cities and areas of high population density. Several treatments for sinus problems are worse than no treatment at all, ___________ some spray preparations bought OTC, ___________ 'over the counter'.*

### Transfer

*Think of a few things you can say about the products or services of a company you know well. Write five sentences and use text connectors to link ideas in each sentence.*

# UNIT 79

## CONTRASTING IDEAS

*See also* Unit 43 – Clauses of contrast
Unit 74 – Connecting and sequencing ideas
Unit 80 – Comparing ideas

## A *Sample sentences*

- Although the competition was stiff, we managed to win the first prize.
- We finished the project on time despite problems with the subcontractors.
- Interest rates have gone down. However, we are still facing financial difficulties.

## B *Form and uses*

We can use the following language techniques to contrast ideas:

1 **Clauses of contrast** (see Unit 43)
These consist of two clauses: the main clause and the contrast clause.
We will complete the project on time, even though the schedule is tight.

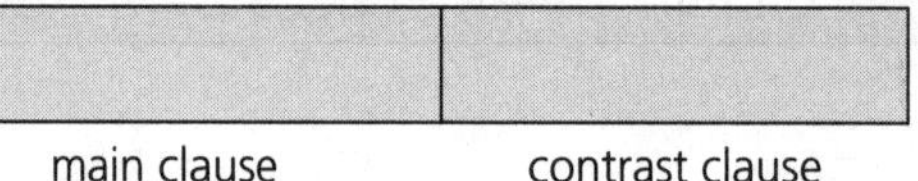


The main conjunctions of contrast are:
*but though although even though while whereas*

Notice the difference in use between **but** and the others:
Local companies are cheap but international companies are more reliable.
Although local companies are cheap, they are not as reliable as international companies.

2 **Phrases of contrast**
The main words to introduce a phrase of contrast are:
*despite in spite of*
Despite/in spite of the machine breakdown, we completed the order.

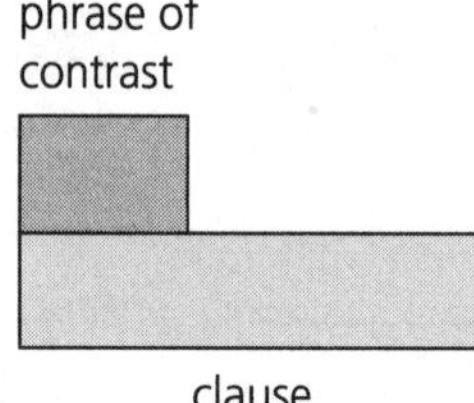


Notice how the above sentence is similar in meaning to the following one:
Although the machine broke down, we completed the order. (clause of contrast)

3 **Sentence connectors of contrast** (see Unit 74)
These are words or expressions which link together two sentences which are in contrast to each other.
We have improved quality. *However*, we still need to reduce wastage.

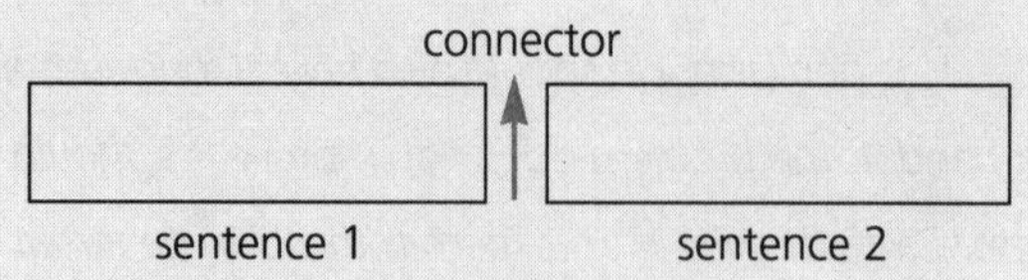


The main sentence connectors are:
*yet however nevertheless still but even so all the same (informal)*

Notice how the above sentence is similar in meaning to the following ones:
Despite the improved quality, we still need to reduce wastage. (phrase)
Even though we have improved quality, we still need to reduce wastage. (clause)

## Exercise 1

*Select one sentence from the left and an appropriate one from the right and connect them using one of the connectors in the middle.*

| | | |
|---|---|---|
| Aircraft engines are well maintained | but | not all of them are implemented |
| Many flight control systems are automatic | Even so | it is sometimes difficult to determine the cause of accidents |
| Leading airports are incredibly busy | Yet | accidents are unavoidable |
| The flight recorder records information about a flight | | pilots have overall control |
| Accident reports contain important recommendations | However | there are very few accidents |

## Exercise 2

*The sentences below all contain a main clause followed by either a clause or a phrase of contrast. Rewrite the sentences using the words given in brackets. The first has been done for you.*

1 We sold the subsidiary even though it was profitable. (despite)
We sold the subsidiary despite its profitability.

2 We realised a good price despite the weakness of the world markets. (even though)
3 We believe the company will benefit, though our decision was difficult. (in spite of)
4 Profit margins have been very tight despite the strength of our core business. (although)
5 The world market will improve while the domestic situation will deteriorate. (in spite of)

## Exercise 3

*Rewrite the following sentences using the words or constructions given in brackets.*

1 Both imports and exports may fall next year. However, the levels are likely to be different. (clause of contrast)
2 Although it is easy to boost exports, it is more difficult to control imports. (sentence connector)
3 Export initiatives improve short-term performance, but do not necessarily lead to long-term customers. (phrase of contrast)
4 Some customers are looking for cheap solutions while others are looking for business partners. (*in contrast*)
5 Although a full order book improves a company's confidence, it does not guarantee survival. (sentence connector)
6 A full order book boosts morale. However, it also stretches a company's cash flow. (clause of contrast)

## Transfer

*We use clauses of contrast when we talk about things that do not turn out as one would expect.*

*Example:*
Although the economy as a whole is improving, our sector is still quite depressed.

*Now write five similar sentences yourself about your area of work. Remember to use the different constructions you have practised in this unit.*

# UNIT 80

## COMPARING IDEAS

*See also* Unit 53 – Comparison of adjectives
Unit 74 – Connecting and sequencing ideas
Unit 79 – Contrasting ideas

## A *Sample sentences*

- Our new hardware processes orders much faster than the old system.
- We should lease the equipment rather than purchase it.
- National offices of the same organisation usually vary in terms of corporate culture.

## B *Form and uses*

We can use the following language forms to compare ideas:

1 **Clauses of comparison.**
These consist of one or two clauses:

One clause:

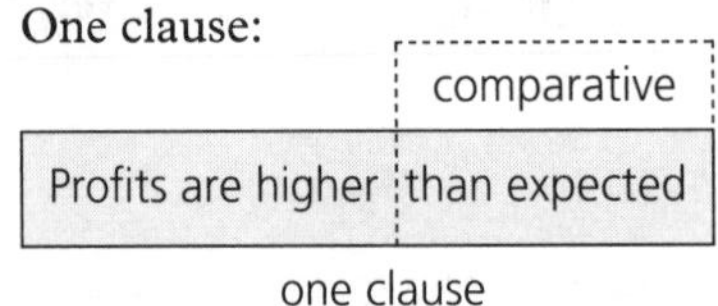


Two clauses:

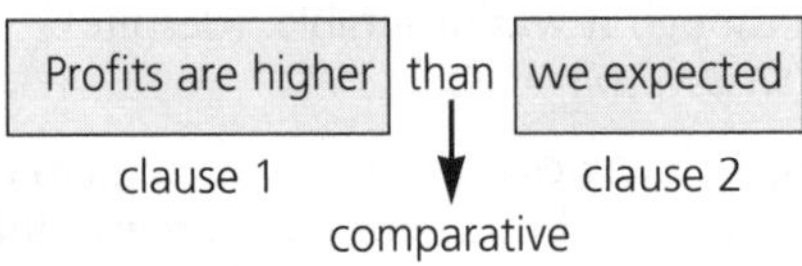


We can form clauses of comparison with the following language forms:

**a** a comparative word + **than**:
Increased competition means that prices are lower than they were last year.
Finding cheaper suppliers is always easier than finding reliable ones.
(Notice the verb … *ing* after the preposition **than** – see Unit 13.)
Last year we increased our prices more than them.
(Notice the object form after the preposition **than** – see Unit 59.)

**b** **rather than**:
We should lease the equipment rather than buy it.
(Here **than** is a conjunction and therefore the verb **buy** takes the same form as **lease,** i.e. infinitive without **to**.)

**c** **as … as…** and **not so … as…**
We have now bought as many units as we need.
They are not so/as profitable as us.
(Notice the object form after the preposition **as** – see Unit 72.)
Datapost is just as fast as sending it by air.
(Notice the verb …*ing* after the preposition **as** – see Unit 13.)

2 **Expressions of comparison:**
*in comparison with* *compared to/with*
Their prices are very low in comparison with ours.

3 **Words and expressions of similarity and difference:**
*the same as* *different from* *similar to*
Their product range is the same as last year. (*not*: the same like/of)

Verbs of similarity:
*conform to* *match* *resemble* *look like* *correspond to*
I'm afraid your terms just don't match our needs.

Verbs of difference (with the preposition **from**):
*differ* *vary* *diverge* *deviate*
Quality must not deviate from the standards we have set.

## Exercise 1

*Read the text below which is part of an annual report from an investment bank. Identify the language forms which compare ideas, then classify them according to the headings which follow.*

### How has it been for you?

This year has been a year for borrowers rather than for savers. The drop in interest rates has been faster and more dramatic than anyone would have suspected just six months ago – from 10.5 per cent in January to 7 per cent now. And, of course, savers have faced the same cuts as borrowers. The table below gives a rough guide to how different types of investment have performed. As you can see, Gilts and Unit Trusts have done well in comparison with Building Society accounts. However, you should bear in mind that the final figures won't correspond exactly to the returns quoted for Gilts and Unit Trusts because buying and selling costs are excluded. The big question is: Will next year look like this year? Should savers use the same strategies as this year? Or should they employ different tactics from this year? I'm afraid that as long as the economic outlook continues to swing, we must expect rates to vary from month to month.

Average percentage returns on investment

| | |
|---|---|
| Gilt | 13.8% |
| UK Unit Trust | 13.4% |
| Building Society | 6.6% |

| Clause of comparison | Expression of comparison | Expression of similarity/difference |
|---|---|---|
| | | |

## Exercise 2

*Each of the following sentences contains a mistake. Correct it.*

1 The business plan was more easy to develop than we expected.
2 In comparison to last year, I think our results will turn out to be considerably better than we forecast.
3 With the new videoconference unit it's almost as good as to have our partners in the same meeting room.
4 We have checked and the new model conforms with the EC standards in terms of higher fire resistance.
5 Their products are not so durable as ours; in fact I'd say that they are not at all the same than ours.

## Exercise 3

*Write sentences comparing the three cars described in the table below. Use the given prompts. The first has been done for you.*

1 same as
*The acceleration of the Jasper is the same as the Bravo.*
2 larger than
3 compared to
4 similar to
5 not so … as
6 as … as

| | Triano | Bravo | Jasper |
|---|---|---|---|
| Engine size | 2,492 cc V6 | 1,725 cc | 1,525 cc |
| Top speed | 210 km/hr | 215 km/hr | 160 km/hr |
| Acceleration 0–100 km | 7.5 sec. | 8.5 sec. | 8.5 sec |
| Fuel economy | 9 lit/100 km | 8.5 lit/100 km | 7 lit/100 km |

## Transfer

*Think of two or more products or companies that you know well. Write at least six sentences comparing them.*

# UNIT 81

## CHECKING and CONFIRMING INFORMATION

*See also* **Unit 84 – Agreeing and disagreeing**
**Unit 90 – Requesting information and action**

### A *Sample sentences*

- I didn't quite catch what you said about raising extra capital.
- What exactly do you mean by 'discretionary payments'?
- Let me just go over the main points again. Firstly, …

### B *Form and uses*

The following techniques may be needed by the speaker and listener to manage the flow of communication:

| | | |
|---|---|---|
| asking for repetition | asking for clarification | asking for verification |
| asking for spelling | repeating information | correcting information |

1 **Asking for repetition:** If you didn't hear, you can use one of these phrases:
*Sorry?* (with a rising intonation)
*Pardon?* (with a rising intonation)
*Pardon me?* (with a rising intonation) (AmE)
*Excuse me?* (with a rising intonation) (AmE)

Another strategy is to state your problem and then make a request.
Stating your problem:
(I'm) sorry. I didn't (quite) hear/catch what you said.
I missed that last part.
Making your request:
Could you repeat that/say that again, please?
Would you mind repeating that, please?

If you didn't understand, you can state your problem and then make a request.
Stating your problem:
(I'm) sorry. I don't quite follow you/see what you mean.
I don't understand what you've just said.
Making your request:
Could you go over that again, please?

2 **Asking for clarification**: If you feel the speaker is being vague or imprecise, you can use one of the following expressions to ask for more precise information:
What exactly do you mean by 'discretionary payments'?
What is the precise purpose/function of this payment?
Could you tell us a bit more/Could we have some more details about the new regulations, please?

3 **Asking for verification**: If you want to check that you have understood what the speaker has said, you can use these expressions:
Did you say the end of *January*? (stressed, to check it is January rather than another month.)
You *did* say January, didn't you? ('did' is stressed)
Is it true/a fact that we will be moving at the end of January?

4 **Asking for spelling**:
Can/could you spell that, please?

5 **Repeating information**: If you are speaking and want to reinforce what you have said, you can paraphrase the information or summarise the main points.
Paraphrasing:
In other words, the AZ120 is technically very sophisticated.
What I mean is/By that I mean that I am sure we can overcome our differences.
Summarising:
Let me just go over/repeat/summarise the main points again.
If I could just bring/draw together the points we've discussed.

6 **Correcting information**: It is quite common to soften a correction by using a polite formula before making the correction:
Excuse me/sorry, that's not quite right. Not fifteen. Fifty.
Sorry, I think you've made a mistake. Fifty rather than fifteen.

# CHECKING and CONFIRMING INFORMATION

## Exercise 1

*Read the following extract from a discussion. Identify examples of the following:*

1 Asking for repetition (REP)
2 Checking understanding (CHECK)
3 Paraphrasing information (PARA)
4 Summarising information (SUMM)
5 Correcting information (CORR)

'Can you explain the effect of falling exchange rates on the company?'

'It's quite simple, really. The effects are numerous but two stand out as very significant. First of all, about 65 per cent of components we use to build our cars are bought in, many from abroad. That means that the value of the national currency affects the prices we pay for these components. It will of course increase the price we have to pay if the currency loses value on the international exchange.'

'Did you say 65 per cent are bought in?'

'That's right – mostly from Korea and Malaysia though also from Japan and Europe.'

'Excuse me, Paul. In fact the largest number of parts come from Japan.'

'Number, yes, but the largest cost involves imports from Korea.'

'Really? You surprise me.'

'Now, where was I? In a nutshell, importing components is affected by currency fluctuation. Now, the second area of influence is in the revenue from sales outside the domestic market or, to put it simply, exports. Clearly a drop in the value of our currency will adversely affect the revenue we receive from export sales.'

'Okay, that's clear. Can you repeat what you said a few minutes ago about margins?'

'Okay – briefly, what I said was that margins had to be improved against a very difficult marketing context. By that I mean we need to improve margins despite a fall in turnover.'

## Exercise 2

*A training organisation telephones a small company in France to explain ways in which the two could work together. Fill in the spaces in the conversation by adding phrases from the box. The first one is done for you.*

So you've got subsidiaries throughout Europe?
No, I didn't say that.
I don't quite follow you
That's exactly right.
No, not exactly.
Could you describe in a little more detail your
Could you repeat that?
In other words,

A: *We're based in Montpellier but we work with colleagues all over France helping to solve clients' training problems.*

B: *I don't quite follow you, so ______________ ?*

A: *Certainly. We are a national company based in Montpellier in the south of France but we operate in all regions of the country, and even throughout Europe.*

B: ______________

A: ______________ *We have agents who look after regions throughout Europe.*

B: ______________ *relationship with these agents?*

A: *Certainly. We advertise our services nationally and we contact local organisations who can help to meet the needs of the companies who contact us.*

B: ______________ *you act as a contact between companies with certain needs and companies who can supply those needs.*

A: ______________ *And we supply support material to local firms.*

B. *So you sell material to help the local firms?*

A: ______________ *We offer to work in partnership with local firms, creating a team to help resolve a particular client's needs.*

# UNIT 82

## LIKES and PREFERENCES

*See also* Unit 15 – Verb ...ing or infinitive + to
Unit 16 – Verb + object + infinitive

### A *Sample sentences*

- I like to read at least two newspapers before I leave for the office.
- I like reading *The Financial Times* because of its international financial coverage.
- I'd like to speak to Mr Brenner, please.
- I prefer going by car to travelling by train, but I'd rather rent one than use mine.

### B *Form*

Note the constructions after the following verbs:

| | like | would like | prefer | would rather |
|---|---|---|---|---|
| object | ✓ | ✓ | ✓ | |
| infinitive with **to** | ✓ | ✓ | ✓ | |
| infinitive without **to** | | | | ✓ |
| **that** + clause | | | (would) ✓ | ✓ |
| verb ...*ing* | ✓ | | ✓ | |
| object + infinitive with **to** | ✓ | ✓ | ✓ | |

### C *Uses*

1 **Like:**
I like the new company logo. (= I think it is good.)
I like visiting clients. (= I enjoy it.)
I like to visit clients in their offices. (= It is appropriate.)
I like my assistant to accompany me on business trips. (*not*: I like that ...)

2 **Would like:**
I would like (to have) the lab report tomorrow, please.
I would like you to send off that report tomorrow, please. (*not*: I would like that ...)
I'd like all the offers in by the end of next week. (contracted form of **would** is **'d**)

3 **Like** versus **would like:**
Do you like whisky? (a general enquiry)
Would you like a whisky? (an offer)

4 **Prefer** and **would prefer:**
We use **prefer** when there are two alternatives; we can also use **prefer** when we only mention the chosen alternative and, therefore, reject any other options:
We prefer fixed interest rates to variable rates. (preposition **to**; *not*: than variable rates)
We prefer receiving payments to making them. (verb ...*ing* after preposition **to**)
I prefer to start the meeting now rather than (to) wait for the others.
I prefer new staff to start on a Monday. (rather than on any other day)

We use **would prefer** for a hypothetical preference:
My staff would prefer fixed interest rates to variable rates. (if they were given the choice)
I would prefer to start the meeting now. (rather than at another time)

***Note:***
What would you like to drink? (an open offer; *not*: what would you prefer?)
Would you prefer/like tea or coffee? (a closed offer)

5 **Would rather:**
**Would rather** means 'would prefer':
A: This is a delicate matter. I'd rather discuss this in private than in the open. (*not*: to discuss)
B: How about your office?
A: I'd rather talk somewhere else than risk an interruption. (*not*: than risking/to risk)
B: Can I make a public statement?
A: Well, I'd rather you didn't just now. I'd rather you waited until I check with the MD. (this is the same as 'I'd prefer that you waited' – see above)

## Exercise 1

*Each of the exchanges below contains one mistake. Underline it and correct it.*

1 A: I'd not rather go via Amsterdam.
B: So you'd prefer to have a direct flight to Stockholm?

2 A: Do you like tea or coffee?
B: Coffee would be very nice, thank you.

3 A: How do you run your monthly meetings?
B: I like that they are very informal, more of an open discussion.

4 A: Do you send out a formal agenda?
B: Yes, naturally I prefer have an agenda than no real plan.

5 A: Would you like to check the minutes now?
B: No, I'd rather we look at them later.

## Exercise 2

*Elena and Karin are in Barcelona for a business meeting. They are planning their evening. Change the underlined phrase for an alternative, using the words in brackets. Do not change the original meaning. The first is done for you.*

Elena: What do you think of this hotel?
Karin: It's very good but <u>I think the Hotel Opera is better</u> (prefer).
*I prefer the Hotel Opera.*

Elena: Yes, the Opera is splendid. I often stay there. Now, about this evening. <u>How about going</u> to a fish restaurant near the port? (like)
Karin: I think <u>it would be more enjoyable to go</u> to a restaurant in Las Ramblas. (prefer) Also, <u>I like meat better than fish</u>. (rather)
Elena: Sure, that's okay! What time shall we meet?
Karin: Not too late. <u>It would be better for me if we did not have</u> a late night tonight. (prefer not)
Elena: Fine. We can meet at 8. <u>Which do you think is better</u>, to meet here or in Las Ramblas? (prefer)
Karin: I'll come to your hotel. That's the easiest.
Elena: Okay, fine. Now, I'll have to go soon, but what about another drink? <u>What do you want?</u> (like)

## Exercise 3

*Robin Ogrizovich is visiting a customer, NIM S.A., in Lisbon. Use the following flow chart to complete the dialogue. Some phrases are already written for you. Use the prompts to write the others. Include different forms of **like, prefer, rather**.*

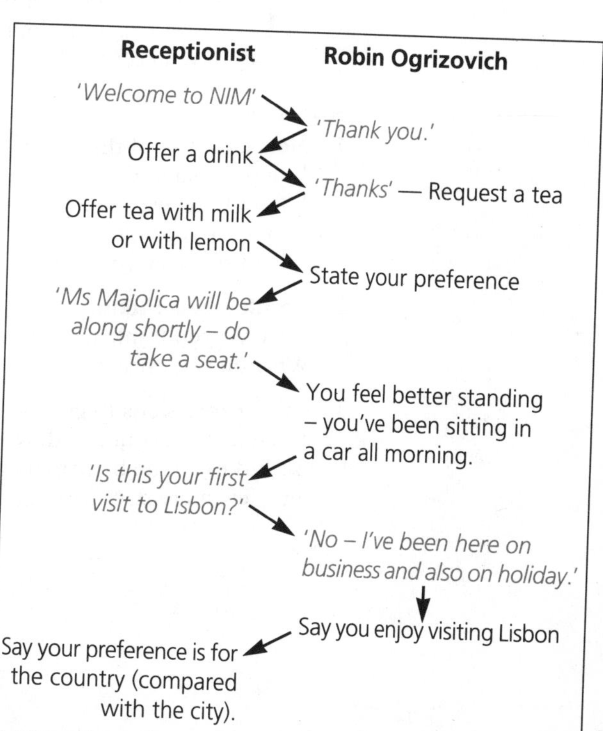

Receptionist
Robin Ogrizovich
'Welcome to NIM'
'Thank you.'
Offer a drink
'Thanks' — Request a tea
Offer tea with milk or with lemon
State your preference
'Ms Majolica will be along shortly – do take a seat.'
You feel better standing – you've been sitting in a car all morning.
'Is this your first visit to Lisbon?'
'No – I've been here on business and also on holiday.'
Say you enjoy visiting Lisbon
Say your preference is for the country (compared with the city).


## Transfer

*Imagine you welcome a visitor to your company or town. Write five sentences asking her about likes and preferences, then write five sentences about your own likes and preferences.*

# UNIT 83

## ASKING FOR and GIVING OPINIONS

*See also* Unit 77 – Asserting and downtoning information
Unit 84 – Agreeing and disagreeing

### A *Sample sentences*

- Do you think that a loan will solve the present cash flow crisis?
- In my opinion we should look at the long-term implications of the restructuring.
- I tend to think that the problems we are facing show a fundamental flaw in our whole philosophy.

### B *Form and uses*

1 We can express our opinions on a scale from *strongly* to *weakly*. Below is a list of expressions to introduce the opinion:

| | |
|---|---|
| *strongly* ↑ | I'm convinced/sure/positive that ... |
| | I strongly believe that ... |
| | I have absolutely no doubt that ... |
| | I definitely/certainly think that ... |
| | I really *do* think that ... |
| | I really feel that ... |
| *neutrally* | In my opinion |
| | I think/consider/feel that ... |
| | I believe that ... |
| | As I see it, ... |
| | To my mind ... |
| | From my point of view ... |
| ↓ | I'm inclined to think that ... |
| *weakly* | I tend to think that ... |

2 Similarly we can ask for opinions on a scale from *forcefully* to *tactfully*. Below is a list of expressions to ask for an opinion:

| | |
|---|---|
| *strongly* ↑ | Do you really think that ...? |
| | Do you really believe that ...? |
| | Are you absolutely sure/convinced/positive that ...? |
| | Don't you think that ...? |
| *neutrally* | Do you think ...? |
| | Do you believe that ...? |
| | Do you consider that ...? |
| ↓ | Am I right in thinking that ...? |
| *tactfully* | Would I be right in thinking that ...? |

***Notes***

1 Notice the use of the positive and negative of **think**:
I think we should tell the bank now. (positive)
I don't think we should tell the bank now. (negative; *not*: I think we shouldn't tell ...)
I think so. (positive)
I don't think so. (negative)

2 **Think** versus **mean**:
What do you think about the proposal? (= What is your opinion?)
What do you mean? (= What do you want to say?)

3 Other expressions to give opinions:
As far as I am concerned, we should talk to the bank now.
According to the bank manager, interest rates are due to fall soon and we should hang on for a few more days. (*not*: according to the bank manager's opinion)

# 83 TASKS

## ASKING FOR and GIVING OPINIONS

### Exercise 1

*Complete the following phrases by adding a word from the box opposite, then complete the sentences in any suitable way.*

| consider mind strongly convinced inclined |
|---|

1 *I ______________ believe that …*

2 *I'm ______________ that …*

3 *Do you ______________ that …?*

4 *To my ______________, this is a really innovative idea, but …*

5 *I'm ______________ to think that …*

### Exercise 2

*The following is part of a discussion about the procedures followed by air traffic controllers. The opinions are expressed very strongly and asked for very forcefully. Rewrite the discussion using the weaker and more tactful forms given in brackets.*

Arne: Are you absolutely convinced that the job is done badly? (think)
Bob: I'm sure that the procedures are regularly contravened. (inclined)
Arne: Do you mean to say our controllers do not follow standard procedures? (consider)
Bob: I'm convinced they don't. (tend)
Chris: I definitely think this is most serious. (see)
Delia: I really feel that accidents can be caused by not following the ICAO guidelines. (opinion)
Bob: I have absolutely no doubt that that is true. (feel) Look at Tenerife. I'm sure that the disaster occurred there because the rules were broken. (view)

### Exercise 3

*A group of three editors working for a publishing company are discussing two possible designs for the cover of a mathematics textbook. Here are the two designs.*

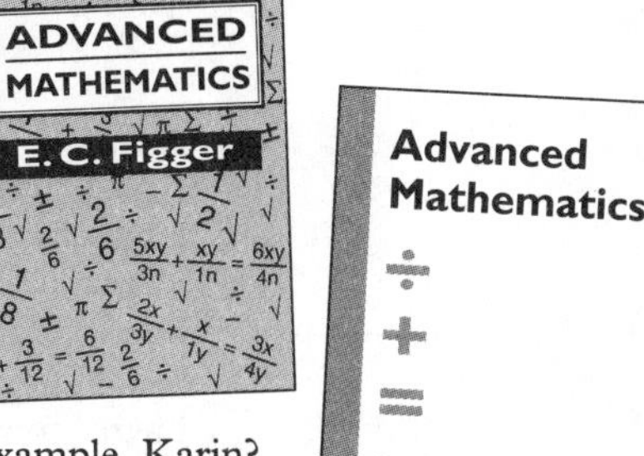


*The discussion is as follows. Steps 1 and 2 are described in detail with examples of what Chris and Karin say. You should write steps 3–5.*

1 Chris asks Karin for her opinion.
Chris: Am I right in thinking that you prefer the second example, Karin?

2 Karin answers, explaining that she strongly prefers the second version.
Karin: I really do think that, yes. It's much clearer – I strongly prefer the more minimalist design. I really believe that the title is clearer and I have absolutely no doubt that the author's name does not need to be so big. I definitely think that the shapes look better than all these formulae. I'm positive that the tints are better too – you can read the title easily, the printing is very good.

3 Chris asks for Jean's opinion.

4 Jean argues (neutrally and weakly) for the first design, mentioning the following points:
- it is stronger
- title is clearer
- author's name is very important
- formulae say more about what is in the book
- tints are better

5 Finally Chris argues (neutrally and weakly) for the second design, claiming:
- agrees with Karin
- author's name not so important
- shapes clearer than the formulae
- he prefers the tints in the second design and the characters in the title are clear enough
- easier to read

### Transfer

*Write a paragraph stating your opinion on some topical problem in your company, or something that has recently been in the news. Express some views strongly, others less strongly.*

# UNIT 84

## AGREEING and DISAGREEING

***See also* Unit 83 – Asking for and giving opinions**

### A *Sample sentences*

- I absolutely agree with you that ambitious targets are what this company needs.
- The team members are now in agreement about the need to change our approach.
- Sally agrees with Alan's suggestion to a certain extent, but she still thinks that the new pay scales should be phased in gradually.
- I'm afraid we can't agree to such long credit terms. That would spell disaster for our cash flow.
- They want 90 days' credit? We couldn't possibly accept that.

### B *Form and uses*

We can use the following scale to show the range:
*agreement → partial agreement → disagreement.*

We can also distinguish between *agreeing with someone* and *agreeing to something.*

| | Agreeing with someone | Agreeing to something |
|---|---|---|
| **agreement** | I totally agree with you<br>I fully/completely agree<br>I'm in total agreement with you there | I totally accept that<br>I fully/completely agree<br>I'm all in favour of that |
| **partial agreement** | Up to a point/To a certain extent I'd agree with you, but ...<br>You may have something there but ...<br>You could/may be right, but ... | Up to a point/to a certain extent I'd accept that, but ...<br>That may be so, but ...<br>That may/might be right, but ... |
| **disagreement** | (I'm afraid) I can't agree with you<br>I don't agree | (I'm afraid) I can't accept that<br>I don't accept that |

***Notes***

**Agree** and **accept**:
I agree with you. (with someone; *not*: I am agree with you)
I agree with Alan's suggestion. (with something; = I have the same opinion as)
I agree with you about/on the need for change. (= to share the same opinion about/on something)
I agree to your credit terms. (agree to something = to be willing to accept/allow something)
I agree to review your credit position in a few months. (agree to do something; *not*: accept to do something)
I accept your suggestion. (to accept something; *not*: to agree something)

# AGREEING and DISAGREEING

## Exercise 1

*Match the phrase on the left with an acceptable continuation from the list on the right. The first has been done as an example.*

| | |
|---|---|
| You may be right up to a point. | There's just one detail I would question. |
| I can't agree with you. | But I can't agree with your conclusion. |
| I'm in complete agreement. | But we need to consider another question too. |
| I agree with the first part of what you say. | I see it totally differently. |
| I agree with most of your analysis. | As you say, there is clearly no alternative. |

## Exercise 2

*Provide responses to the following statements using the prompts given and then select the best ending from the choices given below.*

1 The price of oil is too high. (disagree strongly)

2 If a major producer decides to leave OPEC it has a severe impact on world oil markets. (agree)

3 In the short term demand for oil will remain stable but in the long term it should recover. (partially agree)

4 A large fall – to below $10 a barrel – is unthinkable. (disagree)

5 A stable price of between $25 and $30 is fine. (agree)

6 Political factors have a huge impact. (agree)

**a** In fact any departure has quite an effect.
**b** Many countries use their oil power to extract advantages in other respects.
**c** The price has fallen to below that figure in the past.
**d** It's a comfortable price for both producer and consumer.
**e** It's a price arrived at by market forces.
**f** However, it's always difficult to make long-term forecasts.

## Exercise 3

*Provide one word in each space to complete the following sentences.*

1 *I can't ______________ that. It's quite untrue.*

2 *I agree ______________ provide more support.*

3 *I agree ______________ to a point.*

4 *You're mainly right, ______________ I'm not sure about the last part of your argument.*

5 *I'm sorry, I disagree ______________ you. It's not quite like that.*

6 *Okay, I agree ______________ your request.*

7 *I ______________ your basic argument but I can't go ______________ with all the details.*

## Transfer

*Think of any topical issue in a country you know well. Imagine a friend writes to you expressing a range of opinions on this question. Write a brief reply indicating agreement, partial agreement and disagreement with different opinions in your friend's letter.*

*Possible subjects: politics, economic policy, environment, tourism, business, education.*

# UNIT 85

## CAUSE and EFFECT

***See also* Unit 44 – Clauses of cause or reason**

### A *Sample sentences*

- The sharp drop in interest rates has led to benefits for many small companies.
- Due to the cut in interest rates, many small companies have collapsed.
- The bank is going to reduce rates. As a result we will be able to invest more.

### B *Form and uses*

1 **Verbs and verb phrases**. We can view the relationship in two directions:

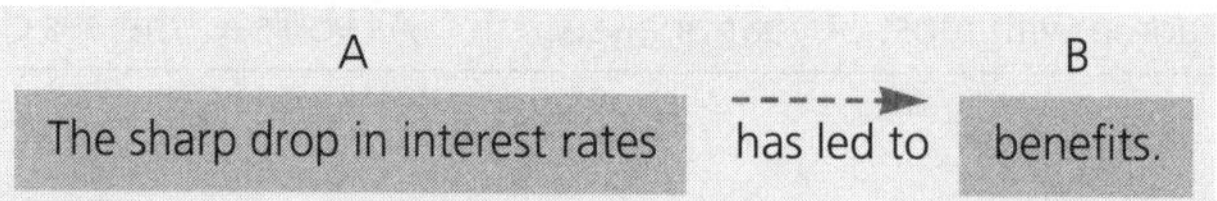


Here A = the cause; - - ► = verb linking the cause to the effect; B = the effect.

Other verbs and verb phrases with a similar meaning are:
*lead to*  *result in*  *bring about*  *give rise to*  *account for*  *be responsible for*

This time ◄- - - = verb linking the effect to the cause.

Other verbs and verb phrases with a similar meaning are:
*arise from*  *stem from*  *be attributable to*

2 **Clauses of cause** (see also Unit 44). Here a subordinating conjunction links the effect and the cause:

The other main subordinating conjunctions are:
*because*  *as*  *since*

3 **Phrases of cause**. Here an adverb phrase introduces the cause:

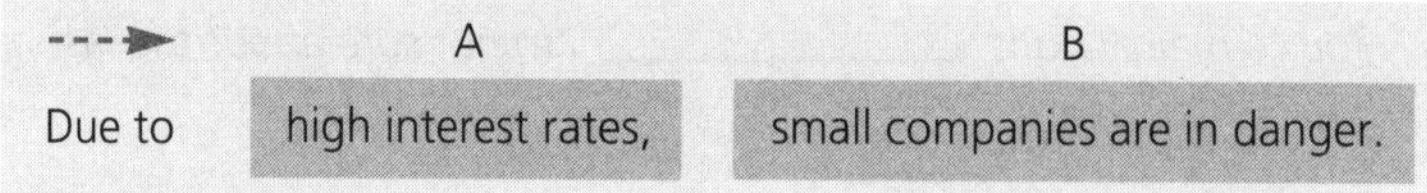


Other expressions with a similar meaning are:
*because of*  *due to*  *owing to*  *on account of*  *as a consequence of*
We always put a noun phrase after these expressions:
Because of low interest rates, small companies are stronger. (*not*: because of interest rates are low)

4 **Sentence connectors of cause.** Here a cause in one sentence is linked to an effect in the following sentence by a connector:

The connector points backwards to the cause and forwards to the effect.

Other connecting words and expressions are:
*therefore*  *so*  *accordingly*  *consequently*  *as a consequence/result*
*hence* (formal)  *thus* (formal)  *because of this*  *that's* (*the reason*) *why* (informal)

## Exercise 1

*Reverse the order of the cause and the effect by using the verb given.*
*The first has been done as an example.*

1 Poor economic policy has led to a severe crisis in manufacturing. (result from)
A severe crisis in manufacturing has resulted from poor economic policy.

2 The fall in inflation stems from strict government control of the money supply in the past five years. (bring about)

3 Lower taxation led to a spending boom at the end of the last decade. (result from)

4 Higher government spending is partly attributable to higher unemployment. (account for)

5 Lower tax revenue arises from increased numbers of business failures. (give rise to)

6 Retail price rises result from increased energy costs. (result in)

## Exercise 2

*Read the extract from an agency news report on an air accident in Moscow. Underline cause with a straight line and underline effect with a wavy line.*

*You work for the aircraft manufacturer. Write a brief memo summarising the cause and effect relationships described in the report.*

The Russian Civil Aviation Authority investigation into the Air Diver 660 crash in Moscow has revealed the cause of the accident to be an explosive rupture in one of the aircraft's engines. The rupture itself was probably the result of metal fatigue. Once the plane landed at Moscow, it caught fire and passengers were unable to escape with the necessary speed, due to a malfunction in a door. A steward tried to force the door but his action led to the door jamming. The door would not open and there was therefore a delay in passengers escaping from the plane.

**Memo**

Subject: Air Diver 660 crash - Moscow 25 September 19..
To: Jan Levi, Production Manager.

## Exercise 3

*The following text contains four phrases of cause. Underline them. Then rewrite the text, changing each phrase of cause into a clause of cause.*

*Here is an example:*
Because of a poor harvest the cost of grain is higher this year.
Since the harvest has been poor, the cost of grain is higher this year.

The British engineering company Harrow tried, unsuccessfully, to sue a German competitor, Bauer, for breach of copyright. However, the court ruled that Harrow had never correctly registered the patent of the item concerned. On account of Harrow's mistake, the product had never been patented. Because of the non-existence of the patent, Bauer did not contravene any law of ownership. As a result of the court's ruling against Harrow, the company had to pay large legal fees. Also, due to the publicity surrounding the case, Bauer expect sales to benefit.

## Transfer

*Think about regional or national economic policy in your country. Write six sentences containing cause and effect relationships.*

# UNIT 86

## OBLIGATIONS and REQUIREMENTS

*See also* Unit 20 – **Must, mustn't and needn't**

## A *Sample sentences*

- There is always resistance to change, but we must find ways of coping with it.
- These changes require us to modify our thinking radically, but we mustn't be dissuaded by the scale of the task.
- We forbid food and drink to be taken into the operating room.

## B *Form*

We can view the notion of obligation under the following headings:
- obligation to do something
- obligation not to do something, i.e. prohibition
- no obligation

We can also view the notion from the point of view of the person/situation causing the obligation (*the obliger*), and the person receiving the obligation (*the obliged*).

Here is the range of verbs for the obliger:

| Oblige someone to do something | Oblige someone not to do something | Not oblige someone to do something |
|---|---|---|
| require<br>force<br>compel<br>make<br>demand<br>oblige | prohibit<br>forbid<br>ban | not require<br>not force<br>not compel<br>not make |

Here is the range of verbs for the obliged:

| Obliged to do something | Obliged not to do something | Not obliged to do something |
|---|---|---|
| must<br>have to<br>need to<br>be required to<br>be supposed to<br>be forced to | must not/mustn't<br>not be allowed to<br>not be permitted to<br>be prohibited from<br>may not<br>cannot/can't | need not/needn't<br>not have to<br>not need to |

## C *Uses*

1 To oblige someone to do something:
The changes require us to modify our thinking. (require/force/compel/oblige someone to do something)
The changes have made us re-evaluate our current practices. (*not*: make someone to do something)
The workers have demanded that we look at safety conditions. (demand that someone does something)

2 To oblige someone not to do something:
The law prohibits companies from discriminating on the basis of sex. (prohibit/forbid/ban someone from doing something)

3 Not to oblige someone to do something:
So far the environmental health officer hasn't forced us to reduce noise levels.
They've asked for equipment guards, but they haven't made us buy them new work clothes.

4 To be obliged to do something:
Companies must provide adequate rest time for their employees. (must do something)
Do we have to do what he says? Isn't there an alternative? (have to do something)
Companies will be required to provide opportunities for teleworking. (to be required to do something)

5 To be obliged not to do something:
Companies mustn't/can't/may not start trading until they have registered their activities. (modals + infinitive without **to**)
A company is not allowed/permitted to continue trading once the receiver has been called in. (not allowed/permitted to do something)
He is prohibited from dealing on the Stock Exchange after his recent conviction for insider dealing. (prohibited from doing something)

6 Not obliged:
You needn't follow their advice if you don't agree with it. (needn't do something)
Managers don't have/need to have any formal qualifications. (don't have/need to do something)

***Note***
Often **must** and **have to** have the same meaning. Sometimes we use **must** for an 'internal' obligation – something that the speaker feels is necessary – and **have to** for an 'external' obligation – imposed from outside.

Compare the following sentences:
We must take radical measures. (We feel they are necessary.)
We have to take radical measures. (Others feel they are necessary.)

# TASKS 86

## OBLIGATIONS and REQUIREMENTS

### Exercise 1

*Read the letter opposite which is about new restrictions on a painkilling drug. Then complete the table which follows.*

**Drug Regulation Council**
Bewlays House Grafton St Dublin 1

Dr Patrick McGinty
Senior Consultant
Abbotsville Medical Centre
Clondalkin
Dublin 2

17 March 19–

Dear Dr McGinty

I am writing to inform you of new restrictions placed on the prescribing of the analgesic drug Anagic. The drug is an effective pain relief agent but cases of misuse have been widely reported.

As a result the Drug Regulation Council has issued new regulations in prescribing Anagic.

- Doctors must write the entire prescription by hand.
- Prescription for persons under the age of 16 is prohibited.
- The dosage must be clearly stated on the prescription.
- The form in which the drug is to be taken has to be specified.
- Doctors are obliged to sign and date the prescription.

The new restrictions do not compel doctors to retain invoices or similar documents relating to the supply of Anagic for more than 12 months.

Safe Custody regulations apply but entries in a Controlled Drug Register are not required.

Yours sincerely

*Iva Pill*
Iva Pill
Drug Regulation Council

| New obligations | No obligation | Obligation not to do something |
|---|---|---|
| | | |

### Exercise 2

*Below is a newspaper report on a campaign by an environmentalist group concerned about dumping chemicals in the sea. Complete the spaces in the report by adding one word from the alternatives in the box.*

*make restricted permitted allowed forced need ban supposed force*

# Chemical restrictions inadequate, say Greens

The environmental pressure group GreenPlanet has called on the government to __________ all dumping of chemical waste at sea.

At present dumping chemical waste is heavily __________ but under certain circumstances disposal at sea is __________ . Companies dumping waste at sea are __________ to get a licence for all such operations. However, the law does not __________ the registration of certain types of chemical waste. GreenPlanet say the present restrictions are inadequate.

A spokesman for GreenPlanet said 'We believe all companies dumping waste material at sea should be __________ to apply for licences. If chemicals are involved, the dumping should not be __________ . Only a major public appeal will __________ the government take the necessary steps.'

A representative of the Ministry of the Environment said the present restrictions were adequate. 'We don't __________ to introduce any changes,' she said.

## Exercise 3

*Imagine you are the owner of a ship which has to be registered with the National Merchant Navy of Honduras. You telephone the Department of Maritime Safety in Honduras and ask a series of questions about ship registration.*

*Write the dialogue based on this outline.*
*Note: (+) = obligation to do something*
*(–) = no obligation to do something*

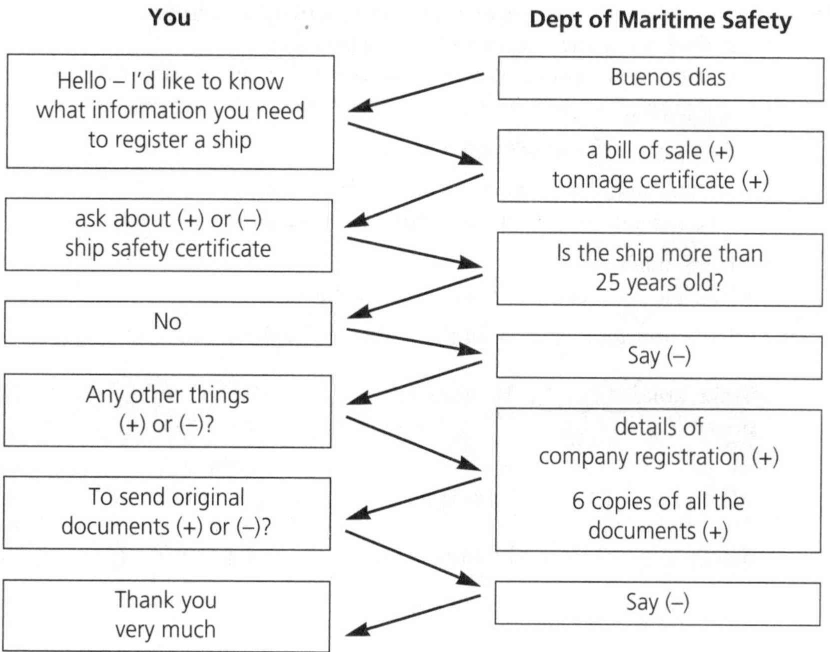

You
Dept of Maritime Safety
Hello – I'd like to know what information you need to register a ship
Buenos días
a bill of sale (+)
tonnage certificate (+)
ask about (+) or (–)
ship safety certificate
Is the ship more than
25 years old?
No
Say (–)
Any other things
(+) or (–)?
details of
company registration (+)
6 copies of all the
documents (+)
To send original
documents (+) or (–)?
Say (–)
Thank you
very much


## Transfer

*Write a brief note to a colleague explaining certain obligations and requirements concerning work in your office. Say what she is obliged to do, not obliged to do and obliged not to do.*

*Example:*
You needn't start at the same time every day, but you must be here for the core time between 10 and 12 and 2 and 4. You are not allowed to be in the building after 8 o'clock in the evening without permission.

# UNIT 87

## ABILITY and INABILITY

*See also* Unit 19 – **Can and could**

## A *Sample sentences*

- We are pleased to inform you that we can extend your credit line from the beginning of next month.
- Our improved profits enable us to consider new investments.
- We regret to inform you that we are unable to offer you the job.
- After training, everybody in this department should be capable of using the PC.

## B *Form*

We can view the concepts of ability and inability in terms of:

1 making someone able or something possible:
Our improved profits enable us to consider new investments.

2 being able:
As a result we can take on new staff.

3 making someone unable or something impossible:
The regulations prevent us from extending your credit line.

4 being unable:
Therefore we can't increase your overdraft.

Let's now look at some of the language for these concepts

| Make able/ possible | Be able | Make unable/ impossible | Be unable |
|---|---|---|---|
| enable<br>allow<br><br>permit | can<br>be able to<br><br>be capable of | prohibit<br>prevent<br><br>stop | can't<br>not be able to/<br>be unable to<br>be incapable of |

## C *Uses*

1 Making someone able or something possible:
The arbitration clause allows us to have this case heard before an arbitrator.
(i.e. **allow** etc. + object; *not*: allow/permit/enable to do)

2 Being able:
We can select any arbitrator. (= normal ability)
We are able to choose any arbitrator we like. (= exceptional ability, i.e. it is unusual or surprising that we can do so)
A good arbitrator should be capable of bringing the two sides to the dispute together quickly. (**capable of** + verb …*ing*)

3 Making someone unable or something impossible:
The bad weather has stopped us having our annual sales meeting. (stop/prevent/prohibit someone from doing something or stop/prevent/prohibit something from happening)

4 Being unable:
I'd like to stay for the reception, but I can't. (= something prevents me)
He is just incapable of keeping to the agreed deadlines. (**incapable of** + verb …*ing*)

***Note***

She can speak English very well. (*not*: She can English very well)
She knows how to do it. (*not*: She can it)

# ABILITY and INABILITY

## Exercise 1

*Complete the following sentences using an appropriate verb from the box.*

can't
capable
prevented
allow able
prohibited
permitted

1 I don't have my chequebook so I __________ write you a cheque.
2 The bank will not __________ us an increased overdraft.
3 We only have a small production plant. We are not __________ of meeting such a massive order.
4 In a few years, if we expand, we will be __________ to supply orders of that size.
5 Employees are __________ to use the company car park.
6 Sorry, entry to the public is __________ .
7 The government __________ us from exporting to that country.

## Exercise 2

*Read the following extracts from a brochure advertising Cellphone services. Complete the spaces with an appropriate form of one of the verbs in the box.*

stop enable capable prevent can allow

**Direct Call**
All your sales staff __________ call your office at any time with the convenience of a private telephone network. Naturally it also __________ calls from your office to any cellphone connected to your network.

**Keysystem DC 5000**
This data communication tool is based on Cellphone technology which __________ you to access mainframe computers, information databases and electronic mail systems.

**Security System**
Whatever system you choose, you can add your own personal number and password and so __________ any unauthorised access to your personal communications system. You can even __________ authorised users contacting you by using an automatic disabling device for those occasions when you do not want to be disturbed.

**VoxBank**
This is a message sending and receiving system __________ of sending 256 messages to other VoxBank users at any one time. So you can alert the whole sales team to a price change or a supply problem with just one call.

## Exercise 3

*Below is part of a distribution contract between a tractor manufacturer, Hrubesch of Budapest (Hungary) and a distributor, Gornik of Gdansk (Poland). Look at the prompts in brackets and change the given verb for another one, either negative or positive. In each sentence include a verb expressing ability or inability. The first is done for you.*

**Distribution agreement**

1 *Introduction – purpose of agreement.*
(The agreement **makes it possible** for Gornik to market Hrubesch tractors in the territories of Poland and Russia.)
The agreement allows Gornik to market Hrubesch tractors in the territories of Poland and Russia.

2 *Limitations on Hrubesch sales in the territories.*
(The terms of the agreement **make** direct sales by Hrubesch **impossible** in the above territories, except to Gornik).
Under the terms of the agreement, Hrubesch __________________ except to Gornik.

3 *Restriction on other agents.*
(It **is not possible** for Hrubesch to sell to other agents in the territories).
Under the terms of the agreement, Hrubesch __________________ in the territories.

4 *Prices.*
(It **is possible** for Gornik to fix prices suitable for markets in the territories.)
Under the terms of the agreement, Gornik __________________ in the territories.

5 *Returned tractors.*
(At the end of the period, Hrubesch **shall be able** to buy back unsold products at 70 per cent of original sale to Gornik if both parties agree.)
If at the end of the period, Gornik has __________________ of the original sale price.

6 *Name of tractors.*
(Any change in name Hrubesch **is not possible**.)
Any change in the name of Hrubesch __________________ .

## Transfer

*Think of any restrictions or legal obligations you know about. Write five sentences stating what you (or another party) can or cannot do.*

# UNIT 88

## SCALE of LIKELIHOOD

*See also* **Unit 18 – May and might**
**Unit 83 – Asking for and giving opinions**

## A *Sample sentences*

- The opening up of Eastern Europe is bound to lead to many business opportunities.
- We are likely to see an upturn in the European economy this year; however, it is unlikely that unemployment will start falling before the middle of next year.
- Once the currencies stabilise, we may get an agreement on pricing.
- They can't possibly expect us to reduce our prices still further.

## B *Form and uses*

If we consider that the scale of likelihood goes from 100 per cent certainty to 0 per cent certainty, we can identify the following segments. (The numbers below are only a general indication, not exact values.)

| 0 | 25 | 50 | 75 | 100 |
|---|---|---|---|---|
| impossibility | improbability | possibility | probability | certainty |

Now let's look at the language for each of these categories.

| | |
|---|---|
| Certainty | I am (**absolutely**) **sure** / **certain** / **positive** **that** sales will increase<br>Sales will **definitely/certainly** increase<br>Sales are **certain** / **sure** / **bound** **to** increase |
| Probability | It is (**very**) **likely/probable that** sales will increase<br>Sales are (**quite**) **likely** to increase<br>Sales **should** increase |
| Possibility | Sales **may** increase<br>Sales **might** increase |
| Improbability | It is (**very/highly**) **unlikely that** sales will increase / **improbable that** sales will increase<br>Sales are **unlikely to** increase |
| Impossibility | I am **sure** / **certain** / **positive** **that** sales **won't** increase<br>Sales **definitely/certainly won't** increase<br>Sales **cannot** (**possibly**) increase |

## C *Uses*

1 **Definitely** and **certainly**. Notice the position of the adverbs in statements of certainty and impossibility:
Unemployment will definitely/certainly rise.
Unemployment definitely/certainly won't rise

2 **Likely** and **unlikely**. These adjectives can take two constructions:
It is likely/unlikely that unemployment will rise. (adjective + **that** clause)
Unemployment is likely/unlikely to rise. (adjective + infinitive with **to**)

3 **May** and **might**. Some speakers feel there is a slight difference in the strength of these two words:
Unemployment may increase. (50%)
Unemployment might increase. (45%)

## Exercise 1

*A pharmaceutical company has released a report on sales, research and future prospects. Match the situation on the left with a corresponding description of likelihood on the right. The first has been done as an example.*

| | |
|---|---|
| The company is having an excellent year. | This should be reversed over the winter months. |
| The sales of hospital equipment have remained constant. | We are certain that the future of the company is very secure. |
| Research into new drugs has been very encouraging | The end-of-year profits are bound to be up. |
| Over-the-counter (OTC) drugs show a slight fall in sales. | This may be related to government cuts in hospital spending. |
| The share price has continued to rise. | We are likely to see important additions to our product range. |

## Exercise 2

*A team of seismologists and civil engineers visits the site of a major road bridge, damaged in an earthquake. Together they produce a report on the likelihood of further damage being sustained by the bridge and on the repair operation.*
*Read the report. Underline 7 expressions of likelihood. Then complete the brief memo to your Head Office outlining the main points in the report. Include comment on the likelihood for the 7 points in the report. Use different expressions to those in the report. Here is an outline for your memo.*

**Azir Bridge: Earthquake damage – Preliminary Report**

**Risk of further quakes in the area**
The area concerned is very prone to earth tremors and two major earthquakes (more than 5 on the Richter scale) had been reported in the last thirty years before the recent one. It is therefore quite likely that another quake will affect the area in the next twenty years. It is difficult to predict the time of such a quake. However, the history of the area suggests a future earthquake of more than 7 on the Richter scale is highly improbable. However, small tremors of less than 2.5 are considered practically certain.

**Present condition of the Azir Bridge**
The bridge sustained serious structural damage in the recent earthquake. Any further tremor in the next few days, including one as low as 2.5 on the Richter scale, is bound to result in further damage, and the bridge might actually collapse.

**Recommendations**
It is advised that the bridge be demolished and replaced. This is sure to last over 15 months. Present cost estimates would certainly top $30 million.

**MEMO**

To: Head Office
Re: Azir Bridge Earthquake

1. Further quakes and/or tremors

2. Present condition

3. Recommendations

## Transfer

*Think about the development of tourism in your country in the short, medium and long term. Include your views on the likelihood of certain things happening or not happening.*

## ADVISING and SUGGESTING

*See also* **Unit 21 – Shall and should**

### A *Sample sentences*

- We are not ready to discuss layoffs yet. Why don't we fix a time for a meeting next week?
- First you should look at your current staffing needs.
- The consultant suggested that we should survey the market to find out the going rate.

### B *Form and uses*

We can classify suggestions under the following headings:
- suggestions involving the speaker
- suggestions to another person
- reported suggestions

**1** Suggestions involving the speaker:

| | |
|---|---|
| *Shall we* / *Why don't we* / *Let's* | discuss this now? |
| *I suggest we* / *We should* / *We ought to* | vote on this point now. |

**2** Suggestions to another person:

| | |
|---|---|
| *Why don't you* / *How about* | get some outside advice? / doing a random study? |
| *I suggest you* / *(I think) you should* | survey the market |
| *I (would) advise you* / *It's advisable* | to approach a reputable agency. |
| *I (would) recommend* | one of the major banks. |

**3** Reported suggestion:

| | |
|---|---|
| *The consultant advised us* | to review the company's operations. |
| *He recommended* / *He suggested* | that we (should) list our strengths and weaknesses. |

Note the following constructions:

How about (doing) something:
How about (giving) a brief overview? (*not:* how's about; *nor*: to give)

Suggest (that) someone does something:
I suggest (that) you give a brief overview.

Suggest something:
I suggest a brief overview.

Advise someone to do something:
I advise you to summarise the current situation.

Recommend that someone does/should do something:
I recommend that you summarise the current situation.

Recommend (someone to do) something:
I recommend (you to give) a brief overview.

# ADVISING and SUGGESTING

## Exercise 1

*Each sentence below contains a mistake. Underline the mistake and correct it.*

1 He suggested me to go to Kiev as soon as possible.
2 How about to have a meeting next month?
3 I recommended you to come, but you didn't.
4 I suggest to commission an independent report.
5 Why we don't stop now and continue tomorrow?
6 We should to think about this in more detail.
7 It is suggested to improve fire precautions.

## Exercise 2

*Chairing a meeting or a discussion may involve advising and making a lot of suggestions. Use the prompts below to write suitable sentences for chairing a discussion.*

1 Everyone has arrived and everyone is talking. It's 10 a.m., time to start the meeting. What do you say?

2 You want to start with *Item 1, Research and Development Update*. What do you say?

3 You know that Michelle has a report on this. Ask her to start.

4 Henri asks a question – but there is no time to answer it now. You know that another person, Joelle, could help him. What do you say to him?

5 The meeting decides that more money is needed to sponsor research into a new type of security camera. You know that a sister company is involved in some related research. Recommend contacting them.

6 It's 11.30 a.m. Time for coffee. What do you say?

7 During the coffee break a colleague, Karen, has a good idea. Suggest that she tell the meeting about it when you start again.

8 The meeting has restarted. Recently an outside consultant reported that a small team of three specialists should be set up to investigate ways to improve image on night-time photography. Report his suggestion.

9 Suggest that John writes a letter to the Chicago Institute of the Visual Image.

10 Suggest ending the meeting and having another one in four weeks.

## Exercise 3

*Here is part of an Incident Report on an oil drilling platform in the North Sea. Read the report and notice in particular the section containing recommendations.*

*Write a brief memo to the onshore Safety Officer, outlining the recommendations in the report opposite.*

**MEMO**

To: Peter Smalbord (Safety Officer)

From:

Re: Fire incident, Puffin, Drilling Platform Alpha Dos

The report into the above incident ...

**KITE OIL COMPANY**

**Incident Report**

**Date:** 12 October 19—
**Place:** Drilling Platform Alpha Dos, Puffin Rig, Gyda.

**Incident:** Fire (category 7)

**Description of events**
Rolf Halbo, Maintenance Engineer, was checking a valve on T45 gangway when he noticed smoke coming from a bin on gangway U28 below. He went below and looked in the bin and found abandoned overalls smouldering in the bottom of the bin. He took a fire extinguisher from Fire Point 128 and immediately extinguished the fire. The lid of the bin was not secure.

**Recommendations**
Improved housekeeping.
Issue order that no overalls be placed in bins.
Remove bins during potentially hazardous work, e.g. welding.
Further investigations required to determine exact cause of fire.
All lids to bins should be firmly secured.

**Indications**
Welding work was in process on T55 gangway above.

Report Approval:

| Witness | Shift Supervisor | Rig supervisor |
|---|---|---|
| R E Halbo | Yves Marchand | Trond Horscht |

## Transfer

*Write a short letter or memo to a colleague suggesting ways to improve communications within your company. Also, suggest a meeting to discuss your ideas.*

# UNIT 90

## REQUESTING INFORMATION and ACTION

***See also*** **Unit 41 – Questions**

## A *Sample sentences*

- Does your bank offer numbered accounts?
- Could you tell me if your bank offers numbered accounts?
- I'd like to know what you charge for these special services.
- Do you think you could send me the information before the end of the week?
- Do you happen to know which banks offer numbered accounts?
- Would you mind repeating that, please?

## B *Form*

We can make a request with either a *direct question*, an *order* or a *request*:
Does your bank offer numbered accounts? (direct question – see Unit 41)
Please fax me the information this morning. (order)
Would you mind repeating that please. (request)

If we are requesting information, the request comprises:
- **please** and/or a polite formula
- a question word
- a request

If we are requesting action, the request comprises:
- **please** and/or a polite formula
- a request

The language we use is very similar; so we use (I) to indicate a request for information and (A) to indicate a request for action.

1 The polite formula:
If you expect the other person to do what you ask (A), or to know the information that you want (I), use:

| | | |
|---|---|---|
| *Could you* (A) | *I'd like you to* (A) | *I wonder if you could* (A) |
| *Could you tell me* (I) | *I'd like to know* (I) | *I wonder if you could tell me* (I) |

If you are not sure whether the other person will do what you ask (A), or knows the information you want (I), use:

| | |
|---|---|
| *Do you think you could* (A) | *Do you know* (I) |
| *I wonder if you could* (A) | *Do you happen to know* (I) |
| *Would you mind* (A) | |

2 The question word when you ask for information:
If it is a **wh**-question, use the **wh**-question word, i.e. **who, what, which, when, where, why**, or **how**.

If it is a **yes/no** question, use **if** or **whether**.

3 The request:
We use the statement word order in polite requests for information:

| | *subject* | *verb* | |
|---|---|---|---|
| Could you tell me when | you | can deliver | the goods? |

## C *Uses*

Now we can grade these requests on a scale from **direct** to **indirect** (very polite). For a list of formulae to introduce the request, see Appendix 11.

# REQUESTING INFORMATION and ACTION

## Exercise 1

*Identify which of the following sentences ask for information (I) and which ask for action (A). Identify the two most direct forms (D) and the two most indirect forms (IND).*

1 I wonder if you'd mind sending me a new manual for the Creatif software Version 5.0? ☐

2 Can you tell me who I need to write to for such a manual? ☐

3 Do you think you could tell me if a newer version is planned? ☐

4 Perhaps you could send me a product list with prices? ☐

5 I'd like to know the name of a local supplier. I live in Osaka. ☐

6 Please send me a form so that I can become a registered user. ☐

## Exercise 2

*A customer visits a bank and asks a series of questions about the bank's services. Each question contains a mistake. Underline the mistake, then correct it.*

1 Can you tell me what are the kinds of current account available?
2 I'm wondering if you know the normal bank charges on overdrawn accounts?
3 Could you tell me do you send statements every month?
4 I like to know what interest you pay on a deposit account.
5 Would you mind say me what is the current level of interest you charge on loans?
6 I'd like that I have an appointment to discuss my cash flow problem with a loans officer.
7 I wonder if you mind checking whether a cheque I paid in last Monday has been cleared?

## Exercise 3

*Imagine you are on the telephone, discussing computing and word processing problems with your Creatif software User Service Centre. You have heard that there is something called* ***fragmentation****. Use the prompts below to request either information or action. Your question should be appropriate for the given answer.*

**1** *Ask what this is.*

*Q:*

*A: It happens when files are broken into fragments – small parts – for storage on your hard disk.*

**2** *Ask if it affects the files you write.*

*Q:*

*A: No, but it makes some actions slower – such as retrieving or saving files.*

**3** *Ask what the solution is.*

*Q:*

*A: You can compact the hard disk. To do this you need a special program, called Compact.*

**4** *Ask if Compact is already supplied with your Creatif software.*

*Q:*

*A: No, you have to buy it separately.*

**5** *Ask him to send you this Compact program.*

*Q:*

*A: I suggest you contact your computer store.*

**6** *Ask if Compact is difficult to run.*

*Q:*

*A: No, it's very easy. but you must not run it from Creatif. You must run it from DOS.*

**7** *Ask if you can call again if you have any problems with it.*

*Q:*

*A: Of course not. Please do.*

## Transfer

*Think of a conversation with a supplier of goods or services that you use. Write six requests, three for information and three for action.*

# PART 3

# *APPENDICES*

# APPENDIX 1

## PREPOSITIONAL VERBS

*See also* **Unit 33 – Verb + preposition**

**agree to** something (= accept):
They have agreed to our proposal to speed up the whole project.
**agree with** somebody/something:
I agree entirely with you.
**allow for** something:
In the winter we must allow for delays of up to 3 weeks.
**amount to** something:
The consultancy fees amounted to more than we had expected.
**apologise for** something:
I must apologise for keeping you all waiting.
**apply for** something:
We have just applied for membership of the European Marketing Scheme.
**approve of** somebody/something:
After watching the way George handled the crisis, I have to say I completely approve of his action.
**attend to** somebody/something:
I will attend to this matter as soon as possible.
(*Note*: to attend a meeting)
**complain** (**to** somebody) **about** somebody/something:
I'm going to complain (to them) about their poor delivery.
**conform to** something:
All our products conform to European standards.
**consent to** something:
They have consented to a display of their new products at the show.
**consist of** something:
The equipment consists of three main parts.
**depend on** something:
My answer depends on who is asking the question.
**hear about** something:
Have you heard about the new appointment?
**hear from** somebody:
I hope to hear from you after you have looked at our proposal.
**hope for** something:
We are hoping for a big improvement in productivity next year.
**insist on** something:
They have insisted on putting back the date of signature.
**look at** somebody/something:
Have you had a chance to look at our proposal yet?
**look for** somebody/something:
We are looking for enthusiastic agents in all parts of Europe.
**look forward to** something:
We are all looking forward to meeting you.
**pay** (somebody) **for** something:
We must pay (them) for the spare parts before the end of the month.
**refer to** something:
If you refer to the appendix at the end of the contract, you will find all the numbers of the components.
**rely on** somebody/something:
You can rely on them; they are totally dependable.
**succeed in** something:
Congratulations! You have succeeded in getting the Saudi contract.
**think about** something (= concentrate on):
At present we are thinking about your offer and will get back to you shortly.
**think of** something (= consider):
We are thinking of setting up a joint venture, but we would like some more information about the trading possibilities first.
**wait for** somebody/something:
We must contact them; they are waiting for our answer.

# APPENDIX 2

## OBJECT + PREPOSITIONAL VERBS

*See also* **Unit 34 – Verb + object + preposition**

**accuse somebody of** something:
They accused the Finance Manager of falsifying the company's accounts.
**advise somebody of/about** something:
Please advise us about any changes in the legislation.
**compare somebody/something with** somebody/something:
Of course you can't compare Peter with George. He was in a different league.
**congratulate somebody on** something:
We'd like to congratulate you on your appointment.
**convince somebody of** something:
We just can't convince them of the superiority of our products.
**describe something to** somebody:
Let me describe the main parts to you.
**divide/cut/split something into** something:
I've divided my presentation into three main parts.
**do something about** somebody/something:
We must do something about Sarah. She seems very unhappy.
**explain something to** somebody:
First of all I'd like to explain the operating system to you.
First of all I'd like to explain to you how the system operates.
**interest somebody in** something:
Finally we have managed to interest them in the new model.
**prefer somebody/something to** somebody/something:
In fact we preferred the old model to the new one.
**prevent somebody from** something:
They have prevented us from delivering the goods.
**protect somebody/something from** somebody/something:
The new legislation protects us from unfair competition.
**provide somebody with** something:
We would be happy to provide you with references.
**remind somebody of** something:
Let me remind you of the recent changes in the organisation.
**spend money on** something:
Last year we spent a lot of money on new equipment.
**tell somebody about** something:
Please can you tell us about the new developments.

## APPENDIX 

### PHRASAL VERBS

***See also* Unit 35 – Verb + adverb (phrasal verb)**

**break down**
I'm going to call the engineers because the machine has broken down again. (stop working)

**bring about**
The new appointments should bring about radical changes in the organisation. (cause)

**call off**
I'm afraid I'm going to have to call off the meeting. (cancel)

**call round**
The next time that you're in the area, please call round. (visit)

**close down**
After long negotiations they have decided to close down the plant. (stop the operations of)

**come along**
As you are here, why don't you come along for a meal with us this evening? (come)

**fill in**
Before the appraisal interview, make sure that you fill this form in. (complete by writing in relevant information)

**find out**
Can we find out how long they have been buying from ABC? (discover)

**look over**
I'd like half an hour to look over the figures before the meeting. (examine quickly)

**make up**
I don't believe that story about the contract in China; I think he made it up (invent)

**move in**
Everything is ready at the new offices; we're moving in next week. (take possession of new premises)

**put on**
Why don't you put on the booster? It'll run the job much faster. (turn on)

**send back**
If you don't like the goods, you can always send them back. (return)

**speak up**
I'm sorry. I can't hear you very well. Could you please speak up? (speak louder)

**speed up**
This is a very busy period for us; so we need to speed up production. (make faster)

**throw away**
Please make sure that you throw away all the old literature.

**turn down**
It's a very attractive offer, but I'm going to have to turn it down. (reject)

**turn up**
You don't need a ticket to get in; you just turn up. (arrive)

**walk through**
On the next part of the tour, we are going to walk through the despatch hall.

**write down**
They've quoted a price but they haven't written down the part numbers.

## APPENDIX 

### VERBS OF SPEAKING

***See also* Unit 39 – Reported speech (1)**

*accept add affirm agree allege announce answer argue assert claim comment communicate convey declare demonstrate disclose divulge emphasise explain highlight imply indicate inform maintain notify prove recount reply report restate reveal show state stress suggest transmit tell*

## APPENDIX 

### VERBS OF COMMANDING, REQUESTING, QUESTIONING AND REPORTING

***See also* Unit 40 – Reported speech (2)**
**Appendix 11 – Requesting**

1 Commanding:
*brief command direct instruct request require tell*

2 Requesting:
*ask beg call for implore invite press urge*

3 Questioning:
*ask demand examine inquire investigate query question*

4 Reporting:
Some of these verbs take a subordinate clause (1). Some take an infinitive with **to** (2); and some take both (1, 2).
*convince* (1, 2) *encourage* (1, 2) *entreat* (2)
*indoctrinate* (2) *invite* (2) *motivate* (2)
*persuade* (1, 2) *threaten* (2) *urge* (1, 2) *warn* (1,2)

## APPENDIX 

### NOUNS

***See also* Unit 48 – Nouns**

1 The following nouns have only a plural form (**-s**) and take a plural verb:
*archives arrears assets* (belonging to a company)
*contents customs* (taxes) *funds* (money)
*headquarters outskirts premises* (buildings)
*savings surroundings thanks*

2 The following nouns are uncountable singular:
*accommodation advice baggage equipment furniture information luggage machinery permission progress traffic travel trouble weather work*

We're planning to invest in new *machinery*. (uncountable)
We're planning to invest in new *machines*. (countable plural)

3 Uncountable common nouns:
**a** These nouns ending in **-ics** are usually singular:
*economics tactics politics mathematics ethics*
**b** *News* is always singular.
**c** Substances are often singular, e.g. *oil, butter, petrol, coal* and *wine*. They can be used as countable nouns when they mean 'a type of':
We now sell three butters. (three types of butter)

# APPENDIX 7

## ADJECTIVE DERIVATIONS

*See also* Unit 51 – Adjectives versus adverbs

| Ending | Noun or verb | Adjective |
|---|---|---|
| **-ite** | define | definite |
| **-ful** | use | useful |
| **-al** | economy | economical |
| **-ive** | product | productive |
| **-able/ible** | agree | agreeable |

| Ending | Noun or verb | Adjective |
|---|---|---|
| **-(i)al** | manager | managerial |
| | accident | accidental |
| **-less** | hope | hopeless |
| **-ic** | economy | economic |
| **-ous** | number | numerous |
| **-ing** | interest | interesting |
| **-ed** | interest | interested |

# APPENDIX 8

## ZERO ARTICLE

*See also* Unit 58 – Articles

We do not use an article (**the** or **a**) with certain types of words.

1 Names of meals:
*breakfast lunch dinner supper*
I usually eat lunch in the company canteen.
What do you eat for breakfast?
*But*: I usually eat a small breakfast before going to the office.

2 Institutions:
*school college university church prison hospital*
I went to university in Sheffield, before joining the company.
*cf.* The University of Sheffield has quite a good reputation.
The university in Sheffield has quite a good reputation.

3 Some common words:
*bed work home*
What time do you normally finish work?
I'm usually at home at the weekend.
*most half both*
Most managers have had some overseas experience before joining us.
At least half of the problem was their fault.
Both plans have been approved.

# APPENDIX 9

## CONNECTORS AND SEQUENCE MARKERS

*See also* Unit 74 – Connecting and sequencing ideas

**1 Logical connectors and sequence markers**

**a** Cause:
*therefore so accordingly consequently*
*as a consequence/result hence* (formal)
*thus* (formal) *because of this that's why* (informal)

**b** Contrast:
*yet however nevertheless still*
*but even so all the same* (informal)

**c** Condition:
*then in that case*

**d** Comparison:
*similarly in the same way*

**e** Concession:
*anyway at any rate*

**f** Contradiction:
*in fact actually as a matter of fact indeed*

**g** Alternation:
*instead alternatively*

**2 Textual connectors and sequence markers**

**a** Addition:
*also in addition moreover furthermore besides*
*too overall what's more* (informal) *in brief/short*

**b** Summary:
*to sum up then overall in brief/short*

**c** Conclusion:
*in conclusion finally lastly to conclude*

**d** Equivalence:
*in other words that means namely*
*that is to say or rather*

**e** Inclusion:
*for example for instance say such as*
*as follows*(written) *e.g.* (formal and written)

**f** Highlight:
*in particular in detail especially notably*
*chiefly mainly*

**g** Generalisation:
*usually normally as a rule in general*
*for the most part in most cases on the whole*

**h** Stating the obvious:
*obviously naturally of course clearly*

# APPENDIX 10

## GRAPHICS

*See also* Unit 75 – Describing trends

1 The different types of lines in graphs:
——— a solid line
- - - - - - a broken line
.............. a dotted line

2 The names for the axes on a graph:

The vertical axis is also called the *y* axis and the horizontal axis the *x* axis.

Vertical axis
Horizontal axis

**3** The different types of graphics:

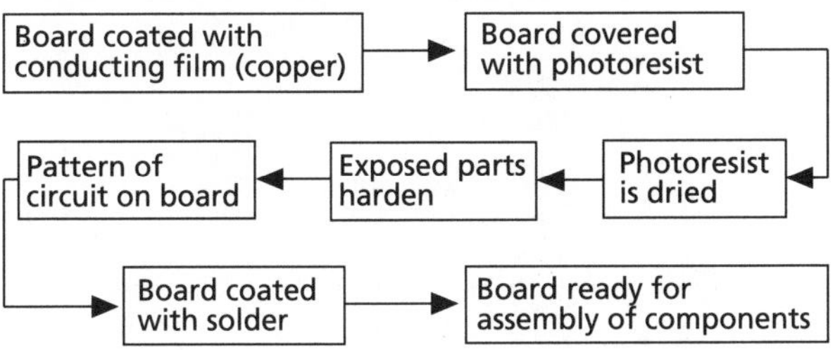


**A flow chart**

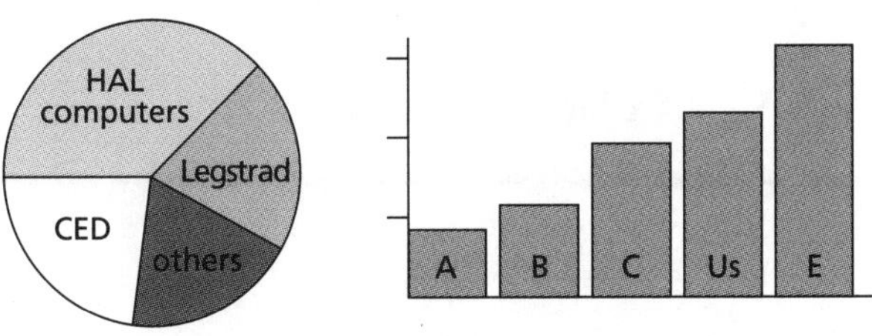


**A pie chart** **A bar chart**

| GNP/GDP % change | Average '81–'89 | '96 forecast | '99 forecast |
|---|---|---|---|
| France | 12 | 28 | 30 |
| Germany | 11 | 32 | 30 |
| Italy | 08 | 31 | 28 |
| Japan | 39 | 25 | 15 |
| UK | 17 | 26 | 32 |
| USA | 23 | 25 | 35 |

**A table**

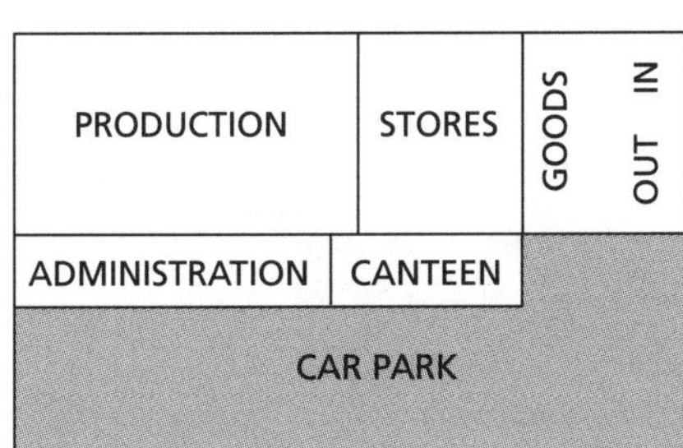


**A plan**

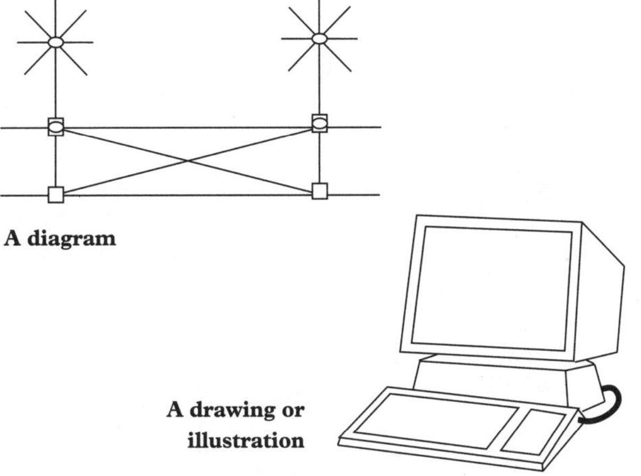

**A diagram**

**A drawing or illustration**

# APPENDIX 11

## REQUESTING

***See also*** **Unit 90 – Requesting information and action**
**Appendix 5 – Verbs of requesting**

The list below shows formulae to introduce the request on a scale from *direct* to *indirect* (very polite).
It also shows which phrases can be used to introduce a request for action (A) and a request for information (I).

*direct*

Please + order (A)
Please tell me … (I)
I want you to … (A)
Do you know … (I)
Can you … (A)
Can you tell me … (I)
Will you … (A)
Will you tell me … (I)
Could you … (A)
Could you tell me … (I), please
I'd like you to … (A)
I'd like to ask you … (A) or (I)
I'd like to know … (I)
Do you happen to know … (I)

Perhaps you could … (A)
Perhaps you could tell me … (I)
Could you possibly … (A)
Could you possibly tell me … (I)
Do you think you could …(A)
Do you think you could tell me …(I)
Would you mind … (A)
Would you mind telling me … (I)

I wonder if you could … (A)
I wonder if you could tell me … (I)
Do you think I could ask you … (I)

I wonder if you'd mind … (A)
I wonder if you'd mind my asking you … (I)
I was wondering if you could … (A)
I was wondering if you could tell me … (I)
I was wondering if you'd mind telling me … (I)

*indirect*

# PART 4

# KEY

## TASKS 1

### THE PRESENT CONTINUOUS

#### Exercise 1 (M)

*Now I am planning a new project.*
*At the moment we are working with our R & D department.*
*At present our department is designing new solutions.*
*Currently they are installing a new network.*
*Currently I am designing a new network.*
*Now we are planning new solutions.*
*Are they now designing new solutions?*
*Are they planning a new network at the moment?*

#### Exercise 2

| Activity at or around the time of speaking | Temporary activity in the present | Fixed arrangement in the future |
|---|---|---|
| (4) | (1) (2) (3) | (5) |

#### Exercise 3

1. Now John is finishing preparations for a meeting tomorrow.
2. Tomorrow morning, Michael, John and Patrizia are having a meeting.
3. Tonight Michael is meeting Felix to discuss the trip to Japan next week.
4. Tonight John isn't meeting Felix and Michael.
5. Next week they are going to Japan.

## TASKS 2

### THE PRESENT SIMPLE

#### Exercise 1

*Softcraft produces computer software for business applications. The company* ***supplies*** *programs for general business applications. In addition, Softcraft* ***develops*** *customised software for individual requirements. Softcraft* ***employs*** *85 people. 40 of these* ***work*** *in program development. The company also* ***uses*** *external consultants.*

#### Exercise 2 (M)

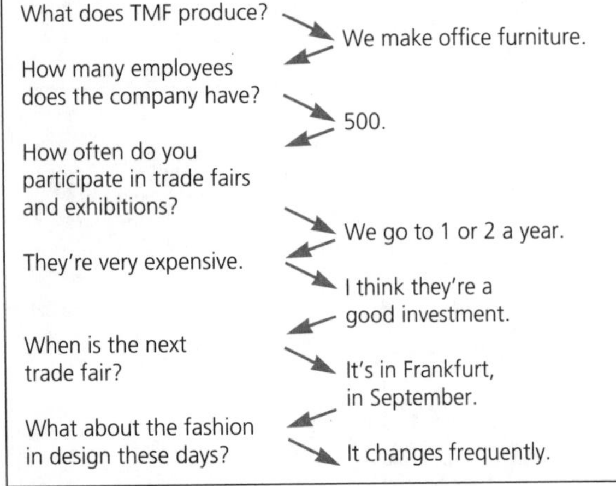

What does TMF produce?
We make office furniture.
How many employees does the company have?
500.
How often do you participate in trade fairs and exhibitions?
We go to 1 or 2 a year.
They're very expensive.
I think they're a good investment.
When is the next trade fair?
It's in Frankfurt, in September.
What about the fashion in design these days?
It changes frequently.


#### Exercise 3 (M)

1. We always provide a good service.
2. I often have face-to-face meetings with new customers.
3. Our company occasionally employs external consultants.
4. I'm usually busy in summer.
5. He hardly ever has meetings in the morning.
6. I hardly ever see the Senior Vice-President.
7. We never write reports.

## TASKS 3

### THE PAST SIMPLE

#### Exercise 1

*On Monday Diano S.p.A.* ***reported*** *increased profits for the year. Exports* ***climbed*** *by 20 per cent last year but domestic sales* ***fell*** *by 5 per cent. Two months ago the company* ***set up*** *new sales offices in France and Singapore. On the Milan Stock Exchange yesterday the company's share price* ***rose*** *by 300 lire to L. 2,155.*

#### Exercise 2

J: When **did you begin** negotiations?
D: We **started** three months ago.
J: And you reached agreement this morning?
D: That's right.
J: Was the original idea yours or Fallon's?
D: At first we **approached** Fallon and we **put forward** some outline proposals.
J: **Did you have** any major problems?
D: No, as you know, we **met** many times and we **reached** agreement yesterday.

#### Exercise 3

*In January 1992 TELCO reported profits of $28m – an increase of 25 per cent. In June TeleResearch (TR) produced a prototype of the Linco Mobile Phone and in October offered Telco a licence agreement. One month later Telco offered to buy the Linco Mobile Phone for $2.5m. TR rejected the offer and then in January 1993 Telco suggested a joint venture. Negotiations began and in June 1993 Telco and TR formed a joint venture company, Linco.*

## TASKS 4

### THE PAST CONTINUOUS

#### Exercise 1 (M)

*I was researching new ideas when they found a solution.*
*Mrs Ford was writing a report when she resigned.*
*The production team were designing a new plant when the Director abandoned the project.*
*The manager was researching a report when I resigned.*

### Exercise 2

1 We **were reviewing** safety procedures when the accident **happened**.
2 While we **were cleaning** the tanks the chemicals **polluted** the river.
3 The plant **was operating** at full capacity before the explosion **happened**.
4 We **turned off** the supply because the pipe **was leaking**.
5 As the equipment **was getting old** we **decided** to replace it.
6 When the fire **started** she **was wearing** protective clothing.
7 While the company **were investigating** the accident the government **introduced** new regulations.
8 The risk of explosion **was** highest precisely when the workers **were repairing** the pipe.

### Exercise 3

*On Monday at 16.30 a construction worker was hurt at the Iribas plant. The foreman said that four men* ***were working*** *on a roof when a crane* ***hit*** *the wall of the building. One of the men* ***slipped*** *and* ***fell*** *to the ground. The crane driver* ***tried*** *to lift a metal pipe when he* ***lost*** *control. A preliminary report identifies three factors which contributed to the accident: the injured worker* ***was not wearing*** *a safety harness. The crane* ***was working*** *in a prohibited area. It* ***was raining****, so work should have been stopped.*

## TASKS 5

### THE PRESENT PERFECT SIMPLE

### Exercise 1

1 Mennis plc have not contacted us recently.
2 I have not spoken to Frank yet.
3 We have not ordered anything today.
4 Paolo hasn't called you yet.
5 Mr Joyce has sent the goods today.
6 She has not arrived yet.

### Exercise 2

*Last year our company* ***reported*** *a small increase in profits. This year we* ***have seen*** *continued improvement and our turnover* ***has risen*** *by 15 per cent. This is very good news in a difficult world market. In fact internationally, the market* ***has fallen****.*
*Naturally, our costs* ***have gone up*** *and so the rise in profits is not so great. It is true that our domestic performance* ***has been helped*** *by the collapse of our competitor, Capra & Pecora, which* ***went out of business*** *in January.*

### Exercise 3

| Activity at some non-specific time in the past with an impact or result in the present or future | Activity within a period of time which is not yet finished | Activity which started in the past and continues to the present |
|---|---|---|
| in Asia there has been increased growth | we have already seen signs of improvement | recent times have been difficult |
| we have been involved in the insurance market | | the world economy has suffered a downturn |
| | | this sector has grown rapidly |

## TASKS 6

### THE PRESENT PERFECT CONTINUOUS

### Exercise 1

1 You've been working for Paulus & Company for many years.
2 You haven't been working for Paulus & Company for many years.
3 Have you been working for Paulus & Company for many years?
4 They've been selling shares since January.
5 They haven't been selling shares since January.
6 Have they been selling shares since January?

### Exercise 2

1 George has been working too hard recently. (period)
2 He has made a lot of mistakes. (point)
3 He has been travelling all over the country. (period)
4 He's even had a couple of minor road accidents. (point)
5 He's asked for some time off work. (point)
6 We've been thinking of ways to help him. (period)

### Exercise 3

**Memo**

To: B.J. McCusker
(Sales)
From: H.V.

Subject: Recruitment of Sales Director (Northern Region)

We've been advertising for six months in national newspapers. We've interviewed five candidates but we haven't been able to fill the position.

This month we've placed an advertisement in the Sales & Marketing Journal.

I've talked to the 'Head Hunting' agency. This seems to be an increasingly probable solution.

Any comments?

## TASKS 7

### THE PAST PERFECT

#### Exercise 1

1 The plane had left when they reached the airport.
The plane hadn't left when they reached the airport.
Had the plane left when they reached the airport?
2 She had already signed the contract when you called.
She hadn't (already) signed the contract when you called.
Had she already signed the contract when you called?
3 You had sent the report before we noticed the mistake.
You hadn't sent the report before we noticed the mistake.
Had you sent the report before we noticed the mistake?

#### Exercise 2

2 We had already sold the shares when the market fell.
3 I had already met Mrs Haan before the Seville Trade Fair.
4 We had already designed a new logo before we designed the packaging.

#### Exercise 3 (M)

*71 per cent of women aged 18–25 had bought clothes in the previous week.*
*62 per cent of men aged 18–25 had bought clothes in the previous week.*
*49 per cent of men aged 26–35 had bought clothes in the previous week.*
*Only 31 per cent of men aged 36–45 had done so.*
*More women than men had bought clothes in the previous week in all age groups.*
*For both men and women the youngest had bought clothes more than older age groups.*

## TASKS 8

### THE FUTURE with WILL

#### Exercise 1

1 I think I'll go to Athens soon. (1)
2 Are you thirsty? I'll get you something to drink. (1)
3 We'll watch a video, then we'll see the production plant. (2)
4 Hold on – I'll just phone Marta to ask her. (1)
5 When you come, I'll introduce you to Maria Penrose, our Finance Manager. (1)
6 There'll probably be a fall in profits in the spring. (4)
7 Perhaps I'll get to Sydney next year. (4)
8 I expect you'll stay in a hotel, won't you? (3)
9 John has arrived. I'll go to meet him. (1)
10 The report will be ready on Monday. (2)

#### Exercise 2

2 It'll be about cost savings.
3 (I think) it'll be easy.
4 I'll call the repair man.
5 I'll telephone her.
6 We won't meet Bergit.

#### Exercise 3 (M)

2 After a verb of mental activity.
I expect there'll be a rise in inflation.
3 A neutral activity as part of a process, e.g. a presentation.
First I'll explain the background.
4 A neutral activity in the future.
The launch will be in January.
5 Activity decided at the time of speaking.
It's time for the news. I'll go and listen, then I'll tell you if there's anything there about share prices.
6 In the main clause of conditional I sentences.
If I go to Warsaw I'll visit Mr Zabrinski, our sales rep there.

## TASKS 9

### THE FUTURE with GOING TO

#### Exercise 1

| Sentence | Action already decided | Intention | Activity based on present situation |
|---|---|---|---|
| 1 | | | ✓ |
| 2 | ✓ | | |
| 3 | | ✓ | |
| 4 | ✓ | | |
| 5 | | | ✓ |
| 6 | ✓ | | |

#### Exercise 2

*'Product A is an old product, nearing the end of its life. As the graph shows, sales for Product A* ***are going to fall*** *whereas sales for product B, which is very profitable,* ***are going to rise****. Because of this, we* ***are going to cut*** *production of A and at the same time concentrate efforts on B. In addition, we* ***are going to launch*** *a new product, C.'*

## TASKS 10

### THE CONDITIONALS (1)

#### Exercise 1

1 If you **come** we'll discuss it in detail.
2 If we **reached** agreement we'd sign the contract the same day.
3 Unless there is a major problem, we'll **need** only one day.
4 If we have good advertising, the product **will be** a success.
5 If there **were** an easy solution, we would have avoided the problems.
6 If we had taken your advice, we **would have spent** more money.

### Exercise 2

2 If the sales are poor we'll change the distribution network.
If the sales were poor we'd change the distribution network.
If the sales had been poor we would have changed the distribution network.

3 If there is high demand overseas we'll increase the Export Sales team.
If there were high demand overseas we'd increase the Export Sales team.
If there had been high demand overseas we would have increased the Export Sales team.

4 If there is a world recession there'll be a drop in the world market.
If there were a world recession there would be a drop in the world market.
If there had been a world recession there would have been a drop in the world market.

### Exercise 3 (M)

2 If you stopped work there would be no protection for your family.
3 If you spent a period in hospital you would have no cover for hospital fees.
4 If your house caught fire you would have insufficient cover to replace lost items.
5 If you had a road accident you would not be covered for legal expenses.
6 If (the worst happened and) you died you would have no life assurance.
7 If you had no life assurance your family would be left with no money.

## TASKS 11

## THE CONDITIONALS (2)

### Exercise 1

**Deposit and payment**
No holiday booking will be accepted unless accompanied by the necessary deposit. A confirmation will then be issued once the deposit has been received. The balance may be paid at any time provided it is not later than eight weeks before departure.

**Changes to bookings**
As you will appreciate, your holiday arrangements are planned many months in advance and on rare occasions it may be necessary to make changes. In the unfortunate event that we have to make major changes, you will be entitled to compensation as shown in Appendix 1. However, you will only be entitled to compensation on condition that you contact our office not later than seven days after notification of the proposed changes. Provided that we can substitute a holiday of similar quality, there will be no entitlement to compensation.

**Misbehaviour**
We reserve the absolute right to terminate without notice the holiday arrangements of any person in the case of misbehaviour likely to annoy other passengers.

**Should you have a problem**
Should you have a problem, remember that our representatives are on hand to help.

### Exercise 2

1 d. 2 f. 3 a. 4 e. 5 b. 6 c.

### Exercise 3

1 Should the policyholder wish to extend this policy, he must notify the company before the policy expiry date.
2 Should the policyholder not contact the company before the expiry date, the company shall be entitled to terminate the agreement.
3 Were the policyholder subsequently to decide to renew the policy, the company would be entitled to charge an introductory fee.
4 However, were the company to decide not to renew the policy, for whatever reason, they must inform the policyholder within seven days.
5 Were the company not to inform the policyholder within the specified time, they may not refuse to renew the policy.
6 The company may terminate the contract:
  a should the policyholder not disclose all the relevant information;
  b were the policyholder not to complete all the sections;
  c had the policyholder failed to pay the full premium by the agreed time.

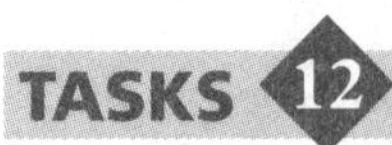

## TASKS 12

## TENSE REVIEW

### Exercise 1

*Mantegna S.p.A. was founded by Leonardo Mantegna in 1952. Until 1955 the company had only a small factory in Verona producing mainly steel pipes. In 1956 a new plant was opened in Milan and the company began manufacturing valves. In 1975 the Head Office was moved to Milan. In 1980 Mantegna rejected an attempted takeover by Echo Inc., Chicago. In the next ten years sales offices were established in 48 different countries. Now the company has a turnover of $450m and produces a range of over 400 products. The company is planning expansion into the automotive sector. Next year there will be a new plant in the United Kingdom and the company plans to open a plant in Boston, Massachusetts in three years.*

## TASKS 13

## VERB ...ING

### Exercise 1

On checking the above file we find that you are correct in thinking the cost estimates for the coming year are excessive. We regret that in calculating labour costs some errors appeared in our analysis. We are presently repeating the study which involves reviewing all the figures.

Working in partnership with Harris & Co is proving very useful and we are sure that there will be many benefits.
We look forward to having a joint meeting soon. We are also involved in calculating costs for the following year and will let you know as soon as they are finished.

We must meet soon, otherwise we risk not having everything ready for the MD in June, but it's not worth fixing a date today, as I don't yet know my movements for the rest of this month.

## Exercise 1 continued

| Subject of verb | Object of verb | After preposition | Continuous verb form |
|---|---|---|---|
| working | reviewing<br>having<br>not having<br>fixing | on checking<br>in thinking<br>in calculating | repeating<br>proving |

## Exercise 2

1 We are interested in **seeing** your plant.
2 **Launching** new products is essential for the survival of the company.
3 We look forward to **hearing** from you.
4 He suggested **meeting** us next month.
5 **Clarifying** our policy is an essential prerequisite to improving products.
6 By delaying we risk **losing** the contract.

## Exercise 3

3 She said the products were old and investing more in R & D was essential.
4 There was a lack of money in the company and she suggested having a rights issue.
5 Overstaffing should be solved by reducing the workforce.

# TASKS 14

## INFINITIVE

## Exercise 1

*'We need **to increase (PS)** research **to develop (PS)** a completely new model. **To have begun (PP)** the research earlier would have cost much less money. However, **to delay (PS)** now will cost even more. Some members of the board appear **to be recommending (PC)** simple modifications to the existing range. This is a very short-sighted strategy. **To rely on (PS)** old models during a fall in the market is quite wrong. We have **to plan (PS)** for the long-term development of our product range. As I said, it would have been better **to have put (PP)** more cash into the project two years ago. Now, **to be talking about (PC)** relying on continued production of a range that is declining is clearly not sensible.*

*'This, to me, is absolutely clear. If we want **to be (PS)** in control of the situation in the future, we have **to understand (PS)** it now.'*

## Exercise 2

**MEMO**
**To:** TR
**From:** SA
**Date:** 14th May

Re. Advertising contract negotiation

It is going **to be** difficult **to reach** agreement with Emmy over the advertising material. Their principal negotiator, Stella Ragione, appears **to want** a large downpayment on signature of contract – probably near 50 per cent. We plan **to tell** her that this is impossible. We are happy **to discuss** the possibility of an advance but personally I believe it would be a mistake **to agree** to anything above 20 per cent. **To clarify** our position immediately could save us time.
I suggest we inform Miss Ragione of our views on the matter. We should also make it clear that Morreille Partnership (Marseille) are happy **to take on** the project and their reputation for high standards is as good as Emmy's. We need **to resolve** this very soon,

## Exercise 3

1 We want to talk about the problem of transport. ☑
2 We delayed **having** a meeting.
3 We decided not to have a meeting. ☑
4 We started to consider the alternatives. ☑
5 We avoided **having** an accident

## Exercise 4

1 **To begin** the research earlier would have cost much more money.
2 **To delay** now will cost even more.
3 We have **to decide** on our priorities.
4 My impression is that **to increase** production is a high-risk strategy.
5 **To invest** more during a fall in the market is quite wrong.
6 It would have been better **to have put** more cash into the project two years ago.
7 **To have commissioned** more market research would have helped.

# TASKS

## VERB ...ING or INFINITIVE + TO

## Exercise 1

1 I'd like **to attend** the conference.
2 I remember **meeting** your colleague in Osaka.
3 I tried **to phone/phoning** you last week but I think you were away.
4 We like **to test** the goods before we despatch them.
5 We tried **asking** for payment on delivery but in practice we had to allow 30 days.
6 We would like **to make** a formal agreement.

## Exercise 2

1 We'd like to have a meeting.
   **b** We want a meeting.
2 We stopped to visit suppliers in Budapest.
   **b** We interrupted our journey so we could visit them.
3 Have you tried sending goods by train?
   **a** Have you experimented with the idea of using the train?
4 We remembered to send publicity material with the goods.
   **c** We did not forget to send the material with the goods.

## Exercise 3

1 I **tried to call** you yesterday but without success.
2 I **remember sending** you a tender for the Apple Project but we have had no reply.
3 We **like to contact** potential customers to check their reactions to tenders.
4 I am sure that if you **stop to think** about our offer you will agree that the price is fair.

# TASKS 16

## VERB + OBJECT + INFINITIVE

## Exercise 1

**OFFICESPACE**

We will <u>help you solve</u> your space problems. We <u>invite you to share</u> in a whole new concept in office design! Our modern office systems <u>allow you to create</u> additional space at little extra expense. We can <u>enable you to redesign</u> working areas to maximum advantage! If you <u>would like us to send</u> you details of this amazing offer, fill in the reply coupon below. Or if you would prefer to telephone us, simply ring 0800 and ask for Freefone OFFICESPACE.

## Exercise 2 (M)

1 I persuaded you to come.
2 Joanne does not allow purchasers to accept gifts.
3 We want the report to be destroyed.
4 She can help new recruits understand.
5 Henry would prefer me to resign.

## Exercise 3

1 The report made us to review our forecasts. ✗
   The report made us review our forecasts.
2 The report failed to identify the cause of the accident. ✓
3 This allows to make further investments. ✗
   This allows us to make further investments.
4 We want that you respect the terms of the contract. ✗
   We want you to respect the terms of the contract.
5 We asked them to advance the order by two months. ✓
6 We would like that you to come to the meeting. ✗
   We would like you to come to the meeting.
7 The contract does not permit that we increase the price. ✗
   The contract does not permit us to increase the price.

# TASKS 17

## WILL and WOULD

## Exercise 1

A: This is the contract for the transport of the order to Singapore. Would you check it for me?
B: Of course. **I'll** do it now.
A: **You'll** see, they **wouldn't** agree to pay the insurance.
B: Really? I think that other company, TransWorld, would pay it.
A: No, on the contrary, they **wouldn't**. But if you like **I'll** ask them.
B: No, **don't**. **I'm** sure **you're** right.

## Exercise 2

Helena: Oh, Martina. You know about the despatch of the KMB order tomorrow? **Would** you check that the transporters will arrive early?
Martina: Of course I **will**, **I'll** phone them now.
Helena: And do you know if they**'ll** reach the ferry terminal in time for the 2 o'clock sailing?
Martina: I spoke to them yesterday. They said they **would**.
Helena: And **did** they agree to bring back the faulty goods?
Martina: No, they **wouldn't** do that this time because the lorry is going on to Bari with other goods. They said they**'d** bring the faulty goods another time.
Helena: I see. That's a pity.

## Exercise 3

1 Excuse me, would you help me book a flight to Manchester?
2 Of course I will. (I'll do it now).
3 If you want, I'll help you unload the goods.
4 Yes it will.
5 No they won't.

# TASKS 18

## MAY and MIGHT

## Exercise 1

1 Stock levels **may** rise in the final quarter of the year.
2 **We may not** have any SuperFix in stock.
3 **We may/might change** to a just-in-time method of procurement.
4 **We may** need to increase the quantity we hold in stock but our present suppliers **might** not be able to meet our needs.
5 If the quality is not good enough **we may/might** change our suppliers.
6 **May** I check stock levels today instead of tomorrow?
7 If you check stock levels today instead of tomorrow **you might** get inaccurate information for the month.
8 **We may already be** using that supplier.

### Exercise 2

1 Yes, it **might** damage our reputation.
2 If we don't, the public **may/might** misunderstand our intentions.
3 We'll have an 'open' day when everyone **may** visit the factory.
4 If we don't, we **may/might not** get the support we want.
5 No, I said they **may** come.
6 I don't know. They **may/might**, or they **may/might not.**

## TASKS 19

## CAN and COULD

### Exercise 1

A: **Can I** see you next week?
B: Of course **you can**. **Could you** come on Monday?
A: No, sorry, **I can't** come then. If it is okay with you, **I could** come on Tuesday.
B: Excellent. **Can you** confirm by fax?
A: Certainly. **I can** do that now. Oh, another question. **Could I** bring my colleague, Mr Lee Wang?
B: Of course **you can**. I look forward to meeting him.
A: Thanks very much. See you next week.

### Exercise 2

2 They **could** find the theory difficult.
3 The manager told Piero that he **could** do the course.
4 After the course you **can** carry out major maintenance.
5 This course was not available last year so Gautier **couldn't/can't have** this qualification.
6 Due to company cuts, the department **could not** spend money on the course.

### Exercise 3

| Ability | | | Possibility | | Permission | |
|---|---|---|---|---|---|---|
| past | present | future | present | future | past | present |
| 5 | 3 | 4 | 6 | 7 | 1 | 2 |

## TASKS 20

## MUST, MUSTN'T and NEEDN'T

### Exercise 1

The colour of the plastic is not right. The liquid must have been (D) too hot. This batch must be (O+) withdrawn but we needn't (–O) stop the production. Obviously we must (O+) check the temperature control. We mustn't (O-) leave it as it is or the same thing will happen tomorrow.

### Exercise 2 (M)

1 Obviously we mustn't pollute rivers.
2 We needn't build an expensive purification plant.
3 We must make small changes to production methods.

### Exercise 3

We had to look at our production control procedures. We didn't need to examine every step in the process, but we had to ask all employees how we could improve the system. Of course, the management fixed the rules: but we had to implement them.

### Exercise 4

1 Miriam is late. She had another meeting this morning but **it must have** finished by now.
2 The goods are faulty so we **needn't** pay for them.
3 The production costs are too high. We **must** reduce them.
4 The system is dangerous. We **mustn't** continue using it.
5 The valve broke so we **had to** replace it.
6 The supervisor says we **have to** report any leakage. Last year we **didn't need to** report small leaks.

## TASKS 21

## SHALL and SHOULD

### Exercise 1

A: Shall we wait for Peter? (Sugg)
B: Yes, he should be along any moment. (Pr)
A: Is he staying all morning?
B: He certainly should. (Obl) We've important things to discuss.
A: While we're waiting, shall (Sugg) I show you the report?
B: No, I shall (Fut) look at it in detail this afternoon. I think you shouldn't (Ad) say anything about it until Peter's here. Should (Cond) it be controversial, he'd want to be the first to know.

### Exercise 2

Picture A – 2
Picture B – 1
Picture C – 3
Picture D – 6
Picture E – 4
Picture F – 5

### Exercise 3

1 Shall we have some lunch now?
2 Should we change the schedule?
3 You shouldn't continue with this!
4 She should arrive at about 5 o'clock.
5 The report should be good.
6 Should you want to see the machine in operation, please contact us.

## Exercise 4

'Friends, I'm going to talk about new production plans. First I shall talk about the 24-hour production line at the Friuli plant, then I want to say something about our new automated line at Rimini. So, Friuli. Production should start in June. I think we should begin with a low output – say about 50 per cent of capacity. In this way any bugs should be eliminated early without creating chaos. Shall I describe the line in detail? If not, you should read the report that should be ready at the end of next week. Now, if we start at 50 per cent capacity, the production output will be about the same as it is now for the initial period. This shouldn't be a big problem ...

# TASKS 22

## ACTIVE

### Exercise 1

1 The cost of living **is rising** faster than ten years ago. (I)
2 We need to **reduce** costs. (T)
3 Manufacturing companies **are experiencing** major problems. (T)
4 Service companies **are doing** better. (T)
5 Unemployment **is increasing** in the United States. (I)
6 Property values **show** a slight fall. (T)
7 In spite of the problems, economists **are** optimistic. (I)

### Exercise 2

1 The bank **is going to raise** interest rates.
2 The cost of borrowing **will increase** by 2 per cent.
3 Many companies **are paying** heavy costs.
4 An interest rate rise **will worsen** industry's problems.
5 A representative **said** the news **would be** a disaster.

### Exercise 3

1 First we load the goods onto the lorry.
2 After that the lorry takes the goods to the port.
3 Then the driver hands over the docket.
4 Next, the customs sign the docket.
5 The driver keeps the docket.
6 Finally we file the docket.

### Exercise 4

1 The Vice-President took an important decision last week.
2 The telephonist has been making/has made too many private calls recently.
3 The nightwatchman has just patrolled the factory.
4 The plant does not manufacture products during the August holiday.
5 The laboratory will test/is going to test/is testing the new product next week.
6 The company doctor checks the employees every month.
7 The maintenance staff are repairing/will repair/are going to repair the production line next Monday.
8 Canteen staff do not cook food at the weekends.

# TASKS 23

## THE PASSIVE

### Exercise 1

1 Staff have been recruited by the Human Resources Department.
2 Finished products are stored in the warehouse.
3 New products are going to be developed by the R & D staff.
4 Goods are manufactured in several locations.
5 The new plant will be opened by the Corporation President.

### Exercise 2

*Liquids A and B are poured into a container. They are mixed and material C is added. The mixture is heated to 220°C and left to cool. Then the mixture is poured into small cans. The tins are closed, labels are applied and the goods are conveyed to the warehouse.*

### Exercise 3

1 50 per cent of our production is going to be made at our Bahrain plant.
2 The company's range of services is being expanded.
3 Our headquarters are being relocated in Malaysia.
4 The commission paid to agents was increased by the Sales Manager.
5 Protective clothing must be worn by employees inside the production area.
6 The merger proposal was being considered for most of last year.

# TASKS 24

## BE (1)

### Exercise 1

*We **are** reviewing salaries at the moment. However they **are** unlikely **to be** increased by more than the current rate of inflation, which **is** 3 per cent. The future strength of the company depends on capital investment. When costs increase too much, capital investment **is** reduced. This **is** sure to affect the profitability and long-term strength of the company. We **are** committed to the development of the company. This has always **been** our objective and will continue **to be** so in the coming decade.*

### Exercise 2

2 One is responsible for half the production, isn't it?
3 And that one is in Athens, isn't it?
4 The Thessalonika plant is the smallest, isn't it?
5 And it's the newest, isn't it?
6 It was opened in 1992, wasn't it?
7 And a new plant will be opened next year, won't it?

### Exercise 3

Dear Mr Antrobus

We were very pleased to hear that you are interested in our new TESPO-2 account. Unfortunately, the documentation will not be ready until next month. Therefore I am enclosing with this letter the preliminary details.

As you are no doubt aware, the TESPO-1 was issued at the end of last summer and has been a great success. We are confident that TESPO-2 will be a great success, too.

We hope that this information is/will be of use to you. However, if there are other aspects that you would be interested in, we would be delighted to talk to you by phone.

Yours sincerely

*M Bailey*
M Bailey
Investment Consultant

## TASKS 25

### BE (2)

### Exercise 1

1 Right.
2 Right.
3 Wrong. Companies are meeting the challenge by **being** more cautious.
4 Wrong. Our advice to new investors is: don't **put** all your capital into one fund.
5 Wrong. This service **has been offered** to clients for twenty years now.

### Exercise 2

2 Originally the project was to have been completed by the end of next year.
3 It is unfortunate that the building company ran into some financial difficulties.
4 Finally, the project was abandoned after we demanded they keep to the deadline.
5 Because there has been a delay/we have been delayed/the project has been delayed, there is a lot of pressure on us to find a replacement.
6 At the moment interested companies are being invited to submit tenders.
7 Originally, all tenders were to have been submitted by the end of last month.
8 To be honest, we are unlikely to be in the new building on time.

### Exercise 3

***There is*** *an airline in France called Air Europa.* ***It is*** *owned by a consortium of French, German, Danish and Dutch companies.* ***There are*** *too many airlines in Europe and* ***it is*** *likely that Air Europe* ***will be*** *bought out by one of the larger national carriers.* ***They are*** *a small company and* ***are*** *unlikely to remain independent. This* ***is*** *a common pattern in Europe where a few years ago* ***there were*** *many more airlines.*

## TASKS 26

### VERBS of SPEAKING

### Exercise 1

*The board met to* ***discuss the*** *new financing arrangements. The Chairman* ***told the*** *meeting that changes were necessary to reduce costs. He* ***asked the*** *Finance Manager to describe the new plan. She first* ***talked/spoke about the*** *reasons for the changes. Then she* ***spoke/talked about*** *the new plan.*

### Exercise 2

*I first heard about the problem when Jane* ***told*** *me about it. We* ***discussed*** *it for an hour. I* ***asked*** *her to* ***tell*** *me the reasons but she couldn't* ***say*** *what the reasons were. We agreed to* ***speak/talk*** *about it again before the meeting next week.*

### Exercise 3

Arione: Pronto, Arione, SpA.
Karamura: Hello, this is Yu-Ling Wu, from Karamura. Can I **speak** to Ms. Rina Arione, please?
Arione: She's in a meeting just now. Can you **tell** me what you want to **talk** about?
Karamura: Certainly. I need to **discuss** our meeting next month. I would like to **ask** Ms Arione for some suggestions for the agenda. When could I **talk** to her?
Arione: I think she'll be free in about an hour. I'll **ask** her to call you, shall I?
Karamura: Oh yes please. Did you **say** about an hour?
Arione: Yes, approximately. She'll call you then.
Karamura: Many thanks. Goodbye.

## TASKS 27

### VERBS of REPORTING

### Exercise 1

| | say | suggest | promise | require |
|---|---|---|---|---|
| infinitive + **to** (1) | | | ✓ | |
| **that** + clause (2) | ✓ | ✓ | ✓ | |
| verb *…ing* (3) | | ✓ | | |
| object (4) | | ✓ | ✓ | ✓ |
| object + infinitive with **to** (5) | | ✓ | | ✓ |

| | explain | advise | warn | claim |
|---|---|---|---|---|
| infinitive + **to** (1) | | | | ✓ |
| **that** + clause (2) | ✓ | | ✓ | ✓ |
| verb *…ing* (3) | | ✓ | | |
| object (4) | ✓ | ✓ | ✓ | |
| object + infinitive with **to** (5) | | ✓ | ✓ | |

### Exercise 2

*The Health & Safety Committee has* ***promised*** *a full investigation into the accident on the drilling rig Puffin in the North Sea. The Minister for Energy has* ***asked*** *the Committee to produce an interim report. The company concerned, General Oil, has* ***admitted*** *responsibility for the accident and has* ***recommended*** *carrying out immediate safety checks on all similar installations. The government has* ***threatened*** *to force the closure of the rig but the company* ***claim*** *this is not necessary. A member of the Committee, Grete Arnheim, has* ***urged*** *the company to* ***agree*** *to a full public enquiry. General Oil has* ***indicated*** *that they do not think this is necessary but that they probably would* ***accept*** *the conclusions of an independent investigation.*

### Exercise 3

1 The labour costs are too high so the Board recommend
  **b** reducing the workforce.

2 The R & D budget has been reduced and the Head of the Department has warned
  **c** that she will resign.

3 The problems require
  **b** an immediate solution.
  **c** that we find an immediate solution.

4 We maintain
  **a** a high level of quality.

5 The results prove
  **b** that we were right to invest.

## TASKS 28

### VERBS of the SENSES

### Exercise 1

1 After work I like looking at television.
  I like **watching** television.

2 I am smelling something strange. Is it a gas leak?
  I **smell/can smell** something strange.

3 I want to look at the results but not in any detail.
  I want to **see** the results …

4 I'm hearing you, please carry on. (note: this is acceptable in American English.)
  **I'm listening**, please carry on.

5 This surface is feeling very good. What is it made of?
  This surface **feels** good.

6 If you watch over here, I'll show you something interesting.
  If you **look** over here …

7 The wine is tasting good.
  The wine **tastes** good/The wine**'s** good.

### Exercise 2

*'Welcome to Oxwell. Now, I'd like to outline the programme for the morning. We're going to* ***hear*** *a presentation by our Vice-President, Robin Robins. Then we'll* ***watch*** *a video about the chemical industry market. Then we'll have an opportunity to talk about the video. After that at about 11.45 Joanna Tarrant will take us* ***to see*** *the plant. You'll be able to* ***watch/see*** *the production process in action. Then we'll have lunch and I promise you'll be able to* ***taste*** *some local specialities.'*

### Exercise 3

Paul: How do you **feel** about the plans?
Angela: I'm optimistic. Do you want to **see** the latest forecasts?
Paul: I can't just now. I'll **look** at them tomorrow. I've got to go and **watch** a demonstration of a new testing machine by Horrowitz & Co.
Angela: Before you go, the laboratory has produced a variation on the RT4 flavour for the new Zappo drink. Have you **tasted** it?
Paul: Yes, it was okay but it **smelt** like bad eggs!

## TASKS 29

### ARISE, RISE, RAISE, LIE and LAY

### Exercise 1

*raise* (T) *rise* (I) *lay* (T) *lie* (I) *arise* (I)

### Exercise 2

1 **b** Different problems arise.
2 **a** The costs have risen every year.
3 **a** We can raise the prices.
  **c** The prices can be raised.
4 **b** If the material lies directly on the floor it will be okay.
5 **a** Lay the picture on the table and we'll see it clearly.
  **b** If the picture is laid directly on the table we'll see it clearly.

### Exercise 3

**MEMO**

**To: Finance Department**
**Re: Trip to Switzerland**

**A problem has arisen over costs for the above trip. The airline has raised prices by 20 per cent so the budget is too small.**

**Please raise the budget to meet the extra cost.**

**Thanks.**

## TASKS 30

### VERBS and ADJECTIVES

#### *Exercise 1*

feel/sound/look/turn/prove/become/seem/appear + **optimistic/pessimistic**.
feel/sound/look/prove/seem/appear/taste/go + **right/wrong**
feel/sound/look/run/become/seem/appear/go + **wild**
feel/sound/look/become/seem/appear/fall + **ill**
feel/sound/look/prove/become/seem/appear + **happy/unhappy**
turn/become/seem/taste/go + **sweet/bitter**
feel/sound/look/turn/prove/become/seem/appear + **sceptical**
feel/sound/look/turn/prove/become/seem/appear + **confident**
sound/look/prove/seem/appear/go + **crazy**
sound/look/prove/(become)/seem/appear + **absurd/sensible**

#### *Exercise 2*

1 Share prices are very volatile and the market
 **a** has grown pessimistic.
2 The company has invested a lot in new products and everyone
 **b** appears confident.
3 After looking at the splendid results the Board
 **c** feels excited about future prospects.
4 Paula has read the report on the product and says she
 **c** remains pessimistic.
5 After a good start the project
 **a** went wrong.

#### *Exercise 3*

**ARDILLA INVERSIONES** (IBERICA)
Calle Gerona 46, Barcelona, Spain

Ms May Ling-Wu
Head of Financial Planning
Ardilla Investments (USA)
Stephenson Building
220–228 Colorado Boulevard
Ohio

14th October 19_ _

Dear Ms Ling-Wu

Thank you for your letter of 8th October.

As you know, the prospects for a good return on investments in Spanish companies have **turned** sour. There is a lot of instability about as a consequence of changes in exchange rates and a general loss of confidence. Share prices have **run** wild, with some companies showing large gains and others large falls.

On the telephone yesterday you **sounded** surprised when I told you that I didn't **feel** confident. My feelings last week have **proved** right. Things **look** bad just now so probably our analysis will **remain** pessimistic. Even the larger investment houses **are** very sceptical about prospects in the short term.

I will contact you at the end of the week but I don't expect prospects to improve until interest rates fall.

Regards

*Maria Isabel Vasquez*

Maria Isabel Vasquez
Investments Consultant

## TASKS 31

### HAVE, HAVE GOT and GET

#### *Exercise 1*

1 The company will get a new director next month.
2 I got your letter yesterday.
3 I've just finished the report.
4 The government hasn't got a workable economic plan.
5 Our competitors haven't got any good products at present.
6 Have you got my letter yet?
7 Does the TS Corporation have any plants in Korea?

#### *Exercise 2*

1 We have gotten a good deal from the negotiations.
 No mistakes. This form is common in AmE.
2 Parlour Smith had major losses last year.
 No mistakes.
3 They hadn't a good management organisation.
 **They didn't have** …
4 Had they the same director then as now?
 **Did they have** …?
5 We've got a new policy on sales discounts.
 No mistakes.
6 Had you got any benefit from the training course you did last week?
 **Did you get** any benefit …?
7 Have you an agent in Morocco?
 **Do you have** an agent …?
8 I got your letter this morning.
 No mistakes.

#### *Exercise 3*

You
Harrow (London)
Does Harrow have a manufacturing plant in Japan?
No
Where do your Japanese sales reps get Harrow goods?
Korea. We have a plant in Seoul.
Does Harrow have any agents in Japan?
Yes we do have agents. We don't have any sole distributor in Japan.
Thank you. Goodbye

## TASKS 32

### MAKE versus DO

#### *Exercise 1*

1 The Chairman made a long speech. (correct)
2 He said the company did a good profit in the year.
 **made a good profit**

3 He said the company would remain independent, though a large competitor had made an offer to buy a 25 per cent stake in the company. (correct)
4 The shareholders could do a choice between independence and prosperity or the uncertainty of being taken over by a large multinational.
**make a choice**
5 The Chairman said that those who recommended selling shares were making a big mistake. (correct)
6 He believed that independently the company could still make progress. (correct)
7 I did a trip in South America and was made welcome everywhere I went.
**made a trip**
8 They made the repairs without doing any complaints.
They **did the repairs** without **making any complaints**.

## Exercise 2

*do an exercise  do a favour  make a speech*
*make a plan  make progress  make money*
*do damage  make a report*
*make an appointment  make a profit*
*make a complaint  do a job*

## Exercise 3

1 HT has to choose between Arrow and Bow.
2 Yes, they have made an offer.
3 They do good work and are cheaper than Bow.
4 HT must make an appointment.
5 To say if there is any reason why Arrow should not do the work.

## Exercise 4

**MONDO INTERNATIONAL**

**Am Eichenwald 270**
**D-8902 Kassel**
**Germany**

Mondo Sport Surfaces
1200 Laird Boulevard
Washington DC
38632 USA

12 May 19__

Dear Bernadette,

Re: Tennis SSR567 Project

Further to my telephone call last week, there is some more news I have to tell you.

We **made** a mistake in the initial design stage. We need to **do** some more research on the effects of high temperatures on the surface areas. Please **make** arrangements for a new test in the Schuster Laboratories. I have **made** enquiries about exactly what we need to **do** and Uli and Rosa are going to contact me as soon as they **make** a decision on the tests.

Please **make** sure Gerd knows about the delay and tell him we'll **do** our best to resolve the problem as soon as possible.

Regards,

*Marcus Pressman*

Marcus Pressman
Assistant Director of Production

# TASKS 33

## VERB + PREPOSITION

### Exercise 1

1 to agree with someone
2 to allow for something
3 to apologise for something
4 to consist of something
5 to hear of/about something
6 to look for/at something
7 to refer to someone
8 to rely on someone
9 to wait for someone
10 to agree to something
11 to apply for something
12 to approve (of) something
13 to depend on something
14 to insist on something

### Exercise 2

A: Have you **heard about** the road transport strike?
B: Yes, it's terrible. We **rely on** the drivers for all our components.
A: We should **think about** using our own drivers.
B: That **depends on** whether they would be happy to drive during a strike.
A: We can **insist on** them meeting their contractual obligations!
B: Yes, but we have to **allow for** the problems they could meet on the roads.
A: That **amounts to** supporting the strike!
B: Perhaps. Anyway, we should have a meeting with our drivers and **hope for** a simple solution.
A: Yes, they might **agree to** move our components.
B: If not, we'll have to **wait for** the end of the strike.

# TASKS 34

## VERB + OBJECT + PREPOSITION

### Exercise 1

2 I want to divide the talk into two parts.
3 Let me compare product A with product B.
4 They'll explain the software to the eventual users.
5 We spend large sums on investment.
6 We must prevent our competitors from gaining an advantage.

### Exercise 2

*We regret that we need to remind **you of** the terms of the contract when you supplied the goods. According to Article 31 Paragraph 4 you would provide **us with** full instructions on the installation of the H50. Your representative, Mr Yogi, has consistently failed to explain **the installation to** our technicians.*

*Six weeks ago we preferred **the H50 to** rival products, but the service you have provided is lamentable. If this problem is not resolved immediately and to our total satisfaction, we will have to refer **the matter to** our lawyers.*

### Exercise 3

**Memo**

**To:** Pat
**From:** AC

I **compared** the Ndlovu product **with** the Rosario product, and Ndlovu is better. It is more expensive. However, I **convinced BR of** the benefits. He **agreed to** buy Ndlovu products. He **asked me to tell you of** the decision.

## TASKS 35

## VERB + ADVERB (PHRASAL VERB)

### Exercise 1

| | | | |
|---|---|---|---|
| 1 | arrive | = | turn up |
| 2 | cause | = | bring about |
| 3 | discover | = | find out |
| 4 | stop working | = | break down |
| 5 | close (a factory) | = | shut down |
| 6 | abandon (a meeting) | = | call off |
| 7 | complete (a form) | = | fill in |
| 8 | reject (goods received) | = | send back |

### Exercise 2

Tomas: What happened?
Janet: First the pump **broke down** and so the supervisor **shut down** production.
Tomas: Then what?
Janet: We **looked over** the pump assembly and saw that the flow into the pump was too fast.
Tomas: And did that **bring about** a pressure build-up?
Janet: Well, I think so, yes.

### Exercise 3

**Fax message**

KronQvist Pyrolavagen 28
Lidingo Sweden
Telephone: 46 87 465873
Fax: 46 87 465877

To: 33 (1) 43245678
Attention: Eva von Heijne
From: Jean

Dear Eva

You can visit Jean any time next week to examine results. Tom is going to arrive tomorrow.

Monday's sales meeting has been cancelled.

Regards

## TASK 36

## SENTENCE TYPES – SIMPLE AND COMPLEX

### Exercise 1

A Simple statement sentence: 1 5 8
B Simple interrogative sentence: 6
C Simple negative sentence: 4
D Simple exclamative sentence: 7
E Complex sentence with subordinate clause: 3
F Complex sentence with relative clause: 2

### Exercise 2

1. We are reorganising the department and recruiting new staff.
2. We are advertising for a new computer analyst because/since/as Irene has retired.
3. The position, which is at supervisory level, carries a high salary.
4. We need a young person who is also a skilled programmer.
5. We will advertise in various countries and in specialist journals.
6. We need someone with experience but not a complete expert.

### Exercise 3

1. We need to increase the quality of our research **which** will be expensive. Our present research, **which is on** a new pocket-sized communications device, **is** potentially very exciting **and** a major technological advance is possible.
2. I work for ABC **which** makes mechanical **and** electrical parts for automobiles. We sell throughout Europe **and** Asia, **but** not in America. Our biggest customers, **who are** Japanese, **are** some of the best known car manufacturers in the world.

## TASKS 37

## CONNECTING IDEAS

### Exercise 1

| | | | |
|---|---|---|---|
| 1 | in the same way | = | similarly |
| 2 | to sum up | = | in short |
| 3 | too | = | also |
| 4 | finally | = | lastly |
| 5 | alternatively | = | instead |
| 6 | yet | = | however |
| 7 | naturally | = | of course |
| 8 | as a rule | = | usually |

## Exercise 2

*In recent years the company has expanded* ***and*** *the workload for the management has increased.* ***Therefore,*** *we have decided to reorganise our management structure. This picture shows the new organisation.*

*We plan to divide the present Administration Department into two, creating a new Finance Department and a Human Resources Department.* ***In addition,*** *the Sales & Marketing Department will be divided into two.* ***Furthermore,*** *a new Management Services Department will be created. We believe communication channels within the company will be simplified,* ***so*** *decision-making will be more streamlined.* ***For example,*** *decisions which solely affect personnel will now be taken at the level of Human Resources.* ***In general,*** *the principle is that decisions should be taken at the lowest practicable level,* ***especially*** *those everyday decisions which will not affect the whole organisation.* ***Naturally,*** *the changes will take some time to be fully understood,* ***but*** *overall everyone should notice immediate benefits.*

## Exercise 3 (M)

2 We sell our goods abroad, **so obviously** we have to set prices with the exchange rates in mind.
3 Fluctuation in exchange rates causes instability. **In addition**, it makes forecasting more difficult.
4 **Although** we prefer a stable exchange environment, we have to accept instability.
5 Our best products are several years old. The F23, **for instance**, was launched in 1986.
6 We need to expand sales abroad, **especially** in America.
7 Sales in leisure products have increased. We **generally** expect a 25 per cent rise during the summer.

# TASKS 38

## SUBORDINATE CLAUSES

### Exercise 1

1 The committee met <u>to discuss a river pollution problem</u>.
2 <u>If the pollution was caused by local industries</u>, they would have to pay compensation.
3 The pollution concerned chemicals <u>which had leaked into the river</u>.
4 The problem was noticed <u>when dead fish were found in the river</u>.
5 <u>Although companies had strict regulations on the disposal of chemicals</u>, mistakes occurred.
6 The enquiry asked <u>what training workers had been given</u>.
7 The Manager said <u>her company had done everything possible to avoid the leakage of chemicals into the river</u>.

| Reported question | Condition | Time | Relative clause | Contrast | Purpose | Reported speech |
|---|---|---|---|---|---|---|
| 6 | 2 | 4 | 3 | 5 | 1 | 7 |

## Exercise 2

| | |
|---|---|
| The Chairman said | that the industry faced a public relations challenge. |
| The industry has suffered setbacks, | some of which could have been avoided. |
| Now we must rebuild our image | which is essential for future prosperity. |
| I don't know | how long this will take. |
| Should we fail, | the outlook will be bleak. |
| We need to look at the alternatives, | choosing those that will be most effective. |
| We must take every opportunity | to explain our case. |
| Having explained our position, | we deserve fair treatment from the press. |

## Exercise 3 (M)

2 The company organised a press conference to answer criticisms.
3 The chairman said that the safety record was/had been relatively good.
4 The Health & Safety Executive supported the company when they investigated safety procedures.
5 Every precaution had been taken so the management was confident.
6 The press wrote articles which exaggerated the problems.
7 Although the company carries out regular checks, accidents can still happen.

# TASKS 39

## REPORTED SPEECH (1)

### Exercise 1

*The Minister* ***reminded*** *the audience that 20 years ago things were very different. He* ***said*** *the time had come to face realities and he* ***believed*** *we had to choose between cooperation or isolation. He* ***warned*** *that major problems would arise if we made the wrong choice and* ***asked*** *if we wanted to be an isolated and friendless country.*

### Exercise 2

***Asked*** *if the policy of the government* ***would change,*** *the Minister* ***said*** *the government* ***was working*** *towards increasing the quality of services and making the economy strong. He* ***predicted*** *that inflation* ***would continue*** *at present levels – around 2.5 per cent – and economic growth, now at 2 per cent,* ***would rise*** *to 4 per cent.*

### Exercise 3

MODA SPECIALE
Via Vittorio Emanuele 11 200
34000 Milano
Telefono 39 (2) 56567888
Fax 39 (2) 56785490

Ref: JS/23/04

Dear Rina

I spoke to Marianne yesterday. I told her **I liked/had liked** the photographs. She said **she would come/was coming** to Milan at the end of next month. She also said **she would bring** the designs and the finished clothes. **She asked** me to remind you that **you still owe her some money**. She said you **said/promised** the money **would be** in her bank last Tuesday but **it hasn't/hadn't** arrived.

Finally, she **asked** if you **would** call her. She said **she would be in all day** Friday.

Ciao

*Juan*

Juan

## TASKS 40

### REPORTED SPEECH (2)

### Exercise 1

| | | | |
|---|---|---|---|
| verbs of speaking | – | agreed | commented |
| verbs of commanding | – | told | instructed |
| verbs of requesting | – | invited | urged |
| verbs of questioning | – | asked | inquired |

### Exercise 2

1 Wrong. The company has told us to adopt Vision 2000 as our aim for the next five years.
2 Wrong. Vision 2000 urges us to adopt a range of internal measures to improve productivity and quality throughout the company.
3 Right.
4 Wrong. Having presented the policy in outline, managers have asked their teams what training they would like.
5 Wrong. Most teams have asked not to have theoretical training courses.
6 Wrong. In fact they have all suggested having project groups to explore the best way to implement Vision 2000.

### Exercise 3 (M)

*The Personnel Manager asked when the new training programme would be introduced. The Training Manager replied that she didn't know. But she added that they had approached a number of outside training organisations. The Personnel Manager asked if he could see the list of suppliers. The Training Manager agreed to let him see the details. The Personnel Manager suggested making a final decision together. The Training Manager replied that she preferred to make the final decision herself.*

## TASKS 41

### QUESTIONS

### Exercise 1

1 Are you agents for Fischer equipment? A
2 Where can I find this type of product? B
3 You're not serious? D
4 Fischer are market leaders, aren't they? E
5 So you believe they're expensive? D
6 Do you think there are better goods available? A
7 Can you tell me how reliable they are? C

### Exercise 2

1 How long time have you been working on the research?
How long have you been working on the research?
2 Could you tell me who were the main partners in the project?
... who the main partners in the project were?
3 And you didn't plan to spend so much money, didn't you?
... did you?
4 You say the forecasts were inaccurate. Who did resign after these forecasts?
Who resigned ...?

### Exercise 3 (M)

1 Can you tell me something about your company?
2 And where are you based?
3 Can I ask if you have an agent?
4 What's the agent's name?
5 And they are in Sydney?
6 I have to go to the agent?
7 And Wall & Martin are the only agents in Sydney, are they?
8 How do I contact Wall & Martin?

## TASKS 42

### RELATIVE CLAUSES

### Exercise 1

Many pharmaceutical companies, which are among the world's largest (ND), invest millions in research into heart disease and conditions which typically relate to the process of ageing (D).These areas, where research costs are phenomenally high (ND), also offer the greatest potential. Research on curative drugs may be less expensive but the rewards are less because the patients, who will get better (ND), will not need the treatment for years and years. On the other hand, conditions like Alzheimer's disease, heart disease or arthritis, which last for years (ND), could involve long periods of treatment. It is these areas, therefore, which offer the best potential for high profits (D). A further point is that such research is intended to produce drugs which will be marketed in the richest countries (D) where profit will be highest (D).

## Exercise 2

2 He said the environment, a key issue, was everyone's responsibility.
3 Lockville, where there used to be a chemical plant, is now a beauty spot.
4 We made mistakes in the past when we knew less than we know now.
5 The captains of industry, on whom we depend, have major responsibilities.
6 The industries which we criticise produce the products which we buy.

## Exercise 3

1 The factory which produces PCBs has closed down.
2 The reprocessing plant which has been the subject of protests is expanding its operations.
3 The factory which is in the town centre, where many people live, is a major employer.
4 Plastics recycling, which is expensive, is only possible in some countries where sophisticated equipment is available.
5 Many products which claim to be environmentally friendly are not.
6 The majority of people, whose houses are centrally heated, contribute to global warming.

# TASKS 43

## CLAUSES OF CONTRAST

## Exercise 1

Janina: Well, **though** (SC) packaging is expensive, it can help promote the product.
John: Yes, of course, **but** (CC) we have to cut the costs. **Even though** (SC) we use our own designers, the costs are very high.
Janina: **Although** (SC) it's an expensive part of the production, it is very difficult to reduce costs.
John: **While** (SC) we agree that it's expensive, we don't seem to be able to decide how to reduce the expense!
Janina: I see packaging as part of public relations, **whereas** (SC) I think you are looking at it only in terms of packing the product!

## Exercise 2

1 The market has probably passed its peak, **although** computer sales are still very high.
2 Costs have come down **though** the advances in computer technology have been considerable.
3 More people own computers, **while** the number of manufacturers has gone down.
4 Machines are more reliable **but** they are more complex.
5 Computing capability has increased **whereas** the physical size of the equipment has diminished.
6 Users experience difficulties with compatibility **even though** a lot of money has been spent on this problem.

## Exercise 3 (M)

***While*** *there are millions of different software programs available, only a few become internationally successful. The best become standards which others follow,* ***but*** *the originals do not always benefit from this. Of course, different programs work with different operating systems,* ***but*** *there are many more programs than operating systems.* ***Although*** *the industry is very competitive, it is dominated by a few big software producers. Many of these are closely connected with the major computer manufacturers,* ***even though*** *there are also many independent software houses. Also, producing new software is not necessarily expensive,* ***whereas*** *innovations in computer hardware certainly involve massive costs.*

# TASK 44

## CLAUSES of CAUSE or REASON

## Exercise 1

*We are offering you the job* ***since*** *you are the most experienced candidate.*
*You are especially suitable* ***because of*** *your work in the oil sector.*
*Your academic record is ideal* ***as*** *we need someone with post-graduate qualifications.*
*We need you to start as soon as possible* ***because*** *we are beginning a new research project this month.*
*We understand that an immediate start is a problem* ***because*** *you are in work just now.*
*You need to tell your present employer today* ***since*** *you want the job.*
*Just say you have to leave* ***because of*** *this offer.*
*I'm sure it will not be a problem* ***as*** *this sort of thing happens all the time.*

## Exercise 2 (M)

1 The advantage in this system is that there is direct supply from production to customer, since there is no intermediate stage.
The disadvantage is that it is difficult to meet sudden orders for large quantities because of very small stock levels.
2 The advantage of this system is that we can give an immediate response to large orders because distribution is handled from a central warehouse.
The disadvantage is that there are increased storage costs because more goods are held in stock.

# TASKS 45

## CLAUSES of PURPOSE

## Exercise 1

1 **For** a new building to be a success it has to be the right design.
2 **In order to** understand design objectives, it is necessary to consider the ultimate function.
3 We have chosen the best architects **in order that** we can be sure of good results.
4 They are preparing sketches **so that** we can consider their basic ideas.
5 The architects explained some principles about materials **so as not to** leave us confused.

### Exercise 2

1 The distribution channels are being changed **in order to** avoid delays at the ports.
2 We need to spend a lot of money **so as to** guarantee a top quality product.
3 We should book in advance **so that** we won't need to worry about space on the ship.
4 Costs will have to be reduced **in order that** we can have increased profitability.
5 The red switch is **to** switch off the motor in an emergency.

### Exercise 3 (M)

*The laboratory is* ***for*** *testing new recipes. Then there is a Production Department* ***to*** *make finished products. Next we have a Quality Control Department* ***in order to*** *monitor quality and maintain standards. Finally there is a Customer Services Department* ***in order that*** *we can deal with matters relating to customer relations.*

## TASKS 46

## CLAUSES of TIME

### Exercise 1

1 After deciding we could not work alone, we commissioned an agency to produce an advertising campaign.
2 Once they had studied the product and the market, they designed a marketing concept.
3 Before agreeing to their proposals, we studied them very closely.
4 While studying the advertising plans, we had many doubts.
5 Once understood, they seemed okay.
6 Whenever we discussed the product launch we had disagreements.
7 Having seen the success of the launch, we are delighted with the agency.
8 The campaign finished, we're now looking ahead to the next one.

| Subordinate conjunction + finite verb | Subordinate conjunction + non-finite verb *...ing* | Subordinate conjunction + non-finite verb *...ed* | Non-finite verb *...ing* or verb *...ed* |
|---|---|---|---|
| 6 2 | 1 3 4 | 5 | 7 8 |

### Exercise 2

1 (E) 2 (E) 3 (?)
4 (=) 5 (L) 6 (=)

### Exercise 3

1 b 2 e 3 d
4 a 5 c

## TASKS 47

## -ING and -ED CLAUSES

### Exercise 1

| Condition | Contrast | Cause or reason | Time | Manner |
|---|---|---|---|---|
| 4 | 1 2 | 5 | 3 | 6 |

### Exercise 2

***Having carried out*** *some market research SALLO identified a gap in the market.* ***Having designed*** *a product, they developed a prototype.* ***Having completed*** *successful tests, SALLO received a patent. The company looked for financial support.* ***Obtaining*** *that, the company developed the production capability.* ***Having set up*** *the necessary production facilities, the company entered production.* ***Developed*** *in only 12 months, the SALLO product could revolutionise cooking.*

### Exercise 3

2 **a** If you install our software you will have more computing power.
**b** With our software installed, you have improved your computing power.
3 **a** If you call our service team your satisfaction will be guaranteed.
**b** As you have called our service team, your satisfaction is guaranteed.
4 **a** If goods are stored in the warehouse they deteriorate.
**b** While stored in the warehouse, goods deteriorate.
5 **a** If the company cuts its workforce, profitability will improve.
**b** While cutting the workforce, the company is improving its profitability.

## TASKS 48

## NOUNS

### Exercise 1

1 The informations you need are in the post.
information is
2 There's three thousand people coming to visit the exhibition.
There are
3 Alison and Sara read the *Times*.
The
4 When I go to The Hague I stay in_Hilton Hotel.
the Hilton
5 The headquarter is in_United States.
headquarters are in the United States.
6 We have had a lot of troubles with the machinery.
trouble
7 Woodpohl makes top quality furnitures.
furniture.
8 Twelve persons work in my section.
people
9 This is an expensive ______ equipment.
piece of equipment.
10 The import agency gave wrong advices.
advice.

### Exercise 2

| | | | |
|---|---|---|---|
| *money* (U) | *cheque* (C) | *profit* (U) | *debt* (C) |
| *assets* (C) | *machinery* (U) | *machine* (C) | *plant* (C) |
| *production* (U) | *product* (C) | *supervisor* (C) | *foreman* (C) |
| *chargehand* (C) | *worker* (C) | *furniture* (U) | *news* (U) |
| *spokesman* (C) | *mathematics* (U) | | |

### Exercise 3

2 Economics is interesting.
3 What is the trouble with the equipment?
4 Where are the headquarters?
5 The university receives funds from the government.
6 The funds are insufficient.
7 The United States consists of 50 states.
8 Your advice last week was good.

## TASKS 49

## NOUN COMPONENTS

### Exercise 1

**Alpo wins Jordan order**

Alpo Holdings has boosted its drive into automobile markets with a $47.5m sales contract to build 2,000 bus bodies for the Jordanian government.

The order equates to 46 per cent of Alpo's bus parts turnover and is backed by a cash deposit and a $37m OECD–supported buyer credit.

### Exercise 2

*a tax concession*
*a machine tool*
*a ten-day holiday*
*an accident report*
*a law court*
*an export licence*

### Exercise 3

```
The plant consists of a car park, the
production facilities, a loading bay and a
despatch area. There is also a storage depot,
an administration block and a canteen.
```

### Exercise 4

2 There has been a disaster involving chemicals that are highly poisonous …
3 There has been an accident at an oil rig in the North Sea …
4 The record for speed in the air has been broken …
5 There is a problem in the level of congestion at airports…
6 The results for the chemicals industry have been a disaster …
7 There has been a row over pollution caused by gas …

## TASKS 50

## GENITIVE FORMS

### Exercise 1

**TT SOFT**

***Tomorrow's software at today's prices!***

Telephone our sales staff and place your order today. We are the country's top suppliers of all types of business applications software ranging from the very latest word processing and graphics packages to sophisticated special applications. Your future's better with us!

Look at these phenomenal savings!

In a special deal for TT SOFT, BELL has slashed 50 per cent off its desktop packaging program Bell Desk 500.

Trumpet's world-beating spreadsheet at $100!!
A state of the art publishing program for $150!!!

*Meet your needs!*
*Meet the needs of your computer!!*
*Meet us with a telephone call on FREEPHONE 505050 NOW!!!*

### Exercise 2

1 The pharmaceutical group Physic's results are encouraging.
2 The first two quarters' turnover has shown a 20 per cent rise.
3 The company's workforce will benefit.
4 All employees' pay packets will include a bonus.
5 A shareholders' meeting scheduled for the end of September will be a cheerful affair.
6 The Chairman of the Board celebrates ten years in that role. (no change)
7 Profits for each year of his tenure have increased well above the industry average. (no change)

### Exercise 3

The **decision of the Board** to raise the dividend was against the advice of the auditor. Now the **company's** shares have been suspended and its AGM has been postponed. The **directors'** passports have been confiscated by the judicial authorities. A spokesman for Mr Sherlock Holmes, the Managing Director, said Mr Holmes had no comment to make. Mr **Holmes'** wife, also a **Board** member, said the investigation was 'a disgrace'.

Meanwhile, the employees of the company reported for work as usual. A **workers'** representative said her colleagues were worried about their jobs.

## TASKS 51

### ADJECTIVES versus ADVERBS

#### Exercise 1

1 reliable – reliably
2 necessary – necessarily
3 erratic – erratically
4 slow – slowly
5 late – late
6 traditional – traditionally
7 competent – competently
8 excellent – excellently

#### Exercise 2

1 The **economic** arguments for reducing the investment are very strong.
2 The plane arrived **late** so I missed the start of the meeting.
3 I am not **interested** in seeing the museums.
4 My last job was in software programming but **now/presently** I work in quality control.
5 Reducing R & D spending is not **economical** in the long term.
6 The Director is in hospital because she has been working too **hard**.

#### Exercise 3

1 The profit forecast is **really** good.
2 **Poor** sales were caused by a drop in confidence.
3 The **present** board has insufficient experience.
4 We are very **interested** in your proposal.
5 The President sounded **optimistic** about the prospects for growth.
6 He spoke **enthusiastically** about the new products.

#### Exercise 4

***Firstly,*** *I'd like you to look at the graph here which compares the sales of the 386 models with the 286s over five years.* ***Clearly*** *there has been a* ***considerable*** *change with the consumer showing* ***greater*** *taste for 386 machines. The* ***gradual*** *decline in the popularity of the 286 reflects the complexity and range of software and the fact that users need to have* ***faster*** *operating machines. As for the 386, sales have indeed increased* ***dramatically****. In response to these* ***important*** *changes, we have* ***naturally*** *concentrated our efforts on developing improved 386 models.*

## TASKS 52

### ADJECTIVE MODIFICATION with ADVERBS

#### Exercise 1

entirely/totally
quite/reasonably
extremely/highly

#### Exercise 2

1 A: It was a good year.
B: How good?
A: Fairly/Moderately good. As good as we could expect.
2 A: There was a small fall in output in the first quarter of the year.
B How small?
A: Very small – only about 5 per cent.
3 A: The exhibition was successful.
B How successful?
A: Extremely/very successful – we met very many prospective customers.
4 A: The report was critical.
B: How critical?
A: Extremely/wholly/very critical. They condemned everything about the plant.

#### Exercise 3

2 The policy was economically catastrophic.
3 Theoretically, the design was innovative.
4 But frankly, it was wrong.
5 Your argument is logically unsustainable.
6 You are academically right.

## TASKS 53

### COMPARISON of ADJECTIVES

#### Exercise 1

| | | |
|---|---|---|
| *slow* | *slower* | *the slowest* |
| *difficult* | *more difficult* | *the most difficult* |
| *modern* | *more modern* | *the most modern* |
| *easy* | *easier* | *the easiest* |
| *capable* | *more capable* | *the most capable* |
| *dry* | *drier* | *the driest* |
| *quick* | *quicker* | *the quickest* |
| *bad* | *worse* | *the worst* |
| *far* | *further* | *the furthest* |
| *much* | *more* | *the most* |
| *a little* | *less* | *the least* |
| *advanced* | *more advanced* | *the most advanced* |

#### Exercise 2 (M)

The Carro XT has more memory capacity.
It has a bigger monitor.
It also has a longer warranty.
It is more expensive.

#### Exercise 3 (M)

Trains are the cleanest form of transport.
Planes are the dirtiest in terms of $CO_2$ emissions.
Planes produce the most $CO_2$ emissions.
Cars are more polluting than trains.
Trains produce the least $CO_2$ emissions.
Cars produce more $CO_2$ emissions than taxis per passenger kilometre.

## TASKS 54

### EXPRESSIONS of FREQUENCY

#### Exercise 1

Lee: I always fly here.
Kerry: Do you? I **never** fly. I **always** come by car.
Lee: By car? How awful! What about this place? I rarely stay in this hotel. Do you often come here?
Kerry: I **nearly always** stay here, though **sometimes** I stay at the place opposite.
Lee: I see. What about your customers – is this a good place for you to meet them? Do you do much business here? I think it's terrible. I **hardly ever/seldom** sell anything!
Kerry: Really? No, I think it's great. I **normally** sell quite a lot here. I have several good customers here.
Lee: Fancy a drink?
Kerry: Thanks, I'll have an orange juice.
Lee: Orange? I **seldom/hardly ever** drink orange. I prefer apple juice.

#### Exercise 2 (M)

1 I never walk to work, I usually go by car. I sometimes take the bus.
2 I often travel abroad. When I travel abroad I almost always stay in a hotel.
3 If I go a long way I always fly. When I arrive at the airport I generally take a taxi to my hotel. I rarely/hardly ever hire a car.
4 We have a regular meeting with the Director of the Department every fortnight.
5 We frequently phone our most important customers.

#### Exercise 3

1 We hold our shareholders' meeting **annually**.
2 I meet my deputy **twice a week**.
3 I send a report to Head Office **every two months**.
4 I telephone our agents **daily**.
5 We publish a profit and loss account **twice yearly**.
6 We produce detailed sales results **quarterly**.
7 I meet the Managing Director every **fortnight**.

## TASKS 55

### DEGREE with VERY, TOO and ENOUGH

#### Exercise 1

1 The price is **very** high but I can still afford it.
2 We don't have **enough people** to meet the order.
3 It doesn't cost **very much** money.
4 The plant at Lagos is very large. In fact, it is too big. (correct)
5 We sold very few products. In fact, we **didn't sell** enough.
6 The country is very small and it has a very large population. It is **too** heavily populated.

#### Exercise 2

*We were **very** sorry to hear that you are not satisfied with the printing work which we sent last week and in particular that the colour red is **too** strong. We checked the work **very** carefully before it was despatched and we felt that it was good **enough** to meet our **very** high standards. However, since you are not happy, our representative will visit you on Friday to discuss the problem. We understand your need is urgent so I hope this is soon **enough** to fit in with your schedule. If it is **too** late please telephone us.*

#### Exercise 3

2 The service you provide is too slow for us. In other words it is not **quick enough**.
3 The quality of the workmanship is disappointing. In fact it is not **good enough**.
4 The report is not long enough. In other words it is **too short**.
5 The conference is not early enough in the year. In other words it is **too late**.
6 The registration fee is very expensive. In fact it is **too expensive**.
7 The venue is far away. In fact it is **very far/too far**.

## TASKS 56

### SO versus SUCH

#### Exercise 1

1 The work was **so** bad that we refused to pay.
2 The payment was **so** late that we contacted our lawyers.
3 After **such** a long time we had given up hope of payment.
4 It was **such** a large debt that we had to try to recover it.
5 **Such** expensive items cost a lot to repair.
6 Cost increased **so** rapidly that we abandoned the research.

#### Exercise 2

The work is so bad that it will have to be redone.
We are so late that the meeting will be over.
It is such a good design that operating it is easy.
With such good progress we will finish early.
Such material can be recycled easily.
Such customers are very valuable.
He argued so convincingly that we accepted his idea.

#### Exercise 3

2 The project has gone well so far.
3 So long as the weather remains good, the building work will be completed before Christmas.
4 Such an excellent performance surprised me.
5 The engine was not so noisy as I had expected.
6 The service we received was so bad that we changed supplier.

## TASKS 57

### ALREADY, YET, AGAIN and STILL

#### Exercise 1

A: I'm afraid we **still** haven't received authority to export the goods.
B: Has the Trade Department contacted you **yet**?
A: No, not **yet**. I'll telephone them **again** to see why there's such a delay.
B: Okay. Our customers have **already** complained about the delay and I **still** can't give them a delivery date.
A: I know. I'll call you **again** this afternoon.

#### Exercise 2

1 She has ↑ arrived. (already)
2 She has ↑ not arrived. (still)
3 Has she arrived ↑? (yet)
4 She has not arrived ↑. (yet)
5 I'll telephone his office ↑. (again)
6 We hope to see Eddie Roberts ↑ soon. (again)
7 We are ↑ developing a new system ↑. (again)
8 We ↑ use an American consultant. (still)

#### Exercise 3

1 A is still/again the top selling product.
2 Sales for C are again/still the lowest.
3 The PDS market share is again/still 28 per cent.
4 At the end of the third quarter we have already reached the target for the end of the year.
5 Sales have not reached 20,000 units yet.

## TASKS 58

### ARTICLES

#### Exercise 1

| Zero article proper name | Indefinite article countable, first mention | Definite article second or subsequent mention |
|---|---|---|
| 1 15 | 4 5 6 10 11 | 3 7 12 |
| **Zero article plural countable nouns, general meaning** | **Definite article a specific meaning is clear** | **Zero article uncountable, first mention** |
| 2 | 8 9 14 16 | 13 |

#### Exercise 2

1 The University of Leeds is one of the biggest in England. It is also an important centre for medical studies.
2 Butter is a major agricultural product in the European Union. Another is rape seed oil. Most of the butter is consumed by EU countries.
3 The Super Motor Company makes a range of high-performance cars, including the luxurious Grosso 55XT. This is a perfect example of modern automotive engineering.

#### Exercise 3

**Make the right connections in Dubai – the business centre of the Middle East**

When it comes to selecting **a** base for your regional headquarters, Dubai is **the** logical choice. **The** city has become **the** region's leading centre for trade, transport and distribution, industry, conferences and exhibitions. For good reason. Dubai encourages enterprise. **A** state-of-the-art telecommunications system puts you in instant touch with **the** world. 60 international airlines link Dubai with over 100 cities worldwide. And **the** city boasts sophisticated banking, finance and other services, as well as world-class office accommodation. And **the** lifestyle is great too!

## TASKS 59

### PRONOUNS

#### Exercise 1

1 Paul designed the system himself.
2 Jane is my boss. We have worked together for years.
3 I understand that your company has an office in Buenos Aires. Our company has one there too. Ours is in the south of the city. Where is yours?
4 Mary called in. She left a package for John. Can you take it to him?
5 Hernandez and Fernandez make life difficult for themselves.

#### Exercise 2

1 Oh, Mr Beard! Mrs Ford phoned. She asked me to ask you to phone her back as soon as you can.
2 JJD make plastic joints. They have supplied our company, Thomson Boro Ltd, for years. They have always provided us with good service but a recent supply was very poor quality. I telephoned their sales rep. I told him/her about the problem and he/she said it would be resolved easily.
3 The suppliers phoned a moment ago. They said the goods were damaged in transit and that the responsibility is not theirs. They are sending one of their representatives here tomorrow to discuss the problem. In any case, the goods are useless. We must not pay for them.

## Exercise 3

Our products are sold throughout the world. We (PS) export to more than 30 countries. We (PS) have a network of agents and technicians based in service centres in 15 countries. We (PS) pride ourselves (R) on the excellence of our after-sales service. Your needs are also ours (P) and so we (PS) guarantee to provide you (PO) with the best service in the sector. We (PS) make the products and you (PS) use them (PO).

Hambro – do yourself (R) a favour!

Hambro – you (PS) call us (PO) – we (PS) serve you (PO)!

Hambro products – they (PS) work for you (PO)!

## TASKS 60

### DEMONSTRATIVES

## Exercise 1

*'The company sent us a letter.* ***That*** *(1) was the first indication that they were interested in the proposal. We read* ***this*** *(2) with much interest because they were offering us something we had asked for: a 50 per cent share in royalties on all the products they made, obviously meaning all* ***those*** *(3) we agreed to let them make.* ***This*** *(4) is it – here – read it. And then can you put it on* ***that*** *(5) file over there? I need to show it to* ***that*** *(6) consultant fellow who's coming in later. Now look … I want to say* ***this*** *(7). We should not necessarily accept what is on offer. Accepting it straight away …* ***that*** *(8) would be a mistake.'*

| | | | | | | | |
|---|---|---|---|---|---|---|---|
| **1** | B | **2** | B | **3** | RC | **4** | RW |
| **5** | RW | **6** | CS | **7** | F | **8** | B |

## Exercise 2

**Editor/Eastern Europe**

This is an opportunity to work in a research organisation publishing economic surveys on Eastern Europe. This is a new position created to meet growing demand for products in this area.

Those applicants with a good economics degree, experience in publishing and a good knowledge of the region should write with a concise CV to Steven Wright, Personnel Officer, PO Box 456, London SE22 5RF.

**Could you help to influence economic policy in London or Brussels?**

Government Economic Service offers the chance to work at the heart of economic decision-making in this country.

GES staff provide specialist advice to most government departments. To this end we put both micro and macro economic principles into practice, balancing industry specific principles against those which affect the whole economy. We offer preparation for European Commission recruitment competitions. In order to qualify for these competitions you should have post-graduate experience in economic research, well-developed communication and analytical skills, problem-solving abilities and a serious motivation towards a career in the European Community.

If you possess these qualities send for further information and an application form to Steven Wright, Personnel Officer, PO Box 456, London SE22 5RF.

## Exercise 3

MS: What are **these** two tables?

CL: Good question, now let's look at them. **This** one shows how we calculate investment income, while **this** shows an example.

MS: I see. Could you explain them?

CL: Of course. The basic calculation is like **this**. The investment multiplied by interest rate multiplied by running period in days – all **that** over 100 × 360.

MS: I see. And in **this** example, it's for **this** much – 100,000 francs?

CL: Yes, the interest rate – **that's** 7.5 per cent, the time is three months, **that's** 3 times 30. If you finish the calculation you have **this** much: 1,875 francs.

## TASKS 61

### SOME and ANY

## Exercise 1

1 I haven't seen **any** examples yet.
2 There **weren't any** questions so the meeting ended. *or* There were **no** questions so the meeting ended.
3 We don't need **any** help with this.
4 I didn't have **any problems** coming to see you. *or* I had **no problems** coming to see you.
5 The meeting was longer than **anyone** would have wanted.

## Exercise 2

**1** a **2** b **3** c **4** b

## Exercise 3

Customer: I'd like **some** information about upgrading software please. I understand that last month you were offering Grapho 5.1 free of charge to users who had bought 5.0 in January or February. I bought mine in January but I haven't received **any** information and now the free offer is closed.

CSC: Yes, I'm sorry, that's correct. **Anyone** who was a registered user should have received news of the offer.

Customer: I didn't receive **anything**.

CSC: I'm sorry about that. Have you been receiving our regular newsletter since you bought your Grapho software? There's always **something** in there about offers.

Customer: No, I haven't.

CSC: Hold on please, there's **someone** here I can ask about this ...

## Exercise 3

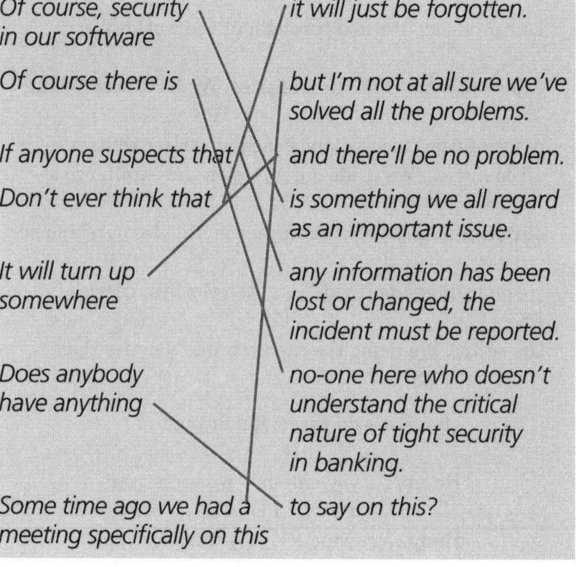


# TASKS 62

## SOME, ANY and RELATED WORDS

### Exercise 1

1 Wrong. I **sometimes** give presentations to other companies.
2 Right.
3 Wrong. I was **somewhat** impressed by her performance.
4 Right.
5 Wrong. So, if nobody has **any** questions, let's move on to the practical demonstration.
6 Wrong. To be honest, we **never** exceed our agreed budget.

### Exercise 2

A: Do you **ever** visit the Asian plants?
B: Well, I'm **not at all/never** sure what will happen next year, though I am tentatively planning a trip **some time/somewhere** in the autumn.
A: And do you plan to go **anywhere** in particular?
B: Well, I suppose if I go **anywhere**, it will be to Korea and Taiwan.
A: Oh, that's interesting. I **sometimes** go out there myself. Usually at very short notice.
B: I see.
A: I must say there is **nothing** that I dislike more than these hastily arranged trips.
B: I agree. **Anything** is better than finding yourself in a meeting without **any** of the right papers.
A: Absolutely!
B: Well, I think we should try to do **something** about it.

# TASKS 63

## QUANTIFIERS (1)

### Exercise 1

4 Several of our products are made from recycled plastic.
7 None of our products are made from recycled plastic.
6 Few of our products are made from recycled plastic.
3 Many of our products are made from recycled plastic
2 Most of our products are made from recycled plastic.
5 A few of our products are made from recycled plastic.
1 All of our products are made from recycled plastic.

### Exercise 2

1 **A few** of our clients responded to the survey.
2 **Most** of them had some positive comments to make.
3 **No** customers thought our products were unreliable.
4 **Much** constructive criticism centred on product distribution and delivery.
5 **Few** customers wanted regular news on our new products and services.
6 **All** respondents said our packaging was good.

### Exercise 3 (M)

All respondents said the organisation was very good.
Few said the seminar rooms were satisfactory.
Most said the level of professionalism was satisfactory.
Many of the respondents said the products and services were satisfactory.
There was much criticism of the seminar rooms.
There was little criticism of the quality of the products and services.

## QUANTIFIERS (2)

### Exercise 1

Not all clients require the same services. Some need a very personalised approach to their problems with several meetings and a few specialist consultations; others can be handled on a more generalised basis with no fee unless some work is actually carried out. In fact, most of our clients feel that we have the right mix of products for them; and many more join us each year. So, we'd like to say that we can do more than please some of the people some of the time; we feel that, all in all, we can satisfy most of the people most of the time.

### Exercise 2

*Most of our competitors have managed to reduce their costs over the last year. All of them have tried to introduce cost-cutting measures. Of course, none of these measures has been an absolute success; and some of them have been a total failure. For example, when Planton tried to save a little money by merging two departments, the results were catastrophic. Few people in the new department were happy to work together as a newly-formed team. Finally, Planton had to invest a lot of money on team-building activities just to solve the new problems which had been created.*

### Exercise 3

*Every day in Britain more than 24 million people go to work. Some of these people work in offices, but most of them work in factories. Of course, there are a few people who can afford not to work. And, unfortunately, there are some people who can't find work. But why do people work? There are several reasons, but the simple answer is that they all need to earn an income. But for most of them, this is not an end in itself. With this money they can buy the goods and services that everybody needs. At the same time, through their work most of them produce the goods and services needed by the population. In this way they are helping to ensure that a high standard of living is maintained for the community as a whole.*

# TASKS 65

## BOTH, EITHER and NEITHER

### Exercise 1

2 Simone speaks both Italian and Spanish.
3 Either we continue or we stop investment.
4 Not only is Singapore a vibrant business centre, it is also in the centre of a spectacular economic region.
5 We neither sell nor rent equipment.

### Exercise 2

1 Neither Philip nor Arne is the right candidate.
2 Both Marta and Juana wrote to me with good proposals.
3 Both Edith and I criticised the poor quality of the printing.
4 Either you or I can book the seminar rooms.
5 Akira is not only a very creative designer but he also works very efficiently.

### Exercise 3

Marina: Can we meet during week 33?
Uta: Yes, I think so. I'm quite busy but I'm sure we'll find a time.
Marina: How about Monday or Tuesday?
Uta: I'm afraid I'm very busy on **both** Monday **and** Tuesday. I could manage **either** Wednesday **or** Friday.
Marina: Let me see. I can manage **neither** Wednesday morning **nor** Wednesday afternoon. Friday? Yes I can manage **either** the morning **or** the afternoon.
Uta: Friday morning would be okay. Can we say 10 o'clock?

# TASKS 66

## EACH and EVERY

### Exercise 1

| | |
|---|---|
| **day:** | each day every day |
| **people:** | neither word can be used with **people** as it is a plural noun. |
| **departments:** | each of the departments |
| **managers:** | each of the two managers |
| **two years:** | every two years |
| **equipment:** | neither word can be used with **equipment** as it is an uncountable noun. |

### Exercise 2

We've checked all the facts down to every last detail.
We've serviced all the equipment, including each device we checked in the summer.
We've reviewed all the news thoroughly and listened again to every item.
We've checked all the premises and every building seems to be empty.
We've appraised all the personnel and each interviewee completed a questionnaire.
We've counted all the money again down to every last coin.

### Exercise 3

2 We have tried to get accommodation in all the hotels in Prague but every bed/room is taken.
3 We have given him a lot of sound advice but every/each suggestion/recommendation falls on deaf ears.
4 I think I left my baggage on the plane; each of my two bags has my name on it.
5 We need to renew a lot of our existing machinery as nearly every machine in the plant is more than 20 years old.
6 It is important to make progress, but we need to take each/every step with care.
7 There is so much traffic on the roads that I think it would be a good idea to tax each/every vehicle according to its engine size.
8 Overseas travel can be very tedious, especially when each/every trip involves a weekend away from home.
9 To analyse work, you can take each/every job/task and subdivide it into its constituent parts.

## TASKS 67

### COMPOUNDS with EVERY

#### Exercise 1

Every product<u>s are</u> made using the finest quality woven fabric.
Every/each product is made ...

Everything <u>what</u> you see being printed here is based on traditional checked patterns.
Everything you see ...

<u>Everyone</u> of our fabrics is made using the best quality cloth available.
Each *or* Every one ...

Almost <u>every time when</u> you visit a top fashion fair in Milan or Paris you will see examples of our fabrics.
Almost every time you visit ...

<u>Every where</u> we enter competitions we receive some recognition of our high standards.
Everywhere we enter ...

We can finish <u>everything material</u> in any way you want, including various special effects.
We can finish every material *or* everything ...

Every <u>dyes</u> we use <u>contain</u> only natural colours.
Each/every dye we use contains ...

#### Exercise 2

1 **Everyone** in this workshop has done an apprenticeship with an engineering company.
2 More than 400 machine tools are produced here **every day**, except Saturday and Sunday.
3 **Each** production line runs continuously, for 24 hours.
4 **Every** eight hours a supervisor checks the level of output.
5 **Everything** is maintained by our own team of fitters.
6 All the production is distributed to agents **everywhere** in Europe.

#### Exercise 3

1 We design **everything** we make.
2 **Everyone** here **receives** a productivity bonus.
3 **Each** worker is entitled to 30 days' paid holiday.
4 **Every decision is** taken by the Board.
5 A new worker is elected to the Board **every two years**.
6 **Everywhere** you go here you see examples of our company's good organisation.

## TASKS 68

### NUMERALS

#### Exercise 1

A/one million.
Five billion.
Four million three hundred and eighty-five thousand five hundred and sixty-seven.
Five point three million US dollars.
Seven point two billion German Marks.
Five thousand seven hundred and fifty-three yen.
Ten dollars twenty (cents).
A/one hundred pounds.
Three pounds ninety-nine (pence).
Four point five six.
A quarter.
Seven eighths.
Three thousand one hundred and fifty-six.
Three point one five six.
Twenty-six degrees Celsius/Centigrade.
One thousand two hundred and fifty degrees Celsius/Centigrade.
Forty-four point five kilograms.
Twenty-two point four seven grams.
A/one hundred and two kilometres.
Five hundred metres.
Two hundred and twenty-five centimetres.

#### Exercise 2

*'Hannah? There's an important message about the Marketing Two Thousand conference. It's on the twenty-third of May and on the twenty-second of June. It starts at ten thirty/half past ten/ten thirty a.m. and finishes at three o'clock/three p.m. It's in room two oh four at the Harrow Conference Centre which is at a hundred and eighty-nine Beechlands Parade, N ten seventeen EG. The phone number is oh eight one two double nine five oh double five. The cost for each participant is a hundred and ninety-five pounds plus seventeen point five per cent VAT and there will be between eighty and a/one hundred participants. Finally, the lunch, which lasts for one and a half hours, will be at the Black Swan Hotel and will cost seventeen pounds fifty.'*

#### Exercise 3

*The actual sales were a/one hundred and three thousand seven hundred and sixty-four units compared with the forecast sales of a/one hundred and twenty thousand, a percentage difference of minus thirteen point five three. In terms of turnover, actual turnover was one point five nine million dollars, compared with the forecast turnover of one point seven five million, a drop of nine point one four per cent on the forecast.*

*Note*: In large numbers **and** is deleted in American English.

## TASKS 69

### TIME(1)

#### Exercise 1

The night shift comes on **at** (TW) 10 p.m. and works **for** (TD) eight hours, so the morning shift starts **at** (TW) 8 a.m. Staff work continuously, with no official breaks **during** (TD) the eight hours, but in practice there are opportunities for short breaks **during** (TD) the shift.

**During** (TD) the night most of the work is routine maintenance and only 20 or so workers are on duty. **In** (TW) the morning when the day shift starts we work at 80 per cent of full production capacity. Well, at least we do **in** (TW) the summer and autumn months, **up until** (TD) about the end of November when production is reduced to about 60 per cent.

We don't work **on** (TW) Sundays of course – the factory closes, except in an emergency.

#### Exercise 2

1 The meeting will be held **on** 5th July 1994.
2 The project began **in** June.
3 We'll have a 20-minute break **at** 4 o'clock.
4 The report won't be ready **until** we've collected all the field survey data.
5 The work, which has already started, will be finished **by** the end of the week at the latest.
6 Make sure you've read the survey before our meeting next week.
7 We'll work all day and relax **in** the evening.

#### Exercise 3

1 The accident occurred on Thursday night.
2 The accident happened at 12.30 a.m.
3 The fire lasted from 1 a.m. until 2.30.
4 The job will be advertised until the end of next week.
5 Applications must be submitted by the end of next month.

## TASKS 70

### TIME (2)

#### Exercise 1

1 Wrong. We finished the project **in** time; so we had three days to spare.
2 Right.
3 Wrong. **During** the two-week period, we had no technical support at all.
4 Wrong. Before **starting** on the next study, there will be a short training course.
5 Wrong. **Next** year we are sure to see the results of our efforts.
6 Right.

#### Exercise 2

2 during/at
3 by/on
4 for
5 before
6 between
7 at … in … in

#### Exercise 3

**During** the day the sea had been very rough. **At** 16.00 the helicopter arrived bringing the replacement drillers. These were needed as 2 of our crew had gone sick **the previous night.** The new drillers are to stay with us **until/till** the end of next week. They have just worked **for** 2 months onshore and are happy to have a change. **During/in** the evening the sea calmed down and we were able to start working comfortably again. However, just **after** the evening shift started, the computer went down again. The computer technicians were called in and **by** 22.00 they had the computer running again. **After** that, there were no problems **during** the night shift. The morning shift reported for duty **on** time at 06.00.

## TASKS 71

### PLACE

#### Exercise 1

A: What field of business are you **in**?
B: Computers.
A: Oh, that's interesting. I have a sister who used to be **in** computing but she's **in** prison now.
B: Prison?
A: Yes – software fraud.
B: Oh dear! Are you American?
A: No, I'm **from** Canada. And you?
B: Florence, Italy.
A: Oh how beautiful. I was there a few years ago with my wife.
B: Really?
A: Yes, we flew **to** London, hired a car **at** the airport, had a look **around** London, took a ferry **across** the Channel, drove **through** France, **over** the Alps…
B: You didn't go **through** Monte Bianco?
A: Mont Blanc? No, we went a longer route, **over** Col di Tenda. Then we drove south **to** Florence. What's the river **in** Florence? I never remember.
B: The Arno.
A: Oh yes, Florence is **on** the Arno.
B: Where did you stay?
A: I don't remember, **in** a hotel. Maybe **at** the Grand Hotel, is that possible?
B: The Grand? No, I don't know that one. Did you go anywhere else **in** Italy?
A: Sure – we went **to** Rome. We walked **along** the Via Appia Antica for six hours! It was wonderful! Then we had to leave. We flew **out of** Rome.
B: It sounds a good trip.
A: It was great! Say, have you ever been **to** Canada?
B: Yes I have. I stayed with a friend **near** Vancouver – about 40 miles away.

## Exercise 2

*The beet is taken **off** lorries and stored **in** piles **outside** the processing area. The beet is sent **along** a system of channels **into** the processing area. It is shredded and dried **in** a huge cylindrical drier. Dried shreds of beet are packed **in** bags and sold as animal feed. The sacks of animal feed are stored **in** a large warehouse before being loaded **onto** lorries for despatch. The main sugar production involves treating the liquid sugar which comes **out of** the beet **in** the drying process.*

## LIKE, AS and SUCH AS

### Exercise 1

*As (C) you know, we have an important decision to make. As (C) we plan for the new year, we have to decide if we want to continue advertising through sponsorship, as (C) we did this year, or change our policy. As (C) sponsorship is expensive, to stay with it is not a small decision. On the other hand, other forms of advertising, television as (P) much as (P) printed word advertising, may be less effective. As (P) marketing manager, I do of course have a personal view on this.*

### Exercise 2

1 F – they are independent.
2 T.
3 T.
4 F – he suggested advertising in a magazine similar to *Construction Weekly*. He may also mean that *Construction Weekly* is a good place to advertise.
5 T – or to see the annual report itself.
6 F.

### Exercise 3

*The Munich Trade Fair was **as** successful **as** in previous years. The last day was **like** a carnival – there was such optimism from everyone involved. A fair always has useful advantages, **like/such as** meeting new customers, seeing competitors' work, meeting friends and of course it gets a lot of publicity. But a lasting benefit is always that a good stand at an international exhibition **like/such as** Munich clearly shows that we are a leading player in the world market.*
***As** we know, a high profile is essential to maintain our reputation for strength in the market.*

## CLASSIFYING INFORMATION

### Exercise 1

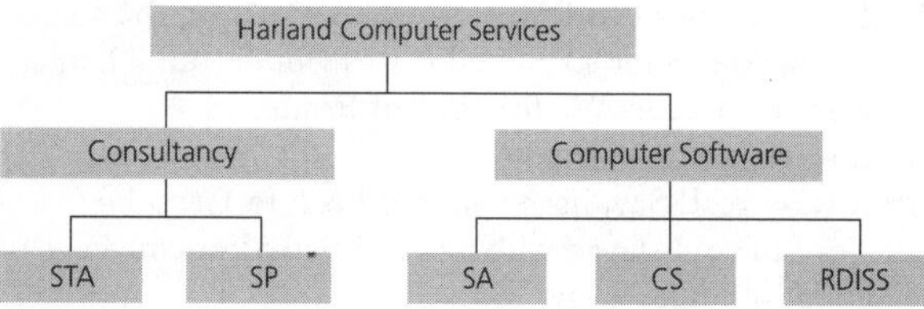


### Exercise 2

1 The products can be divided in four types.
**into**
2 The market is consisting of four main categories of product.
**consists of**
3 The company's research projects fall in two main kinds.
**into**
4 The Communications Department comprises of three different sections.
**comprises**
5 The first stage of the project is broken down by three parts: preliminary enquiries, technical research and scheduling.
**into**
6 There are several stage in the project.
**stages**

### Exercise 3

1 Chemco production is divided into six areas.
2 The Paints and Varnishes Division consists of four types of product.
3 The Chemicals Division is split into three kinds of product.
4 The Oils Division comprises two varieties of oil.
5 The Pharmaceuticals Division involves two categories of product.
6 The Foods Division contains four types of product.
7 The Fertilisers Division can be classified into two sorts of product.

TASKS 74

## CONNECTING and SEQUENCING IDEAS

### Exercise 1

| time relationship | cause | contrast | comparison |
|---|---|---|---|
| firstly | that's why | yet | in the same way |
| **concession** | **contradiction** | **alternation** | **addition** |
| anyway | actually | instead | in addition |
| **summary** | **conclusion** | **equivalence** | **inclusion** |
| to sum up | lastly | in other words | for instance |
| **highlight** | **generalisation** | **condition** | **stating the obvious** |
| notably | on the whole | in that case | clearly |

## Exercise 2

*'**To begin with** (TR) we need to consider the long-term implications of the decision to increase our dependence on gas-fired energy production. **For example,** (INC) let us say we do go ahead. **In this case** (COND) we decrease our reliance on coal. **As a result** (CAUSE) we reduce costs because we understand that gas is cheaper than coal. **In fact** (CONTRAD), the case is not proven, **especially** (HL) because we have no way of knowing what the relative costs of coal and gas will be in ten years' time. **However** (CONTRA), **as a rule** (GEN) gas is much cleaner than coal and this is a genuine advantage. **As a consequence** (CAUSE) of these two advantages, gas looks a better option. **In other words** (EQUI), it's cheaper and cleaner so it's better. **In that case** (COND) we don't need to hesitate. **Naturally** (OBV), nothing is so simple. **In short** (SUM), cost is an unknown factor. We don't know which would be the most economical choice.'*

# TASKS 75

## DESCRIBING TRENDS

### Exercise 1

1 Investment shows b) a slight increase.
2 Sales of Product A have b) risen by $5000.
3 After a period of continual increase, the share price a) has remained stable.
4 In the first year costs c) stood at $3000.
5 The price a) reached a peak and then slumped.
6 The cut in production b) is very slight.

### Exercise 2

1 The level of investment rose suddenly. (e)
2 Sales of Product A fell slightly in the final quarter. (b)
3 The Research and Development budget has stabilised over the past few years. (d)
4 At the end of the first year sales stood at 50 per cent of the present level. (f)
5 The share price reached a peak before falling a little and then maintaining the same level. (a)
6 There has been a steady increase in costs over several years. (h)
7 The sudden collapse in share prices has surprised everyone. (g)
8 The value of the shares has shown a steady decline. (c)

### Exercise 3

1 The **graph** compares the performance of three products, A, B and C.
2 The **horizontal axis** shows time over ten years.
3 The **vertical axis** shows the volume of sales in number of units.
4 Product A is represented by the **solid line**.
5 The performance of Product B is shown by the **broken line**.
6 You can see the performance of Product C in the **dotted line**.
7 Clearly **Product A** is the most successful product.
8 Sales of Product B **have maintained the same level** in recent years.
9 Sales of Product C **have declined**.
10 Product A has shown a **steady rise**.

# TASKS 76

## DESCRIBING the ORGANISATION

### Exercise 1

*The DSA Corporation consists of three **divisions,** Building Materials, Construction and Civil Engineering. DSA **is based in** New York and comprises four **subsidiaries,** KAF Inc., Halcon, Conway and RoadCo. Each of these is **headed by** a Senior Vice-President who **reports to** the **parent company**.*

### Exercise 2

*KAF Inc. is a building materials manufacturing company in Detroit. KAF **is headed by** the Chief Executive Officer, **supported by** the Board of Directors, which **consists of** four people. The staff in each of the four departments **are accountable to** a Vice-President who is also on the Board. In each department, a managerial team of directors **supports** the Vice-President. In the Sales Department, one director **is responsible for** exports, the other **is in charge of** domestic sales.*

# TASKS 77

## ASSERTING and DOWNTONING INFORMATION

### Exercise 1

1 I'm inclined to think that the results are satisfactory. (NA)
2 I feel that there are one or two small problems here. (NA)
3 What we need is a new direction in policy. (A)
4 It could be said that the chances of success are limited. (NA)
5 It's important that we conclude these negotiations this week. (A)
6 I tend to think there's likely to be a fall in interest rates soon. (NA)
7 I'm sure that there's no point in meeting Mr Roach. (A)

### Exercise 2

2 I tend to feel I can't go any lower.
3 Under no circumstances may the password be given to anyone else.
4 I think we can expect extremely good sales.
5 I really believe we can expect very disappointing results.
6 Perhaps you might look at the alternatives.
7 There appears to be a huge difference in our positions on this.
8 We don't seem to agree with you!
*or* It seems we don't agree with you!

## Exercise 3 (M)

H: Maybe I could suggest that I be a sole agent in Norway?
B: That's quite impossible!
H: Then I'd be inclined to ask for a slightly lower price.
B: That really is impossible.
H: It seems to me that discounts sell goods.
B: What sells goods is good salesmanship!
H: I think that all the agents here will give discounts.
B: I really don't agree with you. And in any case it seems that we're going to make discounting illegal according to the contract.

## TASKS 78

### EQUATING and INCLUDING IDEAS

#### Exercise 1

*Some of the most important American companies,* ***notably*** *Allen Morland and KRD, are experiencing problems in their home markets.* ***In particular,*** *a growth in competition from S. E. Asian producers is affecting formerly secure positions. The leading producer in Korea,* ***namely*** *Reto Inc, has gained a large market share,* ***(0 marker)*** *23 per cent.* ***In other words,*** *there are big changes happening in the world market. There is a lot more competition.* ***Technically speaking,*** *we are witnessing a diversification due to increased market penetration by hitherto unknown producers. There are no easy ways to face these changes. There are plenty of inappropriate short-term solutions,* ***such as*** *governments erecting trade barriers,* ***for example.***

| Highlighting example | Introducing example | Reformulation | Designation |
|---|---|---|---|
| notably<br>in particular<br>for example | such as | technically speaking | namely<br>in other words |

#### Exercise 2

*A major international airline,* ***namely*** *World Air, has recommended immediate checks on part of the hydraulic system of a popular aeroplane,* ***(0)*** *the AD780. The centre of concern is the actuating cylinders,* ***in other words,*** *the device in the hydraulic system which expands or contracts when pressure is applied. The warning comes after three critical reports, including,* ***for example,*** *last week's ICAO survey of 700 transatlantic airliners,* ***notably*** *several AD780s. The report from ICAO noted,* ***in particular,*** *concern over the hydraulics in several planes.*

## Exercise 3 (M)

The patient has a bad sore throat, or **technically speaking** he has inflammation of the pharynx. He also has chronic sinusitis **or, put simply,** he has a bad sinus problem. He needs a course of antibiotics, **such as** penicillin. He should also have a long rest, and **in particular** give up singing in a rock band. If the problem does not improve, he should see the consultant, **(0)** Doctor Battiato, who is an expert in these acute throat disorders. Problems of this nature seem to have become more common, **especially** in cities and areas of high population density. Several treatments for sinus problems are worse than no treatment at all, **notably** some spray preparations bought OTC, **that is to say** 'over the counter'.

## TASKS 79

### CONTRASTING IDEAS

#### Exercise 1

Aircraft engines are well maintained but accidents are unavoidable.
Many flight control systems are automatic. Even so, pilots have overall control.
Leading airports are incredibly busy. Even so, there are very few accidents.
The flight recorder records information about a flight. Yet it is sometimes difficult to determine the cause of accidents.
Accident reports contain important recommendations. However, not all of them are implemented.

#### Exercise 2 (M)

2 We realised a good price even though the world markets were weak.
3 We believe the company will benefit, in spite of our difficult decision.
4 Profit margins have been very tight although our core business has been strong.
5 The domestic situation will deteriorate in spite of the improvement in the world market.

#### Exercise 3 (M)

1 Although both imports and exports may fall next year, the levels are likely to be different.
2 It is easy to boost exports. However, it is more difficult to control imports.
3 Despite the improvement in short-term performance, export initiatives do not necessarily lead to long-term customers.
4 Some customers are looking for cheap solutions; others, in contrast, are looking for business partners.
5 A full order book improves a company's confidence. Nevertheless it does not guarantee survival.
6 Although a full order book boosts morale, it also stretches a company's cash flow.

## TASKS 80

### COMPARING IDEAS

#### Exercise 1

| Clause of comparison | Expression of comparison | Expression of similarity/difference |
|---|---|---|
| rather than for savers<br>faster and more dramatic than ... | in comparison with Building Society accounts | the same cuts as<br>won't correspond exactly to<br>Will next year look like ...<br>the same strategies as<br>different tactics from<br>expect rates to vary |

#### Exercise 2

1 The business plan was **easier** to develop than we expected.
2 In comparison **with** last year, I think our results will turn out to be considerably better than we forecast.
3 With the new videoconference unit it's almost as good as **having** our partners in the same meeting room.
4 We have checked and the new model conforms **to** the EC standards in terms of higher fire resistance.
5 Their products are not **as** durable as ours; in fact I'd say that they are not at all the same **as** ours.

#### Exercise 3 (M)

2 The Triano engine is larger than the other two.
3 The Jasper is very economical compared to the other two/the Triano.
4 The top speed of the Triano is similar to the Bravo.
5 The Jasper engine is not so big as the Bravo/the other two.
6 The Jasper is as fast as the Bravo.

## TASKS 81

### CHECKING and CONFIRMING INFORMATION

#### Exercise 1

*'Can you explain the effect of falling exchange rates on the company?'*

*'It's quite simple, really. The effects are numerous but two stand out as very significant. First of all, about 65 per cent of components we use to build our cars are bought in, many from abroad. That means that the value of the national currency affects the prices we pay for these components. It will of course increase the price we have to pay if the currency loses value on the international exchange.'*

*'Did you say 65 per cent are bought in?'* ***(CHECK)***

*'That's right – mostly from Korea and Malaysia though also from Japan and Europe.'*

*'Excuse me, Paul. In fact the largest number of parts comes from Japan.'* ***(CORR)***

*'Number, yes, but, the largest cost involves imports from Korea.'*

*'Really? You surprise me.'*

*'Now, where was I? In a nutshell, importing components is affected by currency fluctuation* ***(SUMM)****. Now, the second area of influence is in the revenue from sales outside the domestic market or, to put it simply, exports* ***(PARA)****. Clearly a drop in the value of our currency will adversely affect the revenue we receive from export sales.'*

*'Okay, that's clear. Can you repeat what you said a few minutes ago about margins?'* ***(REP)***

*'Okay – briefly, what I said was that margins had to be improved against a very difficult marketing context.* ***(SUMM)*** *By that I mean we need to improve margins despite a fall in turnover.'* ***(PARA)****.*

#### Exercise 2

A: We're based in Montpellier but we work with colleagues all over France helping to solve clients' training problems.
B: **I don't quite follow you**, so **could you repeat that?**
A: Certainly. We are a national company based in Montpellier in the south of France but we operate in all regions of the country, and even throughout Europe.
B: **So you've got subsidiaries throughout Europe?**
A: **No, not exactly/No, I didn't say that.** We have agents who look after regions throughout Europe.
B: **Could you describe in a little more detail your** relationship with these agents?
A: Certainly. We advertise our services nationally and we contact local organisations who can help to meet the needs of the companies who contact us.
B: **In other words**, you act as a contact between companies with certain needs and companies who can supply those needs.
A: **That's exactly right.** And we supply support material to local firms.
B: So you sell material to help the local firms?
A: **No, I didn't say that/No, not exactly.** We offer to work in partnership with local firms, creating a team to help resolve a particular client's needs.

## TASKS 82

### LIKES and PREFERENCES

#### Exercise 1

1 A: I'd not rather go via Amsterdam (I'd **rather not** ...)
2 A: Do you like tea or coffee? (**Would you like** ...)
3 B: I like that they are very informal, more of an open discussion. (I like **them** to be **very informal**)
4 B: Yes, naturally I prefer have an agenda than no real plan. (I **prefer to have** ...)
5 B: No, I'd rather we look at them later. (I'd rather we **looked** at them later).

### Exercise 2

How about going to a fish restaurant near the port?
**Would you like to go** to a fish restaurant ...?

I think it would be more enjoyable to go to a restaurant in Las Ramblas.
I think **I'd prefer to go** ...

Also, I like meat better than fish.
Also, **I'd rather eat meat**.

It would be better for me if we did not have a late night tonight.
**I'd prefer not to have** a late night tonight.

Which do you think is better, to meet here or in Las Ramblas?
**Which do you prefer**, ...?

What do you want?
**What would you like to drink?**

### Exercise 3 (M)

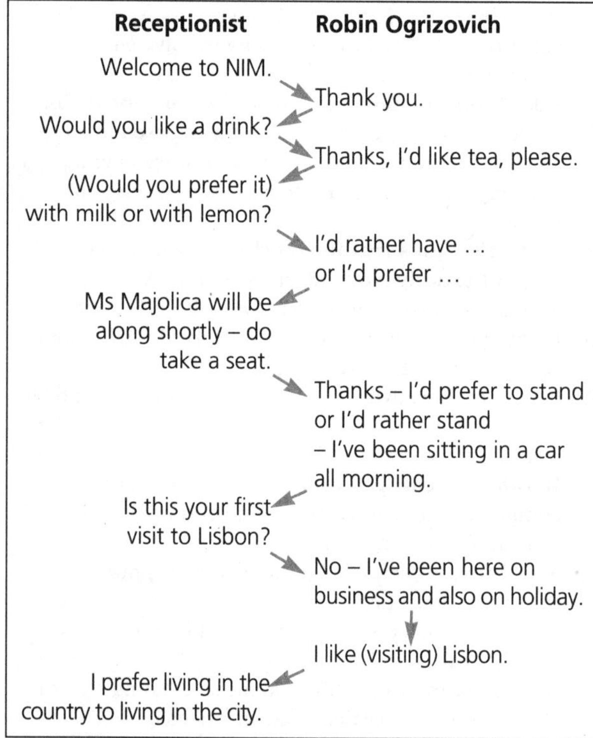

Receptionist
Robin Ogrizovich
Welcome to NIM.
Thank you.
Would you like a drink?
Thanks, I'd like tea, please.
(Would you prefer it) with milk or with lemon?
I'd rather have ...
or I'd prefer ...
Ms Majolica will be along shortly – do take a seat.
Thanks – I'd prefer to stand
or I'd rather stand
– I've been sitting in a car all morning.
Is this your first visit to Lisbon?
No – I've been here on business and also on holiday.
I like (visiting) Lisbon.
I prefer living in the country to living in the city.


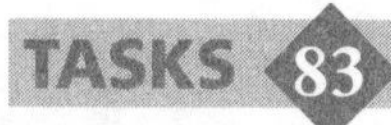


## ASKING FOR and GIVING OPINIONS

### Exercise 1

1 I strongly believe that ...
2 I'm convinced that ...
3 Do you consider that ... ?
4 To my mind, this is a really innovative idea, but ...
5 I'm inclined to think that ...

### Exercise 2 (M)

Arne: Am I right in thinking that you think the job has been done badly?
Bob: I'm inclined to think that the procedures are regularly contravened.
Arne: Do you believe that our controllers don't follow standard procedures?
Bob: I tend to believe they don't.
Chris: As I see it, this is most serious.
Delia: In my opinion, accidents can be caused by not following the ICAO guidelines.
Bob: I feel that that is true. Look at Tenerife. From my point of view, the disaster occurred there because the rules were broken.

### Exercise 3 (M)

3 Chris: What do you think, Jean?
4 Jean: Yes, I tend to prefer the first design. I'm inclined to think it is stronger. In my opinion the title is clearer and, as I see it, the author's name is very important. I feel that the formulae say more about what is in the book. I tend to think these tints are better too.
5 Chris: Well, I'm inclined to agree with Karin. I believe the author's name is not so important and I tend to feel that the shapes are clearer than the formulae. I think I prefer the tints in the second design and the characters in the title are clear enough. As I see it, the second design is easier to read.

## AGREEING and DISAGREEING

### Exercise 1

You may be right up to a point. But we need to consider another question too.
I can't agree with you. I see it totally differently.
I'm in complete agreement. As you say, there is clearly no alternative.
I agree with the first part of what you say. But I can't agree with your conclusion.
I agree with most of your analysis. There's just one detail I would question.

### Exercise 2 (M)

1 I can't go along with that. It's a price arrived at by market forces.
2 I totally agree. In fact any departure has quite an effect.
3 I agree up to a point. However, it's always difficult to make long-term forecasts.
4 I'm afraid I can't agree. The price has fallen to below that figure in the past.
5 That's true. It's a comfortable price for both producer and consumer.
6 I agree with you. Many countries use their oil power to extract advantages in other respects.

## Exercise 3

1 I can't **accept** that. It's quite untrue.
2 I agree **to** provide more support.
3 I agree **up** to a point.
4 You're mainly right, **but/although** I'm not sure about the last part of your argument.
5 I'm sorry, I disagree **with** you. It's not quite like that.
6 Okay, I agree **to** your request.
7 I **accept** your basic argument but I can't go **along** with all the details.

# TASKS 85

## CAUSE and EFFECT

### Exercise 1

2 Strict government control of the money supply in the past five years has brought about the fall in inflation.
3 A spending boom at the end of the last decade resulted from lower taxation.
4 Higher unemployment partly accounts for higher government spending.
5 Increased numbers of business failures give rise to lower tax revenue.
6 Increased energy costs result in higher retail prices.

### Exercise 2

The Russian Civil Aviation Authority investigation into the Air Diver 660 crash in Moscow has revealed the cause of the accident to be an explosive rupture in one of the aircraft's engines. The rupture itself was probably the result of metal fatigue. Once the plane landed at Moscow, it caught fire and passengers were unable to escape with the necessary speed, due to a malfunction in a door. A steward tried to force the door but his action led to the door jamming. The door would not open and there was therefore a delay in passengers escaping from the plane.

**Memo**

Subject: Air Diver 660 crash - Moscow 25 September 19--
To: Jan Levi, Production Manager.

An explosive rupture in an engine was responsible for the crash. This was probably the result of metal fatigue.

Once landed, passengers could not escape quickly because of a malfunction in a door. An attempt to force the door caused it to jam.

The door would not open and this brought about a delay in passengers escaping.

### Exercise 3

*Underlined phrases of cause*

The British engineering company Harrow tried, unsuccessfully, to sue a German competitor, Bauer, for breach of copyright. However, the court ruled that Harrow had never correctly registered the patent of the item concerned. On account of Harrow's mistake, the product had never been patented. Because of the non-existence of the patent, Bauer did not contravene any law of ownership. As a result of the court's ruling against Harrow, the company had to pay large legal fees. Also, due to the publicity surrounding the case, Bauer expect sales to benefit.

*Underlined clauses of cause* (M)

Since Harrow made this mistake, the product had never been patented. As no patent had ever existed, Bauer did not contravene any law of ownership. Because the court ruled against Harrow, the company had to pay large legal fees. Also, since a lot of publicity has surrounded the case, Bauer expect sales to benefit.

# TASKS 86

## OBLIGATIONS and REQUIREMENTS

### Exercise 1

| New obligations | No obligation | Obligation not to do something |
|---|---|---|
| * to meet new regulations<br>* to write prescription by hand<br>* dosage clearly stated<br>* form in which drug is to be taken has to be specified<br>* doctors must sign and date the prescription | * retain invoices for more than 12 months<br>* entry in Controlled Drug Register | * prescription to persons under 16 is prohibited |

### Exercise 2

**Chemical restrictions inadequate, say Greens**

The environmental pressure group GreenPlanet has called on the government to **ban** all dumping of chemical waste at sea.

At present dumping chemical waste is heavily **restricted** but under certain circumstances disposal at sea is **permitted**. Companies dumping waste at sea are **supposed** to get a licence for all such operations. However, the law does not **force** the registration of certain types of chemical waste. GreenPlanet say the present restrictions are inadequate.

A spokesman for GreenPlanet said 'We believe all companies dumping waste material at sea should be **forced** to apply for licences. If chemicals are involved, the dumping should not be **allowed** . Only a major public appeal will **make** the government take the necessary steps.'

A representative of the Ministry of the Environment said the present restrictions were adequate. 'We don't **need** to introduce any changes,' she said.

## Exercise 3 (M)

| You | | Dept of Maritime Safety |
|---|---|---|
| | ← | Buenos días |
| Hello – I'd like to know what information you need to register a ship. | → | |
| | ← | First, a bill of sale is required. And you have to send a tonnage certificate. |
| Am I supposed to provide a ship safety certificate? | → | |
| | ← | Is the ship more than 25 years old? |
| No. | → | |
| | ← | Then you don't need to. |
| Is there anything else I need to do? | → | |
| | ← | Yes. You are obliged to send details of your company registration and you must send 6 copies of all the documents. |
| Do I have to send original documents? | → | |
| Thank you very much. | ← | No you needn't. |

## TASKS 87

### ABILITY and INABILITY

#### Exercise 1

1. I don't have my chequebook so I **can't** write you a cheque.
2. The bank will not **allow** us an increased overdraft.
3. We only have a small production plant. We are not **capable** of meeting such a massive order.
4. In a few years, if we expand, we will be **able** to supply orders of that size.
5. Employees are **permitted** to use the company car park.
6. Sorry, entry to the public is **prohibited**.
7. The government **prevented** us from exporting to that country.

#### Exercise 2

**Keysystem DC5000**
This data communication tool is based on Cellphone technology which **enables/allows** you to access mainframe computers, information databases and electronic mail systems.

**Direct Call**
All your sales staff **can** call your office at any time with the convenience of a private telephone network. Naturally it also **allows** calls from your office to any cellphone connected to your network.

**VoxBank**
This is a message sending and receiving system **capable** of sending 256 messages to other VoxBank users at any one time. So you can alert the whole sales team to a price change or a supply problem with just one call.

**Security System**
Whatever system you choose, you can add your own personal number and password and so **prevent** any unauthorised access to your personal communications system. You can even **stop** authorised users contacting you by using an automatic disabling device for those occasions when you do not want to be disturbed.

#### Exercise 3 (M)

2 *Limitations on Hrubesch sales in the territories.*
Under the terms of the agreement, Hrubesch **is not allowed/permitted** to sell tractors in the territories, except to Gornik.

3 *Restriction on other agents.*
Under the terms of the agreement, Hrubesch **is not permitted/allowed** to sell tractors to other agents in the territories.

4 *Prices.*
Under the terms of the agreement, Gornik **can** fix its own prices suitable for the markets in the territories.
*or* **shall be allowed/permitted** to fix …

5 *Returned tractors.*
If at the end of the period, Bornik has any unsold Hrubesch tractors, Hrubesch **shall be permitted/allowed** to buy them back at 70 per cent of the original sale price.

6 *Name of tractors.*
Any change in the name of Hrubesch **is prohibited.**

## TASKS 88

### SCALE of LIKELIHOOD

#### Exercise 1

| | | |
|---|---|---|
| The company is having an excellent year. | → | The end-of-year profits are bound to be up. |
| The sales of hospital equipment have remained constant. | → | This may be related to government cuts in hospital spending. |
| Research into new drugs has been very encouraging. | → | We are likely to see important additions to our product range |
| Over-the-counter (OTC) drugs show a slight fall in sales. | → | This should be reversed over the winter months. |
| The share price has continued to rise. | → | We are certain that the future of the company is very secure. |

#### Exercise 2

**Azir Bridge: Earthquake damage – Preliminary Report**

**Risk of further quakes in the area**
The area concerned is very prone to earth tremors and two major earthquakes (more than 5 on the Richter scale) had been reported in the last thirty years before the recent one. It is therefore <u>quite likely</u> that another quake will affect the area in the next twenty years. It is difficult to predict the time of such a quake. However, the history of the area suggests a future earthquake of more than 7 on the Richter scale is <u>highly improbable</u>. However, small tremors of less than 2.5 are considered <u>practically certain</u>.

**Present condition of the Azir Bridge**
The bridge sustained serious structural damage in the recent earthquake. Any further tremor in the next few days, including one as low as 2.5 on the Richter scale, is <u>bound to</u> result in further damage, and the bridge <u>might</u> actually collapse.

**Recommendations**
It is advised that the bridge be demolished and replaced. This is <u>sure to</u> last over 15 months. Present cost estimates would <u>certainly</u> top $30 million.

## Exercise 2 continued (M)

**MEMO**

To: Head Office
Re: Azir Bridge Earthquake

**1. Further quakes and/or tremors**
Further quakes are very probable and small tremors are certain. However, a major earthquake is highly improbable.

**2. Present condition**
The bridge is badly damaged. Further tremors in the area are almost certain and if they happen the bridge may collapse.

**3. Recommendations**
The bridge needs to be replaced. The team is positive that repairs will take over 15 months and costs are sure to top $30m.

# TASKS 89

## ADVISING and SUGGESTING

### Exercise 1

1 He suggested <u>me to go</u> to Kiev as soon as possible.
He suggested **that I** (**should**) **go** to Kiev as soon as possible.
2 How about <u>to have</u> a meeting next month?
How about **having** a meeting next month?
3 I recommended <u>you to come</u>, but you didn't.
I recommended **that you came**, but you didn't.
4 I suggest <u>to commission</u> an independent report.
I suggest **commissioning** an independent report.
5 Why <u>we don't</u> stop now and continue tomorrow?
Why **don't we** stop now and continue tomorrow?
6 We should <u>to think</u> about this in more detail.
We should **think** about this in more detail.
7 It is suggested <u>to</u> improve fire precautions.
It is suggested **that we** improve fire precautions.

### Exercise 2 (M)

1 Shall we start?/Let's start.
2 I suggest we start with *Item 1, Research and Development Update.*
3 Michelle, how about you starting with your report on this?
4 Henri, I recommend you speak to Joelle, she could help you on that.
5 I would recommend that we contact …
6 It's 11.30 a.m. Why don't we stop for a coffee?
7 I suggest you tell the meeting about this when we start again/Why don't you tell the meeting …?/You should tell the meeting …
8 The consultant recommended that a small team of three specialists should be set up.
9 John, I'd advise you to write a letter to the Chicago Institute of the Visual Image.
10 We ought to stop now and have another meeting in four weeks/Why don't we stop now? I recommend that we meet again in four weeks.

### Exercise 3 (M)

**MEMO**

To: Peter Smalbord (Safety Officer)
From:
Re: Fire incident, Puffin, Drilling Platform Alpha Dos

The report into the above incident recommended improved housekeeping. It also advised that no overalls should be placed in bins and that the bins should be removed during potentially hazardous work, like welding.
The report also advised that further investigations are necessary to determine the exact cause of the fire.
Finally it suggests that lids to bins should be firmly secured.

# TASKS 90

## REQUESTING INFORMATION and ACTION

### Exercise 1

1 I wonder if you'd mind sending me a new manual for the Creatif software Version 5.0? (A) (IND)
2 Can you tell me who I need to write to for such a manual? (I) (DIR)
3 Do you think you could tell me if a newer version is planned? (I) (IND)
4 Perhaps you could send me a product list with prices? (A)
5 I'd like to know the name of a local supplier. I live in Osaka. (I)
6 Please send me a form so that I can become a registered user. (A) (DIR)

### Exercise 2

1 Can you tell me what <u>are the kinds of current account</u> available?
… what **kinds of current account are** available?
2 <u>I'm wondering</u> if you know the normal bank charges on overdrawn accounts?
**I wonder** if …
3 Could you tell me <u>do</u> you send statements every month?
Could you tell me **whether/if** you send …
4 <u>I like</u> to know what interest you pay on a deposit account.
**I'd like** to know …
5 Would you mind <u>say me</u> what is the current level of interest you charge on loans?
Would you mind **telling me** …
6 <u>I'd like that I have</u> an appointment to discuss my cash flow problem with a loans officer.
**I'd like to have** an appointment …
7 I wonder if <u>you mind</u> checking whether a cheque I paid in last Monday has been cleared?
I wonder if **you'd mind** checking …

### Exercise 3 (M)

1 I was wondering what this is.
2 Can you tell me whether it affects the files I write?
3 Do you happen to know what the solution is?
4 Do you know if Compact is already supplied with the Creatif software?
5 I wonder if you'd mind sending me this Compact program?
6 Do you know if Compact is difficult to run?
7 Would you mind if I call again if I have any problems with it?

# INDEX

Numbers indicate pages A = Appendix

# INDEX

# INDEX